OF BEARDS AND MEN

OF BEARDS AND MEN

The Revealing History of Facial Hair

CHRISTOPHER OLDSTONE-MOORE

THE UNIVERSITY OF CHICAGO PRESS

CHICAGO AND LONDON

Christopher Oldstone-Moore is a senior lecturer in history
at Wright State University in Dayton, Ohio.

The University of Chicago Press, Chicago 60637
The University of Chicago Press, Ltd., London
© 2016 by Christopher Oldstone-Moore
All rights reserved. Published 2015.
Printed in the United States of America

24 23 22 21 20 19 18 17 16   2 3 4 5

ISBN-13: 978-0-226-28400-2 (cloth)
ISBN-13: 978-0-226-28414-9 (e-book)
DOI: 10.7208/chicago/9780226284149.001.0001

Library of Congress Cataloging-in-Publication Data

Oldstone-Moore, Christopher, 1962– author.
    Of beards and men : the revealing history of facial hair /
Christopher Oldstone-Moore.
        pages ; cm
    Includes bibliographical references and index.
    ISBN 978-0-226-28400-2 (cloth : alk. paper)
    ISBN 978-0-226-28414-9 (ebook)
    1. Beards—History. 2. Mustaches—History. 3. Men—Social
life and customs. I. Title.
    GT2320.O43 2015
    391.5—dc23
                                        2015010764

♾ This paper meets the requirements of ANSI/NISO Z39.48-1992
(Permanence of Paper).

Dedicated to

JENNIFER

and

CAROLINE, AILEEN, AND MARILEE

with love beyond words

CONTENTS

Introduction: Male-Pattern History   1

1 Why Do Men Have Beards?   5
2 In the Beginning   19
3 The Classic Shave   38
4 How Jesus Got His Beard   63
5 The Inner Beard   79
6 The Beard Renaissance   105
7 The Shave of Reason   130
8 Beards of the Romantic Imagination   151
9 Patriarchs of the Industrial Age   174
10 Muscles and Mustaches   198
11 Corporate Men of the Twentieth Century   213
12 Hair on the Left   235
13 Postmodern Men   260

Conclusions   289

Acknowledgments   293
Notes   295
Index   329

INTRODUCTION

MALE-PATTERN HISTORY

There is a growing trend in today's world: beards. The consumer-products giant Procter & Gamble has noticed, reporting in early 2014 that this growth of hair has reduced demand for Gillette razors and shaving accessories. A scholar contributing to the *Atlantic* declared 2013 "a landmark year for men's facial hair."[1] The cornpone prophets of *Duck Dynasty* and the whiskery Boston Red Sox grabbed headlines, as did the crimes of Amish beard-cutting rogues, a kerfuffle over a BBC presenter's facial fuzz, the campaign of Sikhs in the US Army to overturn its beard ban, and the revival of mustaches in France and Turkey, not to mention increased observance of "Movember"—Mustache November.

Is this the dawn of a new era or just another bump in the road? Only time will tell. One thing is certain: changes in facial hair are never simply a matter of fashion. The power of beards and mustaches to make personal and political statements is such that, even in the "land of the free," they are subject to administrative and corporate control. That Americans do not have a legal right to grow beards or mustaches as they choose was confirmed by the Supreme Court's 1976 ruling in *Kelley v. Johnson*, which upheld employers' authority to dictate grooming standards to their employees. Such infringements of freedom are a strong hint that something more than style is at stake. In fact, beard history fails to reveal fashion cycles at all, presenting instead slower, seismic shifts dictated by deeper social forces that shape and reshape

1

ideals of manliness. Whenever masculinity is redefined, facial hairstyles change to suit. The history of men is literally written on their faces.

Judith Butler, one of the luminaries of gender studies, has argued that our words, actions, and bodies are not simply expressions of ourselves; they are the way we form ourselves as men and women. Our identities, in other words, are made and remade by what we do and say.[2] In this sense, cutting or shaping facial hair has always been an important means not just to express manliness but to *be* men. Society enforces approved forms of masculine personality by regulating facial hair. We arrive, then, at the first principle of beard history: *the face is an index of variations in manliness.* As religions, nations, and movements formulate specific values and norms, they deploy hair, as well as other symbols, to proclaim these ideals to the world. When disputes arise about contrasting models of masculinity, different treatments of facial hair may indicate where one's loyalties lie.

The idea that facial hair is a matter of personal choice remains popular despite abundant evidence to the contrary. Choosing to wear a beard in modern America, for example, can still get you drummed out of the military, fired from a job, disqualified in a boxing match, eliminated from political contention, or even labeled a terrorist. This reality relates to the second principle of beard history: *facial hair is political.* Because ideas of proper manliness are bound up with social and political authority, any symbol of masculinity carries political and moral significance. This explains why facial hair has the power to outrage and why it is subject to social controls.

Another misconception holds that shaving or not shaving is a matter of convenience, and that developments in razor technology explain the prevalence of smooth chins over the past century. The truth is quite different. Shaving is as old as civilization itself, and the absence of modern conveniences has never prevented societies from taking advantage of the symbolic power of removing hair. We arrive, then, at the third principle of beard history: *the language of facial hair is built on the contrast of shaved and unshaved.* Using this basic distinction, and its many variations, Western societies have constructed a visual vocabulary of personality and social allegiance.

History teaches us to be cautious about declaring the current beard trend the dawn of a new era. A few star athletes and Hollywood extroverts notwithstanding, a smooth face is still very much the norm. The popularity of beard clubs proves it. They thrive on the proposition that growing a beard or mustache is an adventurous thing to do. In fact, substantial changes in facial hair norms are rare in history, and when they do happen, they are signs of significant historical shifts. We should, then, bear in mind a fourth principle of beard history: *understanding the forces shaping the male face requires the long view.* Historians who focus on one place and time may miss the larger picture that emerges over many centuries. Beard history is like a mosaic: the image becomes sharper the further back one stands.

All of these dimensions can be seen in the example of Alexander the Great, who changed the course of Western civilization and also the face of masculine respectability. By conquering Egypt and Persia, Alexander made himself and his fellow Greek-speakers masters of the known world. Yet he chose a look—portraits, statues, and coins depict him as youthful and clean-shaven—that was widely disparaged in Greek tradition as unmanly. Why would he do so? More to the point, why did respectable Greek and Roman men enthusiastically emulate him for the next four hundred years? The answer is that he viewed himself as a demigod and wished to look the part. Because the artists of his day depicted mythic heroes like Achilles and Heracles as eternally youthful and beardless, he shaved himself and encouraged his followers to do the same. He was very persuasive. In classical times, elite men—or lesser men who aspired to greater honor—adopted Alexander's style to imply something heroic in themselves. It was not a fad or fashion trend but powerful symbolism. Only after many prosperous centuries for ancient barbers did an alternate philosophy of masculine honor arise, finally breaking the power of the shaven ideal.

Each chapter in this book describes a distinct era in beard history, from the emergence of great cities in Mesopotamia and Egypt to the rise of the smooth-skinned "metrosexual" in our own time. In the twenty-three centuries since Alexander set the precedent, shaving has been the default mode of masculine style, punctuated by four great beard movements. The first, initiated by the Roman emperor Hadrian in the second century, persisted for about a hundred years. The second, in the High Middle Ages, saw kings, nobles, and knights complementing their armored splendor with full beards. This movement, however, was incomplete. Churchmen shaved, especially after the eleventh century, when they were positively required to do so by canon law. This was part of the church's deliberate effort to define its own brand of manhood, with its own special claims to spiritual and political authority. This hair dualism dissolved by the late fourteenth century, however, when laymen adopted the clergy's shaven style. The Renaissance generated a third beard movement, inspired in great measure by opposition to medieval churchly values and styles. The fourth and final outgrowth of beards was comparatively brief, spanning just the latter half of the nineteenth century. In this talkative and rather more self-conscious era, men did not hide their aspiration to fashion a new masculinity for the modern world.

To measure the tides in our present day, one must see them against this extended backdrop, appreciative of the social forces that interact with the styling of the body. If one scans corporate conference tables, capitol chambers, and military mess halls, it is not yet possible to discern a beard movement. When facial hair becomes desirable, or even acceptable, for soldiers, managers, and legislators, we will know that a new chapter in the story of masculinity has begun.

Limitations of space and sources dictate that this initial exploration of beard history focus primarily on elite men in Western Europe and North America who had time and resources to shape their bodies as they deemed appropriate, and whose choices dictated social norms. Men outside these centers of power could not ignore the styles established by the elite but were forced either to conform as best they could or to stand defiantly apart. Even so, writing the story of manly hair in other regions, and among minorities and other non-elite groups, remains an important task for future writers.

Our voyage across time begins in prehistory, in the far-off evolutionary past. Some would argue that natural selection has determined and still determines the meaning of beards. With this idea in mind, evolutionary biologists and psychologists have strived valiantly to untangle the natural riddle that is the human beard.

1

WHY DO MEN HAVE BEARDS?

Civilization is at war with nature. That is true at least with regard to facial hair. In the heat of this centuries-long battle, on which billions of dollars are spent each year, few have paused to consider how the war began in the first place. Why did nature give men—and some women— beards? How did they end up with a band of hair on their cheeks and chins that society requires they scrape off every day? If one hopes to discover the meaning of beards, it makes sense to start with these basic questions. And that will require us to peer into the mists of the evolutionary past.

It is tempting to think that beards are a holdover from our much hairier progenitors, that for whatever reason this trait survived as we developed into the naked ape. Yet bonobos, our closest relative in the animal kingdom, lack hair around their mouths—precisely where the human beard grows. It would seem that, if anything, human beings have *added* hair to their faces, even as they lost it most other places. Even if our ape ancestors had had hairy faces, a question would remain: Why did women lose this hair while men retained it? As it is, a hairy chin and upper lip are virtually unique to the human male.

The beard is also distinctive as the last of the sexual traits to manifest itself in a man's development, other than baldness. Biologists have determined that both beard growth and baldness are stimulated by androgens, such as testosterone, and that the rate of growth varies

1.1 Male Bonobo.

according to naturally occurring cycles of hormone secretion. One scientist reported in the journal *Nature* in 1970 that he had measured an increased rate of beard growth (by weighing the clippings from his shaver) on days before he traveled to visit his distant lover.[1] He surmised that his androgen levels spiked as he anticipated sexual activity, causing his beard to grow faster. Later studies found that androgen production followed a five- or six-day cycle, as well as a daily cycle, with facial hair growth reflecting its variation. A California scientist reported in 1986 that both illness and jet lag affected the rate of his beard growth, apparently by disrupting these hormonal rhythms.[2] More recently, biologists have mapped some of the endocrine pathways that link androgens with hair follicles in the face and scalp. It is clear that male hormones are part of the mechanism of beard growth and hair loss, but this does not explain why these androgens have evolved this function.

The Evolution of Beards

Beginning with Charles Darwin himself, evolutionary theorists have pondered the origins of the beard. In *The Descent of Man* (1871), Darwin described a process of sexual selection that operates in tandem with natural selection in shaping the course of human development. Natural selection changes a species by favoring individuals with traits that enhance their chances of survival and procreation. When it comes to procreation, however, there is another level of selection as individuals within a species compete with one another for the favor of sexual partners. Darwin reckoned that, for the purposes of this competition, animals evolved many secondary sexual characteristics that functioned either as weapons to defeat sexual rivals, such as horns or tusks, or as ornaments to attract potential mates, such as colored hair and feathers. Individuals with the more appealing ornaments or stronger weapons would succeed in reproducing themselves and propagating their distinctive traits. Darwin assigned the human beard to the category of ornament, and imagined that it had the power to attract women.[3] Over the millennia, the theory goes, bearded men were more successful in procreation than their smoother competitors, and the human beard evolved into its present form. In short, men now have beards because our prehistoric female ancestors liked them.

But Darwin saw a problem with this idea. Anthropologists of his day reported that human populations varied widely in the fullness of the male beard. It was believed that Native Americans, for example, were nearly incapable of growing them. Darwin surmised that some ancestral women in some particular places must not have liked the beard and because of that prejudice continually selected against it. That is, the beard functioned as an ornament only among peoples who in fact considered it to be an ornament. To help resolve this conundrum, Darwin invoked still another evolutionary process: the inheritance of acquired characteristics. Before Darwin, Jean Baptiste Lamarck had argued that species change over time by passing along newly acquired traits to their offspring. If a giraffe, for example, spends a lifetime stretching its neck to reach food in the treetops, its progeny will be born with longer necks. Though many a schoolteacher or professor might dismiss the the inheritance of acquired characteristics as un-Darwinian, Darwin repeatedly invoked this this principle in *The Descent of Man*, and did

1.2 Charles Darwin.

so again on the matter of beards. Noting anthropological observations of peoples who were relentless in plucking unwanted facial hair, and referring to (very dubious) experiments that appeared to show that surgical alterations in animals could be passed on to the next generation, he concluded that "it is also possible that the long-continued habit of eradicating the hair may have produced an inherited effect."[4] In other words, men who cut or pulled their facial hair would beget boys who grew less facial hair as adults. The inheritance of acquired characteristics thereby completed a process begun by sexual selection, leaving some groups of men with great thick beards and others with almost none. This analysis assigned women a great deal of influence over beard evolution: they chose more or less bearded men according to their tastes, and men plucked their hairs to accommodate them, which in turn led to permanent physiological changes.

By making the evolution of beards a matter of taste rather than survival, however, Darwin failed to provide a truly Darwinian explanation, that is to say, an answer based on the process of natural selection. In fact, his tactic raised more questions that it answered. What made the beard a strongly attractive ornament for some but loathsome to others? If it was simply a matter of taste, why were the passions it stirred strong enough to cause some prehistoric women reject would-be mates? Was it simply a matter of vanity? In the face of such questions, evolutionary biologists after Darwin had their work cut out for them.

As it now stands, theorists have proposed three basic solutions to the beard conundrum. The simplest, which Darwin himself considered and rejected, is that beards have no purpose at all. Accidents happen in evolution as in everything else. A gene preferred in natural selection for, say, its role in making the skin more resilient, may have the secondary effect, not in itself significant, of giving that skin a certain color. The difficulty in discerning any obvious survival value in facial hair makes it a possible example of this phenomenon. But most scientists have been reluctant to let it rest there. For one thing, insignificance is an unprovable supposition. It is impossible to say for certain that beards are simply along for the ride, at least not until all the functions of all the human genome are discovered. Scientists seek reasons for things, after all, and it is far more interesting to suppose that beards serve a purpose, obscure though it may be.

A second possible solution builds on Darwin's idea that beards are ornaments that charmed prehistoric women and can presumably still charm women today. Adherents of this line of thought have worked to replace Darwin's reliance on vague notions of taste with more concrete psychological and biological explanations for women's preferences. A third theory takes the opposite approach, arguing that hair is a threat device useful in intimidating rival males and establishing dominance. Women, then, have been attracted, not to the beard as such, but rather to the social dominance that impressively bearded men achieve over other men.

The challenge for scientists is to figure out ways to test these competing theories. How can one tell if the beard functioned in the evolutionary past more as a lure to females or as a threat to males? One approach is to observe the role of analogous, sex-related ornamentation in animals—feathers, ruffs, antlers, and so forth. Another is to test male and female reactions to bearded faces to see if there are still echoes of the primitive impulses that motivated our ancestors thousands of years ago.

Ornaments

Darwin's beard-as-ornament theory has found significant scientific affirmation over the years. One adherent is evolutionary psychologist Nancy Ectoff, who argues that the pursuit of a good-looking partner is "a universal part of human experience," one that "provokes pleasure, rivets attention, and impels actions that help ensure the survival of our genes."[5] Ectoff and others who study physical attraction have found abundant evidence that men are attracted to certain physical attributes in women. Male predilection for blondes, for example, has been demonstrated by psychological experiments time and time again. So too has a preference for high hip-to-waist ratios, as well as high cheekbones and large eyes. Women, by contrast, seem less likely to base their judgments of men on physical qualities, and they show less agreement about what the ideal man should look like—other than that he should be tall (though not too tall). Evolutionary theorists generally explain women's less superficial approach to mating by pointing to the evolutionary logic of female reproduction. Given a woman's more limited ability to bear offspring, and her sizable commitment to raising children, it is in her interest to find a man who is helpful and reliable rather than just handsome. This does not mean, however, that looks do not matter. Many studies have found that women take appearance into account, and some women consider physical attractiveness extremely important. Research further indicates that when they do take physical appearance into account, women focus primarily on the face. All this points to reasons why women might value the quality of a man's beard.

When they look at men's faces, women may be unconsciously evaluating the genetic quality of potential partners. This idea is suggested by studies of animal behavior. Some species of birds, such as peacocks, develop exaggerated colors or tails because sexual partners prefer them. The longest-tailed peacocks reproduce the most, and over the generations the tails get longer and longer. Why do the females care so much about size and color? Is there something meaningful about these displays, or is it just putting on a show to bamboozle female birdbrains? In 1975 the evolutionary biologist Amotz Zahavi suggested that displays like long feathers are in fact not a lie but an honest advertisement of better genes. According to Zahavi's "handicap principle," displays such as oversize feathers or a buck's broad antlers come at significant physiological cost to their owners in terms of energy and nutrition. Animals that mount an impressive show, then, are demonstrating their health, and thus their desirability as sexual partners.[6] In the 1980s, several researchers suggested still another purpose for sex-related displays: signifying resistance to disease. Because an incidence of disease tends to diminish the quality and size of feathers, ruffs, antlers, and so forth, a good display would indicate the male was healthy. A showy male is thus advertising his excellent immune system as well as his success at finding food. The same may be true of beards. Prehistoric women knew a healthy man by his face.

This "good genes" notion was reinforced by hormonal research in the 1990s, when biologists developed the "immunocompetence" theory. According to this idea, not only do big physical features represent good health, they are a direct demonstration of strong immunity to disease, in that the high levels of androgens required for such displays actually *increase* the risk of disease through suppression of the immune system.

Testosterone suppresses the immune system in order to ensure the viability of sperm (which are treated by the body as alien cells); a healthy male with big secondary sex traits (and therefore high levels of testosterone) is, then, even more genetically impressive for his ability to ward off disease with reduced immunity.[7] In the animal world, healthy males with big tails, horns, or whatever are in effect saying to females, "Look what I can do with one immunological hand tied behind my back!" Perhaps the human beard is analogous to the tail feather or the antler. It too is a male display generated by testosterone—a billboard of genetic competence. Do women notice? Do they swoon? That's what many psychologists have tried to find out.

In the past five decades, dozens of experiments have charted impressions and reactions to different sorts of male faces in order to assess stereotypes and biases involved in selecting sexual partners, spouses, employees, or political candidates. All have shed light on the beard-as-ornament theory. There is a nearly unanimous finding that a beard makes a significant difference in both men's and women's initial perceptions of a man. A beard almost always made a man appear older and more masculine. But does it also make him more attractive? On this matter, studies have reached contradictory conclusions, depending on the subjects tested and the way the questions were asked. Sometimes the beard was deemed very attractive, sometimes very much not so.

A University of Chicago study published in 1969 established that both men and women found bearded men more attractive than shaved men.[8] A few years later, however, students at two other Midwestern universities rated bearded men (in photographs) to be less kind, good, and handsome than beardless men.[9] Soon after, undergraduates in Tennessee and California affirmed the original Chicago findings, assigning bearded men higher marks for maturity, sincerity, generosity, and good looks.[10] Such contradictory findings inspired researchers at the University of Wyoming to conduct a survey that simply asked undergraduate women straight out whether they preferred men with facial hair. Of the 482 women who filled out a questionnaire, only 17 percent favored beards, while many expressed their outright distaste; about 42 percent liked mustaches.[11]

By the late 1970s, the count stood at two studies in favor of, and three against, the desirability of beards. This back-and-forth continued for the next two decades—with a few split decisions. A 1978 experiment involving Canadian undergraduates, for example, found bearded faces rated higher for confidence, intelligence, and happiness, though not likeability.[12] In 1984 researchers again reported that young men and women rated bearded faces more likeable and physically attractive.[13] A 1990 study that asked 228 professional personnel managers, averaging thirty-one years of age, to judge pictures of six equally qualified male job applicants, found that they deemed bearded men more attractive, more composed, and more competent.[14] This was contradicted by a later experiment, published in 2003, in which university undergraduates were asked to evaluate hypothetical job applicants based on resumés and photographs. This time, there was a bias against bearded men, though bearded candidates were deemed only marginally less attractive.[15] A study of the perceptions of women at a Kentucky university published in 1996 found an even more negative perception of beards. Faces with beards were rated older, more aggressive, less socially mature, and less attractive.[16] By the first decade of the twenty-first century, eight studies had found beards attractive, while eight had found them unattractive. Another two had mixed results. It is safe to say that anyone hoping to find decisive evidence for the beard-as-ornament theory faced frustration. Inconsistent lab results are the product of differing methods and conditions but may also reflect the triumph of nurture over nature, which is to say, our cultural preferences have overwhelmed residual primitive instincts that promoted the evolution of beards. On the other hand, it may simply be that the ornament theory is wrong, and that the beard evolved instead as a social weapon.

Weapons

The inconclusiveness of evidence for the beard-as-ornament theory provides an opening for the competing theory of beard as weapon. But how can beards help men fight? Sociobiologist R. Dale Guthrie has offered one explanation: intimidation. The prevalence in the animal kingdom of male competition to establish sexual dominance is apparent, with male displays found everywhere in "spots, splotches, stripes, manes, ruffs, dewlaps, elaborate tails, crests, plumes, gaudy color patterns, wattles, inflatable pouches, combs, throat patches, tufts, beards, and many other ornaments."[17] The peacock's grand display of vibrant feathers, by Guthrie's account, functions less to attract females than to overawe rival males; their message is not so much "pick me" as "back off, I'm tougher." Among apes, tooth-baring and other mouth gestures play an important role as social signals. Jaws and teeth are the primary weapons in most of the animal world, and much primate male ornamentation seems to relate to the mouth and jaws, including contrasting colors in the lower face and hair ruffs that exaggerate the line of the chin. Our human ancestors might have been similar. Primordial human bullies intimidated their contemporaries by baring their teeth and growling in a menacing way. They might add to that effect by sticking out their chin. Guthrie points out how common it is to refer to a square or set jaw as a sign of strength or aggression. By contrast, a receding jaw is "weak," and people might be observed retracting their jaw as a sign of horror or retreat. Hairy chins work to the same purpose. They make the mouth and face seem larger and thus more threatening.

While Guthrie may be right that a beard is a threat signal, there is no exact analogy for the human beard in the animal world. When apes bare their teeth, it is the teeth, not the rather less impressive chin hair that bears the message. Beards, moreover, can have the opposite effect, making the mouth and teeth appear smaller rather than larger. The weapons theory, like the ornament theory, could use some independent verification. If beards are meant to intimidate men rather than impress women, one would expect to observe indifference in women and fear in men in psychological tests. Champions of the beard-as-weapon theory can find support in the fact that subjects in the psychological experiments have indeed rated bearded men as more "masculine" and "dominant." In the 1969 Chicago study, which found beards attractive, investigators demonstrated that the beard was more impressive to men than to women.[18] A group of students were shown a drawing of an older, mustached man with a younger, clean-shaven man and asked to describe their relationship. Most male students—though not female students—spoke of the older man's seniority and authority. When another group of male and female students was shown a similar drawing—this time with the young man bearded rather than shaved— the female response was unchanged, but the male students tended to refer to the two men as equals conferring together. The beard had raised the younger man's social stature in the eyes of male viewers. It may have been that the beard made him look older rather than more intimidating. Even so, a sheaf of studies in subsequent decades has confirmed that for both men and women a bearded man appears more potent, fierce, and aggressive.[19] The Kentucky undergraduates who rated bearded men as less attractive also judged them to be older and more aggressive. Notably, the men in this study tended to assign higher ratings of aggressiveness to bearded faces than women did.[20]

The notion that the beard might be a sort of threat signal was further confirmed as recently as 2012 in a study of New Zealanders' and native Samoans' reactions to images of men. The same men were rated by men and women as older, more aggressive, and of higher status, but also less attractive, if they had beards. The researchers also showed pictures of the men with angry grimaces, and the bearded versions appeared to people of both cultures as especially threatening. This, the authors concluded, was evidence that a beard was indeed a threat device that helped scare off male competitors.[21]

Though these results support the weapon theory, it is not entirely clear why subjects viewed bearded men as more aggressive. In some experiments, the association of aggression and antisocial behavior may be the result of the beard's cultural implications rather than its jaw-enlarging effect. After all, beards have in recent decades been more obviously a statement of political nonconformity or antisocial activity than of attacking and biting. The scary association may be with drug culture or radicalism rather than physical dominance as such. The best hope for the weapon theory is to suppose that the aggressiveness associated with beards is indeed the echo of primal threat signals rather than cultural stereotypes.

Recent studies have offered fresh support for the ornament theory as well. Specifically, it has been discovered that women like stubble. This was first reported as an accidental finding in 1990 by a team of psychologists led by Michael Cunningham who were investigating the precise facial features that determined male facial attractiveness. The team identified twenty-six parameters, including eighteen dimensional measurements, such as height and width of the eyes, nose, and mouth, along with variations of hair and clothing. University women in Georgia, Illinois, and Kentucky then rated the attractiveness of numerous photographed male faces.[22] Large eyes were found to be the best indicator of an attractive face, the same as in male ratings of female faces. For male faces, prominent chins and cheekbones were also strongly correlated with good looks. The authors of these studies took this to be proof of their "multiple fitness" hypothesis, which suggested that women were attracted both to "neonate" (babylike) features like large eyes and to "mature" masculine features such as a strong chin. Mustaches and beards, however, did not appear to be part of "multiple fitness," for they were again associated with lower attractiveness ratings. The researchers surmised that beards detracted too much from the "neonate" qualities women liked.

That women did not find beards attractive was nothing new, but in one of their trials, the researchers stumbled upon a positive correlation of attractiveness with scruffiness. The study deliberately excluded faces with mustaches or beards from the experimental sample, but some of the photographed faces nonetheless appeared smoother than others. The women's responses showed a surprising preference for faces with a more visible (though shaved) beard. The researchers interpreted this to mean that the *capacity* to grow a beard was a favorable "mature" feature, whereas an actual beard would obscure the desirable neonate qualities of the face. In short, stubble was the sort of balance women were looking for: masculine, but not too much. This result was pure serendipity. Stubble was a factor that asserted itself even when no one was looking for it.

At first, the researchers did not give this result much thought. But in retrospect, it seemed revealing of both what might be right and what might be wrong with beards from the female perspective. The desirability of the *potential* but not the *actual* beard may explain the widely variant results in studies of facial hair. Women want it both ways. Different female subjects in somewhat different circumstances may see the balance of masculine/too masculine differently, with the beard being rated up or down accordingly. This result reinforces the argument of evolutionary psychologist Nancy Ectoff, who has described male attractiveness as a delicate balancing act. Women are attracted to a look of strength and dominance, she maintains, including a strong chin and jaw enhanced by a beard, but this attraction is counterbalanced by a desire for other qualities in a mate, such as dependability and a willingness to invest resources in children.[23] Thus, overly masculine faces are rated as less attractive by women because they lack sufficient goodness and sociability.

Surveys of German men in 2003 and English women in 2008 confirmed the stubble effect.[24] Subjects in the latter study were female undergraduates at Northumbria University who rated male faces altered by computer software to show them with no facial hair, light stubble, heavy stubble, light beards, or heavy beards. The women judged the lightly stubbled versions most attractive, followed, in order, by heavily stubbled, lightly bearded, clean-shaven, and fully bearded. It was clear that some balance between minimal and maximal masculine traits was most desirable, with a general preference for a shaved face over full beard. Women, it would seem, would rather not have to choose between beard and no beard on a man's face. This result was again confirmed by a 2013 study in which Australian women rated photographs of men with heavy stubble (about eleven day's growth) as more attractive than either fully bearded or fully shaved versions of the same faces.[25] It is tempting to hope that this may be the happy ending to the rollercoaster ride of inconsistent results in beard research. The stubble theory, however, still cannot escape the difficulties of earlier studies, that is, the contamination of cultural bias. It so happens that stubble has been stylish in the early twenty-first century, and it may have been fashion trends rather than evolution that impelled university women to fill out their surveys the way they did.

Fifty years of psychological research has arrived, then, after many twists and turns, at an indeterminate conclusion: beards are, and are not, attractive. They are intimidating to some degree, though it is not clear exactly why. The primary obstacle in this quest to uncover the origins of beards is the inability to reproduce the conditions of primitive human life tens of thousands of years ago, and to understand the preferences of prehistoric men and women. A thorough analysis of the human genome may eventually reveal new secrets, but until that time it will be necessary to reconcile ourselves to the limits of biological science in explaining the meaning of beards. This is, however, no reason for despair. In the final analysis, biology may be the least important factor in determining why men grow, trim, or cut their beards as they do. We humans have a way of transgressing the bounds of nature, of assigning to the body new purposes and interpretations that evolution never intended. Our bodies are subject to culture as much as to biology, and this is especially true of hair, which is relatively easy to manipulate.

If civilization rather than evolution ultimately determines the meaning of hair, it should be possible to formulate a sociological theory of beards. Many have tried to do so. Some have taken a Freudian approach, in which hairstyles and hair rituals derive their power from expressing or suppressing the libido. Others investigators have theorized about the use of hair and beards in establishing social and gender distinctions; these ideas have managed to explain many, though not all of the uses of hair in social communication. Recently, French anthropologist Christian Bromberger acknowledged social scientists' failure to explain the meaning of hair.[26] As an expert in Middle Eastern anthropology, Bromberger was intrigued by the ways in which, from the tenth century to the present day, Muslims and Christians have differentiated themselves through facial hair, as have Latin Christians from Greek Christians. Bromberger knew it was more than this, however. Hair could also help define male and female, distinguish conformists from dissenters, and indicate contrasts between refined civilization and primitive naturalism. What he recognized in all of this complexity was unfinished business. He called for the study of "hairology" that would map contrasting attributes of hairstyles—artificial/natural, long/short, hirsute/hairless, light/dark, smooth/nappy—and the social oppositions they were meant to indicate. Such a hair dictionary, as it were, would serve to translate a wide range of explicit and implicit social messages.

The dream of hairological theory is a pleasant one, but it will not easily be achieved. Even if the detailed patterns of affinity and opposition were worked out for a given society, it would provide at best a kind of snapshot of social codes. It would capture a moment in the ebb and flow of human history, but not the ebb and flow itself. In fact, the meaning of facial hair is most visible in change rather than stasis. Watching the film from beginning to end is the only way to understand the plot that drives events. The same is true of the history of facial hair. Following the twists and turns of the unfolding story of beards, shaving, and manliness casts new light on both the past and the present, allowing us to read the conscious and unconscious messages we send with our hair.

2

IN THE BEGINNING

Shaving is as old as civilization. The Sumerians and Egyptians, the founders of Western civilization, used copper and bronze razors to tame their facial hair. Ancient men shaved themselves for a number of reasons but one of the most important was to distinguish two different sorts of men: the bearded lords and the shaven priests.[1] Each had a distinct claim to authority and power. The patriarchal lords conquered and ruled the land, while the priests secured favors from the gods. Patriarchs took pride in their natural hair as a sign of manly potency, while priests took care to shear away the impurity and arrogance of hair so that they might enter the divine presence. Sumerian and Egyptian rulers could not hope to rule without access to both of these forms of manly power. You can tell this by their faces.

King Shulgi Pleases the Gods

The history of Western civilization began in Sumer, the southern portion of Mesopotamia, the land between and around the Tigris and Euphrates rivers in what is now Iraq. There the Sumerians built great cities, erected enormous temples, dug irrigation canals, and laid roads. They also formed a professional priesthood, invented writing, devised legal codes, and organized armies and governments. To this day we eat the plants and animals they learned to cultivate and herd—wheat, oats, cattle, sheep, goats, and chickens—and we measure time and space as they taught us to, marking out twenty-four-hour days, seven-day weeks, and twelve-month years. One of the greatest Sumerian kings was Shulgi (ca. 2094–2047 BCE), a legend in his own day and a paragon of Mesopotamian manliness. To know his story, and the way he presented himself to his subjects, is to know the importance of facial hair in the opening chapters of our civilization.

The two representations in figure 2.1 are both King Shulgi.[2] In the first, he appears shaved and bare-chested, humbly carrying an excavation basket in the ritual dedication of a temple. In the second, he looms in a rock carving as a conquering warrior, crushing enemies under his feet. He wears a great beard and carries an axe and bow, all symbols of strength and command. Which was the true look of the great king? The answer is both and neither. These images were stylized representations of different aspects of royal power. The contrasting facial hair was the primary mark of distinction between Shulgi in his role of chief priest and Shulgi in his capacity as conqueror and lawgiver. As lord and protector of his people, a Sumerian king needed to command both of these primary forms of masculine power.

According to dozens of hymns sung in his praise, including one he wrote himself, Shulgi was the best at everything. He was a god begat by gods who surpassed all mortals in mind and in body. He was a warrior, swift of foot and skilled in arms. He was also a scribe and diviner, who surpassed all others in his skill with words, numbers, and divine signs.[3] In true Sumerian fashion, he used these awesome gifts to honor the high gods, for that was the foundation of his royal authority. To be the greatest of kings, in other words, he had to be the greatest of worshippers, and in the hymn he wrote about himself, he bragged about one particularly astonishing feat of worship in his seventh year on the throne.

By his own account, Shulgi was at Nippur on the holy day of *eshesh*. Nippur was home of the temples to the chief gods Enlil and An, the storm god and the god of heaven, respectively. From this holy city he ran alone a hundred miles to his capital city of Ur, taking only two hours to complete the trip. After a bath and a brief rest, Shulgi performed sacrifices to Nanna, the moon god, in the great stepped temple Shulgi had

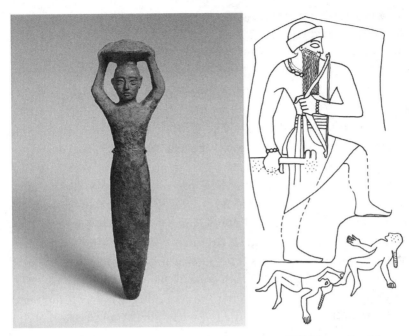

2.1 (*Left*) King Shulgi: temple dedication statuette, 21st century BCE. Metropolitan Museum (www.metmuseum.org). (*Right*) King Shulgi: drawing of a rock carving at Darband-i-Gawr, Iraq, 21st century BCE. Courtesy of Claudia E. Suter.

recently completed for him. Completing his feast-day celebrations in Ur, the tireless king hit the road again, running the hundred miles back to Nippur in order to repeat his sacrifices and celebrations for Enlil and An. In this way he miraculously officiated at the same festivities in his two principal cities on the same day. As if this was not enough, Shulgi boasted that he completed the return trip in a hailstorm. "My heart full of happiness, I sped along the course, racing like a donkey foal journeying all alone . . ."⁴ Without a doubt, he was the long-distance champion of piety.

For Shulgi, serving the gods was job one, and statues of him as a shaved priest embodied this part of his kingly charisma. But he had other responsibilities as well. He was also the lawgiver, head judge, and military commander in chief. In these roles he presented an impressively bearded face. Shulgi was a two-faced character not because he was a liar, but because he hoped to impress his subjects with the full range of his royal magnificence. It may well be that he shaved himself like a priest for important rituals like temple dedications, and otherwise let his beard grow long. On the other hand, Shulgi's beard in the cliff carving, like those in many other representations of Mesopotamian kings, appears grandiose and unnatural, suggesting it may have been a costume for show. What is clear, however, is that Shulgi wished to appear shaved or bearded as the occasion demanded.

When he presented himself like a priest, Shulgi was drawing on very old traditions. From before recorded history, Sumerian priests removed the hair on their heads and faces, and in many cases also cast off their clothes when entering the presence of the gods. Textual evidence indicates that for thousands of years of Near Eastern history, priests, diviners, scribes, and physicians continued to shave as a sign of their professional calling.[5] Written records from the period after Shulgi's time tell of diviners (*baru*) being initiated after long training with the formula "The barber hath done his handiwork upon him."[6] The ancient Israelites also followed this tradition.[7] In the book of Numbers, the Hebrew God gives Aaron the following instructions regarding the Levites, the priesthood of Israel:

> Take the Levites apart from the rest of the Israelites and cleanse them ritually. This is what you shall do to cleanse them. Sprinkle lustral water over them; they shall then shave their whole bodies, wash their clothes, and so be cleansed.[8]

The Levites did not remain shaved in normal circumstances; rather, this practice demonstrates how shaving was in the ancient Near East an essential component of ritual preparation for divine service.

There are several reasons why this was so. Like many cultures even now, the ancients thought hair was an integral part of the body, and so cutting it off expressed self-denial, humiliation, or sacrifice. The most common ritual of hair-cutting in the ancient world occurred in mourning the dead, where cutting or tearing the hair or beard, along with tearing clothes or lacerating the skin, bespoke pain and loss. In Egypt, tomb paintings of all periods show both men and women tearing hair and clothing in a display of grief.[9] Egyptian gods of the afterworld were also depicted holding curved strands of their hair in a typical gesture of mourning.[10] Readers of the Hebrew Bible are familiar with the destruction of hair in mourning. A vivid example is the prophet Jeremiah's description of mourners approaching Jerusalem to present offerings at the temple: "They had shaved off their beards, their clothes were rent and their bodies gashed."[11]

The primary purpose of shaving for priests, however, was not mourning or suffering but purification. The hair, standing in for degraded humanity, was scraped and washed away, freeing the supplicant of arrogance, deformity, and pollution. It was a form of decency approved by the gods, and it comes as no surprise that from an early date kings and nobles in at least some Sumerian cities adopted shaving as the norm. Indeed, the earliest rulers of Sumerian cities were the chief priests, but before many centuries passed, they had to combine this function with the role of commander of the armed forces. For a time, temples were the home of the king, and the priesthood served as administrators of the city-state. But as the state grew, and war and defense become more prominent in the affairs of the city, kings built palaces and augmented the priestly administration with political and military functionaries. Even so, the primary legitimacy of government remained rooted in serving and securing the favor of the gods.[12] The normative status of the shaved face is clearly illustrated in the so-called Standard of Ur, a decorated box dating to about six hundred years before Shulgi's time, which depicts the Sumerian king, nobles, and soldiers as entirely bald and beardless. The first known statue of a shaved king carrying a dedicatory excavation basket on his head dates from about the same time as the Standard of Ur, underscoring the ritual inspiration for the practice of shaving.

The Standard of Ur depicts the king at war as well as at peace. Early kings were necessarily warriors, but Sumerian rulers still preferred to emphasize their religious credentials, such as temple-building and cultic sacrifices.[13] A little more than two centuries before Shulgi, however, a new sort of ruler stormed onto the scene, the fearsome Sargon of Akkad, whose inscriptions are all about war and conquest. He overwhelmed the Sumerian cities with his ferocious army and incorporated them into the first empire to stretch the entire extent of Mesopotamia. Sargon was not a Sumerian but a foreign conqueror who did not bother to pose as a priest-king. Instead, he presented himself as a charismatic, bearded hero who was assigned to world dominion by the chief god Enlil.[14] His grandson Naram-Sin improved on this heroic model of kingship by declaring himself a god who ruled as a junior ally rather than as a servant of the greater gods. As one would expect, Sargon and Naram-Sin's propagandists endowed them with a magnificent grandeur exemplified in the bronze head found at Nineveh, most likely of Naram-Sin.[15] The intimidating warrior beard had made a dramatic comeback in Mesopotamia.

When Naram-Sin claimed, like the Egyptian pharaohs, to be a god, Sumerian traditionalists were outraged.[16] In the years after his death they spread a story that Naram-Sin had sacked the Sumerian holy city of Nippur, desecrating the temple of the chief god Enlil and provoking Enlil to unleash foreign armies to destroy his empire. This myth does not appear to reflect historical events so much as the anger of those who opposed the shocking hubris of the Akkadian conquerors. From this point onward, tensions between hairy kings and purified priests remained a recurring theme. A priestly text preserved from Babylon in the eighth century BCE, long after Naram-Sin's time, denounces the king Nabu-suma-iskun for desecrations of the temples and their holy rites, complaining, among other things, that the king had committed the unforgivable sacrilege of entering the inner sanctuary unshaven, bringing with him forbidden objects.[17] In the Sumerian restoration that followed the fall of the Akkadians, rulers like Shulgi put razors to good use to signal their respect for the temples, the priesthood, and old customs. On the other hand, neo-Sumerian kings did not wish to abandon entirely the awesomeness of Sargon and Naram-Sin's divine and bearded majesty, which had proven an effective means of promoting royal power. As a result, later Sumerian kings like Shulgi decided to have their cake and eat it too.

Halfway through his reign, Shulgi was beset by military threats to his empire. Around this time he too declared himself a god, the first king to do so since Naram-Sin. It was time for him to play warrior-god rather than priest-king. Official hymns now praised Shulgi for his strength in arms, his awesome stature, and his likeness to a sturdy tree or noble lion. It was said that a his lapis lazuli beard overlaying his holy chest was a wonder to behold.[18] This description sounds like a description of some long-lost statue, which it probably was. Lapis lazuli is a precious blue stone that traditionally decorated images of gods. Shulgi had a

2.2 Bronze portrait head of Sargon or Naram-Sin from Nineveh, 23rd century BCE. Scala/Art Resource, NY.

godlike beard suited to his new status as the divine lord of Mesopotamia.

Shulgi's successors for the next half century followed his example, honoring the gods and the priesthood while also claiming divinity for themselves. They continued to represent themselves with two sorts of faces, as evidenced by royal seals. The seals of Shulgi's dynasty follow

2.3 Cylinder seal impression depicting enthroned King Ur-Nammu, 21st century BCE. HIP/ Art Resource, NY.

a standard form showing the king enthroned receiving a supplicant. In most cases the king is presented with a tremendous, waist-length beard, such as that of Ur-Nammu, father of Shulgi (figure 2.3). Ibbi-Sin, a successor of Ur-Nammu and Shulgi, had many such seals, but others have been found that show him in an identical pose but without a beard (figure 2.4). The best clues to explaining the differences between these seals are their origins. The shaved king was unearthed at Nippur, the Sumerian holy city. The bearded Ibbi-Sin seals hail from elsewhere, usually the royal capital of Ur. It appears that the king adopted a more traditional, purified guise for his priestly subjects in Nippur and a more godlike, magisterial style in the capital. Whether or not Ibbi-Sin literally shaved when visiting Nippur, his smooth-faced official image was suitably conciliatory to those who told the still-remembered stories of Naram-Sin's bearded arrogance.

Ibbi-Sin was the last king of the Sumerian era, and the long tradition of royal shaving died with him. The Babylonian and Assyrian rulers of later centuries hewed strongly to Sargon's model of heroic, bearded kingship, not bothering with the alternate image of priestly or scribal

2.4 Cylinder seal impression depicting enthroned King Ibbi-Sin, 21st century BCE. Metropolitan Museum (www.metmuseum.org).

power. One Assyrian king of the eighth century BCE called himself Sargon II, while no one thought to name himself Shulgi II. Mesopotamian rulers of the last two millennia BCE always presented themselves with majestically braided and beribboned hair on the chins. This did not mean the end of shaving in the ancient Middle East, however. The Hittites, who built a great empire from their base in Asia Minor between the fifteenth and thirteenth centuries BCE, developed traditions very much like the bygone Sumerians. Hittite kings did not claim to be gods, but their closeness to the gods was manifest in their religious labors. Though great warriors, Hittite kings would not hesitate to break off a campaign in order to perform important religious rites in their capital.[19] Like the Sumerians, the Hittites believed shavenness was next to godliness. In their art, even the gods were clean-shaven, excepting only the chief god, who wore a grand beard. In the Hittite world, only this lone patriarch at the apex of the divine hierarchy wore the ultimate emblem of authority. This idea mirrored that of the Egyptians, builders of the ancient Near East's most prosperous and stable society.

Hatshepsut Acquires Bearded Authority

Shulgi's claim of divinity was rather novel in Mesopotamia, and unheard of among the Hittites, but nothing new in Egypt, where kings had always been hailed as gods. The pharaoh was an absolute ruler, acting simultaneously as sole landowner, commanding general, high judge, and chief priest. As in Sumer, it was the task of the ruler to please the gods, preserve order, and promote prosperity in his realm. Hatshepsut (r. 1479–1458 BCE) was one of the more successful pharaohs in this respect, ruling a peaceful and prosperous Egypt for more than twenty years.

As commander of the armies, Hatshepsut was a successful conqueror. An inscription in the tomb of a high official testifies, "I saw [Hatshepsut] overthrowing the Nubian nomads, their chiefs being brought to him as prisoners. I saw him destroying the land of Nubia while I was in the following of his majesty."[20] In the majestic temple dedicated to Hatshepsut's memory at Deir el-Bahri, bold deeds and grand achievements are extolled in word and image. One accomplishment the temple commemorates is an expedition to the exotic land of Punt, on the Horn of Africa, and the acquisition of five boatloads of tribute, including bags of gold and incense, ebony, ivory, and furs. The inscription also boasts of thirty-one myrrh trees, of which "never was seen the like since the beginning [of time]."[21]

All was well in Egypt, but not all was as it seemed. Hatshepsut, referred to in records as "him" and as "king," was in fact a woman, the first female king of Egypt. Other women had ruled as regents, or as the unofficial power behind the throne, but Hatshepsut attained full powers in her own name, including the divine status reserved exclusively for the pharaoh. She attained this status, remarkable in a society so bound by tradition, step by step. Born a princess, the daughter of a pharaoh, she became queen, or "God's Wife," when her half-brother and husband ascended to the throne. When her husband died, she ruled as coregent with her young stepson, still hailed as God's Wife. Within a few years, however, Hatshepsut had convinced loyal courtiers and priests in the capital city of Thebes that she had the political talent and divine approval to rule on her own, paving the way for her coronation as king.

Some modern historians have imagined Hatshepsut to be an ambitious and unscrupulous woman who usurped power for her own selfish glory.[22] The truth is that she was capable ruler, and her ability was recognized by the male elite. This acceptance was not easily won. In particular, Hatshepsut had to reassure her people that she was a traditional pharaoh in every respect other than her sex. She promoted herself, therefore, not as a reformer, but as a restorer and guardian of tradition. In case anyone should doubt it, she had it emblazoned in large hieroglyphs on the walls of her memorial temple. "I have never slumbered as one forgetful," she declared in stone, "but have made strong what was decayed. I have raised up what was dismembered. . . ."[23] Reassuring though this was to her subjects, she still had the tricky problem of how to present herself in public and in official art. Luckily for her, Egyptian kings had adopted a highly stylized appearance, featuring shaved heads topped with wigs and crowns, and decorative, artificial beards. It was a relatively simple matter for a female pharaoh to adopt male hair and clothing, and fully look the part. For all intents and purposes, she was a man.

In fact, she was the only one in Egypt with a long beard. In contrast to Mesopotamian practice in her time, Egyptian nobles, as well as priests, shaved both their heads and faces.[24] It comes as no surprise, then, that finely crafted copper razors have been found in Egyptian archeological sites. High-born Egyptians enjoyed the superiority of shaven purity and the proper regularity of their well-ordered wigs. The king alone was permitted the distinction of a beard, assuring him the highest masculine status.[25] It was not a real beard, however, and was never meant to be. Egyptian art routinely depicts the strap that held it on the ruler's chin. Narrow and curved, the carefully shaped beard was a symbol of royal authority just like the crown and scepter.

Egyptians accepted the idea that the pharaoh was a human being who assumed the office of divine ruler. It was just one further step for them to accept that a woman could assume the office of manhood. In this respect the tradition of artificial beards helped Hatshepsut make the symbolic transformation from queen to king. When she was chief queen to Tuthmose II, she was depicted in art as a normal female consort. When her husband died and she assumed the regency, she was still represented as fully female and described as Chief Queen and God's Wife, though also sometimes as "King of Upper and Lower Egypt."

2.5 Head of Hatshepsut from Hatshepsut's Temple at Deir el Bahri, 15th century BCE. Metropolitan Museum (www.metmuseum.org).

As she solidified her hold on power, she experimented with new titles and new imagery for herself.[26] In temple paintings early in her rule, she appeared in her usual feminine dress but sometimes stood in a stereotypical male pose, wearing the tall crown of a king. By the seventh year of her reign she abandoned all compromise and presented herself as entirely male, with attributes including the iconic beard, retaining only the female pronoun in official inscriptions. For Hatshepsut, donning the beard was the ultimate statement of her power. It made this wife and mother the patriarch of Egypt.

Some two decades after Hatshepsut's death, her stepson and successor, Tuthmose III, attempted to expunge Hatshepsut's kingly image from temple walls and strike her from the official list of kings. It may be that Tuthmose was taking revenge against his pretentious stepmother, but if so, why did he wait twenty years? The timing suggests that the real reason was not rage against Hatshepsut herself but lingering discomfort with the idea of a female pharaoh. Rather than allow this precedent to stand, the Egyptian patriarchy decided to remove disturbing images of the woman with a pharaoh's beard.

King David's Ambassadors Are Cut Short

About four and a half centuries after Hatshepsut's time, King David ruled in Israel. His small kingdom was never the equal of Egypt or the great empires of Mesopotamia, but David's personality looms large in our imaginations, thanks to the Hebrew Bible. He had a memorable story: a shepherd boy who felled the giant warrior Goliath against all odds with an ordinary slingshot. He was the youngest of eight brothers hand-picked by God to lead his people from obscurity to glory.

One of the stories told in the Bible about David's reign recounts his war with the neighboring Ammonites. When the king of the Ammonites died, David sent emissaries to show his respect for the late king and his successor. The new ruler, however, convinced that David's men were spies, determined to humiliate them. According to I Chronicles, he seized the ambassadors, ordering that their beards be shorn and their robes cut off up to the hips. He then sent the ravaged emissaries back to Jerusalem.[27] When David heard how shamefully his men had been treated, he took pity on them, commanding them to stay in Jericho until their beards grew back. The Ammonites could hardly have done anything more shocking. The shearing of David's ambassadors was tantamount to plucking David's own beard, always portrayed in the Bible as a sign of grave dishonor. The prophet Isaiah, for example, referred to the abuse he received at the hands of his enemies: "I gave my back to those who struck me, and my cheeks to those who pulled out the beard; I did not hide my face from insult and spitting."[28] Having provoked David, the Ammonites appealed to their allies for help and prepared for Israel's inevitable revenge.

This beard war illustrates how facial hair had become a central feature of manly honor in the later centuries of Mesopotamian civilization. After the fall of Shulgi's dynasty nine centuries earlier, Sumerian society had disintegrated beneath conquering waves of foreigners, and the era of shaved kings came to an end. Priests continued to use their purifying razors, but royal and noble men were ashamed to be without impressive facial hair. In part, the insistence on beards was an assertion of warrior prowess. In the centuries after the fall of Ur, Mesopotamian kings favored vigorous, forceful images for themselves, as Shulgi himself had sometimes done. In Babylonian and Assyrian art, the greater the beard, the higher the rank. And it was not just a matter of size. Gods, kings, and high officials typically wore them square cut, elaborately curled, and braided.[29] One popular form, dubbed by scholars the "heroic king" style, featured the "flying beard," that is, a flowing beard bent backward as though the king were riding at top speed into battle.[30] Mesopotamian kings after Shulgi's time founded their legitimacy primarily upon their military prowess, and also family lineage and personal charisma. The king was a patriarch more than he was a priest, and great beards were the rule. Even a king like David, for whom service to God was critical, was first and foremost a patriarch. In II Samuel, the God of Israel established a covenant not only with David, but also with his royal descendants. In other words, God recognized David as the patriarch of the Hebrews, whose primary task was to win battles and beget a dynasty. Shaving was not for Hebrew kings, nor for his personal representatives.

For Mesopotamians, the awesomeness of bearded manliness was not merely symbolic; they believed that hair itself it contained a masculine life force critical to fortitude and strength. As a living, though detachable, part of the self, hair was seen by peoples of many cultures as a vital substance that carried part of a person's essence. As such, it had great potential for magic spells, both good and evil. One had to be careful about where one's hair might end up. Magical texts from Mesopotamia discuss, for example, the danger of witches who stealthily collected hairs from their victims in order to work their dark magic upon them.[31] But hair might also be used for good. Clay tablets have preserved ancient recipes for medicines, including some to restore sexual potency, that require a sample of the patient's hair.[32]

Because the beard of a great man was both symbol and essence of his personality, its loss became for the Babylonians, Assyrians, Phoenicians, Israelites, and other Mesopotamians the quintessential sign of dishonor, defeat, or death. No wonder forcible shaving was so grave an insult to David's ambassadors. The Hebrew Bible, our most extensive document from the ancient Mesopotamian world, is chock-full of harrowing tales of lost hair and damaged beards. The story of Samson and Delilah, though it does not involve the beard as such, is a famous example. Before the time of David, Samson was chosen by God to lead Israel as a "judge," or temporary war leader. An angel told his parents that Samson would, from his birth, be a "Nazirite"—someone specially dedicated to God's service—and instructed them that, as a sign of his commitment, no razor was to touch his hair. So long as his hair grew, he would be a man favored of God, bestowed with extraordinary and unconquerable strength.[33]

According to the account in Judges, Samson did not take his Nazirite vow seriously. He repeatedly failed to accomplish his mission to defeat the enemy Philistines. Even worse, he married a Philistine woman, Delilah. He should have been more careful, because it was her nefarious intent to discover the secret of her husband's strength and to betray him to her people. Samson fended off Delilah's questions until finally, nagged to the point of exasperation, he revealed to her that his power was in his hair.[34] The treacherous Delilah then cut his flowing locks as he slept, rendering him unable to resist capture by the Philistine soldiers, who gouged out his eyes and took him to Gaza as a trophy. Samson got his revenge, however. His hair grew back in captivity, which effectively restored his Nazirite vow as well as God's favor. When the Philistines hauled him before a great assembly to mock him, the now-hairy Samson called on God for strength, pulled the temple down upon the assembly, and killed himself and three thousand of his tormentors.[35]

Unlike David's ambassadors, Samson had only himself to blame for the loss of his hair and honor. Like the ambassadors, he was able to redeem himself by growing his hair back. Theorists inspired by Freud believe that these stories reflect a natural tendency of our subconscious to associate beards and hair with the penis and libido. In this sense, the shearing of Samson and David's ambassadors was tantamount to castration. It is not necessary, however, to rely on Freudian theorizing to understand why Mesopotamians saw hair as a vessel for a person's identity, and its loss as a threat to life and honor. In losing his hair, Samson lost his identity as a godly man. David's ambassadors lost their status as honorable courtiers.

About three centuries after David's death, the northern part of his kingdom was conquered and destroyed by a new power in the region, the Assyrians. When it came to bearded grandeur, no one surpassed the Assyrians. In the palaces of the so-called neo-Assyrian empire, stretching across Mesopotamia from the ninth to the seventh centuries BCE, kings paraded the grandest, most elaborate beards ever seen.[36] They were so grand, in fact, that some historians have wondered if they might be artificial, like those of the Egyptian pharaohs. Without much evidence for this suspicion, however, we must imagine that great time and expense was required to ensure than no lesser man could surpass the magnificence of the king.[37]

An impressive display of hair like that of Assurnasirpal II (r. 884–859 BCE) (figure 2.6) was an important indication of what sort of authority he wielded. Assyrians believed that the gods, having chosen a king, would grant him a suitably godlike appearance.[38] Their rulers were warrior kings, and the king's beard was the mark of his extraordinary physical prowess. Images of the king were to be venerated like those of the gods, and great care went into the design and execution of every detail of a royal statue. Everything had to be just so, as indicated in a letter from a priest to King Esarhaddon (r. 681–669 BCE):

> We have now sent two royal images to the king. I myself sketched the royal image which is an *outline* . . . . The king should examine them, and whichever the king finds acceptable we will execute accordingly. Let the king pay attention to the hands, the chin, and the hair.[39]

As chief patriarch, the Assyrian king was depicted with the most elaborate and impressive beard, as the most imposing man of his people. Foreigners and prisoners included in the great reliefs on the palace walls

2.6 Assyrian King Assurnasirpal II, carving from a palace in Nimrud, 9th century BCE.

were shown subordinating themselves to him, scraping their smaller beards or shaved faces on the ground in obeisance and humiliation.[40]

The Assyrian king's awesome manliness stood in particular contrast to the beardlessness of his eunuch servants. The Assyrians were the first in Mesopotamia to employ eunuchs extensively at court, and documents of the time regularly distinguished "bearded" and "unbearded" courtiers. Yet despite their subordinate status, eunuchs could still claim a measure of masculine power. In fact, their exclusion from patriarchy ensured their credibility and authority in the palace. As reliable servants rather than rivals, "unbearded" courtiers were granted great responsibilities, including leading armies in battle. In Assyria, then, the absence of facial hair took on a new social role, distinguishing eunuchs, as it previously had priests, from other men. For priests and eunuchs in the Mesopotamian world, service was power, and by this means they established an alternate type of masculine authority.

Later, when the final books were added to the Hebrew Bible, the Jews inscribed history's first beard-protection statutes. The Jews of Judea, who had not suffered defeat at the hands of Assyria, were conquered by Nebuchadnezzar's Babylon in 587 BCE and their leaders exiled to that fabled city. The fall of Babylon to the Persians, in 538 BCE, allowed the Jews to return to Jerusalem, newly determined to restore their identity as the chosen people, set apart from all others by their covenant with God. The regulations in Leviticus and Deuteronomy, intended for this purpose, included a new hair code.[41] Leviticus commands that priests "shall not make bald spots upon their heads, or shave off the edges of their beards, or make any gashes in their flesh. They shall be holy to their God, and not profane the name of their God."[42] In another passage, this instruction is extended to all Jewish men.[43] Partial beard shaving and gashing of the flesh were mourning rituals that enacted a kind of ritual death in sympathy with the deceased. Under the new code, such practices would make a man unclean and were forbidden. One reason to ban razors, then, was to maintain purity. But another, equally important reason, was to distinguish the ways of the Jews from those of non-Jews. After stating another anticutting rule, Deuteronomy explains, "For you are a people holy to the Lord your God; it is you the Lord has chosen out of all the peoples on earth to be his people, his treasured possession."[44] While shaving of the entire body is prescribed in Numbers for initiation into the priesthood, it seems that this ritual was a one-time transformation, after which the new, sanctified hair was not to be shaved off again.[45] In this manner, the priests would remain "holy to the Lord."

In setting Jews apart as a sort of antitype to the Mesopotamian norm, Leviticus and Deuteronomy sanctified facial hair as a sign of holiness and distinctiveness, designations with profound consequences even today. Conservative Jews and Muslims have found in these scriptures a divine mandate for beards, and a means to demonstrate their faith. We will return to these consequences in later chapters. For now, it is enough to recognize that the Jews had articulated for all time a vision of holy beardedness.

A beard, as this survey of ancient Mesopotamia and Egypt reveals, has never simply declared that one is a man. Rather, one's beard, and other hair, announce what *sort* of man one is. For some societies, the removal of hair was an act of purification suited to the priesthood, or to royals and nobles engaged in solemn ritual observances. A beard, by contrast, was the sign of a lawgiver, warrior, or patriarch whose authority derived more from worldly deeds than from divine service. In some times and places, particularly Sumer and Egypt, shaved gentility was preferred for kings and laymen, so that they might project a quality of divine favor. The beard never lost its association with manly dominion, however. Even in well-shorn Egypt, the pharaohs strapped on ornamental beards to elevate themselves above the level of ordinary men. Sumerian kings like Shulgi and Ibbi-Sin maneuvered to have it both ways, showing one face or another to suit the circumstance. Over time, the emphasis on shaved purity faded in Mesopotamia, while hair was invested with increasing religious and social significance. Hair was proof of life, divine favor, dignity, and strength, and its loss entailed dishonor and destruction. The Hebrews carried this logic to its furthest extent, reversing ancient formulas and declaring the preservation of beards, not their removal, to be a sign of purity and devotion. Beards triumphed. Yet just two centuries after Leviticus insisted on its preservation, manly hair was attacked by one of the world's greatest conquerors.

3

THE CLASSIC SHAVE

When his Macedonian and Greek army conquered the vast and powerful Persian Empire, Alexander the Great reshaped the political landscape of the known world and greatly extended the power and reach of Greek language and culture. One of his greatest legacies, however, was so subtle, or rather so obvious, that it has been entirely overlooked: he forever changed men's faces. Before Alexander's time, a respectable Greek man was fully bearded. Afterward, he was shaved. By shaving himself, and ordering his officers and infantrymen to do the same, Alexander set a standard that would endure unchallenged for the next four hundred years. After that long stretch, natural hair regained favor only through the relentless efforts of defiant philosophers, and then only for a brief time. This great transformation was certainly not a fashion trend. It makes no sense, after all, to speak of four-hundred-year fashion cycles. On the contrary, changing facial hair mirrored competing ideals of manliness. The razor's ultimate victory was to have profound consequences then and now.

Alexander Changes the World

The revolution that overthrew the reign of beards occurred on September 30, 331 BCE, as Alexander prepared for a decisive showdown with the Persian emperor for control of Asia. On that day he ordered his men to shave. What can explain this unprecedented command? In Alexander's view, his difficult situation required it. As the climactic battle with the Persian emperor approached, Alexander had many worries. Though he and his men had proved invincible in three years of battle against large Persian armies in Asia Minor, Egypt, and Syria, Alexander now faced a truly vast army gathered by Persian emperor Darius to put an end to his invasion. When Alexander's Macedonian and Greek troops reached the crest of a hill near Gaugamela (in what is now northern Iraq), they were chilled to discover below them a vast carpet of orange flames—countless thousands of campfires lit by their massed enemies. Some ancient historians wrote that Darius commanded a million men, while others offered the more believable figure of a quarter million. Even at the lower figure, Alexander was outnumbered five to one. Uncharacteristically accepting the cautious advice of his commanders, he delayed his attack, ordering his men to camp for a day while he assessed the terrain and his own situation. One major difficulty was that the battlefield was a wide plain, offering no natural protection for his smaller army.

Facing these pressures, Alexander took several unusual precautions: he confronted the anxieties of his men by performing, for the only time during his campaigns, a sacrifice to the god Phobos (Fear);[1] he dispensed with his usual rousing speech on valor, instead quietly instructing his commanders to remind the soldiers that success depended on every man concentrating on his own assignment;[2] and his final command before the battle was the deployment of razors. The ancient historian Plutarch, writing many centuries later, tells us that "when all preparations had been made for battle, the generals asked Alexander whether there was anything else in addition to what they had done. 'Nothing,' said he, 'except to shave the Macedonians' beards.'"[3] When the commander Parmenio asked the reason for this strange order, Alexander replied, "Don't you know that in battles there is nothing handier to grasp than a beard?"

There is no reason to doubt that Alexander gave such an order, but there is ample cause to doubt Plutarch's explanation. Stories of beard-pulling in battles were just that—stories from myth rather than history. It is possible, of course, that the soldiers nervously shared tales of hair-pulling disasters and that Alexander hoped to make them feel less vulnerable. On the other hand, given the powerful association of hair with manly strength, an idea that featured prominently in ancient Greece's most popular work of literature, the *Iliad*, shaving could just as likely have made the men feel *more* vulnerable. In any event, no Greek or Macedonian leader before this time had required his soldiers to shave.

Plutarch and later historians misunderstood this order because they neglected the most relevant fact, namely that Alexander himself shaved. Every image, especially the famous statue by Lysippus (figure 3.1), depicts a smooth-faced Alexander, distinguished by the graceful turn of the neck and, in Plutarch's words, "the melting glance of his eyes."[4] Whatever else might be said or believed about the benefits and dangers of beards, the most obvious result of Alexander's command was to make his troops look more like him. This would have had a far greater psychological effect than any hypothetical protection against grabby Persians. Symbolically, he was calling upon his men to identify with their smooth-faced leader, and to distinguish themselves from the inferior, bearded Asians they confronted. Alexander wished above all, as he told his commanders before the battle, that each man see himself as a critical part of the mission. They would certainly see this more clearly if each of them looked more like their heroic commander.

Alexander's subsequent triumph at Gaugamela established a new political, economic, and cultural order throughout the Middle East. After his death, only a few years later, Alexander's generals divided the vast new empire among themselves and established a collection of kingdoms administered by Greek-speaking colonists. The Hellenistic Age had dawned, and though Alexander himself was gone, his glorious image lived on in the smooth faces of Hellenistic rulers, courtiers, and soldiers. From Macedonia to Mesopotamia, it was a complete about-face for respectable men: a new look for a new era. Even in Egypt, which had a long tradition of shaving, the Pharaohs had worn an elaborate, false beard. In the Greek world, however, beards were dethroned as a symbol of masculine authority. How and when this great transformation took place is clear enough, but not why. Why did Alexander shave in the first place, and what sort of manliness was he trying to project? To find answers, it is necessary to step a bit further back in time.

3.1 Marble bust of Alexander the Great, 2th century BCE. Photo by Andrew Dunn.

Alexander's choice to shave himself and his soldiers was surprising because there were strong prejudices in Greek culture against it. From time immemorial, Greek and Macedonian men had been ashamed to lack a beard. A smooth chin on a grown man was everywhere taken as a sign of effeminacy or degeneracy. This stereotype was so thoroughly engrained in classical Greece that comic playwrights like Aristophanes could count on it for big laughs from their audiences. In one play, for example, Aristophanes made fun of one of his contemporaries, the tragic playwright Euripides. The story was that Euripides had infuriated Athenian women with his portrayal of female characters. To improve his reputation, Euripides concocted an absurd scheme to have his effeminate friend Agathon dress in drag and infiltrate women's meetings in order to defend him. When Agathon refused, Euripides was reduced to an even more desperate plan. Taking Agathon's razor—a feminine rather than masculine implement—he recruited his very reluctant father-in-law to be shaved and dressed as a woman. The ensuing scene was the typical stuff of comic farce:

> *Euripides*: Well! why mm, mm? There! it's done and well done too!
> *Father-in-Law*: Alas, I shall fight without armor![5]

Any respectable Athenian man would have felt the same. Without his beard, a man was stripped of his "armor," unmanned and humiliated.

More serious social critics, such as the writer Theopompus, took an even dimmer view, damning what Aristophanes mocked. In his diatribes against the Macedonian courtiers surrounding Alexander's Macedonian (bearded) father, King Philip, Theopompus decried their "shameful and terrible deeds. "Some would shave themselves and make themselves smooth," he complained, "although they continued to be men. Others would mount each other although they had beards."[6] It would be unwise to take Theopompus too literally. He was slinging mud at his political adversaries. The relevant point is that he considered it a scandal for men to shave themselves to appear like women or youths. Men who shaved were deviants, either laughable or dangerous, depending on one's point of view. Some Greek cities, wishing to stamp out this social threat, even passed laws requiring men to grow their beards.

The corollary to this negative opinion of shaving was a positive opinion of facial hair. The bearded men of classical Greece took as models the long-haired and bearded warrior-heroes of Homeric verse. In the *Iliad,* Homer's epic tale of the Greek conquest of Troy, the beards of the Greek kings Menelaus and Agamemnon were specifically associated with their masculine authority. Likewise, the power of Zeus, the father of the gods, was symbolized by his flowing hair and beard. Early in Homer's *Iliad*, the goddess Thetis made a very intimate and effective appeal to Zeus on behalf of her son Achilles by stroking his beard.[7] This sensual appeasement of the ultimate male ego succeeded in persuading Zeus to restore Achilles to King Agamemnon's graces.

Men of all ranks acknowledged the majesty of great beards and laughed at Aristophanes's jokes about shaved men. Philosophers and physicians also backed this pro-beard prejudice. The medical works attributed to Hippocrates (only some of which were written by him) put forward several different theories about the physiology of hair, but all shared a notion that hair in general, and the beard in particular, was a manifestation of male superiority. Greek scientists agreed that men had greater "vital heat" than women or children, and that this heat—a life force rather than just warmth—accounted for men's greater hair-iness as well as their greater size, strength, and reasoning powers. In connection with this notion, many Greek medical writers discussed the importance of semen, which they believed to be the purified essence of vital heat. Introduced into a woman's womb, this concentrated life force produced new life. Flowing within men's bodies, it produced a profusion of hair. Even Greek physicians who supposed that women had some semen believed that no woman could sustain a masculine level of vital heat. One medical text, for example, discussed the cases of two women who had stopped menstruating and started growing facial hair, after which they became sick and died. It was surmised their bod-ies could not handle the abnormal buildup of semen caused by the fail-ure of their feminine cycles. Only men's bodies were strong enough to grow beards and live.[8]

It made perfect sense to Greek physicians that vital heat would produce hair. The author of a medical text entitled *Nature of the Child* explained it thus: the flow of semen acted on certain kinds of porous flesh to cause hair to grow, much as a plant would grow from fertile soil. Because both men and women had semen, both sexes grew hair on their bodies, particularly on the head, where the semen was stored. But there were two differences in men's bodies. First, they had greater heat, which made the skin more porous, and second, they had more semen to nourish the hair. The beard could also be explained by the way semen flowed in the body. Stored in the head, it traveled from there to the rest of the body when required, particularly during sex. For men, the hair on the chin grows thick "when the fluid in its course from the head during intercourse is delayed by its arrival in the chin, which projects forward of the breast."[9] Presumably, men had sex facing downward most of the time, and this would make the face the repository of more semen, and more hair growth.

The great philosopher Aristotle did not quite agree with this view. He reasoned that hair was residue from the evaporation of moisture that built up in the pores of the skin. Even so, he agreed that hot fluids, including semen, were the ultimate source of hair, and that this explained why men had more hair as well as more strength and reasoning power. Men with "strong sexual passions" had especially full, thick beards because of an abundance of semen, but these men were also more likely to go bald from the depletion of that semen through repeated intercourse.[10] More sex, more hair loss. "That is why," Aristotle concluded, "no one goes bald before the time of sexual intercourse, and also why that is the time when those who are naturally prone to intercourse go bald." In spite of the apparent flaws in his theory, including his unwillingness or inability to explain female hair, Aristotle found reasons to support the general consensus that both the growth of hair and its opposite, baldness, were intrinsic to the greater vitality and capacity of males. In this way Greek science and philosophy conspired with literature and common opinion to bolster admiration for facial hair. Men had every reason to grow their hair with pride because it signified their privileged nature and their authority over women and children.

Given this prejudice, why would Alexander shave? Was it not shameful, deviant, and demeaning? As someone tutored by Aristotle himself, Alexander could not have been blind to the apparent absurdity of a war leader attempting to "fight without armor." On the contrary, Alexander was the most image-conscious leader the world had yet seen. He was careful to hire all the best public relations people: an official historian, Callisthenes; an official painter, Apelles; and an official sculptor, Lysippus. His choice to shave was therefore a carefully calculated move.[11]

During his years of world conquest, Alexander's propaganda machine portrayed him as a true superhero. Callisthenes cast Alexander as the new Achilles, the demigod hero of the legendary battle of Troy, and

Alexander played the part with gusto. After conquering most of Asia, which was far more than Achilles could have claimed, Alexander preferred to liken himself to another demigod, Heracles, who was known for accomplishing seemingly impossible tasks. It stood to reason that Alexander would attempt to look like these heroes, and because painters and sculptors of his day rendered gods and heroes in the immortal splendor of youthful, beardless nudity, he did his best to follow suit. With limitless self-confidence, Alexander dared to do what no self-respecting Greek leader had ever done before: shave his face. Audaciously, he cast himself in an otherworldly image of ageless perfection, taking advantage of the fact that he was still only twenty-two years old when he led his forces into Asia. He did not, of course, shed his clothes in public, though Lysippus's famous full-body bronze portrait *Alexander with a Lance* (now lost) was indeed nude. For the real conqueror, a smooth, youthful face with flowing curls of hair was the best he could do. In this way life imitated art: it was as though Heracles had stepped straight out of a vase painting to lead the Macedonians and Greeks into a new golden age.

One question remains, however. Why had classical Greek artists chosen to render mythic heroes such as Achilles and Heracles nude and beardless, and what sort of heroism was that? Before 500 BCE, a period art historians refer to as "archaic," Greek painters had invariably depicted heroes and gods in the image of actual Greek warriors, that is to say, fully clothed, long-haired, and bearded. The great exception was Apollo, who was stuck, as it were, in eternal youthfulness. In the decades that followed, however, artists began to make significant changes, and by the end of the fifth century, most heroes and gods had shed both their clothes and their beards, excepting only the most senior gods, Zeus and Poseidon. Achilles lost his beard almost immediately after 500 BCE, and his clothes a generation later. It was the other way around for Heracles; first he was rendered without clothes and later lost his prodigious beard as well.

To some extent, the artists who made Achilles youthful and smooth-chinned were following verbal cues in the *Iliad's* descriptions of him. He was said to be *kalos*, or "beautiful," a word that in classical times (after 500 BCE) was used most commonly to describe attractive young men whom older men admired.[12] Artists may also have had in mind Homer's

3.2 Achilles binding the wounds of Patroclus. Vase painting, 5th century BCE.

description of the god Hermes late in the *Iliad*: "He took the form of a handsome young prince, with the first slight traces of hair on his lips and cheeks, in the loveliest prime of youth."[13] A beardless Achilles or Hermes in this sense reflected the homoerotic interests of classical Greeks of the elite class. The artist of the cup shown in figure 3.2 gave Patroclus a beard, suggesting that he was an older admirer of Achilles. The social life of ancient Greece, particularly in the privileged classes, was largely segregated by sex, and a pattern developed of intimacy between older and younger men. The older man, called the *erastes,* typically initiated a relationship with a youth, known as an *eromenos* or *paidika,* and acted as the youth's mentor and lover. The beard was the distinguishing feature of a mature *erastes,* just as beardlessness was the sign of the youthful *eromenos.*[14] The passage from youth to manhood, signified by the first appearance of a beard, was a sublime and poignant

3.3 (*Left*) Bearded Heracles with lion skin and club, by the Niobid painter, 5th century BCE. Photo by Marie-Lan Nguyen. (*Right*) Unbearded Heracles slaying the Hydra. Pottery fragment, 4th century BCE.

moment, when a young man reached his fullest glory. This is what Socrates referred to when he declared his opinion that all men "who had just grown up" were beautiful.[15]

It is understandable, then, that artists would make Achilles beautiful in this sense, but what can be said for a beardless Heracles, a hero known for his fierce personality and stupendous physical labors? If any man should be bearded, it was he. Yet Heracles too was stripped first of his clothes, at the beginning of the fifth century, and later his manly hair. The change is illustrated in figure 3.3. In the first image, an early fifth-century vase painting, one sees Heracles with his distinctive club and full beard. The second painting, depicting Heracles in battle with the Hydra, dates to about a century later and reveals the new ideal of a smooth-faced hero. What can explain his beardless nudity?[16]

The answer is that both youth and nudity had come to represent immortality in classical Greek art. In the century before 500 BCE, Greek sculptors began carving statues called *kouroi*, stylized male nudes that were placed in temples or cemeteries to memorialize important men. These statues commemorated particular individuals, but they were not portraits. Indeed, they all looked more or less the same: a youthful male nude with a standard smile and stiff pose. Originally, they were painted to look more lifelike, and recent chemical analyses have revealed that many once had light, downy facial hair painted on their chins. This reinforced the impression of youth at the threshold of manhood that Plato's Socrates so deeply admired. The *kouros* was meant to be an idealized figure who defied time and decay by remaining forever at the apex of vitality, neither young nor old. In this sense he was the image of immortal perfection. The *kouros* was also nude to reveal human excellence in his physical body, and to reenact Greek rites of passage to adulthood that involved shedding the clothes of immaturity to enter the natural birthright of adulthood.[17] After 500 BCE Greek sculptors developed this idea further, rendering gods and heroes as idealized nudes and infusing their forms with movement, life, and grace, as one can observe in Praxiteles's famous *Doryphoros* (Spear-bearer) (figure 3.4).

The real audacity of Alexander's choice to shave is now apparent. He meant others to see him as a hero on a par with Achilles and Heracles. The most impressive thing, in retrospect, is that he pulled it off, and that the Greek world eagerly embraced his example. A smooth-faced man commanded new respect because, like Alexander, he was an improvement on nature, superior to ordinary manhood in the same way that a hero was greater than a common mortal. In the centuries that followed, barbers became a necessary feature of civilized life.

To be sure, there were sticks-in-the-mud like Chrysippus, an Athenian Stoic philosopher who lived a few generations after Alexander and did not approve of this new manly style. He complained that even in cities such as Rhodes and Byzantium, no prosecutor dared enforce the laws still on the books against shaving. Chrysippus was proud that he, and virtually all his fellow philosophers, held the line for bearded manliness.[18] To some degree, it was simple conservatism, but there was principle involved as well. Philosophers were history's first pro-beard lobby, though for centuries they stood little chance of breaking the spell cast by the greatest icon of Greek manliness.

Scipio Leads Rome in a New Direction

It was not long before Greek barbers marched on Rome. The Roman author Varro reported that in the first century BCE a monument was erected in city of Ardea to commemorate the arrival of the first bar-

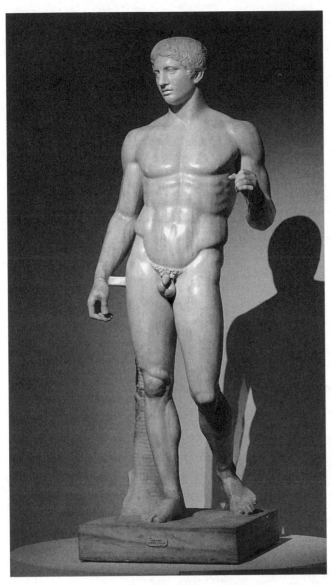

3.4 The Doryphoros (Spear-bearer) by Polykleitos, 5th century BCE. Later Roman marble copy of the original bronze sculpture.

bers in Italy from Sicily about twenty years after Alexander's death.[19] This was the arrival, though not the triumph, of barbers in the Roman world. It would take several more generations for Greek culture and Greek ways to be fully adopted there. By the middle of the second century BCE, however, Romans were also being convinced of the superiority of shaved manliness. According to the first-century CE Roman writer, Pliny the Elder, it was the conqueror of Carthage, Publius Scipio Aemilianus, who was the first Roman to shave every day.[20] Whether or not he really was the first, it made perfect sense to point a finger at Scipio because he was precisely the sort of man who would be inclined to embrace the Greek argument for shaving, and the sort of man whose celebrity would inspire many imitators. To know Scipio Aemilianus is to know why Romans abandoned their beards and adopted the new look of respectable manliness.

Publius Cornelius Aemilianus was born the second son of an illustrious Roman family at the forefront of military and political life. His father was Lucius Aemilius Paulus, who conquered Alexander's Macedonian heirs in 168 BCE. Publius served in his father's campaign with distinction, and by this time he had become, according to a common Roman practice, the adopted son of a childless senator of even more illustrious lineage, Publius Cornelius Scipio. Thereafter young Publius became known as Scipio Aemilianus. The young Scipio's adoptive grandfather was the legendary Scipio Africanus, the man who saved Rome by defeating Hannibal. The newest Scipio had big shoes to fill, and he was determined to do so.

In his quest for greatness, Scipio had the advantage of two famous fathers, one natural and the other adopted, who together secured for him the best possible military and academic education. According to Plutarch, Scipio was surrounded by the best Greek scholars, sculptors, painters, and hunting instructors that money could buy.[21] Not surprisingly, he developed a real passion for all things Greek. As he traveled with his birth father on official visits around Greece, he met Greek intellectuals and collected a library of Greek literature. In 155 BCE, when Athens sent three philosophers on an embassy of friendship to Rome, Scipio was among the crowd of young men who flocked to hear them lecture. He eventually gathered around himself a circle of Greek and Roman historians, writers, and philosophers who attempted to meld the best ideas from the two civilizations. Always a patriotic Roman, Scipio was nevertheless more closely attuned to Greek thinking and manners than his contemporaries.

In spite of his extensive intellectual interests, Scipio was statesman first and foremost, a true political innovator whose career foreshadowed those of later iconoclasts such as Sulla, Pompey, and Caesar. Rather than following the usual practice of building political support through a network of trusted clients and protégés, Scipio relied for political support on his illustrious military record, his reputation for competence, and his personal charisma. When a senatorial rival taunted him for his lack of connections, Scipio's half-jesting reply was telling: "You are quite right; for my concern has been not to know many citizens but to be known by all."[22] This strategy, in combination with his famous name, fostered an aura of greatness that won him unprecedented power. In 147 BCE, the citizenry elected him to the consulship, the chief office of state, even though he was still too young to hold that office. Soon after, the Plebian Assembly selected him to command the final assault on Carthage, bypassing the Senate, which normally made such important military appointments. Scipio's popularity campaign had succeeded brilliantly. In their enthusiasm for a hero, Rome's commoners brazenly trampled long-standing precedent to promote their man. When the younger Scipio followed his adoptive grandfather's footsteps, defeating Carthage yet again, his title "Africanus" and his larger-than-life reputation were secured.

Such was the first Roman to shave every day. His extraordinary face was part of his heroic performance. A man who would be "known by all" did well to seize any opportunity to distinguish himself in the public eye. In an age when Greek ideas, Greek art, and Greek styles were increasingly admired, Scipio presented himself in Alexandrian magnificence. Partly through his example, the shaved face became an emblem of sophistication and statesmanship, inspiring respectable Romans to keep barbers busy for the next three centuries. It seemed that the more ambitious a man was, the more careful he was about this hair regimen. At least that is the impression one gets from Julius Caesar's behavior. The Roman historian Suetonius tells us that Caesar, who took control of Rome a century after Scipio's Carthage triumph, "was so nice in the care of his person, that he not only kept the hair of his head closely cut and had his face smoothly shaved, but even caused the hair on other parts of the body to be plucked out by the roots."[23] A misplaced hair, after all, threatened ruin to his heroic aura. Unfortunately for Caesar, advancing baldness made him appear even older than he was, and he tried his best with a comb-over. Several artists obliged him, however, producing flattering portrait busts with suitably abundant scalps.

Caesar's adoptive heir and successor, Augustus, also cultivated a heroically shaved countenance. The tour de force of Augustan propaganda was a memorial statue now called the *Augustus of Prima Porta*, which was commissioned at his death by his widow Livia (figure 3.5). It was a larger-than-life effort to bestow Alexandrian charisma upon the Roman emperor by fusing recognizable features of the real Augustus with the idealized youthfulness of classical Greek sculpture, notably the widely admired *Doryphoros* (figure 3.4). Like similar images of Achilles, Heracles, and Alexander, it affirmed the emperor's divine status by placing him forever at the apex of life, neither young nor old. And though Augustus was not nude, he was not entirely covered either. What Scipio Aemilianus had started, this sculpture fully accomplished. The ruler of the known world had successfully appropriated the shaven image of divine heroism.

Rome dominated the Western world, and so did shaving. A smooth face was the mark of a refined and honorable man, cast in the image of heroes, both mythic and historic. It was not a fashion statement but an ideal, and it would take more than just time to dislodge it. In fact, it would take nothing less than history's first beard movement to reform both the ideal and style of manly honor. This was the project of professional philosophers, who persistently held out for shagginess during the long era of smoothness.

Emperor Hadrian Chooses Wisely

Some historians still repeat the fable that the Roman emperor Hadrian (r. 117–138) grew a full beard to cover blemishes on his face. This is the fabrication of a frequently faulty Roman history composed some two hundred years after the emperor's reign. More savvy historians tell us that Hadrian grew his beard to look Greek, and thus sophisticated and

3.5 Augustus of Prima Porta. Marble statue, 1st century. Vanni Archive/Art Resource, NY.

philosophical.[24] This explanation is far better, but still not quite right. It makes no sense to say he wanted to look Greek. After all, Romans had been looking Greek since Scipio Aemilianus began shaving three hundred years earlier. As for looking philosophical, this also misses the point. Hadrian was less interested in looking intellectual than he was in appearing virtuous. His new facial hair presented not the look of contemplation but the face of stoic fortitude, self-discipline, and good judgment. With his beard, Hadrian was declaring to the world that his mind and character, not birth, luck, or divine intervention, were the true foundations of his authority. He got these ideas from the philosophers.

When he was still a general, and not yet emperor, Hadrian looked like any other decent Roman, that is to say, smoothly shaved. He was a serious young man, eager to imbibe the wisdom of Roman politicians and Greek philosophers. Like many of his class he spoke fluent Greek, and he eagerly sat at the feet of the greatest minds of the age. The most persuasive to Hadrian was Epictetus, the leading champion of Stoicism, a school of Greek philosophy especially popular among the Romans. Hadrian spent many months in Greece as a military officer, and some of those days at the home of Epictetus in Nicopolis. The Stoics believed in living and acting in concert with universal laws of nature, and for this reason they were the most militant proponents of growing beards. If beards were given by nature, they argued, why would men refuse to grow them? Why would they seek to deny their true selves? One can easily imagine Epictetus reproaching his noble Roman admirer with sarcastic comments about powerful generals afraid to face up to the calling of true manliness. Thus chastened, Hadrian found the courage within himself to return to Rome with a leonine face.[25] In so doing, he reversed four centuries of Greco-Roman tradition and won a great victory for Western civilization's first beard movement.

To understand just what Hadrian was saying with his new look, it is necessary to consider the philosophy of beards that stood behind it. During the previous four centuries of shaving, professional philosophers had routinely suffered abuse for their defiantly woolly faces. Virtually all philosophers wore beards, though there were differences in style among the various schools. The Sophists often kept well-groomed and curled beards. The Peripatetics, devotees of Aristotle's thought,

3.6 Emperor Hadrian. Marble bust, 2nd century. Photo by Marie-Lan Nguyen.

and the Epicurians, searchers for the source of earthly happiness, both favored well-trimmed beards. Stoics preferred fuller beards, though not so ragged as those of the Cynics, who in their disdain for the body allowed their hair to grow long and tangled.[26] Pride of place as father of the beard movement must be granted to Musonius Rufus, a Roman Stoic of the first century and onetime mentor to Epictetus.

Musonius's philosophy is now known through lectures and sayings collected by later writers. One of these lectures was a critique of shaving that amounts to a true manifesto. "The beard," it declares simply, "should not be shaved from the chin." In pruning a plant, Musonius argued, the wise man takes away only that which is useless. A beard is not like that; it is not useless. It is rather "a protection provided to us by nature . . . a symbol also of the male, just as the crest is for the cock and the mane for the lion. Therefore the part of one's hair that is bothersome ought to be removed, but nothing of the beard."[27] In defense of this conclusion, Musonius invoked Zeno, the founder of Stoicism, who had once stated, "One must cut one's hair for the same reason as one must let it grow—that is, following nature."

Here, then, was the essential principle of Stoicism applied to masculinity and the male body. Men who shaved ran the risk of denying their own manly nature in a vain attempt to make themselves attractive to women or boys. Such men, Musonius said, were "broken by luxurious living and completely emasculated." Here he was appealing to old Greek associations between shaving and sexual perversion, but he was also advancing a new line of reasoning that would resonate with future beard advocates like Epictetus: though a beard did not make a man virtuous, a virtuous man would wear his beard because he wished to acknowledge his own manly nature, and live in accord with its solemn responsibilities. The virtues of fortitude and self-control were given to men by nature, as were beards. It was up to them to accept all such natural gifts, and to live accordingly.

Though Dio Chrysostom, a later contemporary of Musonius, was identified as a Sophist rather than a Stoic, he held very similar opinions. At one point in his writings, Dio complained about the citizens of Tarsus, who had ridiculed him for his long hair. Dio retorted that the real shame was not his long hair but the Tarsans' smooth faces. How terrible it was that young men shaved their faces and even their legs, imagining they became more attractive by being effeminate. "Thus ridicule and scorn are being showered by the clever younger set upon the artistry of Nature."[28]

In the following generation, Epictetus established himself as the philosophic champion of beards, and the man who, through Hadrian, finally broke the spell of the classic shave. It is easy to imagine how the great Stoic confronted the future emperor. "Young man, whom do you wish to make beautiful?" the philosopher had said in one of his recorded discourses:

First learn who you are, and then, in the light of that knowledge, adorn yourself. You are a human being . . . Your reason is the element of superiority which you possess; adorn and beautify that; but leave your hair to Him who fashioned it as He willed. Come, what other designations apply to you. Are you a man or a woman?—A man. Very well, then, adorn a man, not a woman. Woman is born smooth and dainty by nature, and if she is very hairy she is a prodigy, and is exhibited at Rome among the prodigies. But for a man *not* to be hairy is the same thing, and if by nature he has no hair he is a prodigy, but if he cuts it out and plucks it out of himself, what shall we make of him? Where shall we exhibit him and what notice shall we post? "I will show you," we say to the audience, "a man who wishes to be a woman rather than a man." What a dreadful spectacle![29]

After harangues like this, it is no wonder that Hadrian determined to return to Rome with visual proof of his rationality and manliness.

Had Hadrian not been the first to adopt the new style, then his near successor Marcus Aurelius would have been, for Aurelius was even more deeply committed to Stoicism. The magnificent statue of Aurelius in equestrian and bearded glory, now in the Capitoline Museum in Rome, is a fitting memorial for this revered emperor, even if the ideological significance of his personal appearance has not been fully appreciated (figure 3.7). Hadrian and Aurelius initiated a new masculine style in Rome and Greece that lasted a century. Leading men now opted for the natural manliness promoted by philosophy rather than the heroic manliness modeled on iconic conquerors of the past. With their ample hair, several generations of Romans and Greeks declared that wisdom and virtuous character were the true basis of manly honor and imperial rule, not some mindless imitation of idealized heroism.

It comes as no surprise that the new enthusiasm for beards during the second century stimulated renewed scientific interest in facial hair. Galen, whose encyclopedic writing established him as the most influential medical authority in late ancient and medieval Europe, revived Hippocratic and Aristotelian theorizing on the matter of facial hair. As Marcus Aurelius's personal physician, his writings on beards confirmed his master's Stoic moralism. Male hairiness, Galen argued, confirmed gender roles and the superiority of men, whose hair helped them per-

3.7 Emperor Marcus Aurelius on horseback. Replica of bronze statue from the 2rd century. Photo by Jean-Pol Grandmont.

form hard, outdoor work. According to Galen, however, the real value of beards was moral rather than physical, for nature made the body "appropriate to the character of the soul." A woman was not given a beard by nature because she does not have an "august character" and therefore "does not need an august form."[30] In writing this, Galen was channeling classical ideas from before Alexander, when beards were essential to male dignity.

If Roman civilization had persisted in its second-century condition, distinguished men might have banished barbers from empire for good. But it was not to be. Economic decline and political turmoil threatened Roman civilization in the century following Aurelius's reign, and emperors were hard-pressed to maintain social cohesion and imperial authority. In this troubled era, a long succession of short-lived emperors abandoned philosophy and resorted to assassination and coup d'état. These usurpers also discarded longer beards, tending to favor a fearsome stubbled look. As Rome reeled from one political crisis to the next, it was apparent that some form of restoration was needed. In the late third century, Emperor Diocletian propagated new images of himself, some of which depicted him in an old-fashioned style: wearing a toga, with short hair and a clean-shaven face. The idea was to imbue his image with divine mystique, particularly in eastern provinces where he hoped to establish an emperor cult, as part of his larger plan to restore social order and reform the imperial administration. The era of bearded virtue was over. It was back to the future for the imperial state.

Diocletian's successor Constantine followed this path as well. He strengthened and solidified the state and forged an alliance with the burgeoning Christian movement. He also perpetuated the new (old) imperial image of the original caesars. The most striking example was a colossal statue of himself installed in a massive new basilica he built near the Roman Forum (figure 3.8). The statue's most outstanding features were its size (thirty feet tall), the cross held in one hand, large eyes, and classical, Alexandrian youthfulness, all of which invested the ruler's form with superhuman majesty. Subsequent fourth-century emperors all followed Constantine's lead, establishing Christianity as the official religion of the empire while looking as much as possible like the shaven emperors of old. All of them, that is, except Julian "the Apostate."

Julian Grows Nostalgic

During his brief time in power between 361 until his untimely death in battle in 363, Constantine's nephew Julian attempted to put the empire on a different track to recovery. He chose a different back-to-the-future scenario than his uncle, modeled on the wise Marcus Aurelius, not the divine Augustus. Like Aurelius, Julian found his solace in Stoic philosophy, not Christianity. He styled himself after Aurelius, the paragon of philosophic self-restraint and benevolent wisdom, and grew a thick, full beard to match.

Ironically, Julian hoped to be revered for his humble virtues of ascetic self-denial. Following the motto of Marcus Aurelius, he strove to "have the fewest possible needs and do good to the greatest possible number." He ostentatiously avoided luxuries and comforts and openly disapproved of popular entertainments like plays and chariot races.[31] His scolding pride and anti-Christian policy rubbed many of his subjects the wrong way. He infuriated Christians by insisting upon the res-

3.8 Emperor Constantine. Head from monumental statue of the 4th century. Photo by Jean-Pol Grandmont.

toration of traditional religion, and non-Christians by hectoring them about their love of sports and entertainment.

These and other grievances motivated some wits in Antioch (where Julian had established temporary headquarters in preparation for an invasion of Persia) to publish a satire of their haughty emperor during the new year's celebrations of 363. His beard became for them a symbol of his retrograde boorishness, and they delivered many cutting remarks about it, including a suggestion that it might be put to better use as material to make ropes. Julian responded with a little satire of his own titled *Misopogon*, or "Beard-Hater," meant to mock both himself and his Antiochene critics. He wrote that he had "out of sheer perversity and ill-temper . . . added to [my face] this long beard of mine, to punish it, as it would seem, for this very crime of not being handsome by nature."[32] This was, of course, a joke. In Julian's text, however, jokes soon gave way once more to invective, and the emperor unleashed a torrent of disparagement on his subjects for their disregard for moral restraint, religious propriety, and social decorum. Julian's conceit was to accept the beard as boorish indeed, but still far preferable to the smooth-faced degeneracy of his subjects. He told the citizens of Antioch that though he had a dirty beard, "you . . . by your soft and delicate way of living, or perhaps by your effeminate dispositions, carefully make your chins smooth, and your manhood you barely reveal and slightly indicate by your foreheads, not by your jaws as I do." Men will soon be sorry when they discover that their distaste for manly discipline and rule of law leads to the collapse of their authority over their own households. With his messy beard, Julian would continue to stand firm against feminine wantonness and social dissipation. Just months after his clash with the citizens of Antioch, however, Julian died of wounds suffered in battle. It was truly the end of an era, for Julian would prove to be the last non-Christian emperor, as well as the last exponent of the first beard movement.

The fall, rise, then fall again of beards in classical civilization reflected a cultural struggle over the true source of masculine virtue: was it natural reason or divine genius? Would a man do better to model himself on the philosopher or on the hero? Before Alexander, both learning and prejudice favored beards as the mark of masculine virtue. Though artists devised a type of beardless masculinity during Greece's golden age, this was an idealized image not meant to represent mortal men. It took the audacity of Alexander, who claimed to be the equal of the demigods Achilles and Heracles, to bring this ideal to life. Lesser men followed his lead, setting a new masculine standard for Western history that still asserts its power today. Philosophers, however, held out for a different idea of manliness. The aspiration to transcend nature, they argued, was a serious mistake. A truly good man cultivated natural virtues of self-discipline and sound reason. They offered themselves as the bearded alternative and called upon all men to follow their lead. For a time, starting in the reign of Hadrian, these ideals triumphed. But it was not long before the glamorous Alexandrian ideal asserted itself once more, much to the regret of holdouts like Emperor Julian.

The eventual collapse of the western empire and the triumph of Christianity throughout the Roman world dropped the curtain on both the classical shave and its antithetical beard movement. Manliness was henceforth shaped in the context of Christianity rather than classical art or philosophy. The beard controversies of the classical era, however, carried forward into the new age, articulated the context of Christian theology. In the Middle Ages that followed, Christian arguments were devised both for and against beards, and though early theologians at first adopted a stoical defense of natural hair, later reformers successfully revived heroic shaving on an entirely new basis.

4

HOW JESUS GOT HIS BEARD

Jesus is the most recognizable bearded man in Western civilization. Though he has been portrayed in a variety of ways over the centuries— laughing or weeping, with lighter or darker skin, more or less thin— one can always count on his flowing hair and medium-length beard. Jesus simply wouldn't look like Jesus without it. The consistency of this image over time provides a false sense of authenticity, as if we knew what he really looked like. We don't. The bearded Christ is not a portrait; it is cultural convention developed over a very long period of time. In the first centuries of Christian history, believers experimented with different images of Jesus, and during this time it was more common to see him without a beard than with one. How and why Jesus's beard became an essential part of his image reveals a good deal about the meaning Christian civilization has assigned to facial hair. The bearded Christ is the product of a time when theology and symbolism were artists' prime motives. The face of Christ was meant to convey something of the nature of a man who was both human and divine. To tell the story of Jesus and his beard, it is best to begin at the end.

Jesus Defies Description

As his followers grew in number, the Jewish rabbi, Jesus of Nazareth, found himself in conflict with both Jewish and Roman authorities. The Romans had little tolerance for disorder, and though they hardly cared about religious disputes among their tumultuous Jewish subjects, they were brutal in the defense of their authority. When Jesus was denounced by religious leaders as a threat, the Romans were content to put him to death. A Roman execution was a public, elaborate, drawn-out affair—a true festival of pain. In 71 BCE, after Spartacus's great slave revolt in Italy was crushed by Roman armies, six thousand rebels died in slow agony on six thousand crosses stretching for mile after mile from the gates of Rome. This form of torture was particularly agonizing, lasting many painful hours before death arrived by asphyxiation. The Gospels report that Jesus's anguish began when soldiers of the Roman garrison in Jerusalem tossed a purple robe on the condemned prisoner's shoulders and a crown of thorns on his head. They mocked him with blows and spit and derisively scrawled "This is the King of the Jews" on his cross. After nine hours of misery it was finished.

After he was buried, rumors spread that Jesus had come back from the dead, though some of his own followers found this hard to believe. Near the end of his Gospel account, St. Luke tells of two disciples who were walking to a village near Jerusalem debating the recent end of the Jesus movement. A man came up to them and asked what they were discussing. The apostles were surprised that the stranger was so poorly informed about recent events in the city. They told him of Jesus's arrest and crucifixion, and their disappointment in the death of the supposed liberator of Israel. There were dubious reports he was alive, but they had not seen him. The newcomer was astonished at their despair. Did they not know that the Messiah was to suffer first before entering glory? Reaching the village, the two disciples asked the stranger to stay with them for the night. When the newcomer sat down for supper, broke the bread, and said the blessing, they suddenly recognized him as the risen Lord. Only when he reenacted the last supper did he become seen and known. At this moment of realization, however, Jesus vanished from sight.

Luke was writing for Christians several generations removed from the time of Christ. No one living had seen him, nor had the faithful preserved a physical description of the "Son of God." In this little story, Luke was assuring believers that the physical absence of Christ was not a problem; after all, even his followers had failed to identify him after the crucifixion. It was important only that the faithful know Christ's teaching and remain in ritual communion with him. In other words, Christians must see by faith rather than with their eyes.

In spite of Luke's admonitions, Christians had an unquenchable desire to see Christ for themselves, and to represent him in human form. This desire was complicated not only by a lack of eyewitness accounts, but also by his composite nature: according to doctrine settled by the Council of Nicea in the fourth century, Jesus was both wholly human and wholly divine. He was, therefore, a paradoxical being who was difficult to explain, much less visualize. Not surprisingly, early symbols of Christ were abstract, such as a fish or a stylized "good shepherd" modeled on conventional depictions of Hermes, the patron god of shepherds. Even so, portraits of a human Jesus proliferated. A letter attributed to Eusebius, the influential bishop of Caesarea in Palestine during the early 300s, describes his having seen many old paintings of Christ and the apostles Peter and Paul that believers had placed in their homes; in particular, he remembers one woman bringing him an image of Paul and Christ "in the guise of philosophers" (which was to say, with long beards). Eusebius confiscated the painting from the woman, declaring that such images diminished the sublime majesty of Christ.[1] Eusebius told this story in his response to Constantia, the sister of the Roman emperor Constantine, who had asked him to send her a true likeness of Christ. The bishop, of course, declined, insisting that there could be no true image, only an inadequate rendering of his brief time on earth "in the form of a slave."[2] Constantia, however, might be forgiven for expressing a common yearning to come into the presence of the human Christ. The doctrines of the church, after all, affirmed that he had been a man in the fullest sense. Was it not right to imagine him that way in art?

The Classical Jesus

For the first five centuries of Christian art, Jesus was more likely than not to be beardless because this image best suited Roman sensibilities. Early Christians worked from what they knew, and this was representations of pagan gods such as Apollo, Hermes, or Sol Invictus. In classical art, these gods were depicted with long, loose locks, and smooth, youthful faces that indicated their freedom from aging and death. It made perfect sense to think of Jesus in the same way. One of the most popular early representations of Christ was as the good shepherd, usually a curly-haired young man carrying a lamb to safety across his shoulders (figure 4.1). The Gospel of St. John has Jesus say, "I am the good shepherd; the good shepherd lays down His life for the sheep" (John 10:11). With this image in mind, Christians quite naturally pictured Christ looking like Hermes, the messenger god, a frequent emissary between mortals and gods who was also a patron of travelers and herdsmen.[3] Artists often showed Hermes lovingly carrying a lamb on his shoulders, and Christians followed suit. The parallels between Hermes and Christ were irresistible: both were divine messengers and shepherds of souls. Ancient Christians also drew a connection between Christ and Dionysus, the god of wine and ecstatic experiences. Jesus's first miracle, after all, had been turning water into wine.[4] According to legend, both Hermes and Dionysus had, like Christ, passed into the underworld and returned again to the living. In art both gods were rendered in classical fashion as immortal youths, impervious to aging and death. Their long, flowing hair was another late classical convention intended to suggest abundance of life and vitality. It made perfect sense to early Christians that Christ would look like these gods.

Still another association was with the god Sol Invictus (Invincible Sun) whose worship was instituted by the Roman emperor in 228. As in the case of Hermes and Dionysus, biblical and theological formulas helped make this connection, for Christ was said to be "the light of the world" (Matthew 4:16) and the "sun of justice" (Matthew 5:45; also John 1:4–5, 9). A mosaic dating from the late third century, found under the Vatican, shows Christ in the image of the Sun-God, with the characteristic rays emanating from his head. Sol was often equated with Apollo, the god of youth, wisdom, and light, and so it was natural for Sol to be represented, once again, as a long-haired, beardless youth. Whether Christ was compared to the shepherd god, the god of wine, or the sun god, it made sense to see Christ as youthful and beardless.

By 300, as we have seen, Roman emperors were shaving again, in imitation of the early emperor-gods Julius Caesar and Augustus. A beardless Christ would therefore look like an emperor as well as a god.

4.1 Marble statue of the Good Shepherd, 3rd century. Album/Art Resource, NY.

This would fit particularly well with the overarching theme of St. Luke's gospel, which presented Christ as the true king who has come into the world to supplant mortal rulers.

Beyond their evocation of imperial and cultic images, Christian artists had a practical use for the youthful Christ figure. When they depicted scenes from the gospels, a smooth-faced Christ would appear godlike in contrast to ordinary bearded men.[5] A striking example of this effect is seen in the carvings on a sarcophagus created in the year 353 (figure 4.2). This stone burial box served as both tomb and memorial to Junius Bassus, a Roman official and Christian convert, and was decorated with richly carved scenes from the Old and New Testaments. Though the stories and characters in these scenes are biblical, the visual language is distinctly Roman. The figures appear in Roman garb, and each scene is set in a framework of classical Roman architecture. In the center, Christ appears as ruler of the world, seated on the vault of heaven (held up by the sky god Caelus), looking like an emperor-god, with the written law or Gospels in one hand. At his side are two apostles, who are differentiated from their master by their ordinary short hair and curly beards. Christ, with his rounded cheeks appears, in fact, to be little more than a teenager. The designer was clearly more worried about making him appear too old than too young. Though strange to the modern eye, it was sensible to the Roman audience, because Christ looked more like a god than those around him.

Of course, long hair and beardlessness were not the only ways ancient artists indicated divinity. The nimbus, or halo, had been used to mark the divine status of emperors, and in Christian painting it was now assigned to Christ and the saints. Some images had Jesus surrounded by an aureola, a sort of halo around the entire body, which was borrowed from very ancient traditions originating beyond Europe. Beardlessness complemented these symbols. It was like a halo in that it distinguished the extraordinary from the ordinary face.

This is not to say that Jesus never appeared with a beard in these early centuries. Bishop Eusebius, as we recall, confiscated a picture of Jesus with a long beard. Some images were modeled on Zeus, the chief god of Greek mythology, or Asclepius, the god of healing, both of whom were customarily portrayed wearing thick, dark beards. These

4.2 Detail of Christ with apostles from the Sarcophagus of Junius Bassus, 4th century. Erich Lessing/Art Resource, NY.

were, however, the exceptions rather than the rule, until the sixth century. By the seventh century a single, consistent image prevailed, featuring long, typically brown hair and a moderate-length beard. This was the medieval, as opposed to classical, Jesus. Why and how did this metamorphosis occur? And what does this transformation say about facial hair and manliness in Christian culture? The answers to these questions are to be found in the transitional centuries between classical and medieval art, during which both types of Christ images appeared side by side, sometimes even in the same work of art. This juxtaposition helps to explain the thinking that led Christian art in a new direction.

Transitional Centuries

Though the youthful-heroic look predominated in early Christian art, there really was no official, standard image, and early Christians felt no compulsion to be consistent. Christ figures with quite different looks were often present in the same churches, or even in the same work of art. Facial hair in these images indicated an intentional choice to convey something about Jesus. A notable example of this is in the dazzling mosaics that decorate the sixth-century church of Saint Apollinaire Nuovo in Ravenna, Italy. On one side of the sanctuary, among other images, is a series of scenes illustrating the teaching and miracles of Christ. On the opposite wall is a parallel sequence depicting Christ's betrayal, passion, death, and resurrection. The clothing is the same in both series, but the teaching and miracle-working Jesus is beardless, while the Jesus on the other side has longer hair and a beard that

4.3 Christ performing the miracle of the loaves and fishes. Mosaic in the Church of St. Apollinare Nuovo, Ravenna, Italy, 6th century. Alfredo Dagli Orti/Art Resource, NY.

4.4 Christ on the road to Calvary. Mosaic in the Church of St. Apollinare Nuovo, Ravenna, Italy, 6th century. Scala/Art Resource, NY.

seems to get longer as the story progresses.[6] In the first sequence, in other words, Jesus appears as he had in countless earlier paintings and carvings, that is, as an eternally youthful figure who stands out from the ordinary, bearded men around him. In the picture illustrating the miracle of the loaves and fishes, for example, his long hair and smooth face give him, from a modern perspective, a rather feminine look (figure 4.3). In the trial and death scenes on the opposite side of the nave, Christ is again distinguished from ordinary men, but this time by his longer beard, as one can observe in his procession to the crucifixion (figure 4.4). The reason Jesus is portrayed so differently in the same work of art has long puzzled art historians, but it is evident that the designers of the church wished to suggest that Jesus was a different sort of savior in the two main phases of his earthly life.[7] In the first phase, he is a god among men; in the second, he is not immortal in the same sense. Instead, he is the suffering Son of Man who triumphs over death in the resurrection.

To make better sense of this contrasting symbolism, it is helpful to examine other artworks that include both a bearded and a nonbearded Jesus. One of these is the Antioch Chalice, an elaborately decorated silver cup created in Constantinople in the late fifth or early sixth century. On one side is a seated, smooth-faced Christ stretching his hand in the gesture of speech. On the opposite side is a bearded Christ in an identical position, but holding a scroll. These symbols indicate that the beardless Christ is teaching, while the bearded Christ is in heaven, possibly at the last judgment.[8]

Still another example can be found in Rome, in the fifth-century ceiling mosaics of the Church of Santa Costanza. In one area of the ceiling, a youthful, almost beardless Christ is seen delivering the law to the bearded saints Peter and Paul before ascending to heaven; sheep in the foreground represent the Christian faithful who will look to the apostles for guidance and protection. In another vault nearby, executed at the same time and in the same style, a heavily bearded Christ sits enthroned on the globe as ruler of the world, attended by a beardless saint or angel. These two images are inverses of each other, reflecting their contrasting settings: one on earth, one in heaven.

These three examples, from Ravenna, Constantinople, and Rome, all follow a similar pattern. The Christ of the passion and ressurection is bearded; the teaching and miracle-working Jesus is not. In each case, his hair contrasts with those around him, reinforcing his uniqueness. On earth, a smooth-faced Christ is the divine man among bearded mortals. In the world above, he is the bearded Son of Man, in striking contrast to the smooth-faced angels who populate heaven. Christian art was quite consistent on this last point: angels (always male) have the long-haired, youthful look of eternal life. In their heavenly company, Christ needed to look different, more human. In the final analysis, contrasting hair was a valuable method to indicate that Christ was neither a man nor an angel, that wherever he might be, and whatever he might be doing, he is like no other.

The Iconic Christ

At the time these different Christ figures were created, a new artistic style was becoming popular, the icon. This was a portrait of a holy figure such as Christ, Mary, a saint, or an angel that was used in private and public worship as a focus of veneration. It was a visual object that made a divine person present and accessible to the worshipper, lifting his or her mind and spirit toward the sacred.[9] The purpose of this image was different from the narrative or symbolic representations of earlier art. Context and narrative faded away in favor of a "true" likeness that manifested the inner, spiritual character of holiness and created a mystical link to the divine presence.[10]

Creating a single, true likeness of Christ was a special problem for icon painters, who needed to portray, in a single face, the teaching, miracle-working, suffering, and resurrected Christ. Without action or specific context, the icon painter could not rely on the visual contrasts used by designers of narrative scenes. The solution to this problem can be seen in one of the earliest preserved icon paintings, a sixth-century portrait in the monastery of St. Catherine on Mount Sinai (figure 4.5). Produced in Constantinople, the capital of Orthodox Christendom, it presents Christ before a background of distant buildings and golden stars that suggests both heaven and earth. Within the figure itself, however, the visual logic of the heavenly, bearded Christ prevails over the beardless, earthly Christ. For one thing, there are no mortals in the scene from whom Jesus must be differentiated. For another, the inert form and golden hues accentuate the heavenly setting over the earthly. The iconic Jesus, then, is not the divine man among mortals. He is the Son of Man in heaven. And artistic tradition had depicted Christ in heaven as bearded, to make him more human and to distinguish him from angels.

In the icon painting, Christ's beard also helped establish the right balance in representing his divine and human natures. If Christ was too heavenly, distant, and angelic, he could not also be the compassionate savior who shared in human suffering. The point of the icon, after all, was to make Jesus intimately present. It was necessary to give the Christ figure a human touch, and the painter of the St. Catherine icon managed this by endowing him with an ordinary, medium-length beard, representing neither the youthful immortality of a classical god nor the full, philosophic, or Zeus-like hairiness one sometimes finds in earlier representations.

When one considers the overall impression of the St. Catherine image, it becomes apparent how different components of the portrait work to harmonize the grandeur and modesty of Christ. On the

4.5 Icon of Christ offering a blessing. Monastery of St. Catherine, Sinai, Egypt, 6th century. Gianni Dagli Orti/Art Archive at Art Resource, NY.

one hand, he appears with an unworldly golden halo around his head, golden stars above, and a jewel-encrusted Bible in his arm. On the other, he greets you at eye level with two fingers raised in a comforting sign of blessing. His face is likewise both impressive and modest. He is a bearded man with extraordinary, flowing hair and a firm demeanor, yet his beard is moderate and ordinary, and his features mild. Having struck upon an effective visual formula for the complex personality of Christ, artists have more or less faithfully reproduced it ever since.

Church Fathers Promote Beards

The visual logic of iconic art was the primary reason for Jesus's beard, but it drew powerful reinforcement from theology. The development of icons occurred at a time when many leaders of the church strongly approved of facial hair. The so-called Fathers of the Church were theologians of the first six centuries whose writings were afterward taken as authoritative. These men promoted a positive view of facial hair as part of their assertion of a male-dominated gender order. The masculinity of Christ, as well as his humanity, was very important to them.

The earliest proponent of Christian beardedness was the influential theologian Clement of Alexandria (ca. 150–ca. 215). Clement was a Christian convert steeped in Greek philosophy who lived in the time of the first beard movement. He channeled Aristotle and Epictetus in his discussions of manliness and hair, though he added a tone of divine insistence lacking in these earlier authors. Epictetus had hoped to shame men into growing beards, but Clement threatened them with damnation. "God planned," he wrote, "that woman be smooth-skinned, taking pride in her natural tresses, the only hair she has . . . but man He adorned like the lion, with a beard, and gave him a hairy chest as proof of his manhood and a sign of his strength and primacy." It was, he insisted, "a sacrilege to trifle with the symbol of manhood."[11] Clement's contemporary, Tertullian, the first great Latin Christian writer, also defended beards as proof of a supposedly natural gender order. His *On the Apparel of Women* was primarily concerned with female indulgence and vanity, though he also reprimanded men who dyed their hair or cut their beards too closely.[12] Both Tertullian and Clement were eager to steer their Christian readers away from self-indulgence and disorderly desire. To their thinking, modesty involved acceptance of the body as God made it, and an embrace of the male superiority it supposedly demonstrated.

For Christians of the late Roman Empire, however, the human body became more controversial. Many saw it as corrupt, a burden to the soul, and an impediment to spiritual renewal and eternal life. Many enthusiasts sought a spiritual transformation and resurrection that would literally leave the body in the dust. The new byword was "virginity," and true holiness was redefined as the total abandonment of sexuality, and therefore of social and family life. This new asceticism sought to gradually release the soul from the chain binding it to an earthly prison, so that at death it could emerge from the abandoned body in spiritual perfection. The most influential exponent of this view was the theologian Origen (185–254), a onetime student of Clement. Origen believed that the triumph over the body did not have to wait for death but could begin immediately in the life of faith. Origen praised the ascetic life and the denial of physical urges, going so far as to castrate himself as an act of liberation. With Origen and others of his stripe, the denial of sexuality involved overcoming the limits of the body and also of gender. Many expected that in the life to come, masculinity and femininity would become irrelevant in the angelic perfection of the soul.[13]

The problem with this view, in the minds of many Christians of the time, was that the denial of the body and of gender difference could not be confined to heaven but threatened to overthrow the gender order on earth as well. Origen and other writers like him provoked a backlash in the fourth century, as Christian authors recoiled from this frightening precipice. St. Jerome (347–420), for one, was caught on the horn of this dilemma. He was a man deeply committed to the ascetic life, an admirer of monasticism and even of Origen himself. But the more radical implications of Origen's thought frightened him, so he tried to find a middle ground: a theology of self-control rather than renunciation. He also emphasized the importance of the body and of bodily resurrection. In spite of Paul's declaration that in Christ there is no male or female, Jerome believed that in the life to come men will still be men, and women will still be women. Gender, in other words, is so fundamental that even death and salvation cannot dissolve it. Though Jerome had been both a beneficiary of and mentor to powerful Christian women, he rejected both the spiritual resurrection and women's claims to spiritual equality that would be its result.[14]

In this regard, Jerome was in perfect harmony with most Christian leaders of his day, who agreed that it did no good for women to stroke their hairless cheeks and dream of a resurrection that would void their inferior status. The Church Fathers favored the notion that resurrection was a restoration rather than a transformation. Neither a man's gender nor his beard would disappear in heaven. On the contrary, they would be restored in fuller glory, all blemishes of body and soul erased. St.

Augustine (354–430), the single most influential Church Father in Christian history, also favored the idea of bodily resurrection and the preservation of sexual traits (though not of sexuality) in the eternal life. The body would be a spiritualized body, however, attaining a kind of perfection impossible in earthly life. Speaking as a Greek sculptor might have, he envisioned that the resurrected body would attain the beautiful proportion of the peak of life.[15] Augustine made clear that hair would be included in this restoration, though he surmised that the number of hairs rather than their lengths would be preserved.

The fact that Augustine, unlike classical artists, included beards in resurrected perfection indicates that he, like other Church Fathers before him, viewed masculinity as fundamental to creation, not just a physical attribute but a quality of the soul, manifest particularly in the virtues of fortitude and nobility. In his commentary on Psalm 33, Augustine interpreted the mention of David's beard as a reference to his spiritual strength.[16] Similarly, he interpreted the reference to Aaron's beard in Psalm 133 to denote Aaron's authority and, allegorically, the apostles who bravely confronted the world with the Gospel. "The beard," Augustine explained, "signifies the courageous; the beard distinguishes the grown men, the earnest, the active, the vigorous."[17] It was symbolic of spiritual virtue, with the definite implication that men had stronger spirits than women. As an ornament of the manly soul it was beautiful rather than practical, and offered a small glimpse of the fuller beauty of the life to come.[18]

When theologians like Jerome and Augustine praised masculinity and beards in defense of the gender order, they provided a theological basis for a bearded Jesus. The fact that Jesus was a man was essential to his authority, and his beard was essential to his being a man. Christ's manliness, in turn, legitimized both the existing social order and the dominance of men in the church.

After centuries of experiment and change, the image of Christ became fixed in many key respects, particularly in regard to his hair. The almost universal agreement on a bearded Jesus in Christian art since the seventh century originated in an effort to humanize the divine Christ, but in many eras, including our own, it has instead had the effect of making him appear archaic and unworldly. On the other hand, every age can recognize the masculinity of Christ in the standard image, and this has been an important visual prop for male authority in the world. Lest women think that we all are all one in Christ, Christ is emphatically not female. The bearded Christ reinforces the notion that beards are literally heavenly and underscores the even more ancient association of facial hair with wisdom and authority. Men, being more akin to Christ, thus affirmed for themselves their privileged station in the kingdom of God and entitlement to leadership in the church.

5

THE INNER BEARD

Any man who wonders why custom requires him to shave every day must turn his thoughts back to the Middle Ages, when ancient models of manliness were cast aside and replaced with new ones that eventually shaped modern customs. As in ancient Mesopotamia, medieval culture produced competing types of manhood, each with its distinctive hairstyle, yet by the end of the Middle Ages, one masculine mode—beardlessness—had emerged triumphant. This was the church's doing. Though the iconic Christ remained bearded, medieval Christianity embedded in the European mind a link between shaving and goodness, and secured the ascendancy of the razor in Western civilization.

This linkage took time. It was not an obvious or self-evident principle, nor did it have any currency beyond the territories of Latin Christianity. It arose from the particular convictions, conflicts, and confluences of medieval European life. Twelve hundred years ago, when Charlemagne built the first great state of the medieval era, the reformation of the manly face was already underway.

Charlemagne Has Himself Crowned

Charlemagne, or Charles the Great, was king of the Franks and conqueror of Europe during his long reign from 768 to 814. His domi-

5.1 (*Left*) Bearded Charlemagne of the medieval imagination. Reliquary bust said to contain part of Charlemagne's skull, 14th century. Erich Lessing/Art Resource, NY. (*Right*) Mustachioed Charlemagne of history. Bronze statuette, 9th century. Erich Lessing/Art Resource, NY.

nance over Europe was a great achievement, not to be matched for the remainder of the Middle Ages. Naturally, he became a legend in later centuries, taking on the role of the ideal king. As a result, there were really two Charlemagnes: one of fable, and one of history. One Charlemagne triumphed magnificently against the Moors in Spain; the other did not. One captured Jerusalem from the heathens; the other did not. One had a great white beard; the other did not. As a rule, the masculinity of the medieval imagination was more full-throated and full-bearded than it was in actual practice. Real life was more complicated, and more interesting.

The mythic-hero version of Charlemagne emerges most vividly in one of the popular hits of the Middle Ages, the *Song of Roland*, an epic poem written down about three centuries after the great king's death. In this fantasy, Charlemagne is the perfect patriarch: strong, wise, and fatherly. Roland is his perfect vassal: brave, dedicated, and loyal. As a great king, Charlemagne's most important physical attribute is his great white beard, for it tells the story of his soul.[1] When his beloved nephew Roland volunteers for the dangerous mission of leading his rearguard forces in the Frankish march home from Spain, the ruler of the Franks wants to say no, and he slowly strokes his beard before reluctantly agreeing. Roland and his small force are then ambushed, and he bravely stands his ground, slaying hundreds of Arabs with his magnificent sword, Durendal, all the while thinking only of serving his emperor "of the lovely beard." The news of Roland's tragic fate breaks Charlemagne's heart, "who does not raise his head at all, but only plays with his beard and his moustaches, while tears collect on his eye-lashes."[2] Recovering from his agony, the emperor rides forth to exact his revenge, his flowing beard tumbling majestically over his breastplate. In the end, Charlemagne is triumphant but saddened. His wisdom and might have prevailed but at great personal cost. Sadly, he soldiers on. In the final stanza, news arrives of a pagan assault in Italy. "'God!' he says, 'My life is sorrow.' He weeps, tugging his white beard."[3]

The fictional Charlemagne's manly virtues show themselves in his magnificent hair. When acting as loving father, he is said to have a "lovely beard," when a warrior, a "flowing beard," and when a wise ruler, a "white beard." By the same token, the sorrow of manly responsibility is felt in the self-inflicted agony of beard-pulling. This equation does not mean, of course, that all men, or even all patriarchs, actually had great beards. In fact, long beards were more common in myth than in history, and were less in evidence in Charlemagne's time than during the twelfth century, when the *Song of Roland* was composed. The real Charlemagne did not tug his beard tragically because he did not have one. He did not sit on a throne like a white-bearded statue because he had places to go and people to see.

The actual, mustachioed Charlemagne was, in his own way, just as impressive as his bearded legend. For one thing, he was physically imposing, standing six feet, three inches, with a thick frame, making him truly a giant among men at a time when people were on average much shorter than they are today. Unlike his mythic antitype, however, the historical Charlemagne was far less interested in crusading in Arab lands than in civilizing his own half-Latin, half-German, largely impoverished kingdom. To accomplish this, he marshaled both the military prowess of his German nobles and the civilizing powers of the Roman church. Charlemagne himself reflected his two-toned society. On the one hand, he spoke German and ruled in the manner of a German chieftain. In German tradition he kept several wives, even if only one them was official. On the other hand, he studiously practiced speaking and writing in Latin, he wore Roman-style clothing, and he gathered around himself the best scholars and wisest counselors the church had to offer. Under their guidance, he founded schools, stocked libraries, built monasteries, and promoted the moral and social teachings of the church, even if it meant he had to curb some of his own German tendencies.

One of those tendencies was to favor long hair and beards. Earlier rulers of the Franks had been famous for their uncut hair and flowing beards, but Charlemagne's father had dispossessed the old dynasty, and both father and son rejected its old, hairy ways. Charlemagne cut his hair short, in the Roman, churchly fashion, and limited his facial hair to a bushy mustache. He may have found inspiration in a famous statue of the great Theodoric, the Gothic ruler of Italy three centuries earlier, who wore a similar decoration. In any case, the mustache worked for Charlemagne as a sort of compromise. It was German, but not too far from the Roman preference for modesty in hair.[4]

The crowning achievement of Charlemagne's reign was precisely that. On Christmas morning in the year 800, Pope Leo III crowned him Roman emperor, a title not known in Western Europe for over three centuries. In a ceremony that was carefully choreographed and imbued with deep symbolism, the German and Latin worlds were formally fused to create a new state and a new society. It began with pope and king praying together, prostrate before the altar of old St. Peter's Basilica in Rome, the spiritual home of the Roman Catholic Church, which the first Christian emperor, Constantine, had built nearly five hundred years before. High above the assembled courtiers and clergy, the ancient glory of Christian civilization rose in classical columns and glittering mosaic images of popes and apostles. On a high arch above the great altar, giant figures of Emperor Constantine, St. Peter, and the enthroned Christ gazed down through a mystical haze of incense. Inscribed on this arch were old but timely words: "Constantine has founded this royal hall for Christ because the world has risen in triumph to the stars with Him as guide and leader."[5] And so, in this "royal hall" of St. Peter's, the world seemed to rise in triumph again under a new emperor. After king and pope lifted themselves from the floor, the ruler of the church placed the imperial crown on the king's head, anointed him with holy oil, and prostrated himself at the feet of Europe's master. On cue, the assembled clergy proclaimed him "pious Augustus, crowned by God."[6]

Charlemagne was not really the Augustus of old, of course. He did not have the shaved face of the original Augustus, nor of Constantine, who towered benevolently above him. The new age was certainly not a restoration of ancient Rome. Charlemagne was, after all, still a German, and he still had his mustache. On the other hand, he wished to be known as pious and crowned by God. In that respect, less rather than more hair was appropriate, not only because it was the Roman style, but also because the church had begun to articulate a new alignment between piety, goodness, and shorn hair.

This equation of holiness and hair-cutting had taken root in the wreckage of the old Roman Empire well before Charlemagne's time. At first, it was simply a pragmatic choice. As German tribes swept over Europe, subduing Latin Europe, the Latin-speaking clergy struggled to retain their independence, cohesion and authority. To reinforce their separate identity, they assiduously maintained the short, Roman hairstyle. Taking their cue from the classical past, and also from St. Paul's rejection of long hair in the First Letter to the Corinthians, church authorities formally legislated short hair for all clergy.[7] Beards were not specifically regulated but fell under the general rule of moderation. Because the German nobility proudly grew their hair long, this instruction helped differentiate churchmen from laymen. A council of bishops meeting in Portugal in the year 563 prohibited clergy from wearing long hair "like pagans."[8] This ban was repeated by later councils throughout Western Europe, and by 721, Pope Gregory II was threatening long-haired priests in the province of Rome with excommunication. It was clearly more than a matter of decorum; short hair had become an essential symbol of priesthood and holiness.

By the time Pope Gregory issued his command, a new, even more radical type of haircut was spreading among Western clergy. Short hair, it seems, was not enough. Beginning in sixth-century Gaul (modern-day France), men entering the priesthood had the tops of their heads

shaved bald, leaving a distinctive *corona,* or crown of hair. This practice, known as the tonsure, was soon adopted throughout Europe,
along with an explanatory myth that it was done in imitation of St.
Peter, the founder of the church. Symbolically, the crown of hair was
also associated with Christ's crown of thorns. Pope Gregory I (Gregory
the Great, 540–604) provided the authoritative explanation of the tonsure, whose logic was later extended to beard-shaving as well: "What
do we understand in a moral sense by hair, but the wandering thoughts
of the mind?" Therefore, "the shaving of the head then is the cutting off
all superfluous thoughts from the mind. And he shaveth his head and
falls upon the earth, who, restraining thoughts of self-presumption,
humbly acknowledges how weak he is in himself."[9] In this way, hair was
linked with sin, and its removal became a kind of purification. Without
really knowing or trying, the medieval church had reconstituted a very
ancient logic of hairless purity.

Early on, this notion of shaving away sins involved beards as well
as the crown of the head for monks. They were professionals in the
truest sense of the word, for they professed, that is to say, they took
a vow of humility and service. Even more than ordinary priests, who
at the time were allowed to marry and have families, they renounced
the world. Because they undertook a higher standard of spiritual discipline, it made sense that monks would shave off even more of their hair.
Regular shaving for monks (about once a month) became the law of the
land in 816, when Charlemagne's son, Louis, issued a new set of regulations for monasteries. Not to be outdone, many priests opted to shave
their beards as well, as did many laymen, according to the report of a
scandalized Arab observer, Hārūn ibn Yaḥā. The inhabitants of Rome,
he wrote in 886, "young and old, shave off their beards entirely, not
leaving a single hair."[10] He was told it was the Christian thing to do. This
clearly made no sense to Hārūn, for it rejected the natural link between
patriarchy and beardedness that even western Europeans acknowledged. What he failed to recognize, however, was that the Latin church
was formulating an alternative form of patriarchy based on the unique
spiritual authority of celibate professionals. This new symbolism of holy
hairlessness scandalized not only Muslims but also Orthodox Christians
of the Byzantine Empire.

In centuries of arguments between Catholics and Orthodox Christians, stretching from Charlemagne's time to the final breach two centuries later, Orthodox divines rehearsed a long list of theological objections to wayward Westerners, almost always including the reprehensible practice of priestly shaving. It was, they said, contrary to the regulations of the early church, not to mention degrading for the clergy.[11] Westerners like the monk-scholar Ratramnus (d. 868) rose to the defense. Building on ideas articulated by Pope Gregory the Great, he spoke of the heart, or spirit, residing in the head. The hair of the face and head represented a barrier of worldliness that stood between God and the soul. "The face of the heart," he wrote, "ought continually to be stripped of earthly thoughts, in order that it may be able to look upon the glory of the Lord with a pure and sincere expression, and to be transformed into it through the grace of that contemplation."[12] For a monk like Ratramnus, beardlessness was an important facet of holy living.

For all his success, Charlemagne's empire did not survive beyond the 800s. Europe broke down into smaller kingdoms, counties, and cities. In the political wreckage, the church grew even more powerful. It alone unified Europe, and the pope was the only man who could claim the allegiance of all Europeans. In the 900s, however, in the eastern portion of Charlemagne's old empire—Germany and Italy—a new line of kings arose to establish, in name at least, the "Holy Roman Empire." These rulers claimed the old powers of Charlemagne and vied with the popes for mastery in German and Italian territory. As this competition between church and royalty intensified, battle lines were drawn both on maps and on men's faces.

Pope Gregory VII Draws the Line

Before he became pope in 1073, Gregory VII was known as Hildebrand, a monk, papal counselor, and standard-bearer for church power. Energized by a wave of religious enthusiasm that swept Europe in the 1000s, reformers like Hildebrand embraced a bold vision of a Christendom ruled not by rough and semiliterate feudal nobles but by pure and righteous churchmen. As pope, Gregory's first priority was to secure the power to appoint bishops and other high church officials, which up to that time had been largely in secular hands. In short order, he found himself toe to toe with Henry IV, the young king of Germany, who was equally determined to retain his own grip on church offices.

In January 1077, this struggle between the forces of sword and spirit came to a head on a remote mountaintop. Pope and king were traveling to meet each other to settle their dispute, and their paths crossed high in the Alps at Canossa Castle. At the moment, the pope had the upper hand. Almost a year before, he had invoked the authority of God in officially stripping Henry of his royal title, the first pope ever to take such drastic action. He had also excommunicated the king, declaring him cut off from the mother church and its soul-saving grace. By the pope's decree, Henry's subjects were released from any obligation to obey their royal master, prompting many lords and bishops to renounce their sovereign. King Henry was now a desperate man. His authority and his future hung in the balance, and only the pope's satisfaction could save him.

Pope Gregory sat comfortably within the wintry walls of Canossa Castle, secure in his righteousness. Henry literally stood outside in the cold, begging to come in and seek the pope's pardon. For two days in succession, Henry slowly walked barefoot up the winding, icy road to the castle gate, dressed in a plain, penitential woolen tunic, to kneel and tearfully plead for forgiveness, only to be denied admittance and forced to trudge back down to the village below. When Henry appeared again for a third day, the pope, surrounded by advisors who counseled mercy, finally relented. The king and five German bishops entered the castle, kneeling before the pope to receive his absolution, along with the symbolic kiss of peace. Henry promised in writing to obey the pope's decisions concerning the church. The pope then celebrated mass with his former adversaries and hosted a sumptuous banquet.

Gregory had good reason to be pleased. He had got what he hoped for, but, strangely enough, so did Henry. By reconciling himself to the church, he was restored as the legitimate king. His subjects were once again obligated to obey him, and in the years ahead, he rebuilt his power to the point where he was able to force Gregory himself out of Rome and place for a time his own man on the papal throne. The back-and-forth between Henry and Gregory reflected the new character of medieval politics at this time, and for several centuries after. Neither kings nor popes could rule without consideration of the other. There were two entrenched powers with two discrete systems of law (canon law and civil law), two hierarchies (ecclesiastical and noble), and two primary forms of manly dignity—professional and patriarchal. Naturally enough, there were also two contrasting masculine styles: shaved and bearded.

In their quest to strengthen the church, reformers like Gregory sought to imbue churchmen with a higher sense of professionalism. The essence of medieval professionalism—the very origin of the word—was the fulfillment of a vow to give oneself wholly to the service of God, especially in learning and prayer. To eleventh-century reformers like Pope Gregory, the truest model of professionalism was the monastery. A monk did not live to serve himself or his family, only God. He denied himself sex, children, and wealth so that he might give himself entirely to the church. Reformers dreamed of raising the entire clergy to this high standard and began to insist that all priests model themselves on monks. Like monks, they were to hold their offices as a calling, not a source of income. They should not pay money to powerful nobles for their posts (a sin called simony), and they should renounce worldly temptations in a celibate life. Not surprisingly, there were many objections to these new requirements, but Gregory and his allies were adamant. The church must be purified in order to serve God and command his kingdom.

Adopting the professionalism of monks meant looking like monks. Before the eleventh century, only monks had been required to shave. Now it was mandated for all churchmen. Beardlessness was next to godliness. As Pope Gregory engaged in battle with secular power, he vigorously enforced this and other reform measures. He excommunicated bishops for simony, denounced married priests, and strenuously insisted on shaving. In 1080, for example, he sent an urgent letter to the ruler of Cagliari, a Sardinian port city, instructing him to require the clergy under his control to shear off their beards. Those who refused were to have their properties confiscated. In explaining his rule, Gregory claimed that he was enforcing the practice of the church "from its beginning."[13] This was pure fiction, of course. Shaving was an entirely new policy, but the pope was happy to rewrite history for a greater cause.

Perhaps it is a little unfair to blame Gregory for this fabrication. Around the time he was born, earlier reformers had covertly rewritten canon law to make it appear as though beardlessness was authorized by ancient councils. In 1023, a new collection of canon law was published in Rome that included three different statutes requiring clergymen to shave. Canon 208 carried the greatest weight, because it was said to come from the prestigious fifth-century *Statuta ecclesiae antiqua,* or Ancient Church Statues. The new version, however, subtly corrupted the older law: a word in the phrase "Clericus nec comam nutriat nec barbam radat" (Clergy should neither grow long hair, *nor* shave the beard) was changed, so that it now read "Clericus nec comam nutriat sed barbam radat" (Clergy should not grow long hair but *should* shave their beard).[14] The adulterated regulation also declared that those of the Roman fellowship who disregarded this rule were to be expelled.[15] Beginning with a council of bishops meeting at Bourges (France) in 1031, church councils throughout Europe moved to enforce this and similar regulations.

The advance of clerical shaving created a dramatic contrast between churchmen and laymen, just as it was supposed to do.[16] The clergy became rather proud of their unique style and often guarded it jealously. When fashionable young knights adopted a smooth look in Burgundy and Germany in the early eleventh century, many clergymen reacted with alarm. Shaving was a spiritual act for churchmen but perverse in laymen. William of Volpiano, a Burgundian monk, repeatedly denounced vain men who sported outlandish clothes, indecent hose and shoes, and smooth faces. His protégé, Bishop Siegfried of Gorze, later issued similar denunciations of German nobles, warning that "with these exterior changes, it is the mores themselves which are changed," a corruption that threatened to unleash on the Holy Roman Empire a plague of crime and sin.[17] Othlonus, a monk and scholar in Regensberg around the same time, included among his written works an account of a layman who was reproached by his priest for the sin of shaving. "Because you are a layman," the priest said, "according to the custom of the laity, you ought not to go around with a shaved beard, but instead you, in contempt of divine law, have shaved your beard like a cleric."[18] After the layman reneged on his promise not to shave again, he was captured by his enemies and had his eyes gouged out, which

Othlonus interpreted as divine punishment for his heinous offense. A century later, churchmen were still complaining about the shaving vanities of young dandies. Alain of Lille, a scholarly (and shaven) French monk in the early 1200s, mocked vain men who "over-effeminize themselves with womanish adornments," including tight shirts, small gloves and narrow shoes, and "set frequent ambushes with the razor for their sprouting beard."[19] From the perspective of the church, the wrong sort of shaving sent the wrong signal, undermining the essential link between beardlessness and holy professionalism. To shave in order to look youthful and handsome was both effeminizing and vile.

The ideal of holy hairlessness, now enshrined in church law, remained in force until 1917, when a beard finally ceased to be an excommunicable offense in the Catholic church. The ambition of the church to rule the world for God inspired its leaders to marshal its forces and raise its standards. Fundamentally, professionalism attempted to supplant patriarchy, or rather to become the new patriarchy. It may seem odd that celibate, shaved men claimed superiority over noble, bearded ones. The key to this paradox was that medieval thinkers saw in a hairless face not the absence of something but the presence of something better. The removal of the physical beard made way for the inner beard.

Abbot Burchard Offers an Apology

In the century after Pope Gregory's battle with the Holy Roman Emperor, the church continued to gain prestige and strength. More than ever before or since, the holy professionals—monks and nuns—were held up as model Christians leading the ideal life. Landowning families donated their wealth as well as their sons and daughters to this great cause, and both old and new orders spread like holy wildfire.

At the forefront of this expansion was a new order, the Cistercians, who were admired throughout Europe for their quiet, austere routine of work and prayer. In their quest for simplicity, they sought out rural and isolated settings, built grand but plainly designed abbeys and cloisters, and trimmed back the elaborate processions and rituals popular in other monasteries. Even now, in their decayed or ruined state, the unornamented walls, arches, and windows of Cistercian abbeys evoke a timeless peacefulness, far removed from the selfish striving of the world. The cloistered life was not always as serene or as selfless as it was meant to be, however. In 1160, Abbot Burchard, who was in charge of several hundred monks and lay brothers at the Cistercian abbey of Bellevaux, in eastern France, found himself embroiled in a controversy about beards.

Cistercian houses consisted of two ranks—regular ordained monks and lay brothers. The lay brothers were recruited from the peasant class, and their calling was to labor in the monastery's fields and workshops rather than to pray in the choir stalls, as the regular monks did. In most houses they outnumbered the regular monks. The lay brothers wore a darker-hued robe and, by rule, wore medium-length beards to distinguish them from the shaven monks. Discipline among the bearded brothers, as they were often called, was occasionally a problem, and Burchard had received word of unruliness at Bellevaux's daughter monastery at Rosières. Using a metaphorical turn of phrase, Burchard warned the lay brothers there that if they did not mend their ways, they might end up having their beards burned. He was making clever reference to a phrase in the book of Isaiah, in which the prophet warns that any garment mixed with blood would become fuel for the fire. In Burchard's phrasing, the brothers needed to save their own garments—their beards—from the metaphorical flames by avoiding boasting, dissention, and vanity. But the lay brothers felt threatened rather than moved by Burchard's words: Why did he scorn their beards? Were the brothers required to grow them so that the monks might abuse them and their hair?

As he pondered these objections, Abbot Burchard realized that a discussion of facial hair might be, as it were, a teaching moment for the lay brothers of his order. The result was history's first book about beards, the *Apologia de Barbis* (Explanation of Beards).[20] Burchard delighted in the complexity of his subject. He looked at how a beard can represent the moral self, signify right social manners, and reflect the glory of God's creation. Beards were, he thought, a marvelous demonstration of God's creative power and a fascinating example of "wisdom playing with nature."[21] When God's wisdom molds nature in this manner, it leaves a divine imprint that instructs humans about the true order of things.

5.2 Cistercian lay brothers praying. Detail from the tomb of St. Etienne, Aubazine Abbey, France, 13th century. Courtesy of Noël Tassain.

In considering his subject, Burchard would have benefited from the work of his contemporary to the east, the German abbess Hildegard of Bingen, a famous mystic and a natural theorist. Unfortunately, her works on human physiology and medicine were not yet known in 1160, which was too bad, because her scientific explanation of beards was the best ever proposed in the Middle Ages. The ancients had spoken of vital heat, moisture, and porous skin but never figured out a convincing reason why beards grew on certain parts of the face and not others. Hildegard had an answer. Thinking of biblical passages about the life-giving breath of God, she imagined that it was the hotter breath of men that nourished the growth of hair around the mouth. Women did not have beards because their breath was not so warm.[22] To Hildegard this difference of heat and hair had deeper roots in the Genesis creation. "That the male has a beard," she wrote, "and more hair on his body than a woman is because the male is formed from earth and has greater strength and warmth and is everywhere more active than woman. . . . But woman is without a beard because she is formed from the flesh of man and is subordinate to man and lives in greater quiet."[23] Here Hildegard offers a concise, if standard, concept of gender difference in relation to the physiology of hair.

If Burchard had known of Hildegard's ideas, he might have explored this connection between hair and creation. As it was, he relied on the authority of St. Augustine, who thought that all references to beards in scripture indicated masculine qualities of courage, earnestness, and vigor. Burchard surmised that there was more to it than that. The great variety of beards must mean something, and he imagined a typology where different parts of facial hair represented distinct moral qualities. Hair on the chin signified wisdom, hair under the chin was the sign of strong feeling, and hair along the jaw, a projection of virtue. "All in all," he wrote, "a beard is appropriate to a man as a sign of his comeliness, as a sign of his strength, as a sign of his wisdom, as a sign of his maturity, and as a sign of his piety. And when these things are equally present in a man, he can justly be called full bearded, since his beard shows him to be, not a half-man or a womanly man, but a complete man, with a beard that is plentiful on his chin and along his jaw and under his chin."[24]

To this extent facial hair was an admirable thing, but monks rid themselves of this emblem of wisdom and virtue because they pursued an even higher manly calling: the inner beard. In taking up this theme, Burchard stood on the firm ground of well-established medieval theology. Early medieval writers, notably Pope Gregory the Great in the seventh century, had written of hair as an allegorical representation of worldly thoughts, sinful or not, that must be shed in order to bare oneself to God. The twelfth-century abbot and bishop Bruno (d. 1123) put this idea in the clearest terms: "Men who are strong are superior to those who only wish to seem so. Therefore, let our interior beard grow, just as the exterior is shaved; for the former grows without impediment, while the latter, unless it is shaved, creates many inconveniences and is only nurtured and made beautiful by men who are truly idle and vain."[25] What grows inside, Bruno was saying, is the true strength of holy manliness.

Burchard extended this line of thought in his discourse to the bearded brothers. Like Bruno, he argued that actual beards were temptations to vanity. Worldly and powerful men sported braided beards, pointed mustaches, and shaped, forked, or fish-tailed cuts in order to stand out and impress. He advised the brothers to avoid these conceits and "let the beard appear to be neglected in rustic lack of fashion rather than shaped with excessive care into a lustful composition."[26] For the monks, as opposed to lay brothers, this modesty was not enough. "We form the hair of our heads into the shape of a crown by shaving, and shave our beards in order to aim for perfection in mind and spirit while we seek to strip away all that is superfluous and this-worldly from our feelings and desires."[27] Lay brothers, by contrast, do not make the form of a crown on their heads or shave their beards, "because lay simplicity, occupied by the earthly kind of labor, is not learned in the writings that allow one to penetrate spiritual matters." If Burchard hoped to soothe the lay brothers' wounded pride, this argument would not help. He was putting the brothers in their place. There were two sorts of men, ordained and lay, and while each needed the other, the lay brothers were not of the same order as the ordained choir monks.

In the final chapters of his investigation of beards, Burchard considers the afterlife. Christian doctrine was clear that the resurrection of the elect was the resurrection of the physical body, but what did this mean for beards? Men would be bearded in heaven, he affirmed, and they would cease shaving. He was saying, in effect, that when nature and spirit are fully harmonized in the life to come, all external beards would become inner beards and vice versa. By the same token, men would not have to fear for their masculinity. It would be preserved in their bodies and hair. Women would still be women, and beardless. The gender order was eternal, and all saved men, clerical and lay, would eventually enter into the bearded brotherhood of heaven.

We have no record of what the lay brothers thought of Burchard's great discourse. It was, in any case, addressed as much to posterity as to his own charges. Burchard offers us a window into the medieval mind on matters of faith, morals, and manliness. He saw his own body as an allegory of the spiritual life, and the shaving of his face as a feature of a higher calling and superior spiritual authority.

The bearded brothers of the Cistercian order were debarred by rule and by theology from shearing away their facial hair. This was true in other monastic orders as well, and this rule reflected a more general divide between clerical and lay manliness. This dualism was not always strictly observed, however. In some cases, churchmen encouraged laymen also to renounce beards as a sign of moral discipline and religious commitment. These efforts eventually wrought lasting changes.

King Henry Submits to the Scissors

"The Normans are a turbulent race, and unless restrained by a firm government, are always ready for mischief."[28] This was how the English monk and historian Orderic Vitalis explained the tumultuous events in England and Normandy at the beginning of the 1100s. In this period, villages were sacked, churches burned, and hundreds killed as royals and noblemen battled each other for land and power. Vitalis believed the popular myth that the Norman nobility were especially combative because they were descended from the ancient Trojans. That is not true, of course; the Norman nobility were instead descended from Viking raiders who had landed in longboats on the shores of northern France less than two centuries earlier. They had settled down as landholders and adopted the customs of the Franks, who preserved more than other Europeans the cropped hair and clipped beards of Charlemagne's day. Muslim visitors to Frankish lands were particularly unimpressed.

One remarked in the year 965 how dirty and unkempt the Franks were, reporting that "they shave their beards, and after shaving they sprout only a revolting stubble."[29] In spite of their accommodation to Frankish manners, however, Norman lords retained the warlike tendencies of their Viking ancestors. Under the leadership of Duke William, the Normans conquered England in 1066 and established one of Europe's most powerful and enduring dynasties. Matters became very unsettled after William's death in 1087, however, and both Normandy and England fell prey to a long struggle for power between his three sons.

In 1096, the bishops of Normandy tried their best to stem the violence. Gathering in a synod, or regional meeting, they declared the "peace of God." They ordered all people above the age of twelve, on pain of excommunication, to foreswear violence during the holy feasts and the seasons of Lent and Advent. No one was to harm monks, nuns, women, merchants, or church property at any time. The synod also affirmed the church's customary property rights and its power to fill church offices without lay interference. These resolutions for peace reveal the troubles of the Norman world, and as events would show, they were too often ignored.

Henry was the youngest and ablest of the three living sons of William the Conqueror, and over time Normans and Englishmen looked to him to end their troubles. Henry successfully claimed the throne of England in 1100 at the death of his brother William, while the oldest brother Robert, Duke of Normandy, was away on the first crusade. When Robert returned home, he struggled to restore his authority and maintain order in his dukedom, and Henry took advantage, declaring his intention to force his older brother out. Landing with an army on the Norman coast, the king of England gathered around him as many allies as he could muster.

One of those who hurried to Henry's side was Bishop Serlo of Séez, whose diocese was particularly hard hit by internecine warfare and plunder. Both men had something to gain from the other. The bishop hoped for peace and royal support for the church, while young Henry hoped to garner legitimacy in his war against his brother. Henry made a promise to the bishop to take up arms for the defense of the people and the church. Serlo was pleased but sought a sign of the king's good faith. It was Easter, and when the court had gathered for mass, the bishop launched into a fiery sermon, chiding Henry and his men for the vanity of their long hair and beards, which had recently come into style. Long hair was the fashion of women, he declared, and insofar as they imitated feminine softness they lost their manly strength and became more liable to sin. The fashion for long beards was also an abomination. Vain men refrained from shaving their beards, he claimed, "for fear that the short bristles should prick their mistresses when they kiss them."[30] Their bushy faces, moreover, made them look more like Muslims than Christians. Long hair and beards were meant only for penitents who, burdened with sins, may "walk outwardly bristling and unshorn before men, and proclaim by their outward disgrace the baseness of the inner man." He concluded his oration by flourishing a pair of scissors in his hand and calling upon both king and retainers to step forward to be shorn. Dutifully, Henry and his men advanced one by one to receive this extraordinary sacrament. The symbolic sacrifice of hair in return for the blessings of a bishop was deemed on both sides to be an excellent exchange.

Bishop Serlo was really making two different appeals in his scissor sermon. One was to press the king and his men to prove their piety and loyalty to the church. Another was his invocation of the illustrious example of Henry's father, the great conqueror, who had shaved. He reminded them in this way of the good old days of Norman virtue and power.[31] The scissors may have helped. Henry marched to victory over Robert, secured Normandy under his authority, and initiated a successful three-decade reign as heir to his father's domains.

Serlo's correlation of shaving with piety, virtue, and power continued to percolate in the minds of the English and Norman clergy. Writing a generation later, the English monk William of Malmesbury described in his famous history of England the marvelous power of Norman beardlessness during their assault on England. According to Malmesbury, the well-trimmed invaders astonished the English Saxons who imagined they faced an army of marauding priests.[32] Maybe they did think so. The magnificent Bayeux Tapestry offers striking images of smooth-chinned Norman cavalrymen vanquishing mustachioed and bearded Saxon foot soldiers. In Malmesbury's monkish imagination, the English could not have failed to note the striking contrast between themselves and the Normans, and must have been awed by the smooth-faced superiority of the latter, whose higher moral discipline and "invincible spirit" assured their triumph.[33]

Bishop Serlo's confrontation with Anglo-Norman facial hair was symbolic and brief. Henry and his successors soon fell in line with the contemporary standard of moderate beards, and the division between churchmen and laymen remained visible on men's faces as well as in their clothing. As noted earlier, *The Song of Roland*, composed about this time, imagined Emperor Charlemagne ornamented with a dignified white beard. In the middle of the century, however, this secular beard trend was interrupted in dramatic fashion by a French king whose crisis of conscience and desperate need for a new start set secular manliness on a new course.

King Louis Crosses the Line

The medieval church enjoyed two great triumphs in France in the year 1144. Just north of Paris, the new ambulatory and choir on the east end of the Abbey of St. Denis was dedicated in a grand celebration headed by King Louis VII and his wife, Queen Eleanor. This addition was the first glorious achievement of Gothic architecture. Just a few months later, the king was back, leading a solemn procession to bury the bones of St. Denis, the patron saint of France, under the rebuilt choir. In a remarkable sign of humility, the king led the procession in penitential garb, including drab woolen tunic, sandals, and shaved face.[34] Louis VII was determined, after the tumultuous and unsuccessful first years of his reign, to reverse his fortunes, submit to the guidance of God and the church, and win the admiration of his subjects.

The redesign of the abbey and the renovation of the king had a good deal in common. Both were inspired by the religious ideals of the era and sponsored by visionary abbots. The key idea in each case was inner beauty. The true splendor of a Gothic church like St. Denis, or Notre Dame, which was begun soon afterward, was inside rather than outside. The true greatness of a pious man was the same. As Burchard was to write a few years later, the inner beard was more beautiful than its exterior shadow.

The new St. Denis grew from the vision of Abbot Suger, who aspired

to glorify God and French royalty by creating a truly magnificent building. Suger and his master builder assembled a new combination of
architectural elements, particularly an exterior buttress system, which
relieved the exterior walls of most of their weight-bearing duties. This
allowed for the installation of large, stained-glass windows that admitted a flood of colored light. By his own account, Suger was thrilled by
the visual effect, "by virtue of which the whole [church] would shine
with the wonderful and uninterrupted light of most sacred windows,
pervading the interior beauty."[35]

Flooding King Louis with spiritual light was rather more complicated. This was the project of St. Bernard, the Cistercian abbot of
Clairveaux and one of the most dynamic and influential personalities
of medieval history. Louis had been crowned and wed at the tender
age of seventeen to the strong-minded Eleanor, and though he had
been schooled in the quiet confines of St. Denis, he was determined
to prove himself a forceful commander of his armed forces. Unfortunately, Louis soon got himself trapped in two of the most dangerous
political minefields of the age, the politics of the church and of divorce.
When a powerful nobleman, Raoul of Vermandois, divorced his wife to
marry Queen Eleanor's sister, Petronilla, the new couple was summar-
ily excommunicated by the pope. Louis sought to defend his sister-in-
law and her husband and also to confront the pope over appointments
to key bishoprics. His reward was a papal interdict on the royal court,
depriving it of the holy sacraments until he and his noble retainers
mended their ways. Louis lashed out and, ignoring the pleas of pious
Abbot Bernard, launched an ill-advised war against the Count of Champagne, who opposed Raoul's divorce and supported the pope's cause
against Louis.

To the king's dismay, the war degenerated into a bloody stalemate,
and Louis himself witnessed a massacre of villagers by his own troops,
who set fire to a church filled with a thousand men, women, and children who had fled there for safety. The horrors of his war, and Bernard's
continued censures, finally chastened the young king. Frustrated and
confused, Louis sank into depression, retiring to his private chambers
for days on end, barely able to act or speak. Bernard, summoned to
advise the forlorn monarch, urged the king to make a fresh start, repent
his sins, and settle matters with the pope and the Count of Champagne.

Heeding Bernard's advice, Louis made peace and embarked on his penitential march at St. Denis.[36] For him and for France, it was a new beginning. Three years later, again at the urging of Bernard, he personally
led the second crusade to the Holy Land. Though not at all a successful
crusader, his reputation for goodness and piety continued to grow until
his death in 1180.

By presenting himself at St. Denis in the manner he did, Louis VII
was setting two precedents for French royalty: piety and beardlessness.
Over the next three and a half centuries, the former was not regularly
observed, but the latter was. It proved easier to look virtuous than to
be virtuous. Louis would have been most proud of his great-grandson,
Louis IX, who outshone his forebear by leading not one but two crusades and by being canonized after his death.

Both Louis VII's and Louis IX's passion for crusading reinforced
their royal style. Crusading knights often chose beardlessness because
of Frankish tradition, because it fit their religious mission, and because
it helped distinguish them from their Muslim opponents.[37] In Spain,
where crusading was a virtually permanent state of affairs for Christian kings hoping to expand their domains, the Muslims who fell under
their control were required to grow their beards long so that they could
easily be distinguished from their short-bearded Christian superiors.[38]
In the battle for Antioch in the Holy Land during the first crusade, in
1098, it was said that many crusaders accidently killed each other in
street battles, having grown out their beards during the long campaign.
A papal representative, Bishop Le Puy, begged the men to get back to
shaving so this would not happen again.[39] Facial hair thereafter was a
generally reliable sign of whose side you were on. So reliable, in fact,
that it could occasionally be exploited. In 1190, during the third crusade,
an Arab supply ship under the command of the sultan Saladin succeeded
in breaking through a crusader blockade of the harbor of Acre when the
Arab sailors disguised themselves as Westerners by flying flags with the
cross, allowing pigs to roam the deck, and shearing off their beards.[40]

The crusaders' unique blend of religious and military life was insti-
tutionalized with the creation of two crusading orders, the Hospitallers
and the Templars. Brothers of these orders were not temporary military pilgrims but permanent fighting monks. Apart from the fact that
their calling was primarily fighting rather than praying, their vows and

5.3 Statue of King Louis IX of France in the chapel of Plessis Castle, France, 14th century. DeA Picture Library/Art Resource, NY.

lifestyle were similar to those of other monastic orders. They were to remain unmarried and chaste, live in common with other brothers, and observe a discipline of humility and obedience. They were a sort of crossover version of monasticism, existing somewhat ambiguously between a life of the world and a life of seclusion. Their rules about hair were similarly ambiguous. The original rule of the Templars, drawn up in 1129, instructed each brother to wear his hair so that he "can be considered from the front or back as regular and ordained."[41] The same rule applied to facial hair, "so that no excess of vice of the face may be noted." A Templar, in other words, was expected to look like an ordinary monk.

When they followed this rule, the Knights of the Temple had a short beard at most. Later, the brothers switched course, adopting the custom of long beards.[42] There is no record of when or why they did this, but they had at least two good motives. For one thing, this style resolved any uncertainty about the Templars' calling: beards declared unambiguously that they were fighters and not choir-monks. Another advantage was a trademark look. As the permanent guardians of the Holy Land, they were an elite force, not to be confused with knights errant who served temporary tours of duty. Their distinctiveness could also work against them, of course. Muslim forces often killed bearded Christian prisoners on the spot, assuming they were members of the detested order.

The era of the crusades ended in 1291 with the loss of the last Christian foothold in the Holy Land. Just over a decade later, French king Philip IV, grandson of the pious crusader Louis IX, arrested the pope in a dispute over church taxes, and effectively placed the papacy under his control. A decade after this, Philip arrested, shaved, and executed the leaders of the Templar order and seized its property. Philip had no interest in serving the church; he wanted it the other way around. The balance of power in Europe was now shifting decisively away from the popes and bishops in favor of the kings and nobles. One might suppose that the rise of the laity might spell the end of professional shaving as well, but the opposite proved to be the case. Laymen may have shown less respect for churchmen, but they still honored the goodness and discipline of a beardless face. As a result, shaving became almost universal by the late 1300s. With their razors, laymen claimed for themselves the inner beard once monopolized by churchmen.

In the late Middle Ages, facial hair no longer distinguished different orders of men. Instead, it represented qualities to which all men of good breeding aspired, regardless of their station in life. By the same token, facial hair carried negative associations. A marvelous demonstration of this symbolism is an illustration in an edition of Aristotle's *Politics* that

5.4 Monarchy, Aristocracy, and Tymocracy. Illumination from 14th-century French manuscript of Aristotle's *Politics*. Courtesy of Royal Library of Belgium, MS 11201-02.

was presented to the French king Charles V in 1376.[43] Here the artist vividly depicts Aristotle's three basic forms of government in both their good and bad forms. In the first illustration (figure 5.4), the forms of good government appear in stylized tableaux from top to bottom: monarchy, aristocracy, and "tymocracy" (a kind of meritocracy). The fac-

5.5 Tyranny, Oligarchy and Democracy. Illumination from 14th-century French manuscript of Aristotle's *Politics*. Courtesy of Royal Library of Belgium, MS 11201-02.

ing page (figure 5.5) offers visions of these forms twisted toward evil: tyranny, oligarchy, and democracy (mob rule). The contrast between good and bad is apparent in the clothing and facial hair of the central figures in each panel. Men of bad government wear chain mail, carry weapons, and flourish long, bushy, or forked beards. Men of good government, like men of the church, wear robes and are closely shorn. In his effort to illustrate Aristotle's ideas, the medieval artist relied upon commonplace notions of manliness: well-trimmed men are clearly wiser and more benevolent.

This carefully crafted presentation of favorable and unfavorable manliness was the culmination of centuries of church teaching, law, and practice, promoted by men like Pope Gregory VII, Bishops Serlo and Bruno, and Abbot Burchard. It was further advanced by the example of pious crusader-kings, such as Louis VII and Louis IX. These men of faith took pride in their humility, insisting that beardlessness and baldness were emblems of spiritual power that entitled them to honor and authority. Churchmen separated themselves from the warrior patriarchy and, for a time, looked distinctive as well. The propaganda worked so well that in spite of—or perhaps because of—the gradually waning power of the church in political and social life, laymen took up the discipline of shaving and its associated virtues.

A dinner conversation in 1438 serves as a fitting summary of the story of medieval facial hair. Pero Tafur, a Spanish nobleman and adventurer, found himself conversing in Italy with the visiting Byzantine emperor John VIII. The subject was Tafur's beard, or rather the beard he had recently removed upon returning to Western Europe after a long residence in Constantinople. The emperor insisted that Tafur had made a mistake, because a beard was "the greatest honor and dignity belonging to man."[44] Tafur, speaking for the entire Latin West, replied that "we hold the contrary, and except in the case of some serious injury we do not wear beards." Tafur was reading from a script the Roman church had written. Even today, nearly seven hundred years later, the descendants of Western Europe instinctively see goodness, discipline, and honor in a clean-shaven man.

6

THE BEARD RENAISSANCE

In the late Middle Ages, dignified men followed the church's inward-looking example, presenting themselves with the smooth face of virtue. Renaissance men, by contrast, embraced the world more wholeheartedly. They focused less upon the corruption and sin of man, and more upon human skill and potential. A strongly secular ideal of manliness took root and found expression in Europe's second great beard movement. According to the new thinking, the beard was natural, a proud emblem of the dignity of man. Not since the height of the Roman Empire had facial hair played so important a role in defining manliness. This shift did not happen overnight, or without controversy. Powerful men propelled this process of physical reformation, and great ambitions propelled these powerful men.

Two Kings Show Off

In 1520, three young, bright, and ambitious rulers dominated Europe. At the ripe age of twenty-eight, England's Henry VIII was the senior member of the group, having ascended to the throne at the age of seventeen. Francis I of France was twenty-five and had ruled for five years. Charles V, scion of the powerful Habsburg dynasty, was only twenty. He had just been elected Holy Roman Emperor, sovereign of

German and Italian lands, having earlier become king of Spain and the Netherlands. As the greatest rulers on the continent, Francis and Charles were rivals, especially for control of Italy. Both had an interest in securing good relations with Henry of England, but it was Francis who acted first. Soon after Charles was elected emperor, Francis and Henry agreed to seal a new alliance by bringing their courts together in 1520 for a week of banquets, tournaments, and diplomatic talks on a field in English-occupied territory in northern France

Ambitious and well educated, Francis and Henry represented a new generation of royalty in northern Europe. They were Renaissance men, hale and athletic, well versed in classical poetry and modern music. One of Francis's first acts as king was to establish a new college in Paris for the study of classical languages. For his part, Henry was fluent in Latin, French, and Italian, and took particular pride in his musical compositions. Each ruler looked forward to meeting, impressing, and perhaps intimidating the other with his intelligence, grace, and wit. Before he arrived on the continent for the festivities, Henry had a temporary palace of wood built and painted to look like stone. One observer remarked that even Leonardo da Vinci could not have created a more convincing illusion.[1] In the field, Francis erected an immense and ornate royal tent supported by two massive ship's masts lashed together. Along with the glittering show of other noblemen's tents, it inspired the name given to this gathering: the Field of Cloth of Gold.

In their communications leading up to this momentous rendezvous, the young kings vowed not only to honor and entertain one another but to grow beards. From the moment the summit was agreed upon, Henry determined not to shave his beard until he had the satisfaction of meeting his French counterpart. Francis replied with a similar promise.[2] At one level, these two men were engaging in a tradition at least as old as Homer and the ancient Hebrews, in which the beard becomes the token of a vow. It was more than that, however. The young rulers were determined to establish a sort of brotherhood of the beard, and like any pair of brothers, it was as much a rivalry as a partnership.

Each king hoped this beard pact would help him contravene the masculine standards of their day. Not surprisingly, both queens objected to their husbands' plans, and neither man was able to keep his promise in the year before the summit. Henry's case is best documented. His wife,

6.1 (*Left*) King Henry VIII of England, ca. 1520. HIP/Art Resource, NY. (*Right*) King Francis I of France, by Jean Clouet, ca.1530.

Catherine of Aragon, hectored him into abandoning his new beard.[3] Francis also felt compelled to shave, but he renewed his determination in the months leading up to the appointed meeting with Henry. When Henry received word of Francis's renewed effort, he decided to ignore his wife's wishes (not for the last time) in order to meet his counterpart on equal terms.

In June 1520, when the men finally embraced each other, they appeared in full flower. One Englishman remarked that Francis was very tall, with a well-proportioned neck, long nose, hazel eyes, and "hair brown, smooth and neatly combed, his beard of three months' growth darker in color."[4] Henry was more thickly set, with what another observer described as "a red beard large enough to be very becoming."[5] Together at last, the two rulers commenced their friendly rivalry. A central part of the festivities was a "feat of arms," performed before the queens and assembled ladies and noblemen. The kings, each paired with a partner, jousted and fought on foot against other pairs of challengers. The two kings mostly avoided confronting each other directly, but according to French sources, they did finally tussle with one another during a drinking party, when dark-haired Francis bested red-haired Henry in an impromptu wrestling match.[6] Despite this slight embarrassment for Henry, the event went off well, and the two men genuinely enjoyed each other's company. The Field of Cloth of Gold was serious diplomacy, but it was also an excuse for dancing, eating, drinking, and sporting, as well as a convenient excuse for the two men to try out a new look. From this point forward, there was no turning back. The bearded era in northern Europe had well and truly begun.

Why were these kings so eager to abandon long precedent in male deportment? For an answer we must look to Italy, because that is where Henry and Francis were themselves looking. Most Europeans viewed Italy as the fount of Renaissance sophistication and style, and both kings were raised with a fluent knowledge of Italian. Francis in particular was an enthusiast for Italian art and poetry, earning him a favorable mention in Baldassare Castiglione's book *The Courtier,* an influential bestseller in which Italian noblemen discussed the knowledge and graces that courtiers ought to cultivate.[7] As rulers eager to bring themselves and their kingdoms up to date, Francis and Henry borrowed and imitated ideas, tastes, and styles emanating from Florence, Milan, Venice, and Rome. Francis and his courtiers were familiar with Raphael's 1515 portrait of a grandly bearded Castiglione, and this helped solidify in their minds an association of beards with Italian sophistication. Raphael also painted himself with full black beard in 1518. Leonardo da Vinci's sketch of himself in 1512 shows him with long hair and a beard of biblical proportions. About the same time, Raphael honored his black-bearded rival Michelangelo by painting him into his famous fresco in the papal library, *The School of Athens*. If the great artists and writers of Italy were bearded, it was only a matter of time before the rest of Europe would follow.[8]

The precedent set by these rock stars of Italian art and letters was so infectious that even popes could not resist. Julius II, the patron of Michelangelo and Raphael, was a worldly man of politics and war, and while he was rallying his army at Bologna, he determined to grow a long white beard—the first papal facial hair in some 140 years. The clearest evidence of Julius's motives comes from the report of one chronicler that the pope had sworn not to shave again until his French enemies had been expelled from Italy.[9] His was a warrior's vow, reflecting his fighting spirit. He was also inspired, no doubt, by the host of biblical patriarchs and prophets Michelangelo had painted for him on the Sistine Chapel ceiling. Julius did not, however, keep his beard for long. He shaved again in 1512, before the gathering of a church-wide council he had called to counter French efforts to undermine his papacy.[10] As his battles shifted from military to theological grounds, the warrior pope returned to his older guise as a shaved man of the church.

The stories of Pope Julius and Kings Henry and Francis reveal the second decade of the sixteenth century as a transitional moment in the history of facial hair. The pope ended his life a shaved man, and his successor, Leo X, remained beardless throughout his life as well. But the young kings hewed to the new course. For more than a century, laymen had been beardless in imitation of clerical goodness. Now the tables were turned. A secular manhood shaped by a humanist spirit asserted itself, changing masculine style and rocking the church as well. Men of the cloth, still bound by canon law to shave themselves, were forced to reconsider their position. Should they affirm their unique, and supposedly superior, type of manliness, or should they to accede to more worldly ideals and embrace the natural authority of facial hair? The ensuing debate among churchmen, and the urgency many felt to abandon the razor, illustrates more clearly than anything else the fundamental logic of the beard renaissance.

Pierio Valeriano Argues for Beards

The new beard movement of the early 1500s was promoted by proud humanists and ambitious kings, but also by the troubles of popes. The case of Pope Julius's battle beard has been noted, but it was Pope Clement VII's penitential beard, instigated by his misfortunes, that had the most enduring impact. This effect was greatly amplified when a priest and scholar in Clement's papal court, Pierio Valeriano, wrote a book promoting beards for the Catholic clergy. Clement would not have grown his beard, nor Valeriano written his book, were it not for the sack of Rome in 1527, another turning point in beard history.

In 1527, the still-youthful Holy Roman Emperor, Charles V, determined to punish Pope Clement for resisting his imperial authority, and dispatched an unruly army of twenty thousand Spanish and German troops to take Rome. Poorly paid and provisioned, the soldiers were permitted to sack the city, devastate homes, loot libraries and churches, and subject its defenseless citizens to rape, torture, and death. In the course of this chaos, half of Rome's population disappeared, either murdered or scattered. For many days, unburied bodies littered the hot summer streets.[11] One victim was Cristoforo Marcello, a humanist scholar and archbishop of Corfu, who was taken hostage for ransom by Spanish soldiers after his home was ransacked. When the soldiers determined that Marcello could not pay the ransom they demanded, they "bound this distinguished man with chains and left him naked under the open air by the trunk of a tree. Every day they pulled out one of his fingernails, and at last they killed him amid these terrible torments."[12]

These are the words of Pierio Valeriano, who chronicled this new fall of Rome and the lamentable suffering of humanist scholars like Marcello. Pope Clement and many other Romans interpreted their misfortune as God's punishment for their sins, and as a sign of contrition and penance, Clement ceased shaving and encouraged others to follow his example.[13] A few years later, in 1531, he granted official permission for priests to grow beards.[14] The pope's motive may have been penitential, but many churchmen embraced the new order for other reasons. They hoped that it would signify a reinvigorated clerical masculinity. That was certainly the idea Valeriano expressed in a small book entitled *Pro Sacerdotum Barbis*, or *In Support of Beards for the Clergy*, published the same year as Clement's permissive edict. It was the original manifesto of the Renaissance beard movement.

Valeriano praised the pope's penitential intentions, but his mind was not focused on humility. On the contrary, his central theme was the need for the clergy to fortify their manly natures and to recover their lost authority. The lesson of Rome's destruction was that powerful Europeans no longer respected the church as they once had. To reverse this trend, the priesthood would need to replace the timidity, softness, and self-indulgence of shaven manhood with renewed dedication and firmness. Beards were the ideal signs of those qualities.

With this line of argument, *Pro Sacerdotum Barbis* upended the medieval logic of holy shaving, asserting a new Renaissance logic of natural manliness. Valeriano claimed to be at a loss to understand any reason for

6.2 (*Left*) Pope Clement V, by Sabastiano del Piambo, before 1527. Album/Art Resource, NY. (*Right*) Pope Clement V, by Sabastiano del Piambo, ca. 1531.

priestly shaving, and betrayed no knowledge of the medieval theology of the "inner beard." Like the good humanist that he was, he insisted that the laws of nature, the examples of the ancients, and the dictates of honest reason should guide men, not obscure medieval theory. His masterstroke was to expose the fraudulent corruption of canon law in respect to the shaving rule. Valeriano proved that the oldest laws of the church had not banned facial hair, but quite the reverse. The way was surely open for the church to adopt a new course.

The main thrust of Valeriano's argument was an appeal to ancient history and natural law in favor of beards. Not only was facial hair natural, he insisted, it also served a useful purpose. It helped to expel the bad humors from the body, prevented tooth decay and other ailments, and protected the skin from extremes of hot and cold.[15] The ancients had wisely taught that beards were connected with moral strength. Echoing the classical philosophers who had inspired the first beard movement, Valeriano contended that the greatest danger to moral worth lay in "excessive refinement and cowardice, easy living and effeminate ways."[16] The great minds of ancient Greece, as well as the heroes of both Old and New Testaments, including Christ himself, were bearded men.

Valeriano thought that priests should "avoid bitter criticisms, shameful outcomes, the suspicion of effeminacy and calumny, and finally appear as men rather than women. For why should we be ashamed of our beards, if it has been revealed to us what exactly the beard is, and how it adorns the dignified and honorable man, and how much it contributes to the status and reputation of the priest."[17] The problem, as the humanist scholar saw it, was not the excessive worldliness of priests but the reverse. If churchmen were to regain their lost prestige and power, they would have to recover their masculinity.

Valeriano's arguments resonated in the courts and cathedrals of Europe, as the new style rapidly gained ground. In England, an anonymous translator published in 1533 an English version of Valeriano's treatise, declaring himself to be a beard wearer who had suffered much abuse for his choice. Just two years later, in 1535, King Henry commanded his courtiers to grow their beards.[18] This was, of course, not the only big change Henry was making in England. The previous year he had overthrown Roman authority and established himself as the new head of the English church. The beard order, while tied to this momentous event, was not simply a matter of Protestantism. Henry's earlier behavior suggests it would have happened sooner or later, and this provided a convenient occasion. Protestants may have been more enthusiastic about beards than Catholics, but Valeriano's book proves the issue transcended sectarian divisions.

The old ways did not die quickly or easily, however. In France in particular, universities, cities, and law courts attempted to stanch the wave of change by requiring professors, judges, and civic officials to shave. The University of Paris barred professors with long beards from its lecture halls in 1533.[19] In 1540, the Parlement of Paris, the chief court of France, published an Edict on Beards, which forbade beards for judges and advocates appearing in its court.[20] In this time of transition, facial hair became a battlefront in questions of moral order. Was it appropriate for responsible and refined men to allow their faces to become hairy? Gentien Hervet, a scholar in Orleans who was rising to prominence as a professor and orator, tackled this question in three successive lectures, which, upon their publication in 1536, amounted to the most erudite statement on the matter to date. With style and wit, Hervet examined the question from all points of view, presented the case for and against, and offered finally a neutral position of tolerance. There were good arguments on both sides of the dispute, he concluded, and both choices could be seen as sensible.

On purely physical grounds, Hervet contended, the arguments for and against led to a draw, for "nature takes both sides of the argument, by both spontaneously producing the beard and being willing to allow it to be shaved."[21] It made practical sense for some men, such as workmen, to cut their beards short. On the other hand, some men he knew suffered from toothaches or other ailments when they shaved. Reviewing ancient writers, Hervet also found arguments for tolerance. In both Athens and Rome, he claimed, men were free to choose how they managed their hair. Though this was a serious overstatement, his intent was to cast the ancients as advocates of wisdom and moderation. He concluded by citing Plato's argument that wisdom is the only thing that is good in and of itself; and if wisdom was the goal, he wrote, it did not matter whether men wore beards or not.[22]

Though Hervet was clearly not agitating for beards, he concurred with Valeriano's conclusion that there was no reason for clergy to distinguish themselves physically from laymen. Manliness was of one substance, grounded in a common physical nature and partaking of the same virtues of wisdom and moral strength. Greek and Roman poets and philosophers were models of this manliness as much as Christ and the apostles. The fact that both philosophers and apostles were bearded seemed to Hervet to affirm this commonality. Under the weight of Valeriano and Hervet's humanist arguments, the medieval logic of beardless virtue was rapidly crumbling.

This humanist turn alarmed many leaders of the church, particularly as it coincided with the menace of Protestant heresy. One of the most influential voices of the Catholic Reformation in the late 1500s, Cardinal Borromeo of Milan, was also a leader in the counterattack on priestly facial hair. Deploying well-established medieval justifications, including the imperative of abandoning worldly and sinful thoughts, he urged regional councils and diocesan synods around Europe to pass fresh injunctions against priests who failed to shave.[23] For their part, Protestants, beginning with Martin Luther himself, gladly grew out their whiskers as an act of anti-Catholic defiance. Clergymen of the two camps were often identifiable by their faces, and at points during the French civil wars between Protestants and Catholics, priests grew beards to avoid being targeted for Protestant attacks.[24]

Luther and his fellow Protestants argued that the priesthood did not constitute a spiritually privileged caste and should not be set apart as a different sort of men. Like Catholic humanists such as Valeriano and Hervet, they viewed manhood as a single and coherent natural state of being whose God-given virtues and dignity were evident in a noble display of hair.[25] Valeriano had called for the remasculinization of the Catholic clergy, but it was Protestants who embraced the beard most fervently. Johan Eberlin von Günzburg, for example, an early convert to Lutheranism, included the following among his rules for an imaginary Protestant utopia: "All men are to wear long beards. Men with smooth faces like women shall be held an outrage."[26]

Explorers and Poets Discover a Brave New World of Hair

Since ancient times, Europeans had imagined barbarians in far-off lands to be wild, strange, and hairy. When they discovered and conquered new worlds in America and Asia, there were indeed hairy men about, but they were the Europeans themselves rather than the relatively smooth natives. The discovery that "savages" were mostly hairless encouraged Europeans to see their own hair in a more positive light. The beard filled European conquerors with pride, and it gave them another reason to believe themselves superior to non-Europeans. It was Native Americans, who often plucked out their generally thinner beards, who encountered the wild hairy man, and it must have been a shock. Though Columbus arrived in America before the beard movement began, shaving discipline had broken down on his ships, and the Americans were frightened, according to Spanish historian Bartolomé de las Casas, by the Spaniards' whiteness, their clothes, and their facial hair. The Americans "ran their hands over [the Spaniards'] beards, marvelling at them because they had none, and carefully inspecting the whiteness of their hands and faces."[27] Las Casas assumed, like most Europeans, that the Americans were overawed by the superior manliness of the bearded invader.[28] It is more likely they were repulsed. An Indian in Canada is recorded to have said after meeting a Frenchman, "Oh, the bearded man! Oh, how ugly he is!"[29]

Throughout the long and tragic incursion of Europeans into America, the beard was a defining feature of the conquerors. Aztecs, Incas, and other peoples found their greatest enemies to be men riding huge animals, carrying terrible weapons, and growing unsightly masses of hair from their chins. In America the biblical tale of Esau and Jacob was reversed, and the hairy man stole the patrimony of the smooth man.

There can be no question that Europeans were gaining a self-conscious pride in their hair by the 1530s. Prominent men of the proudly independent Swiss city of Basel even founded a club called Zur Haaren (To hairiness!), incorporating the image of a hairy wild man into their emblem.[30] It was history's first bearded men's club, pioneering an idea that has found new life in our own times.

By the mid-1500s the greatest beard movement since the Roman Empire was marching from victory to victory. Poets sang of wonders to behold as Europeans explored new possibilities of self-expression. Before long, different cuts became associated with different sorts of men. An anonymous English poem, the *Ballad of the Beard*, spelled out some of these affiliations in verse:

> The Roman T, in its bravery
> Doth first itself disclose,
> But so high it turns, that oft it burns
> With flames of a torrid nose.

> The stiletto-beard oh! it makes me afeard,
> It is so sharp beneath,
> For he that doth place a dagger in's face,
> What wears he in his sheath?

> But, methinks, I do itch to go thro' stitch
> The needle-beard to amend,
> Which, without any wrong, I may call too long,
> For a man can see no end.

> The soldier's-beard doeth march in shear'd,
> In figure like a spade,
> With which he'll make his enemies quake,
> And think their graves are made.

The grim stubble eke on the judge's cheek,
Shall not my verse despise;
It is more fit for a nutmeg, but yet
It grates poor prisoners' eyes.

What doth invest a bishop's breast
but a milk-white spreading hair?
Which an emblem may be of integrity,
Which doth inhabit there.[31]

There was almost always a mixture of seriousness and mirth in beard poetry. The sexual innuendo of the lines about the pointed stiletto beard betrays the twinkle in the poet's eye, and it is unlikely that soldiers wore spade beards to suggest a grave. On the other hand, it is true that soldiers were often associated with thick beards. Shakespeare's character Jaques, in *As You Like It*, described the typical soldier as "bearded like the pard" (leopard).[32] A writer named Robert Greene, in 1592, also referred to the soldiers' spade-beard, and suggested a young lover would prefer a short, pointed beard, again alluding to what was in his "sheath." But Greene also considered the class differences apparent in facial hair. In a witty commentary on the inequalities of his society, he contrasted the lives of two men, the wealthy "Velveteen-breeches" and the commoner "Cloth-breeches." One of the differences in their lives is in the way the barber treats them. The well-cut pointed beard, carefully shaped spade beard, or curled mustachios were only for the man of means, who could afford to pay for their upkeep. So too were the oils, perfumes, and dyes that placed the wealthy unmistakably above other men. The care that a great beard required must have dissuaded many poorer men from attempting one at all. Cloth-breeches could afford only the basics, namely a plain round cut "like the half of a Holland cheese."[33]

For true believers like a German writing under the pseudonym Johannes Barbatium ("John the Bearded"), who describing himself in 1614 as a "lover of beards," a full, unstyled beard was the best to be hoped for. He commended the "beautiful words" of the Roman poet Ovid:

Don't think it ugly that my whole body is covered with thick, bristling hair. A tree is ugly without its leaves, and a horse ugly if a thick mane does not clothe its sorrel neck; feathers clothe the birds, and their own wool is becoming to sheep; so a beard and shaggy hair on his body well become a man.[34]

What mattered to Barbatium was not the beard's shape but its natural flourish and grandeur. Like other humanists of that era, he viewed the modern growth of hair as a true response to ancient wisdom. Conveniently ignoring evidence of four hundred years of shaving in classical times, and the fact that Ovid's praise for beards represented the boast of the hairy, one-eyed monster, Cyclops, he declared that all ancients had agreed that beards were nature's way of affirming the dignity of natural manliness.

Shakespeare Casts Beards in a Supporting Role

To the extent that his plays reflect the thinking and predispositions of his times, one can find in Shakespeare's works valuable insight into the part facial hair played in masculine identity during the Renaissance. Beards often appeared in his plays as a metaphor for men and masculine honor. His comedy *Much Ado about Nothing* is a notable example. Its central characters are Benedick and Beatrice, comedic opposites of the tragic Romeo and Juliet. Unlike the star-crossed lovers of Verona, the scornful Benedick and Beatrice are determined to have nothing to do with romance or with each other. For Romeo and Juliet, it is love at first sight; for Benedick and Beatrice, disdain at first glance. "I will live a bachelor," Benedick declares.[35] For her part Beatrice insists to her uncle Leonato that she wants no husband:

> *Beatrice:* . . . Lord, I could not endure a husband with a beard on his face, I had rather lie in the woollen!
> *Leonato:* You may light on a husband that hath no beard.
> *Beatrice:* What should I do with him? Dress him in my apparel and make him my waiting-gentlewoman? He that hath a beard is more than a youth, and he that hath no beard is less than a man; and he that is more than a youth is not for me, and he that is less than a man, I am not for him . . .[36]

In this exchange, Beatrice makes her case against men: real men have beards, but like their woolly beards, they are rough and unpleasant.

To overcome their aversion, Benedick and Beatrice's friends trick them into believing that each secretly loves the other, and they obediently respond to love's call. Transformed by romantic passion, Benedick abandons his soldierly garb and sarcastic demeanor and appears fastidiously washed, sweetly perfumed, and freshly shaved. Leonato notes that "indeed he looks younger than he did, by the loss of a beard," and Benedick's associates have no trouble diagnosing him as a victim of lovesickness.[37] Without his beard, Benedick mournfully complains of a toothache, apparently to cover the sweet sorrow of his romantic longing, but as we know from Valeriano's treatise, shaving and toothaches were routinely linked in the Renaissance mind. Shakespeare's audiences would recognize this pain as the price Benedick paid for his desire to smooth out the roughness of his manhood for Beatrice's sake. His friends do not condemn him for reducing himself in this way, but they pity him the ravages of love.

By the end of the play, Benedick must prove himself to Beatrice in more substantial ways than primping and preening. Beatrice demands that he fight for the honor of her cousin Hero, who has been defamed by one of Benedick's friends, and Benedick agrees to do so, denouncing his erstwhile comrade as "Lord Lack-beard"—though there is no reason to think he lacks a beard, whereas Benedick is actually beardless.[38] The beard, that is, has become a metaphor for manly honor. Fortunately, the play is a comedy, and misunderstandings are eventually cleared up. "Lord Lack-beard" mends his ways, and all turns out well. Benedick is able to preserve his manly honor without a duel, and Beatrice gets what she seems to have wanted all along, a man who has the figurative beard of manly honor and courage, but not the scratchy real thing.

The way in which Shakespeare casts beards as a double for manhood in these passages was typical of him and his era. When giving a role to beards in his plays, Shakespeare could draw on long-standing associations, particularly those from the Bible. His audiences would have recognized two common themes: that beards denoted the manly virtues of courage and wisdom, and that an assault on the beard was an affront to honor. Both notions are prominent in *King Lear*. In this tragedy, two of Lear's daughters, Regan and Goneril, despise their doddering father and plan his overthrow. At one stage he pleads with them for respect, asking, "Art not asham'd to look upon this beard?"[39] He is saying in effect, "Have you lost all respect for your father and king?" Indeed they have, and they proceed to force him from the throne. When a loyal courtier, the Earl of Gloucester, helps Lear escape the clutches of his ungrateful daughters, he suffers Regan's wrath as a result. Captured and bound, he has his beard plucked:

> *Gloucester:* By the kind gods, 'tis most ignobly done
>   To pluck me by the beard.
> *Regan:* So white, and such a traitor?
> *Gloucester:* Naughty lady,
>   These hairs which thou dost ravish from my chin
>   Will quicken and accuse thee. I am your host,
>   With robber's hands my hospitable favors
>   You should not ruffle thus.[40]

Gloucester is warning Regan that she dishonors herself by dishonoring him, and that this act will have its own revenge. When, in spite of Gloucester's efforts, Lear's downfall is complete, the former king reflects on his own weaknesses, identifying pride as his primary failure. He remembers that when he was king, "They flatter'd me like a dog, and told me I had white hairs in my beard ere the black ones were there. To say 'ay' and 'no' to everything I said!"[41] Lear was told, in other words, that he had the wisdom of an older man before he was even fully grown. His advisors' flattery and lies tempted him to errors of judgment, which led ultimately to the rebellion against him. Too late he realizes that he has foolishly acted against both nature and truth, including the evidence of his own beard. He would have done better to pay more attention to the signs of nature.

The link between nature and truth was a central concern for Shakespeare, and for Renaissance Europe more generally. The "truth" of bearded manhood was part of this thinking. As a natural feature of manhood, the beard was seen as integral to the masculine personality. What happened to the beard happened to the man, and what happened to the man happened to the beard. This equation is apparent in one of Shakespeare's most famous passages, when the wistful and skeptical courtier Jaques in *As You Like It* declares, "All the world's a stage, and all the men and women merely players . . ."[42] Like a playwright, Jaques then sketches the life of a typical nobleman in seven stages, from childhood to old age and death. The peak stages are identified with particular beards. As a soldier, the young man is "full of strange oaths, and bearded like the pard." Later, as a justice of the peace, he appears "in fair round belly . . . with eyes severe and beard of formal cut, full of wise saws and modern instances."[43] There is a natural link between the man and his costume, even if our lives are at some level just an act.[44]

Sometimes, this costume became part of the joke. In *A Midsummer Night's Dream,* the buffoonish amateur actor Bottom is given the role of Pyramus, described by the director Quince as a "most lovely gentleman-like man":

> *Bottom:* Well; I will undertake it. What beard were I best to play in?
> *Quince:* Why, what you will.
> *Bottom:* I will discharge it in either your straw-color beard, your orange-tawny beard, your purple-in-grain beard, or your French-crown-color beard, your perfit yellow.[45]

Shallow-minded Bottom—definitely not a method actor—is obsessed with the sensationalism of fake beards rather than with the inner character of his role. In his enthusiasm for wearing an impressive beard, he makes a mockery of manly honor, and of himself. In making fun of Bottom's fixation, Shakespeare did not mean to mock beards themselves, or to undermine their function as an appendage of masculinity. On the contrary, comic fools like Bottom reinforced the message of Shakespeare's more serious plays, namely, that there is a natural social order that assigns men their roles and their hair. Secure in the knowledge of this order, one can laugh at lesser men or boys playing dress-up with silly fake beards and absurd dialogues.

The bearded bard of Stratford perceived at an intuitive level the part that facial hair played in the performance of manliness. Other Renaissance men sought to understand this matter logically and scientifically. The leading universities in Shakespeare's day, particularly in medicine, were to be found in Italy. It was there that physiologists first fixed their attention on the natural puzzle of facial hair.

Marco Olmo Pioneers the Science of Beards

In Renaissance universities, professors were not dissimilar to Shakespeare's actors, in that they were expected perform in public with eloquence and panache. The primary stage was the "disputation," a formal public argument at a set place and time in which a scholar would defend one or more propositions against counterarguments raised by the audience. In one case, a man named Albertazzi, who taught logic at the University of Bologna and who clearly wished to advance his reputation and career, announced that on November 28, 1594, at nine o'clock in the morning, he would defend one hundred theses in humanist studies, logic, natural sciences, mathematics, philosophy, and theology.[46] Whether he was successful is not recorded, but it was probably a noisy affair, with friends and critics enthusiastically interjecting praise and opprobrium. A serious disputation between professors might last for days, enhancing or damaging the reputations of the participants. In print too, scholars jousted with one another, or with long-dead authorities, about matters of law, philosophy, theology, and natural science. It should come as no surprise, then, that at the height of the beard movement, the subject of facial hair would become a matter of dispute at Europe's most famous university.

Modern science as we know it was just beginning to take shape in Italian cities during the 1500s. A generation before Shakespeare was born, an Italian-educated Pole, Nicolaus Copernicus, had used mathematics and observation to dispute ancient and biblical theories of the solar system. At the same time, a Belgian professor of medicine at the University of Padua, Andreas Vesalius, drew on meticulous dissections to overthrow long-established errors with respect to human anatomy. By the late 1500s, European academics were gradually shedding their fawning reverence for ancient authorities like Aristotle, Galen, and Ptolemy, and charting a new course for science. This had the effect, of course, of intensifying academic combat. At the dawn of the seventeenth century, Italy produced the Copernicus of beard science, Marco Antonio Olmo (Marcus Ulmus in Latin).

Little is known about Olmo other than that he was from Padua and served as a professor of medicine and natural philosophy at the University of Bologna, Renaissance Italy's largest and most prestigious university. In 1603, he published *Physiologia Barbae Humanae* (Physiology of the Human Beard). In three hundred pages of densely printed Latin, Olmo presented the best science had to offer on the subject of the body, the beard, and manliness.

Olmo was convinced that facial hair had been overlooked and misunderstood in medical science and natural philosophy. Reviewing the literature, he found error everywhere, and his book showed the fire, as well as the scars, of many arguments he had endured with his colleagues. Olmo was convinced that the ancient physician Galen was wrong in believing that hair's primary function was the excretion of waste from the body. He also rejected the argument of Renaissance natural philosopher Julius Caesar Scaliger that facial hair had no use whatever, and that mustaches in particular were a regrettable hindrance. Nature does nothing in vain, Olmo insisted, announcing that through painstaking work he had discovered what the beard was meant to do. "It does not serve the purpose of decoration, age, gender, cleansing, or covering," he wrote, "but is something quite different, and performs a task proper to the powers of the human soul."[47]

The soul is not a typical subject for science these days, but it was for Renaissance science, which fused (some might say confused) ancient Greek science, systematic observations, and Christian theology. Olmo, guided by Christian precepts as much as natural logic, worked from the core axiom that hair was part of the body, the purpose of which is to serve the soul. Therefore, hair must also serve the soul in some way. It does so, he concluded, by providing an outward sign of the "genital spirits" and the maturation of manhood, a manifestation of the life force present in male generative powers. In short, God created the beard as a physical image of the manly spirit.

While Olmo's claim that hair originates from the blood makes little sense to modern physiologists, one can readily sympathize with his insistence that hair is more than an excretion of waste material, for this ancient notion was also wrong. In this sense, Olmo was like his near contemporaries Copernicus and Vesalius, doing battle with ancient errors. Olmo's second main contention, that "the beard inevitably follows the male procreative power of our race," also seems plausible.[48] He observed that when males reach sexual maturity, "the power that makes the beard is advanced by the male procreative faculty to perform its own particular task, which is to clothe and equip certain specific places on the face with hairs, as though the male power of procreation were crying out aloud through the beard, like some kind of trumpeter, that it had arrived."[49] In his analysis, observation proves this proposition in both a positive and negative sense: a sexually mature man will have a beard; conversely, a man without a beard is not capable of procreation. A key piece of evidence for him was the case of eunuchs, who lost both beard and potency if castrated before puberty. He recognized exceptions to the rule, as in the case of bearded women, but rare exceptions need not invalidate the basic principle.

To Olmo, this correlation meant that the beard was intended by nature to communicate the masculine characteristics of a person. On a purely medical level, the beard serves as an "indicator of the temperament of the organs which serve the same power, and in particular of the testes," and "supplies this information in accordance with all its own accidental qualities."[50] That is to say, one should be able to diagnose the constitutional vigor of a man by the shape and fullness of his beard. If Olmo were alive today, he would be proud to know that modern biologists have proposed a similar argument in explaining the evolution of beards (see chapter 1).

Olmo was not content to let it rest there, however. To his thinking, the face was a spiritually significant part of the body, and any sign placed there by nature was very important indeed. He pondered Aristotle's argument that procreation was the divine principle working within the human body, endowing semen with the life force that made procreation possible. As beards and procreation were so closely connected, beards must be directly expressive of the divine life force present in the male body.[51] "Thus the divine origin of man," Olmo reasoned, "which is the work of the divine power of procreation, is opportunely and appropriately indicated in the divine part of the body of the same." As a consequence, "the movements of all the powers of the soul are clear to see on our faces, and can be recognized by the most practiced of men."[52]

This is a grand claim, indeed. In Olmo's defense, it cannot be denied that beards had an ineffable mystique, particularly during his lifetime. Olmo believed he could explain the impressiveness of facial hair in scientific terms, and his conclusions paralleled Shakespeare's views in several ways. The beard was not simply a part of a man. It should be

possible, both believed, to perceive something of the inner man by considering the hair on his face. As Shakespeare implied, King Lear might
have avoided his sad fate had he given more thought as a young man to
the humble condition of his immature beard.

Flemish scientist Jan Baptiste Van Helmont (1580–1644) was another great mind of the era who believed he had discovered the true
meaning of beards. Known today as a pioneer in chemistry, Van Helmont was similar to Olmo in blending physical observation and meta-
physical speculation. Like Olmo, Van Helmont recognized a direct link
between beards, virility, and the soul, but unlike Olmo, he considered
this to be a lamentable rather than an honorable connection. Beards
did indeed signal the condition of the masculine soul, but they were the
unfortunate marks of original sin. By Van Helmont's reckoning, Adam
was created in the Garden of Eden without a beard, but eating the forbidden apple stirred in him carnal lust such that he "deflowered" Eve.
A beard then sprouted on his chin as a sign of shame. "Wherefore," Van
Helmont maintained, "that the first infringer of modesty, and deflow-
erer of a Virgin might be made known, God would that hairs should
grow on the chin, cheeks, and lips of Adam, that he might be . . . like
unto many four-footed beasts."[53] From this reasoning, the Flemish
scientist derived a corollary theory. If beards were sinful, true angels
could not be bearded. If a spirit were to appear on earth with a beard,
one could instantly spot him as evil.[54]

The idea that Adam was beardless in Eden circulated in the Muslim
world as well. But the Muslim interpretation of Adam's new beard was
precisely the reverse of Van Helmont's. According to Mohammad Baqir
Majlisi, a Persian contemporary of Van Helmont, Adam was recon-
ciled with God after the exile and asked the creator for a more pleas-
ing appearance. When he received a black beard, Adam asked what it
was. God replied, "This is your ornament, as well as the ornament of
your men and your children until the Day of Judgment."[55] The beard, in
other words, was a blessing rather than a curse.

Though Renaissance artists frequently depicted a beardless Adam in
the Garden, Van Helmont's notion that a beard was sign of shame was
decidedly a minority view in the West.[56] Most people in his time had a
sunnier view of nature's purposes. On the other hand, nature also produced surprises that scientists were hard-pressed to explain. One of the
more baffling conundrums was the existence of bearded women.

Bearded Women Crash the Party

Renaissance people, seeking to understand the rules of nature, were inevitably fascinated when these rules seemed to break down. A bearded woman seemed definitely to break the rules. Women with thick, full beards were, and are, rare, and each example created great interest, disgust, and sometimes admiration. Were such people really men, women, or hermaphrodites? Was nature unstable? What does it mean when sex and gender become so confused?

The most striking example of Renaissance interest in bearded women is Spanish painter Jusepe de Ribera's 1631 portrait of Magdalena Ventura. All we know about its subject comes from a long inscription on the right side of the portrait. Entitled "Behold a Great Wonder of Nature," it explains that Magdalena was a wife and mother from Abruzzi in southern Italy who, at the age of thirty-seven, began to grow a beard "so long and thick that it seems more like that of any bearded gentleman than of a woman who had borne three children by her husband."[57] Ribera's depiction makes this point very clear. Magdalena has a higher forehead than her husband, who stands meekly in the background, and her beard is far more impressive. Her strong, defiant pose adds to her manly demeanor. At the same time, her femininity is also emphasized: she is shown flanked by a spinning bobbin, suckling her child, and wearing the clothing of a respectable woman of her time.[58] The inscription is not judgmental. The purpose of the portrait was to amaze the viewer with a woman whose hair and face are entirely masculine, but who is in all other respects feminine. Nature, Ribera seemed to say, is capable of pulling some great tricks, and a beard is not always reliably masculine.

Magdalena Ventura was not the only celebrated bearded woman of the Renaissance. The sisters Francesca, Maddalena, and Antonietta Gonzales had created a sensation in France and Italy in the late 1500s for being hairy all over their faces and bodies. The same was true of Barbara Vanbeck, born in Augsburg just a few years before Ribera painted Ventura's portrait.[59] What were Renaissance men, who had invested so much in the symbolism of the beard, to make of all this? Ribera's painting was commissioned by an erudite and powerful Spanish nobleman, Fernando Afán de Ribera, duke of Alcala, who spent much of his career as a diplomat and viceroy in Italy. The perspective of the duke and his

6.3 Portrait of Magdalena Ventura, with husband and child, by Jusepe de Ribera, 1631. Album/Art Resource, NY.

painter was in some respects rather traditional. To them, Ventura's hair was a miracle—a gift—similar to miraculous beards recorded in the Middle Ages. The legends of St. Galla, St. Paula of Avila, and St. Wilgefortis (or Uncumber) are examples, and all share a similar story line. In each case a woman who faced an undesirable marriage was granted the miracle of disfiguring facial hair, which prevented the nuptials and freed her to devote her life to God.[60] St. Galla and St. Paula became holy celibates, but Wilgefortis was supposedly crucified by her angry father, the king of Portugal. The strange tale of Wilgefortis became quite popular in the late Middle Ages, for it fused the older theme of the miraculous beard with the passion of Christ. It also bespoke the suffering of women under male tyranny.

In medieval lore, miraculous beards unsexed specially chosen women, providing an escape from masculine constraints. Ribera's painting of Magdalena Ventura shares with these stories a wonder at the miraculous, yet rejects the element of unsexing. Ventura is represented as a woman who was not liberated from her husband, even if he is pushed to the background. Nor does she escape her motherly duties. Instead, the artist works hard to demonstrate her essential femininity. The message is that the beard may deviate from the order of nature, but it does not undermine either sex or gender.

Attitudes toward the hairy Gonzales girls were much the same. Today, their rare genetic condition is called *hypertrichosis univeralis*. Thick hair grew all over their bodies, not just their faces. The trait, passed from the father, affected one of the sons as well as the three daughters. Like Ventura later, these celebrities of abnormality were much admired, and members of the family were "collected" by powerful families. The father was appointed to a minor post in the French royal court in the mid-1500s, and members of his family later became dependents of the Farnese family in northern Italy.[61] Prince William V of Bavaria ordered full-size portraits of several family members. The large paintings attracted a great deal of attention when they were displayed by William's uncle at Schloss Ambras, his summer palace. Copies of these works, along with new portraits and sketches produced during the late 1500s and early 1600s, were disseminated throughout Europe and reprinted in scholarly books. Just as Ribera's portrait presented Magdalena Ventura as a refined, motherly woman, the portrayals of the

Gonzales women emphasized their sophistication and ladylike deportment. These women were seen as neither saints nor monsters but as
extraordinary people, profligately gifted by nature.

The Renaissance beard movement was built on the prestige of the
natural and the ways in which manly honor was affirmed by natural hair,
but Renaissance men were able to reconcile that commitment with a
belief in the extraordinary. These images of bearded women were an
act of reconciliation, showing women who had acquired qualities of
manliness without actually becoming men. The successful reign of
Elizabeth in England would not have been possible without an acceptance of this idea. Nonetheless, many contemporaries were repulsed by
bearded women and female rulers, seeing them as monsters rather than
wonders. The most ardent champions of the Renaissance beard movement held this view, committed as they were to the notion that beards
were reliable proof of male superiority. Pierio Valeriano declared in 1531,
"It hath been ever a monstrous thing, to see a woman with a beard."[62]
More than century later, the English physician and natural philosopher John Bulwer also declared a woman with whiskers "a monster."[63]
Johannes Barbatium insisted that women might grow hairs but could
never produce a true beard, for they did, they would not be women but
hermaphrodites, or some similar sort of "monstrous nature."[64]

The Italian scientist of beards, Marco Olmo, took a more nuanced
approach. He did not deny that bearded women were true women, nor
did he label them monsters. At the same time, he expressed no awareness of, or interest in, actual cases of hairy women, including the Gonzales sisters, one of whom had been examined by a colleague at the
University of Bologna just a few years before he published his work on
beards. In working out his theory, Olmo relied more on ancient sources
than on experiments or observations. On the subject of bearded
women, he followed Hippocratic texts in describing their condition as
an illness related to the interruption of the menstrual cycle. If a woman
continued to have sex with her husband but did not maintain the usual
menstrual flow, her blood would become overly rich in seminal spirits;
this accumulation of male essence could cause hair to grow like a man's.
Perhaps Olmo was aware that the Gonzales sisters would contradict his
tidy theory. They had plenty of hair on their bodies long before sexual
maturity, and contact with men could hardly explain their condition.

He would have to admit that he did not really know why some women grew beards.

The existence of hairy women was not, in any case, enough to dampen the enthusiasm of the beard renaissance. For more than a century, from the early 1500s to the early 1600s, a nearly unanimous chorus of praise for beards sounded from churchmen, poets, and scientists. Spurred by confident humanism, educated European men turned their attention to human nature and the human body. They found in their bodies and beards validation of their standing as men endowed by nature with virtues of strength and wisdom worthy of social respect.

7

THE SHAVE OF REASON

After more than a century of beardedness, European men once again abandoned facial hair in the late 1600s. What followed was the most smooth-faced century in Western history. This was also the century of absolutism, when European rulers centralized power and demanded a higher degree of elegance, grace, and discipline from their subjects. This turn to a more regulated society followed the upheavals of the Reformation, which had contributed to civil wars across Europe, including the French Wars of Religion, the English Civil War, and the horrific Thirty Years' War in German-speaking lands. The quest for social order required men to discipline their bodies and their faces, and to show they were able and willing to abide by elaborate rules of deportment and etiquette.

The decline of facial hair also coincided with the birth of the Enlightenment, which might be assigned to the year 1687, when Isaac Newton published his scientific masterwork, *Principia Mathematica*. Newton's precise, mathematical explanation of the laws of physical nature became the touchstone of the Enlightenment quest to discover natural laws governing human affairs, including economics, law, politics, and the arts. Only a few years before Newton's book appeared, King Louis XIV of France and his court abandoned their pencil-thin mustaches, the last remnants of the Renaissance beard movement. The turn to reason and the razor were not directly linked, nor were they mere coincidences. As the mastery of nature now seemed more necessary and possible, it was fitting that authoritative masculinity was being redefined as a matter of refinement and education. Natural hair was now less compelling; a carefully shaved face framed by a highly styled wig appeared more befitting the sort of manliness to which this century aspired.[1]

Louis XIV Cuts an Elegant Figure

Hyacinthe Rigaud's famous portrait of King Louis XIV at the height of his power in 1701 vividly illustrates these themes (figure 7.1). It seems incredible to modern viewers that a man bedecked in white tights, flouncy lace, red-ribboned high heels, and huge curly wig would be the very image of masculine greatness. But that is precisely what he was. This is the portrait of one of the most successful, admired, and imitated monarchs in history. The power and glamour of Louis's court ensured that this French style, including the banishment of all natural hair, would rule polite society for more than a century.

Louis hoped to communicate several important messages about himself in this portrait. First, there is nothing small about the Sun King. His robes, his sleeves, and his hair are all big. He was a tall man made even taller by high heels and a towering wig. In this sense he cut an undeniably impressive figure. But size was not the whole story. Clearly he was proud of his legs and wished to show them to great effect. Louis and his court engaged in a sophisticated dance, literally and figuratively, that reflected the well-ordered government and society over which he presided. His serene mastery of the intricate steps of political and social ritual was critical to upholding order and the general good. Everything about him bespoke refinement and grace. There is both profusion and orderliness in his entire aspect, from his billowing ermine robe to his flowing curls. All is exquisitely fabricated and arranged. Nothing could be left to chance, and natural hair was certainly too chancy for such an elaborate show. Though Louis and other powerful men had worn styled beards or mustaches in the middle decades of the 1600s, even that small display of natural endowment was eliminated by 1680. Instead, the royal court employed dozens of wig makers working around the clock to supply the king and nobility with a rather different sort of magnificent and carefully controlled hair.

7.1 Portrait of King Louis XIV, by Hyacinthe Rigaud, 1701.

Rigaud's portrait is a highly styled image of a highly styled man, but it faithfully represents the king's personality and ideals. Louis was the star actor in Europe's greatest stage production, supported by a cast of thousands at the glittering court of Versailles. At the time of this portrait, some ten thousand noblemen and their families lived at court for at least part of the year. There were vast, well-tended parks to walk in, shimmering, gold-trimmed halls in which to eat and dance, and innumerable salons for games and concerts. At the center was the Sun King himself, the source of political energy and social life. For Louis, there was no distinction between care for his body and care for the state. The most favored men at court were those permitted to attend him at intimate moments of his daily regimen, particularly his morning toilette, which, like the rest of his day, was a carefully choreographed ritual. A lucky few were selected each day to enter the king's bedchamber when he arose, putting in a word for themselves or a client as their sovereign changed out of his bedclothes and put on his shoes, stockings, and wig.[2] Every other morning, the king shaved himself as a servant held up a mirror, all the while listening to what favors this or that nobleman wished to ask of him.

There have been few times in history when the arrangement of the body politic was so closely tied to the arrangement of the ruler's body. For all its faults and tyrannies, Louis XIV's tightly regulated regime was a triumph of order after the chaos and trauma that France had suffered during a century of religious and civil wars. The passions and confusions of the Reformation had ignited fires of religious anger between Protestants and Catholics and inflamed fierce political rivalries among aristocratic factions. These fires had finally burned out by the 1590s, and a new order began to take shape. The French nobility surrendered to the monarchy a monopoly of force and violence in return for a lion's share of privileges in the new order centered at Versailles. The weapons of war were cast aside in favor of a graceful ballet of political and sexual intrigue that became ever more sophisticated as time went on. The regulation of body and of manners was a critical piece of this social realignment. As Louis XIV's portrait demonstrated, manliness was reconfigured to emphasize taste and sophistication rather than force or impulse. It is easy to see the appeal of this new model for Europe. France had found a solution to the ills of the age, and other nations scrambled to imitate its example. As the 1600s came to a close, tights, lace, wigs, and razors became absolute necessities for any European man who aspired to social influence.

Although Louis XIV helped promote the new masculine style, and became its greatest exemplar, neither he nor any other king brought it about by his own initiative. Back in the 1620s, in the time of Louis's father, Louis XIII, a worldly churchman named Louis Barbier, the Abbot of Rivière, first appeared in court with a blond wig. Soon after, Louis XIII, afflicted with baldness while still in his twenties, followed the abbot's lead.[3] By 1634, the court employed thirty-four barber–wig makers. This did not spell the immediate end of beards, however, for the king preserved a highly styled chin beard and mustache. Wigs and beards coexisted uncomfortably for a time. But natural hair often contradicted manufactured curls, and placed limits on the variety of wigs one might choose. As a result, the beards began to disappear, and mustaches became smaller and smaller. The king's death in 1643 placed his young son, Louis XIV, on the throne under the care of regents. The new king was more fortunate in his hair than his father, and because he was capable of producing long, curly hair of his own, he forsook wigs. The gentlemen of his court and of the city of Paris nevertheless continued to pay for the services of wig makers. In 1673, Louis, now in his thirties and with thinning hair, finally yielded, ordering flowing curls for himself, and approving the establishment of a new guild of two hundred master wig makers for Paris. Shortly afterward, he also abandoned his small mustache. The era of big hair and smooth faces was well and truly begun. In England, Charles II had anticipated Louis's switch to wigs by a decade, but only after several of his leading nobleman had done so. The impulse toward carefully managed manliness ran deep and strong.

This transition from natural to false hair was not simple or easy. It took some time for people to get used to it, and some stubbornly resisted. The experience of English diarist Samuel Pepys opens a window on the fits and starts of the wig trend. Pepys was an ambitious civil servant in the admiralty who was talented enough, and vain enough, to write a richly detailed account of his life among the London elite. As he rose in station during the 1660s, he urgently kept abreast of fashion. In 1663 he was still uncertain whether to shave his natural hair in favor of a hairpiece; he was looking, he wrote, but not yet buying. In October he made the plunge, ordering his first wig and taking his wife to the wig makers to see it. Fortunately for him, she approved. Part of his worry was cost. The wig and accessories such as storage cases, cleaners, and combs were not cheap, but he reassured himself that it was a valuable social investment. He confided to his diary, "I perceive how I have hitherto suffered for lack of going as becomes my place."[4] Another worry for Pepys was whether others would see his new look as affected. He was very nervous about his first day at the office after his big purchase and was relieved that his new style caused no stir among his superiors. His claim to status as a bigwig had been accepted.[5]

Pepys soon discovered the advantages and disadvantages of hairpieces. In the spring of 1665, he caught a cold that he attributed to failing to wear his wig enough, thereby exposing his close-cropped head to the elements. At one point he had second thoughts about the whole enterprise, and grew back his own hair. In the end, however, he found he had become accustomed to the wig's convenience. He even upped the ante. In the spring of 1667 he bought two new and finer hairpieces from a French maker, and the following Sunday attended church in one of them to "make a great show."[6] The bigger the hair, the higher he rose in society.[7]

As Pepys's case reveals, wigs became the essential accessory of manliness and status in the late 1600s, rendering beards irrelevant and aberrant. Traditionalists lamented this turn of affairs, though their voices were gradually stilled. In western Germany in 1647, Johann Michael Moscherosch, a writer who satirized life in his war-torn homeland, viewed the abandonment of natural hair as dishonest and un-German.[8] John Bulwer, a scientific writer in England in the 1650s, criticized the "beard-haters" of his day, who seemed unreasonably angry that nature had placed hairs around men's mouths.[9] This attitude was mistaken, he argued, because nature had a purpose for all things, including facial hair. Bulwer quoted Marco Olmo with approval, agreeing that nature intended the beard to be an index of the manly soul. As such it was an "impiety against the Law of Nature" to do away with it.

It was no coincidence that Bulwer launched his defense of beards at a time when his political adversaries in England, the so-called Roundheads, supporters of Parliament in its war against King Charles I, had rejected aristocratic long hair and distinguished themselves by cropping their hair and beards.[10] In criticizing "beard-haters," Bulwer was also striking at the "unnatural" and "effeminate" politics of his rivals.

In the later decades of the 1600s, the mighty fortress of beard defense was Lutheran Saxony, where wigs had been banned outright until 1662. Even after this line was breached, however, Saxon scholars and pastors persisted in defending natural manliness. In 1672, Jakob Thomasius, professor of philosophy at the University of Leipzig, illustrious philosopher, and onetime mentor to mathematician and philosopher Gottlieb Leibnitz, lectured on the cultural importance of beards. A generation later, in 1698, a professor at Wittenberg University, Georg Caspar Kirchmaier, published another learned discourse, insisting on the moral worth of manly hair. Sounding like a latter-day Bulwer, he denounced "beard-haters," maintaining that nature gave men beards as evidence of dignity and mastery.[11] Kirchmaier feared the loss of male authority, both individual and collective, if men were to forgo their God-given "ornament."

In this flurry of Saxon fervor, the most accessible and sensible contribution emerged in 1690 from the pen of Samuel Theodor Schönland, a Lutheran minister in Lommatzsch. As a bearded pastor, Schönland was spurred to action by the publication of an anonymous tract attacking clergymen's beards as antisocial and vain. Schönland deployed the traditional defense, quoting Valeriano on health benefits and affirming nature's will "to adorn men with beards to increase their authority."[12] He offered more original arguments as well, discoursing on the beard's positive contribution to male virtues. "A good man hunts out incitements to virtue from all quarters," Schönland wrote. "Why then should he not do this by using his beard?"[13] The beard was a symbolic expression of the masculine ideal: when a man trims his beard to prevent it from becoming tangled and uncontrolled, he is reminded to cultivate his spirit also, maintaining a good humor and avoiding the extremes of gloom or frivolity. When he keeps his beard clean, he thinks also of keeping his whole self undefiled by deception and lies. Avoiding dyes and proudly showing his natural hair encourages a man always to act with honesty and good faith.[14] To Schönland's thinking, the beard was not simply a symbol of virtue, but an instrument of its accomplishment, whose loss would literally and figuratively expose men to worldly temptations.

Schönland's arguments, and those of other Saxon conservatives, proved fruitless, and German Protestants joined Western Europe in submission to the razor. Johann F. W. Pagenstecher, a Calvinist professor of history and law in Marburg, put forth a valiant and learned discourse on the virtues of beards in 1708, and still another in 1714, deploying classical and biblical authorities to explain how beards helped preserve male social authority.[15] But it was too little, too late. The razor and wig were more persuasive, and an engraved portrait reveals that Pagenstecher himself wore a fashionable curly wig and smoothly shaved face.

In the eighteenth century, facial hair was nowhere to be found outside enclaves that deliberately cut themselves off from the mainstream. The Mennonites, a German Protestant sect, were one such group, and their stubborn beardedness became for them a trademark of resistance. After suffering persecution in the 1500s for their rejection of civil authority, the radical, Bible-believing Mennonites, along with a smaller breakaway group, the Amish, withdrew to rural parts of Switzerland, Germany, and France, where they held fast to old patterns of life. Many later emigrated to William Penn's American colony, again segregating themselves from the rest of society. To this day the groups' members are immediately recognizable by their old-style dress and grooming, a true relic of Reformation Europe: bonnets and long hair for women; broad hats and long beards for men. The Amish in particular value their styles of hair and dress as proof of their freedom from the corruptions of the world. As their founder, Jacob Ammann, insisted in 1693, those who want "to be conformed with the world with shaved beard . . . and haughty clothing" should be corrected by the church or be banished.[16] In the rolling hills of Pennsylvania, Ohio, and other states, pockets of the long-lost Renaissance beard movement can still be found.

While beard-wearers in central Europe ran for the hills, an even older and prouder tradition of hirsute manliness was facing an all-out attack from one of the most formidable figures in European history, the ferocious six-foot-eight-inch tsar of Russia.

Peter the Great Shears Away the past

In 1682, when Louis XIV strode the gleaming halls of Versailles at the height of his bewigged power, the vast, if comparatively humbler Russian Empire was ruled by an awkward triumvirate of siblings: Tsar Ivan, a sickly and slow-witted fourteen-year-old; his tall and hale ten-year-old half-brother and co-tsar, Peter; and as regent over both of them, Ivan's twenty-four-year-old sister Sophia. As one might imagine, this arrangement was a recipe for political trouble. One set of powerful families stood on Sophia and Ivan's side, ranged against another group backing Peter. Though Peter was very young, Ivan was visibly weak in mind and body. Intrigue and danger hovered over the Kremlin, and Peter had already witnessed terrible scenes of political violence and revenge, as many of his noble supporters were threatened, exiled, or even killed before his eyes. Only Peter himself was spared, in order to avoid even worse bloodshed.

No wonder the young prince preferred to spend as much time as possible at his retreat outside the city, enjoying the company of foreigners from around Europe who told him stories of the outside world, with its marvelous new technologies and military glories. Peter was especially captivated by dreams of ships, navies, and seagoing commerce, which he quickly recognized to be the secret of national wealth and power. He even learned to speak Dutch because it was the language of Europe's greatest seafarers. The young tsar thought his own homeland distressingly backward and unsophisticated by contrast, and in desperate need of foreign know-how. He regularly welcomed Dutch, British, Austrian, German, and Polish visitors to his little country court (though not the French and Swedes, who were military and political rivals), plying them for all manner of information and expertise. At the same time, he eagerly copied their foreign styles and manners.[17] Even before he became king in his own right, he dreamed of leading Russia into the family of European kingdoms and competing with the great nations on an equal footing. In 1689, while still only seventeen, he made his move and, with the critical support of elite militias and church leaders, ousted Sophia and shoved Ivan aside. The ambitious teenager was now supreme.

Once he had power, Peter faced the daunting task of bending Russia to his will. His two primary weapons were the sword and scissors. With the sword of his military, he defeated adversaries at home and abroad, raising Russia's stature in the world. With scissors in his own hand, and in those of his minions, he sheared off Russian beards, symbolically severing old Muscovy from its traditional moorings and launching it on the roiling waters of European modernity. It seems odd that the new tsar would make so much of beards, but in Russia facial hair was not a fashion choice; it was integral to male identity—a feature from time immemorial of both religious faith and masculine honor. Peter pursued an aggressive war on hair precisely because he knew it would help him uproot the spirit of tradition and resistance.

The turning point came in August 1698, when the twenty-six-year-old monarch was on a European tour. Elite units of guardsmen, longtime allies of Ivan and Sophia, deeply resented Peter's favoritism toward foreigners and foreign ways, as well as pay cuts he had imposed on them. Taking advantage of his absence, they rose up to force him from the throne and put Sophia in his place. The rebels were not wrong about Peter's un-Russianness. While he was away, the tsar, who never grew the obligatory Russian beard, had ditched Russian robes as well, adopting Western-style pantaloons, stockings, and coats. The rebellious guards, in turn, seemed to Peter to personify the Russia he despised: superstitious, unruly, and bearded. The westernized tsar hurried home to force a showdown.

By the time Peter reached Moscow, the uprising had been crushed, but there was still work to do. When prominent nobles gathered to greet their long-absent lord, Peter declared the advent of a new era by producing a pair of scissors and shearing off the beards of his leading courtiers right then and there.[18] A few days later, at a banquet honoring the Orthodox New Year, he sent a court jester around the hall shaving any who had not yet conformed. According to one observer, "It was of evil omen to make show of reluctance as the razor approached the chin, and was to be forthwith punished with a boxing of the ears. Between mirth and the wine cup, many were admonished by this insane ridicule to abandon the olden guise."[19]

With his cutting command, Peter drew a line between the new Russia and the old, and handed his opponents yet another grievance against him. Conservatives were outraged by Peter's neglect of Orthodox Christian customs in favor of what they deemed corrupting foreign ones, particularly tobacco smoking and shaving.[20] Though he had defeated them in the field, Peter knew that the guardsmen and their traditionalist sympathizers would continue to stir trouble. He arrested and tortured thousands who had opposed him, eventually hanging or beheading over twelve hundred people in the autumn of 1698. Hundreds of corpses hung from the walls of the city and the Kremlin in grisly testimony to the tsar's ruthlessness in tearing Russia from its old ways.

To prevent Russians from backsliding, he planned a national tax on beards, but war with Sweden delayed its implementation. In 1705, however, he was ready to move forward, and a decree went out that men of all ranks, other than priests and peasants, were to shave or pay a special tax. Most would be charged thirty rubles, a very serious fine, while nobles, officers, and wealthy tradesmen would pay twice as much. Merchants of the highest ranks would be charged a hundred rubles.[21] Those who insisted on keeping their beards paid the tax and were required to wear a medal emblazoned with a picture of a beard, with the words "money paid" etched underneath. The success of this tactic was evident in the fact that little tax was actually collected. Men preferred to keep their money rather than their hair.

Even if it was nominally their choice, the loss of a beard was very distressing for Russian men. John Perry, one of several English shipwrights hired by Peter to bring foreign know-how to Russia, witnessed this for himself. When the order to shave arrived at the shipyards, workmen whom razors had never touched marched forlornly to the barbers. When one gloomy carpenter returned to work, Perry joked that he had suddenly become a young man and teasingly asked what he had done with his hair. To Perry's great surprise, the carpenter reached into his coat and showed it to him, carefully wrapped in a cloth. The downcast workman said he intended keep it safe at home and to have it placed in his coffin when he died, so "he might be able to give an account of it to St. Nicholas when he came to the other World."[22]

Tsar Peter and the Russian Orthodox church were now locked in a struggle for the soul of Russia, and beards became the visible sign of their confrontation. The carpenter's tale was just one manifestation of this crisis of Russian manliness, religion, and identity. Even now, the battle continues. The resurgence of Russian Orthodox faith after the fall of communism has revived in some conservative quarters a theological passion for beards and revived criticisms of secular, clean-shaved modernism. In 2009, a book by a twenty-first-century Old Believer named R. Atorin raised the banner of Orthodox beardedness, denouncing

7.2 Barber cutting off the beard of an Old Believer. Eighteenth-century engraving. Courtesy of New York Public Library.

shaving as a sin.[23] It was this sort of theological commitment that made Peter's war on beards so intense and so important.

According to Atorin, the fathers of the Russian church had, since the Middle Ages, taught that wearing a beard was an important sign of obedience to God. The creator, it was argued, made men in his image, and that image has material as well as spiritual aspects. To preserve the harmony of body and soul, "the appearance of a human being needs to match the makeup of his soul." A man obeys God by conforming himself intellectually, morally, and physically to this godly image. If he does not follow God's will in the physical sense, he is liable to fall short intellectually and morally as well. Atorin summarizes the implications of this thinking: "A man, when committing the sin of beard-shaving . . . tries to remake his appearance according to his own subjective discretion, which does not agree with God's order."

From the Middle Ages, Russian prelates had indeed insisted on beards as a sign of obedience and orthodoxy, and also as a mark of distinction from Roman Catholic Christians, who, as we know, chose shaving as a ensign of spiritual devotion. In about 1460, the archbishop of Rostov reprimanded a nobleman for "abandoning the image of God" by shaving. A church council meeting in Moscow in 1551, responding to complaints that men were beginning to imitate Westerners in their clothing and in shaving and cutting their hair short, warned believers to refrain from these foreign and un-Orthodox practices.[24] In the following century, there were sharp battles over reforming the liturgy and rituals to bring the Russian church into conformity with supposedly more authentic Greek practices. In the 1660s, a minority of "Old Believers," objecting to these "foreign" reforms, broke away from the official church. The tsars backed the reforms, and the Old Believers became disaffected from the government as well. The split did not yet involve clothing or facial hair, as all elements of the Russian church continued the beard tradition up to Peter's day. Again in the 1690s, the Patriarch Adrian, head of the Russian church, issued warnings that members should not imitate Western Christians who, by shaving, made themselves look like apes and monkeys.[25] The church also condemned the dirty Western habit of smoking tobacco.

When he abandoned traditional dress and ordered men to shave, then, Peter deliberately contravened the church's definitions of masculinity and social order. He desperately needed to find allies within the church, and he enlisted the bishops of Rostov and Pskov to write theological defenses of the new rules. The bishop of Rostov published his opinion that beards were an old but unnecessary custom, and that ancient and medieval arguments for them were no longer relevant. The arguments against shaving, he pointed out, were founded on the Old Testament, especially Leviticus, and not on the New Testament, which superseded it. Moreover, it was neither practical nor necessary to enforce beards in modern times.[26]

7.3 Metropolitan Korniliy (Konstantin Ivanovich Titov), Primate of the Russian Orthodox Old-Rite Church since 2005.

The Old Believers, who already rejected the mainstream authorities, denounced these arguments and held fast to their beards as well as their treasured Russian liturgies and customs. Peter eventually chose to isolate them by positively requiring them to wear beards, clearly identifying them as discredited nonconformists. Peter did not need to eliminate all beards, so long as most of his subjects were modern, shaved men.

Jean Jacques Rousseau Scandalizes Polite Society

After the defeat of beards in central Europe and finally Russia, it was a rare and scandalous thing for a gentleman to neglect soap and razor. It was very daring of Jean Jacques Rousseau, a celebrated though unconventional man of letters, to appear at court with a beard.

It happened in 1752, at what Rousseau later described as a critical point in his life. He was forty years old and highly regarded for his musical compositions. His reputation was such that some powerful friends had arranged a command performance of his new opera, *Le Devin du Village* (The Village Soothsayer), at the Chateau of Fontainebleau before King XV and his court. On this splendid occasion, Rousseau displayed his characteristic mix of nervousness and defiance. He naturally hoped that the court would be impressed by him and his work, but he also demonstrated a perverse willingness to ignore the niceties of good manners. "I was on that day," he reported in his autobiography, "in the same careless undress as usual: with a long beard [*grande barbe*], and a wig badly combed."[27] "Long" in this case meant something like a week's growth. Any length of scruff would have been bad manners at the French court. Convinced, however, that "this want of decency was an act of courage," Rousseau entered the theater in which the royal family would soon arrive.

Conducted to a prominent box, and surrounded by elegant women, the composer began to worry about his appearance and steeled himself with defiant thoughts. His beard was not in itself objectionable, he quietly reasoned, for it was granted by nature and would at many times in history have been considered an ornament rather than a disgrace. Luckily for Rousseau, neither his appearance nor his music caused serious offense. The king was delighted by his opera and even offered him the high honor of a lifelong pension. This unexpected twist of fate was a recurring theme in Rousseau's career. He had defied proper decorum and been rewarded handsomely.

There were more turns of fortune to come. Rousseau declined the king's offer of financial security out of the same contradictory motives of fear and courage that had inspired his bearded appearance at the opera. On the one hand, he felt unprepared for the delicacies and pitfalls of courtly society and was terrified of making a fool of himself when presented as a royal pensioner at court. On the other, he risked losing his independence of thought and action. Even so, his close friends were flummoxed. Denis Diderot, the editor of the great *Encyclopedia* and a leading luminary of the age, berated his friend for neglecting the financial well-being of his lover, Thérèse Levasseur, and her aged mother. The pleas of the great thinker, however, were unable to sway Rousseau from his rough-hewn path.

Rousseau's cheeky display was daring and uncommon, running against, not only courtly decorum, but the widespread association of masculine virtue with refinement of look and deportment. European gentlemen from Spain to Russia followed French and English style trends, albeit not without some grousing about foreign and feminized fashions. It was generally a matter of how far refinement should go. Large wigs, frilly clothing, and shiny accessories might seem excessive to some, but a shaved face was never really questioned (Rousseau notwithstanding) as an appropriate manifestation of gentility. Indeed, the availability of cheap, high-quality steel razors by the middle of the century gave rise to enthusiastic marketing of shaving implements, as well as the manly virtues of shaving, to an ever wider audience of consumers. More men could afford to shave themselves more often and more comfortably. This aspect of gentility, at least, was more accessible and convenient than ever before.[28]

Although shaving was never contradicted in any practical sense, Rousseau was not alone in at least contemplating the alternative. The smooth-faced thinkers of the Enlightenment, particularly those in France, were intrigued by the history and theory of beards, if for no other reason than that it presented a portal into times and thinking utterly unlike their own. As he sat in his splendid theater box, Rousseau was mindful that his scruff had both natural and historical justification.

He may have brought to mind recent scholarly references to beard history in such well-regarded works as Furetiere's *Universal Dictionary* and Calmet's historical and critical dictionary of the Bible. More were yet to come. Diderot's *Encyclopedia* would include, a few years later, a brief entry on beard history, and virtually every decade for the next fifty years witnessed another major work on the subject from a variety of authors.[29]

In 1759, a learned Italian named Giuseppe Vannetti published a study of what he called *Barbalogia,* or "beardology." This work marked a transition from the theological speculations of seventeenth-century writers like Olmo, Van Helmont, and Bulwer to the more naturalistic analysis of the eighteenth century. Vannetti, for example, dismissed Van Helmont's theory of Adam's pre-apple beardlessness by appealing to common sense.[30] As for beards themselves, Vannetti was agnostic. Styles had always changed, he argued, and they always would. The custom of shaving prevailed in his day simply because Italians imitated foreign, that is to say, French, styles.[31]

In 1774, the erudite abbot Augustin Fangé produced a volume entitled *Mémoires Pour Servir a l'Histoire de la Barbe de l'Homme* (Studies on the History of Man's Beard). This was the first analysis of the subject from an entirely Enlightenment perspective, exhibiting a thoroughly systematic and skeptical approach. Fangé enumerated several reasons that facial hair had changed over time and place, including climate, religion, group identity, and social emulation. He knew that the real significance of his subject was in the way hairstyles connected with social ideas and, to his credit, refused to accept the premise, popular with beard apologists, that facial hair served to demonstrate male superiority. "Nothing," he asserted, "is more uncertain than the uses of the beard."[32] He even cast doubt on the notion that men were unique in their beardedness. Women too had beards, he noted, even if theirs differed in quality and quantity. Of course, there had also been notable examples of women with extensive facial and body hair. He surmised from this that men and women were more alike than most people claimed.[33] Fangé did agree, however, that "the author of nature" had seen fit to use hair to distinguish men from women, and that the beard seemed to be an "ornament of virility." But he was unwilling to go beyond that.

Fangé's dispassionate study might well have remained the final statement on this subject for a long time, had it not been followed by decades of profound social and political ferment. In the 1780s, Frenchmen in particular were dissatisfied with matters as they were, and a new generation prepared the way for revolution in their fervor for political justice and social equity. Jacques Dulaure was one of this generation, and his examination of beard history was not so much a scholarly survey of past customs as a vision of a new social order.

Jacques Dulaure Finds his Voice

The Academie du Pont Saint-Michel was not an official body. It was the whimsical name chosen by a group of ambitious young Parisians for their literary club. Meeting weekly at the Café Girard in the heart of Paris, these friends shared their research, poetry, and fiction with one another. At one meeting in 1782, twenty-seven-year-old Jacques Antoine Dulaure presented his essay entitled *Pogonogogia: A Philosophical and Historical Essay on Beards.* Dulaure was a civil engineer trying to become a writer. His first efforts involved the things he knew best, the history of civil engineering and architecture, but he had begun to expand into theater reviews and poetry. Seeking something new and fresh, and hoping to amuse his friends, he delved into the curious lore of hair, soon becoming fascinated with the topic as a novel avenue for moral criticism. This was slightly embarrassing to Dulaure, who, in his later published introduction, apologized for being "led away" by his subject and for abandoning his original intent to produce a learned jest.[34] Even so, his friends liked it and urged him to publish it. It was a measure of wider interest that a London press issued an English edition soon after it appeared in Paris.

Starting on a whim, Dulaure discovered an intriguing theme, but even more importantly, he found his voice as a writer. By writing about beards, he accidently discovered a cause, and he discovered the usefulness of history as tool of social and moral criticism. As a result, the engineer became a historian.[35] When revolution came in 1789, the historian became a politician. Dulaure served for a short time as a representative in the National Convention, until he was forced out in 1793 by the leftist coup that launched the Terror. In many respects, Dulaure's *Pogonogogia* was expressive of the latest and most fervent phase of the Enlightenment, in its greater passion for reform and criticism of the status quo. Inspired by an Enlightenment faith in the authority of nature and reason, he found in beard history two great moral forces ranged against each other: the superficial vanity of fashion and the solid integrity of nature. Society had fallen under the absurd spell of fashion. "Who, in this enlightened age," he asked sardonically, "would put the least confidence in a physician who wears his own hair, were it the finest in the world? A wig, certainly, can't give him science, but it gives him the appearance, and that is everything now-a-days."[36]

Aligned with this antagonism of fashion and authenticity was the conflict between effeminacy and manliness. When men abandoned nature's path, Dulaure reasoned, they rendered themselves effeminate, devoid of the vitality, seriousness, and fortitude they ought to have. Shaving was men's misbegotten effort to depart from nature's calling, resulting in subjection to the tyranny of the trivial. Revitalization of manliness was needed for social renewal. "To write an apology for long beards," he extravagantly declared, "is to recall to men's minds their ancient dignity, and that superiority of their sex which has been lost in Europe ever since the fabulous days of chivalry."[37] There can be no doubt that Dulaure and his young, middle-class friends struggled with their own feelings of inadequacy. They could assign some of the blame for their situation to what Dulaure derided as "our effeminate customs," and dream of finding fresh courage to assert themselves and achieve honor and distinction.[38]

Dulaure's history was a sweeping epic involving a grand contest between champions of honest beardedness—Demosthenes, Hadrian, St. Clement, Francis I—and "unmerciful enemies of bearded chins," such as Alexander the Great, Pope Gregory VII, Louis XIV, and Peter the Great. Hebrews, Persians, Greeks, Romans, Chinese—indeed, peoples all around the world—had reverenced long beards, which proved their innate force and underscored the notion that shaving was the tyranny of jealous rulers. The enemies of beards foolishly ignored the health benefits of facial hair and callously risked the collapse of the gender order. In contrast to Fangé's calm recognition of bearded women, Dulaure derided them as repulsive and declared it appropriate for women to eradicate any show of hair on their faces. According to *Pogonogogia,* the presence of facial hair on women, and the absence of it on men, were signs of social disorder and pointed to its source—the unnatural tyranny of fashion. Distracted by self-indulgence, men "know no other virtue than the talent of being agreeable."[39]

It stood to reason, then, that a return to beards would improve the moral fabric, and Dulaure called upon independent, strong-willed men to lead the way. It sounded like a dare, and though they might thrill to the idea, he and his friends were not quite ready to act on it. Typically for Enlightenment thinkers, Dulaure was more talk than action. Like Rousseau, he was intrigued by the beard as a radical gesture, and especially as an assertion of masculinity, even if he was not ready to grow one himself.

During the eighteenth century, beards were an abstract idea, a concept around which a larger critique of cultural degeneracy could be built. For both Rousseau and Dulaure, fashion, refinement, and superficiality had removed men from a proper grounding in natural honesty and virtue. They looked to a bearded past and anticipated a bearded future. Russian traditionalists like the Old Believers had similar thoughts. They too perceived the beard as a symbol of true moral order and looked to a venerable past, before absolutist rulers like Louis XIV and Peter the Great had imposed smooth and immoral manners upon them. There can be no question that, as Samuel Pepys's experience proves, elite men had invested dignity in artificial rather than natural hair, as well as elaborate conventions of dress and deportment. The reason these conventions did not wither under the assaults of beard champions is that the real benefits of social decorum trumped fantasies of liberated virility.

Revolution arrived in France just a few years after Dulaure's study of beards, and dreams of a new political and social order stirred the hearts of hopeful young men like the little band at the Academie du Pont Saint-Michel. For a time Dulaure was himself a representative in the revolutionary legislature. The king fell from power, and the church was stripped of much of its wealth and influence. It was possible that fashion would suffer a similar defeat. An anonymous pamphlet distributed in the streets of Paris after the fall of the Bastille expressed this expectation. It congratulated the citizens of Paris for recovering the liberty of their medieval forebears, the Franks. "You will again become like them," the text announced, "strong and healthy, like them you will let your beard grow, and you will wear the long hair they favored. Goodbye hairdressers, beauticians and merchants of fashion, now you will cover yourselves with cotton or homespun. From now on you will scorn all the ornaments of luxury, and you will make use of all your physical and intellectual faculties."[40] As it turned out, of course, the revolution proceeded in fits and starts, proceeding from terror to war, Napoleonic glory, and military defeat. The dreams of liberty, equality, fraternity, and beardedness remained unfulfilled as the nineteenth century got underway.

8

BEARDS OF THE
ROMANTIC IMAGINATION

The French Revolution stirred great hopes and fears throughout Europe. The hope was for a new birth of liberty and equality. The fear was the specter of political violence and war unleashed by revolutionary fervor. Many wondered what good could come of revolution if reason were crushed by the horrors of the guillotine. In the face of this grave obstacle, young and fervent romantics throughout Europe dreamed of a new spirit of sensitivity, intuition, and heroism that would quell disorder, foster unity, and achieve true liberty. Many hoped that Napoleon Bonaparte might be the man to secure these dreams, a man of genius able to keep both retrograde royalty and revolutionary terror at bay. Among Napoleon's many early admirers was the German composer Ludwig van Beethoven, who dedicated his passionate and groundbreaking Third Symphony to him. Soon after history's first romantic composer dedicated history's first romantic symphony to Europe's first romantic political hero, Bonaparte betrayed Beethoven's aspirations, quashing the fledgling French Republic, declaring himself emperor, and embarking on a campaign of imperial conquest. The frustrated composer tore up his symphony's title page and removed his dedication. It was painfully clear to him that Europe had not yet found its liberating hero, and that his soaring symphony would call to mind the unfulfilled hopes of a romantic generation.

A few years after Beethoven's disillusionment, Germany, Austria, Italy, and Spain fell under Napoleon's boot, and a deep gloom overshadowed liberal dreams in those countries. The French Revolution, once so full of promise, had become a nightmare. Conservatives raised the standard of resistance, calling on all to rally to monarchy and tradition. Beleaguered republicans clung forlornly to their fading hopes of equality and constitutionalism. Romantics proposed a third way: if men themselves changed, both national restoration and republican freedom would be possible. Like the conservatives, they looked to history; unlike the conservatives, they did not look to the immediate past but to a more distant, medieval past, whence bearded men beckoned as hopeful symbols of a restored future.

Friedrich Ludwig Jahn Looks Back

Outside Berlin in the summer of 1811, gangs of young robbers led by a vigorous, bearded man of middle age assaulted scores of travelers. Hidden among rocks and trees in a stretch of hilly countryside, the predatory bands would emerge suddenly, descend on their victims, wrestle them to the ground, and carry them off to their lair. If the prisoners were lucky, they might be rescued by counterattacking travelers. It was a dramatic scene repeated dozens of times over the course of the summer.

The robbers were not real robbers, however, nor were the travelers real victims. They were teenage boys playing a well-organized game. The mastermind was the boys' rather unusual history teacher, Friedrich Ludwig Jahn. With games like Robbers and Travelers, and gymnastic exercises in a nearby field, Jahn tested his students' physical strength and skill and encouraged them to develop a sense of teamwork and strategy. These Prussian boys were growing up at a time when Germany lay broken and impotent in the grip of Napoleon's revolutionary armies, and it was their teacher's dearest ambition to instill in them a spirit of companionship, resourcefulness, and toughness that would eventually restore German independence.[1] Like many of his generation, Jahn was a true Romantic who believed that human destiny was shaped by spirit and passion. He was convinced that his fellow Germans needed a rebirth of national feeling and pride to regain their freedom, and that gymnastics exercises and field games were the best means to this end. Physical discipline would help revive the medieval spirit of daring, heroism, and honor, which in turn would redeem modern Germany.

Over the next several years, more and more boys and young men joined Jahn's gymnastics club at the edge of the city, where they played, fenced, and trained on a range of apparatus, including the high bar, the pommel horse, and Jahn's own invention, the parallel bars. There could be no mistaking Jahn for a gym teacher, however. He was first and foremost a mythmaker and nation-builder. The young men who flocked to his club were invited into an egalitarian brotherhood of German heroism, replete with a costume of linen trousers, loose gray shirts, and newfangled badges of chivalry. The emblem on each boy's chest featured four dates alongside the word *Turnkunst* (Jahn's coinage to replace the Greek *gymnastics*): 9, the year the Germans secured their freedom by defeating the invading Roman army; 919, the year the chivalric tournaments began; 1519, the end of tournaments; and 1811, the year Jahn revived manly tournaments in the guise of gymnastic games.[2]

The history teacher with the romantic spirit saw the future by looking into the past, or rather, the imaginary past. In a book on German nationality that Jahn published just before establishing his gymnastics club, he urged his countrymen to abandon their slavish admiration of foreign ideas and foreign ways. He called instead for the adoption of specifically German values, styles, and words—like *Turnkunst*. He wore a costume of cheap, durable, unbleached cloth with an open collar, which he imagined was authentically German, and he grew out his beard because he thought this too was both noble and German.[3]

Though he had reason to believe his beard and clothes were historically authentic, his choices were not determined by careful research. The two things he found most distressing in his day were the imitation of all things foreign—especially French—and the loss of German virility. Unbleached cloth and facial hair were emphatically unfashionable, and thus un-French. Beards especially denoted strength, by association with medieval chivalry. In his book on nationality, Jahn waxed poetical about the good old days of hairy masculinity. The ancestral German man was master of many sorts of warfare. "Later came the disappearance of the sword, regarded as superfluous, from his side, of

8.1 Friedrich Ludwig Jahn. Library of Congress, LC-USZ62-41274.

the troublesome beard from his face, and of the heroic courage of our ancestors from his heart."[4] In Jahn's imagination, a new, bearded generation of gymnasts, cunning in field games, fierce with fencing foils, and fearless on high bars and pommel horses, would renew medieval glory for modern Germany.

Jahn's back-to-the-future logic promised a nonrevolutionary path to the revolutionary goals of social equality, national unity, and constitutional government.[5] In his imagination, bearded men, tuning their bodies, minds, and spirits to the heroic German past, could bypass social and political divisions and controversies. No wonder Jahn let his beard grow thicker and longer with each passing year.

In 1813, Jahn and several hundred gymnasts served in the Prussian militia, helping to expel French forces from German lands. He then joined with others to organize a national patriotic student fraternity to promote physical revitalization, constitutional reform, and German unification. Jahn provided the guidebook of gymnastics, again announcing his goal of recovering lost manly traditions.[6] The German authorities knew a threat to the aristocratic order when they saw it and viewed the gymnastics movement with great suspicion. In 1819, an overzealous gymnast at the University of Jena assassinated a critic of the student movement, and the authorities jumped at the opportunity to ban both patriotic fraternities and their gymnastic exercises. Jahn himself was apprehended, banished from Berlin, and placed under a house arrest for several years. The time for unity, constitutionalism, and beardedness had not yet arrived in Germany.

Friedrich Ludwig Jahn may not have realized his particular vision of manliness, but that did not mean the old social and gender order had survived the revolutionary era intact. On the contrary, the American and French Revolutions ushered in a new era of natural hair for men in the Western world. Before these upheavals, men used the artifice of elaborate clothing and false hair to demonstrate superior breeding and social privilege. Afterward, silk stockings, lace collars, high heels, bright ribbons, and powdered wigs were banished for good. In their place a contrary style emerged, featuring black trousers, black coats, black ties, and black hats. This "great renunciation," as one scholar called it, enacted the modern idea of equality by simplifying and standardizing male fashion, emphasizing the natural physique and personal virtues such as sobriety and restraint over wealth and breeding.[7]

The new ideals of this era grounded social rights not in inheritance and rank but in manhood itself. Thomas Jefferson proclaimed in the American Declaration of Independence (1776) that all men were endowed with inalienable rights, and the French Declaration of the Rights of Man and Citizen (1789) insisted that social distinctions should be based on individual merit rather than social rank or entitlement. Not all European states ascribed to these egalitarian ideals, but in the age of the Napoleonic Wars all relied on their male citizenry as never before to fight for their homelands. In both theory and in war, then, manhood became the foundation of the political order.

Sober black clothing and natural hair was the appropriate look for a society founded on male citizenship. The move to a more natural look encouraged thoughts of beards as well, but concern for responsible self-discipline argued against it. The most popular European style in the first half of the nineteenth century was what the French called the *favoris* and English speakers called whiskers. This was a rather more impressive display of natural hair than was permitted in the previous century, but it was still restrained. The mustache, which became an important part of military style at this time, was a special case that will be considered later. The full beard became even less acceptable in polite society when young romantic radicals adopted it as a calling card of social rebellion.

Victor Hugo Causes a Riot

While conservative governments in Germany kept Friedrich Ludwig Jahn and other liberals in check, France remained at the cutting edge of social ferment, and also the leading edge of hair experimentation. In the late 1820s and 1830s, young bearded romantics were the talk of Paris, much of it disapproving. A conservative gentlemen in Victor Hugo's novel *Les misérables,* which was set in 1832, complained that "the nineteenth century is poison; the first little squirt that comes along grows his little goatee, thinks he's a genuine rogue, and leaves his old relatives in the lurch. That's republican, that's romantic. What the hell is romantic about that?"[8] The answer, of course, is that beards were romantic because they were natural and historic, and thus seemed to counter the vanities and corruptions of modern life. Hugo was himself partly responsible for the enthusiasm for beards in the 1830s. He was the brightest light among a new generation of artists and writers who were burning to try new ideas and experience new freedoms. After visiting an exhibit of romantic art featuring historic scenes and historic bearded men, Hugo gave voice to the hairy impulse of his generation.

Though he could not bring himself to wear a beard, Hugo penned a lighthearted, satirical argument for doing so. God had originally made men beautiful, Hugo wrote, with eyes, chin, mouth, and cheeks that expressed serenity, confidence, and strength. But the grandeur of the male face had been destroyed by modern commercial civilization. Men in modern times had become narrow-minded and unimaginative, and it showed in their faces. "The calculations of interest take the place of the speculations of the intellect . . . [and] when interest has superseded intelligence, pride disappears, the nostril contracts [and] the eye grows dull."[9] But God, he wryly proposed, had foreseen this development and in his wisdom provided man with a beard to cover "this ugliness bred of civilization." The moral was "let your beards grow, all ye who are ugly and who wish to be handsome!"[10] When this semijoking piece appeared in print, the controversy of the chin erupted. Hugo was astonished as critics rushed to denounce beards as "repulsive, unpatriotic, Jewish, abominable, and worst of all, romantic!" Champions of good taste pronounced the shaven chin to be classic and dignified, vowing that the French, the most intelligent people in the world, would never allow beards to triumph.

Young and old, radical and conservative, all took the beard question rather more seriously than Hugo had expected, and the excitement of the debate inspired even more young men to let their facial hair grow. Here was an effective way, along with colorful and historic clothing, to offend the priggish middle classes and pierce the smugness of the old guard. It was not necessary for *les jeunes-France* (Young France), as they called themselves, to be consistent about what period of history they evoked with their hair. Some hoped to model themselves on the supposedly pure authenticity of Homeric Greece. Some, influenced by Walter Scott's wildly popular medieval novels, emulated the nobility of knighthood; others, the boldness of Renaissance courtiers. All eras were equally suitable because they all stood in colorful and hairy contrast to darkly clothed, smoothly trimmed respectability.

In 1830, revolution broke out again in Paris, and romantic beards reached full bloom. The deeply unpopular and very unliberal Bourbon king Charles X had done his best to turn back the clock on equality and liberty, but French citizens of almost all ranks had lost patience with his hopelessly outdated and oppressive rule. An early sign of the coming revolt came in February 1830 when conservative guardians of literary taste were bested by Hugo and his romantic supporters in the theatrical riot known as the "Battle of the *Hernani*." *Hernani*, Hugo's untraditional new play set in Renaissance Spain, features a desperate confrontation between three men for the hand of a Spanish noblewoman, which ends rather badly when the lady and two of her suitors commit suicide. To men of taste, the sexual themes, passionate tone, and earthy, contemporary French dialogue were shocking and reprehensible. Alerted to its offensiveness, traditionalists turned out in force at the premiere to demonstrate their displeasure. Hugo and his romantic allies were ready for them. Deeming themselves "knights of the future" and "defenders of artistic liberty," young students, poets, and artists stationed themselves around the theater, resplendent in colorful medieval or Renaissance outfits, long hair, and flowing mustaches and beards.[11] They boisterously cheered the play, and countered conservative jeers and catcalls with gameful rejoinders. The costume drama in the seats overshadowed the one on stage, which proceeded with great difficulty amid the tumult. In the end, the critics pronounced the battle of the *Hernani* a triumph for the romantics, and Hugo collected a handsome price for the publishing rights. It was curtains for the restrained sophistication of French classical theater, and it was a portent of doom for King Charles.

The uprising in the streets of Paris that toppled the king the following July was immortalized by the romantic painter Eugène Delacroix in his monumental work *Liberty Leading the People* (figure 8.2). At the center is Lady Liberty, waving the flag of the republic and beckoning men to follow her toward national liberation. She is a symbol, of course, but so are the men to her right. One is a tanned, scruffy workman who stands in for the French laborer. Next to him is a young, bearded gentleman dressed in his bourgeois black coat, tie, and top hat, and carrying a musket. The man in black is really a mixed metaphor, combining the sober black outfit of the respectable middle class with the beard of Young France. This monumental canvas presented Delacroix's vision of a nation invigorated by a liberal and romantic spirit.

The street battles of 1830 succeeded in overthrowing Charles X, but they did not manage to create a republic. Powerful landed and business interests prevented this by calling in a new king, Louis Philippe, who promised to be more moderate than his predecessor. The old regime was out, but the hopes of idealists like Hugo and Delacroix were

8.2 *Liberty Leading the People,* by Eugène Delacroix, 1830.

dashed. Just two years later, foolhardy radicals prematurely tried again. As described in Hugo's *Les misérables,* "great strapping lads with long hair, beards, and mustaches" took to the barricades once more to fight the new king, only to be routed by shaved and disciplined troops.[12]

Within weeks of this debacle, Louis Philippe's government cracked down on another, even more radical group of hairy men called the Saint-Simonians. In July 1832, dozens of them marched behind their charismatic leader Barthélémi-Prosper Enfantin into a Paris courtroom to face trial and conviction on charges of unauthorized meetings and moral depravity. The heavily bearded Enfantin had declared himself the prophet of a new brand of Christianity that would liberate the world, and especially women, for whom he outrageously advocated complete equality with men. The Saint-Simonians represented a curious mix of religious fervor and scientific calculation. Unlike the artists and poets of Young France, most members of this cult were engineers and scientists who hoped to use science, guided by a generous Christian spirit, to organize an ideal society. It was to be a sort of top-down socialism, planned by a talented elite for the benefit of all.

Though they staked a claim to both science and rational religion, Saint-Simonians were, like their Young France peers, essentially romantic dreamers. Beards suited Saint-Simonians for the same reason they suited other romantics: they were both old and new. Saint-Simonians admired the past in terms of Christian traditions and ordered social hierarchy, but they also yearned for a future in which a scientific elite would rule. The sight of these outlandish men on trial reinforced in the European mind the association of beards with recklessness and revolt. Hair was not simply hair; it was a challenge to the social order.

The revolution of 1830 and the failed revolt of 1832 did not settle political matters in France. Indeed, observers in subsequent years noted how ideological divides found expression in subtle variations of hair.[13] Conservative royalists were, naturally enough, clean-shaven. On the other end of the spectrum, republicans sported sideburns extending to their jaws along with a *mouche*, a small tuft of beard below the lips. Moderate republicans did not grow a *mouche*. If one had a *mouche* and a mustache, but not the long sideburns, a style later referred to as the "imperial," one was a Bonapartist, that is, a supporter of the fallen imperial regime of Napoleon. Liberals, who stood between the moderate republicans and the conservatives, favored mustaches, with or without sideburns. Full beards, of course, were not really acceptable, except for artists and radicals. In a country defined by political divisions, it comes as no surprise that facial hair was deployed as a badge of allegiance, and this studied variation in facial hair helped keep France at the forefront of masculine style during the nineteenth century.

The social threat of long beards was a universal language in the early nineteenth century, understood in America as well as Europe. The contexts and issues varied, but the fear of hairy nonconformity was fundamentally the same. In the same year that Young France shouted at conservative theatergoers in Paris, an American farmer faced the battle of his lifetime in defense of individual choice.

Joseph Palmer Fights for His Beard

Joseph Palmer was an upstanding, churchgoing citizen of Fitchburg, Massachusetts. His choice to grow a long beard, however, was deeply shocking to his straitlaced neighbors. They denounced him as a disgrace, even a monster, and they blanched at his proud refusal to do away with his obnoxious ruff.

In the summer of 1830 matters reached a head. As Palmer waited his turn to receive communion at the town's Congregational church, the minister carrying the bread and wine simply passed him by. Infuriated, the bearded farmer advanced to the communion table, took the cup, and served himself, finally shouting to the assembly, "I love my Jesus as well, and better, than any of you do!"[14] For the good citizens of Fitch-burg, this was the final straw. Some days later, four men armed with shears, soap, and razor seized him in the street, intending to put an end to his offensive whiskers. Palmer was thrown to the ground but, with the aid of a jackknife, managed to escape with his beard intact.

Not to be denied, Palmer's attackers accused Palmer of assault, and he was thrown in jail. Behind bars, he wrote letters to the newspapers declaring that the true reason for his imprisonment was hatred of his whiskers, not the trumped-up charges of battery. For nearly a year, Palmer kept up a stream of public complaints about his jailers and his treatment. Finally, exasperated officials unlocked his cell to be rid of him. Palmer denied his tormenters even this satisfaction by insisting that he would not leave until he had been reimbursed for what he believed to be the exorbitant fees charged for his upkeep. Officers simply lifted him in his chair and carried him into the street. Now free, Palmer had no more trouble about his hair, and he embarked on a long career as a social agitator. At his death in 1875 his family placed a tombstone with the epitaph JOSEPH PALMER. PERSECUTED FOR WEARING THE BEARD.[15]

Palmer's beard was not a nationalist symbol like Jahn's, a romantic statement like those of Young France, or a socialist emblem like Enfan-tin's, but it was just as much a symbol of protest. Palmer was an idealist, and though not really a revolutionary, he was certainly a reformer. He was personally acquainted with the leading thinkers in New England, including Ralph Waldo Emerson, Henry David Thoreau, and Amos Bronson Alcott. He was active in the cutting-edge movements of his day, notably antislavery and temperance, and he eagerly joined Alcott's Fruitlands, an unsuccessful utopian commune. In short, the townspeo-ple of Fitchburg were not wrong to see Palmer as a rebel, even if they were wrong to think that a razor would put him in his place.

Facial hair was especially offensive to New Englanders because it suggested a willful independence that ran counter to the communal ethic of the Puritan tradition. Even social reformers were likely to react negatively to such idiosyncratic displays. It would be hard to find a man with a more radical temperament than Massachusetts-born William Lloyd Garrison, the great lion of the American antislavery movement. But even Garrison took exception to facial hair. In 1829, just months before the attack on Palmer's beard, Garrison, who was just starting out as an abolitionist journalist in Baltimore, displayed his precocious talent for ranting. "Of all the brutal inclinations," he declared, "of all the vulgar rivalships for unenviable pre-eminence—of all fashionable absurdities propagated and maintained by fashionable monsters—there has been nothing half as indecent and ridiculous, as the present rage for sporting huge mustaches."[16] Garrison stood at the cutting edge of American social reform, but the arrogance of a mustache seemed to him the ugly side of American individualism.

Facial hair indeed became a matter of increasing controversy in the 1830s and 1840s, the decades following Palmer's imprisonment. Garrison's tirade is just one example. Self-assertion, whether ideological or not, inclined more and more men to experiment with hair in these decades, provoking, in turn, a reaction from guardians of moral order and good taste.

Americans were generally not so rigid as the stern New Englanders of Palmer's town, and they were more likely to sprout beards than Europeans. But even in the "land of the free," there was widespread resistance to facial hair in these years. Men of cultivation generally reaped the growth on their faces to meet shaven standards of decorum. A sophisticated southern contributor to the *Southern Literary Journal* mused appreciatively in 1838 about historic beards in art and literature, but still found no justification for facial hair attempted by the iconoclasts in his own day. In his eyes, "an undergrowth, like that of our swamps, covers the countenance, and the human face divine is metamorphosed into the image and likeness of a mop."[17] Two years later, a German historian named Hermann Hauff, made the same point, mocking arrogant young men in his country who attempted to project an unwarranted sophistication by growing facial hair. "It is now precisely the opposite of what we see in earlier bearded centuries. Whereas once the rough white-streaked beard commanded the respect of the younger generation, now the youthful, combed, and tediously nourished beard is meant to impress the smooth beaks of elders."[18]

In spite of such dismissive objections, political conservatives infected by the romantic spirit joined others in testing the possibilities of unconventional hair. Their reasons were largely the same as those of leftists, that is, to invoke a vital and authentic masculinity that would legitimate their cause. The early nineteenth century witnessed two forms of conservative facial hair: the aristocratic beard and the martial mustache. Both would prove important in laying the foundations for a new beard movement in the Western world.

Lord Eglinton Puts the Middle Ages on Parade

Archibald Montgomerie, the thirteenth Earl of Eglinton, was not a particularly unusual or gifted member of the Scottish nobility, but his rather ordinary opinions are what make his actions in 1838 so significant. Like many aristocrats of his day, he was alarmed by the pace of social and political change engulfing nineteenth-century Europe. When he announced plans to host a medieval tournament at his faux-gothic castle in Scotland, complete with pageantry, banquets, armor, jousts, and mock battles, he was doing little more than channeling his class resentment against modernity. A major reform of Parliament in 1832 had greatly reduced the power of the aristocracy and increased that of middle-class reformers. The tournament was intended to counter these developments and provide some cheer for a fading nobility. At a time when Sir Walter Scott's 1819 novel, *Ivanhoe,* entranced readers across Europe with the romance of medieval chivalry, it only seemed right that the real-life aristocracy should reclaim its heritage.[19]

Dozens of aristocratic gentlemen from around Britain responded to Eglinton's call to train with broadsword and lance. Eventually, thirteen fought in the tournament in August 1839, arrayed in what they believed to be authentic armor and weapons. These retro knights completed their costume with thoroughly unmodern full beards. On the appointed day, thousands of spectators from around the country—many also wearing period costumes—poured onto the castle grounds in excited anticipation. The festivities began with a grand parade of knights and retainers escorting the "queen of beauty," Lady Seymour, to the lists. Unfortunately, it was at this moment that the skies opened, drenching participants and onlookers alike. A chilled and rapidly diminishing crowd watched the desultory procession slosh through a sea of mud, modern umbrellas obscuring the medieval splendor. After a slow, muddy joust, the remaining festivities were canceled. It seemed a telling fiasco. The romantic excesses of Eglinton's joust were just as foolish and irrelevant as leftist dreams on a Paris barricade. Even the young Queen Victoria laughed when she read about the ridiculous scene.[20]

Mere rain was not enough, however, to dampen ebullient conservative gentlemen like Lord Eglinton and his friends. When the weather cleared a few days later, the parade and joust were restaged for a smaller but drier crowd. Notable painters were present to capture sunlit images of chivalry reborn. Their glamorous work appeared in several commemorative books, which failed to mention the earlier mud. The lasting importance of the tournament lay in the publication of dreamy images of shimmering, bearded knights fighting for age-old virtues of loyalty, honor, and courage. Paintings of the Eglinton tournament contributed to a growing cavalcade of bearded heroism adorning the halls of the great country houses, as well as the houses of Parliament.

Most of the gentlemen who bought suits of armor and grew beards for the Eglinton tournament soon shaved them off again. It was playacting, after all. But another sort of aristocratic facial hair had far more staying power: the cavalry mustache. Even before Eglinton staged his tournament, the mustache had become the essential accouterment of martial panache. Over time, the style filtered upward into the European aristocracy, and downward into the rank and file of Europe's armies. Prince Albert, the consort of Queen Victoria, modeled a notable example of the military-aristocratic mustache. Good thing too, for it helped him win the queen's heart.

Prince Albert Cuts a Dashing Figure

It was like a fairy tale. Long, long ago, the young princess of a great kingdom resentfully turned away old and dull suitors in hopes that a handsome prince would appear to sweep her off her feet. She was Princess Victoria of Great Britain, who became Queen Victoria at age eighteen in 1837. She resisted pressures to marry, insisting that, like Queen Elizabeth of old, she would remain single for the foreseeable future.

8.3 Eglinton Tournament, 1839. Bearded knights escort "Queen of Beauty" Lady Seymour to the lists.

Victoria's great vulnerability, however, was her youth and inexperience. After several public relations blunders, she had managed to make herself unpopular with both officialdom and the public. One of these faux pas was to publicly accuse a lady of her court of adultery, when in fact the unfortunate woman was bloated, not by pregnancy, but by a malignant tumor that soon killed her. Victoria was not politically astute and too often proved petty and impetuous. To those around her, and to her subjects at large, she seemed badly in need of a guiding hand.

The man favored by her relatives for this role was Albert, her slightly younger cousin. The son of a German duke, he was amiable, reliable, studious, and, most helpfully, amenable to the prospect of marrying a foreign cousin he barely knew. Victoria was unconvinced. Though she agreed, under pressure, to host Albert and his elder brother at Windsor Castle in the fall of 1839, she warned her pushy relatives that she would not commit to marrying anyone for at least two or three more years. She had met Albert once several years earlier, and liked him well enough, but now she was queen, and she feared losing the power of initiative that she so thoroughly enjoyed.

All this changed suddenly when, on a bright fall evening, Albert was ushered into the castle. Victoria was smitten. Writing in her journal that first night, she gushed that Albert was "quite charming, and so excessively handsome, such beautiful blue eyes, and exquisite nose, and such a pretty mouth with delicate moustachios and slight but very light whiskers; a beautiful figure, broad in the shoulders and a fine waist; my heart is quite going . . . "[21] A few days after this breathless confession, she sketched a portrait of Albert that captured her adoration. To the queen, her mustachioed and whiskered prince was the very image of manly perfection. Abandoning her former self-control, she proposed to Albert and he accepted.

It is no exaggeration to say that the marriage of Victoria and Albert was one of the more important events in European history. Albert proved to be a steady and wise counselor. Together, Victoria and Albert established a tone of sobriety and earnestness suitable to their pious and industrious subjects, and Albert's attention to technology and industry helped to keep the monarchy relevant in modern times. They raised a large family, and their descendants sat on thrones throughout Europe. The last German kaiser and the last empress of Russia were their grandchildren. None of this great legacy was obvious at the start, of course. Victoria was still unpopular when she married in 1840, and so was her choice of husband. To many of her subjects, Albert was yet another foreign fortune-seeker insinuating himself at the top of society in order to live sumptuously at Britain's expense. The occasional rough treatment the new couple received in the press is a reminder that the vitriol of today's tabloids is nothing new. One broadsheet circulating in the streets before the wedding rhymed:

> Saxe-Coburg sends [Albert] from its paltry race,
> With foreign phrases and a moustachio'd face,
> To extract treasure from Parliament by wooing
> The hoyden Sovereign of this mighty isle [who]
> Welcomes her German with enraptured smile.[22]

A sure sign of Albert's un-English ways was his mustache, which was like a foreign language to the public. He did not look like an English aristocrat, banker, or businessman, who might wear prominent side-whiskers but nothing more. Whether or not Albert's continental style would find favor on the imperial isle, only time would tell.

The new Prince Consort's mustache may have seemed foreign, but it was not unprecedented in Britain. Elite cavalry units—the Horse

8.4 Prince Albert. Engraving by Henry S. Sadd, 1847. Library of Congress, LC-DIG-pga-03230.

Guards, Life Guards, and Tenth Royal Hussars—all sported the fur caps and long black mustaches typical of hussar cavalry units throughout Europe. It is this military mustache tradition that was the ultimate inspiration of the German aristocratic mustache, and thus Albert's hairstyle. The original hussars were Hungarian cavalry units of the seventeenth century, whose fearsome looks and bold tactics were widely imitated by other European armies. The Napoleonic Wars helped spread the hussar style to Western Europe and to western art. One of the best-known renderings of hussar bravado is Theodore Gericault's painting *An Officer of the Imperial Horse Guards Charging* (figure 8.5). Hair is key to the heroism and dash of this Napoleonic officer. There is the horse's mane and tail, the leopard-pelt saddle, the fur hat, and, of course, the fearsome mustache.

For members of regiments that adopted the hussar style, a dark upper lip was absolutely required. In 1806, the hussar name and uniform were introduced into Britain when the Tenth Light Dragoons, at the Prince of Wales's command, became the Tenth Royal Hussars. With this name change came new uniforms and mandatory mustaches.[23] Before long, the old look seemed mundane, and other military units adopted elements of the new mode. A general order in 1830 attempted to halt this proliferation and limit mustaches to Life Guards, Horse Guards, and Hussars, so that these elite forces might be appropriately distinguished. Demand was so great, however, that military commanders soon buckled. The same was true in France, where in 1833 permission was granted for all French soldiers to wear mustaches.[24] By midcentury, virtually all cavalrymen in Europe, and most regular army officers, exhibited the fierce face of a Hungarian raider.[25]

The justification for this trend was the idea that facial hair, along with grandiose uniforms, struck fear into the hearts of enemies, and thus was a sort of weapon.[26] The cavalry, with its speed and noise, was the original vehicle of "shock and awe" tactics, and an impressive get-up was deemed critical to its arsenal. One way mustaches helped, no doubt, was by making men appear older than they really were. Many cavalrymen too young to grow impressive facial hair faked it. Jean-Baptiste Marbot, who was a seventeen-year-old French hussar, recounts in his memoirs that he used black wax to paint on the required look.[27] This was not uncommon. An anonymous writer to the *Times* of London complained in 1828 about the cost in time and money of pro-

8.5 *An Officer of the Imperial Horse Guards Charging,* by Théodore Géricault, 1812.

curing and maintaining fake mustaches for Life Guardsmen. All mustaches had to be a uniform black color, so men of any other coloring, if they could grow one at all, had to use dye.[28]

Though Prince Albert's mustache was uncommon in the British nobility, it granted him an appropriately military and conservative aspect. It also imparted a manly charm and flair that could cause a young queen to take leave of her senses. Before she met Albert, Victoria had laughed at the romantic follies of the Eglinton tournament, but now her attitude shifted. Just three years after Eglinton, the Queen hosted a rare fancy-dress ball at Buckingham Palace for two thousand guests. The theme was chivalry, and Albert and Victoria appeared in the guise of the medieval king Edward III and Queen Philippa. The *Times* of London declared it one of the most magnificent royal entertainments since the seventeenth century.[29] Soon afterword, Albert gave his wife for her birthday a small portrait of himself in armor, painted by Robert Thorburn, which became her favorite likeness of her husband. In her own words, it gave Albert "the gravest manliest look."[30] The medieval Albert was a charming fantasy. With his tall bearing, mustache, and whiskers, he carried it off well. The trick to being a modern prince, it would seem, was to embrace technology, innovation, and change, but to look medieval.

In spite of Albert's growing popularity, and the widespread adoption of mustaches by military officers throughout Europe, there was a concerted effort in every European country to limit mustaches to the military. Officers and aristocrats hoped to reserve the mustache as a distinctive mark of their class. Meanwhile, guardians of middle-class respectability denounced it as arrogant and rebellious on civilian men. When young clerks in Paris presumed in 1817 to sport mustaches and the *mouche* (a small tuft of hair on the chin), they faced widespread derision in the press and on the vaudeville stage.[31] Some firms positively outlawed such displays. In 1818, an English commentator in a respectable journal complained that "the dandyism of the moustache [is] incongruous and coxcombish when pasted on the English countenance."[32] In Spain, the mustache was reserved for military men, and even ordinary soldiers were denied the right to wear them before 1845.[33] The king of Bavaria published an ordinance in 1838 forbidding civilians to wear mustaches, under threat of arrest and forcible shaving.[34]

Outside the regimented life of military men, hair on the lip retained the taint of foolish arrogance, dandyism, or worse. In Prussia in 1840, nineteen-year-old Friedrich Engels, the future collaborator with communist theorist Karl Marx, enjoyed a special thrill in growing a mustache while a university student. He gloried in its power to shock respectable society, including his own parents. For a time he deliber-

ated about making things worse by adding a Renaissance-style romantic beard, but he decided against it. He enticed his friends "with the
courage to defy philistinism and grow a mustache" to sign a pledge to
do so in time for a mustache celebration party.[35] He felt very daring in
all this, and he liked the attention it brought him. Engels never turned
back from this first rebellion against middle-class respectability, later
becoming the fully bearded communist icon of history. Marx himself
followed a similar path, making good use of his immense black beard as
a symbol of defiance.

By the 1840s, bearded and mustachioed liberals and socialists
throughout Europe were facing off against the traditional order. In
France, there was alarm about the spread of facial hair and rebellion
among the working classes. A Paris police report in 1840 lamented that
"we see with pain many individuals belonging to the working class, in
blouses, with beard and moustache, apparently spending more time on
politics than their labours, reading republican newspapers and detest-
able pamphlets published for distribution among them so as to lead
them astray and gradually push them in the most deplorable direction."[36] Britain witnessed the fearful appearance of insurrectionary hair
among its two most disgruntled populations: the industrial working
class and the Irish. Daniel O'Connell, the leader of the campaign for
Irish self-government, got a big laugh in 1843 when he described to one
of his audiences a letter he received from Galway (western Ireland),
"wherein police had orders to watch the arrival of any ship, coach, car
or foreign looking personage in that town, particularly any who wore
mustachios." The crowd roared when O'Connell cast a significant
glance at his son Daniel, who sported a "very well-curled and promising moustache of a sanguinary and *farouche* character."[37]

The Chartists were working-class men who agitated for the Charter,
a manifesto calling for a popular parliament elected by all adult men.
The leader of the most radical faction of Chartists, Feargus O'Connor,
was notorious for his scandalously unshorn chin.[38] In 1848, Lord Palm-
erston, the foreign secretary and one of Britain's leading politicians,
damned the Chartists as "whiskered and bearded rioters."[39] An economic slump in 1847, and news of liberal revolutions in Europe in 1848,
had inspired the collection of millions of signatures favoring the Charter. In advance of a mass demonstration planned for London that sum-

mer, 100,000 middle-class citizens volunteered as special constables to contain the working-class demonstrators. In the event, the crowds proved smaller than anticipated by either side, partly because of heavy rains. With only about 150,000 protestors, the fearsome O'Connor proved unwilling to confront the army of constables arrayed against him. "The day of the Chartists passed off with most ridiculous quiet, and the government is stronger than ever," observed the wife of the American ambassador to Britain, Elizabeth Bancroft.[40] Even so, the British remained jittery about both insurrection and scruff. Bancroft noted in her memoirs that anyone promoting democracy too loudly might be packed off at any time, particularly if he had a long beard.

The English government was secure, but King Louis Philippe of France and the kings and princes of Germany proved vulnerable to a new generation of bearded liberals. For a short time in 1848, royal power was humbled in Paris, Berlin, Vienna, Budapest, and other capitals, as loyal forces retreated in the face of street protests. For a time, it seemed a united and democratic Germany would be born. Liberals from all parts of Germany, including an elderly Friedrich Ludwig Jahn, gathered in Frankfurt to form a federal parliament and write a bill of rights and a constitution for a new country. The old dream of the romantic nationalists seemed to have come true. But it was not to be. The parliament was divided and leaderless. The German princes, like their counterparts in Austria and Italy, regained their balance and swept aside the confused forces of revolution.

Beards and revolt also failed in Russia. In the 1840s, Russian "slavophiles" ramped up their criticisms of what they saw as an overly Westernized autocracy and sharpened their rhetoric in support of national traditions, political rights, and self-determination. In symbolic sympathy with the Russian peasantry, the Russian Orthodox Church, and the Russian past, these reformers grew full beards. They imagined that they were fending off foreign cultural influence, but they were in fact perfectly channeling the pan-European romantic liberalism of their day. Like Friedrich Jahn's gymnasts or the partisans of Young France, the slavophiles sought to create the future from the past. Tsar Nicholas could read the signs and concluded, not incorrectly, that any nobleman who wore a beard was challenging his authority. Nicholas himself wore a mustache in the military manner, but beards were out of the question.

He insisted that it was his critics who had fallen under the spell of foreign, liberal ideas, not himself. He would defend Russia by enforcing the ban on Russian beards.

When Nicholas traveled from St. Petersburg in 1849 to make a formal state visit to Moscow, several prominent slavophile noblemen, including Alexei Khomiakov and the brothers Ivan and Constantine Aksakov ostentatiously appeared in public wearing traditional Russian dress and beards. The response was not long in coming. A circular from the Ministry of Interior, issued to provincial marshals of the nobility, announced that "the tsar is displeased that Russian noblemen wear beards" and warned that bearded noblemen would not secure official appointments.[41]

In Russia, Britain, France, Italy, and Germany, and indeed in every European city, romantic idealists rejected the shaven order and agitated for individual freedoms and constitutional rights. Conservative romantics likewise reacted against the tyranny of modern commerce and pragmatism. Liberals and conservatives mined the past for images of authentic and heroic manhood with which to shape a new future. In the fervent heat of their imaginations, they called forth a primal manliness to correct the errors of the age. Mustaches and beards seemed to them both historic and heroic, yet in view of the failures of the German patriotic student associations, French insurrectionists, neo-chivalric aristocrats, British Chartists, and Russian slavophiles, and liberal uprisings everywhere, they also carried an air of impracticality and tragedy.

The decisive failure of the revolutions that broke out in Berlin, Vienna, Rome, and other important cities in 1848; the collapse of Chartism in England; and the defeat of republicanism in France, with the creation of a new Napoleonic empire in 1852, crushed the forces of romantic liberalism. It would seem that shaven decorum was more secure than ever. In fact, the opposite was the case. When respectable men no longer feared hairy radicals, they no longer feared hair and were free to avail themselves its possibilities. It was as though a dam had burst. Pent-up aspirations to grow facial hair were suddenly let loose. Beards lost their political meaning and became instead tools to restore notions of patriarchy and manly dignity in a turbulent industrial age.

9

PATRIARCHS OF THE
INDUSTRIAL AGE

The spirit of any age, said the celebrated German philosopher Arthur Schopenhauer, takes shape in the design of everyday things like buildings, furniture, ornaments, clothing, and the "the manner in which the hair and beard are cut."[1] In 1851, when he published these remarks, Schopenhauer observed a new spirit in a trend toward beards. The sixty-three-year-old didn't like it one bit. "The beard," he complained, "being a half-mask, should be forbidden by the police. It is moreover, as a sexual symbol in the middle of the face, obscene: that is why it pleases women."

Besides insulting women, the great philosopher gave voice to a fading early nineteenth-century mindset in which facial hair symbolized rebelliousness. In the latter half of the century these political stereotypes were thrown aside, and beards became respectable and widespread. Men no longer grew out their hair to declare their political allegiances but instead to assert their individual and collective rights as men. It was not a matter of class or nation. All levels of European and American society were swept up in the new beard movement. Some prominent men were leaders in the new style, while others were slow off the mark. Abraham Lincoln was famous for his beard, but he was actually a hesitant latecomer to the trend, persuaded only after a very young supporter urged him to keep up with the times.

Abraham Lincoln Hears a Young Girl's Plea

Abraham Lincoln was, for most observers, a surprising choice as the Republican nominee for president in 1860. He was not an accomplished statesman with a distinguished record but a former two-term congressman little known outside his home state of Illinois. He did have several things going for him, however: he was a political moderate with thoughtful charm and homespun humor that engendered trust, and he had an inspiring way with words. He certainly could not rely on good looks, a shortcoming he made light of in his speeches. In a debate during his unsuccessful senate campaign two years earlier, his opponent, Stephen Douglas, had accused Lincoln of being untrustworthy and two-faced. Lincoln quickly retorted, "If I had another face, do you think I would wear this one?"[2] This willingness to make fun of himself did not prevent his opponents from mocking his ugliness and linking it to his backwoods origins and unpolished manners. One newspaper declared that "Lincoln is the leanest, lankest, most ungainly mass of legs, arms and hatchet-face ever strung upon a single frame. He has most unwarrantably abused the privilege which all politicians have of being ugly."[3] Even some Republicans wondered if he was really the right man to lead America through its greatest crisis.

Famous as Lincoln is today, few are aware that he won the general election without any traveling or speeches. In those days it was the custom of presidential candidates to stay at home and maintain a dignified silence through the fall campaign season, leaving it to surrogates and supporters to make their case. Lincoln's photograph did circulate widely, however, and unfortunately for him, the camera did not lie. Though Lincoln was not vain, he did worry that his looks might hinder him in establishing the necessary personal authority to lead the country. This worry must have been on his mind when he received a surprising letter from an eleven-year-old supporter named Grace Bedell. Grace told Lincoln that her father had brought home the candidate's picture, asked if he had any daughters her age who might respond to her, then pressed on to her reason for writing:

> I have got 4 brother's [sic] and part of them will vote for you any way and if you will let your whiskers grow I will try and get the rest of them

to vote for you. [Y]ou would look a great deal better for your face is so thin. All the ladies like whiskers and they would tease their husband's to vote for you and then you would be President.[4]

Lincoln was impressed by the girl's forthright suggestion. In his own hand he responded:

> I regret the necessity of saying I have no daughters. I have three sons—one seventeen, one nine, and one seven, years of age. They, with their mother, constitute my whole family.
>
> As to the whiskers, having never worn any, do you not think people would call it a piece of silly affection if I were to begin it now?
>
> Your very sincere well-wisher A. LINCOLN."[5]

The Republican candidate made no promise to follow Grace's suggestion, clearly uncertain about the impression a change of style would make. As everyone knows, however, he changed his mind after the election, deciding that his elevation to leadership of the nation justified a modest makeover.

Lincoln did not choose his new look capriciously. Not all beards were alike. Lincoln did not choose to wear a full beard, though that was the prevailing style, opting instead for a trimmed beard without the mustache. This was a popular choice among American clergy at this time. One observer at the 1864 general conference of the Methodist Church in Philadelphia noted that almost all clergymen wore such facial hair.[6] By contrast, virtually every officer in both armies of the Civil War wore a full beard or large mustache. Of Lincoln's generals, Ulysses Grant, for example, wore a full beard; George McClellan, a prominent mustache; and it was Ambrose Burnside's great whisker-mustache combination that put "sideburns" in the American lexicon. These contrasts illustrated the great divide between civilian and military styles of facial hair. As noted earlier, mustaches had become the signature of military dash and derring-do, and European nations had begun to require them for their officers. Lincoln deliberately chose a less aggressive look. Though he was not a pacifist like the Amish and Mennonite men who also shunned the mustache as a sign of violence, Lincoln's clean lip nevertheless offered a quiet protest against the strife and bloodshed of his times.[7]

9.1 Abraham Lincoln, by Christopher S. German, 1861. First portrait with a beard. Library of Congress, LC-USZ62-31600.

In February 1861, the president-elect made his way by train to Washington from his home in Springfield, stopping to address crowds along the way. When Lincoln arrived in Westfield, New York, Grace Bedell's hometown, he delivered his usual brief address but concluded with a request: "I have a correspondent in this place, a little girl whose name is Grace Bedell, and I would like to see her."[8] Grace was too far back to hear Lincoln, but she was escorted to the railcar, where Lincoln stepped down, saying, "You see I have let these whiskers grow for you,

Grace." He warmly shook her hand, kissed her, and was on his way. Lincoln had an eleven-year-old girl to thank for catching him up with the times. His tardiness was due partly to the habitual conservatism of a lawyer, partly to his lack of vanity. Lincoln may have paid little heed to the beard bandwagon during the previous decade, but even he could not escape the enthusiasm of his age for natural manliness.

By the time Lincoln headed to Washington, the newest beard movement was already more than a decade old. The critical point in this turn toward hair had come in 1848, when the fires of revolution raged through Europe. Louis Napoleon, the bearded nephew of the great conqueror, was in the thick of it.

Louis Napoleon Breaks the Rules

In most ways Louis Napoleon was not very much like his famous uncle. At age thirty, the original Napoleon, already a conquering general, took the reins of government in Paris and began his quest to dominate Europe. The nephew, by contrast, spent most of his first forty years either in exile or in prison. The great emperor had made his mark with boundless energy and quickness of mind, whereas his nephew-pretender was both slower of wit and softer around the edges. In spite of these contrasts, both shared a sense of destiny—the idea that history revolved around them—and though the younger Napoleon could not claim any great conquests, he did manage a clever escape from prison that demonstrated at least some creativity and acting skills. In this caper, Louis managed to make good use of his signature beard.

In 1840, after a second failed attempt to rally units of the French army to overthrow the government, Louis was sentenced by King Louis Philippe to a long term of imprisonment in a castle in northern France. It took a while, but after six years, the prisoner with the famous name finally found his chance. Renovations of the castle buildings brought crews of workmen into the prison grounds and an idea into Napoleon's mind. What followed was an adventure worthy of Hollywood, complete with disguises, fast talking, and quick thinking.[9]

At 6:30 on a May morning, the plot was put into action. Napoleon's loyal valet, Charles Thélin, who had been allowed by the castle commandant to make regular visits, diverted the work crew from Napoleon's rooms by inviting them to have a glass of wine on the floor below. In the meantime, the prisoner prepared his disguise. He donned a workman's outfit, shaved off his Bonapartist mustache and beard, smudged his face with dirt, and stuck a smoking pipe between his teeth. As a final touch, he pilfered a shelf from the castle library to carry. For good luck, he even thought to select the shelf labeled "N." At this point, Thélin quietly slipped away from his guests and, taking care to tether Napoleon's small dog, distracted the guards at the building doorway with tales of an ill and bed-ridden Napoleon, as their charge, the shelf obstructing his face, walked nonchalantly by.

So far so good, but at this point the escapee's pipe fell and shattered on the pavement, drawing glances from workmen and guards in the courtyard. Napoleon calmly and slowly picked up the pieces, trying to look every bit the poor laborer who could not afford to abandon his broken pipe. Napoleon's co-conspirators later surmised that some of the guards must have recognized his stout shape hunched over in the courtyard but let him pass in a tacit show of support.[10]

The political prisoner reached the front gate, still shouldering his board, and ordered it opened. Without much thought the gatekeepers obliged, and the future ruler of France was gone, heading to a secluded rendezvous with followers on his way to freedom in England. Safely out of the French king's clutches, Louis grew back his wide mustache and pointed chin beard grander than before, and just two years later, when revolution again convulsed France, he grasped a golden opportunity to seize power. The king, his former captor, was overthrown, and a new republic declared. Landing in France to wide acclaim, the new Napoleon relied upon his unsurpassed name recognition to achieve a monumental victory in France's first-ever presidential election. He thus became the first bearded head of state in Europe since the 1600s, helping to usher in new era in masculine style.

Louis Napoleon deserves a great deal of credit for increasing the respectability of beards. His style was widely imitated in France, particularly after he declared himself emperor of the French in 1851. As represented in Hippolyte Flandrin's portrait, the new emperor conveyed the swashbuckling dash of a seventeenth-century musketeer. The popular author Guy de Maupassant described the powerful effect of the

9.2 Emperor Napoleon III, by Hippolyte Flandrin, 1852. Universal Images Group/Art Resource, NY.

emperor's style on Frenchmen, portraying in one of his stories an ordinary middle-class man, who, "after repeatedly contemplating [Emperor Napoleon], followed the example of a great many of his fellow-citizens: he copied the cut of his Majesty's beard, of his coat, his style of wearing his hair, his walk, even his mannerisms."[11] What better way to earn respect than by imitating the dignity of their illustrious ruler? Though widely replicated through Europe, the "imperial" eventually became the stereotyped face of a Frenchman.

In Napoleon, we can observe the military and romantic sources for the beard movement, but there were other, greater factors at work as well. It was really the *failure* of romanticism and revolution, not their success, that finally lifted the social restraints on facial hair. Napoleon himself, though exhibiting a style that was once revolutionary, had become a safe, conservative solution to the political upheavals in 1848. Other democratic uprisings around Europe that year had collapsed even before Napoleon betrayed the republic and declared himself a monarch. Midcentury economic prosperity also reduced political turmoil. As the threat of bearded youths and workers flying red flags on barricades evaporated, so too did the fear provoked by facial hair. Bearded men like Napoleon became respectable, and upright gentlemen were now at liberty to let their beards grow.

No longer fearful, beards and mustaches were newly available for men hoping to bolster their flagging masculine confidence. For decades, men had experimented with more and more hair, particularly sideburns, but now at midcentury they were ready to make the big move. On cue, brave leaders stepped to the fore to advance the cause. One of the most influential was Albert Smith, who, though little known today, was a famous Victorian stage performer who had just as much influence in Britain as Louis Napoleon had in France.

Albert Smith Puts On a Show

Beyond the Swiss chalets was a majestic backdrop of farmyards, forests, and snow-capped Alps. On one side of the village square, fish swam in a pond; on the other, the village clock chimed eight o'clock. A crowd had gathered in anticipation. The man of the hour boldly stepped out from a chalet door. He was smartly dressed, hearty, thick, and bearded, but he was not Swiss. He wasn't actually in Switzerland either. It was Albert Smith mounting a London stage elaborately decorated as a Swiss mountainside. He was opening another of his wildly popular performances of *The Ascent of Mont Blanc*.

Smith was perfectly attuned to what people of his era wished to see. The rising middle classes of Britain loved tales of danger, fortitude, and success, and so he decided in 1851 to climb Europe's tallest mountain, in order to make a show of it. He wasn't by any means the first to reach the summit, but he was in rare company. Only a few hundred men and one woman had been to the top, and none of them was capable of telling the story with Smith's flair. Expertly blending humor and adventure, along with creative vocalization, Smith created a lively cast of amusing characters, vibrant scenes, and a dash of satire. Even a half century later, the novelist Henry James retained vivid memories of seeing *Mont Blanc* as a child: "Big, bearded, rattling, chattering, mimicking Albert Smith again charms my sense . . ."[12]

The first half of *Mont Blanc* was Smith's description of his travels from London to the Swiss village of Chamonix, replete with all the sights, sounds, and personalities that Smith adroitly conjured. One of his most remarkable effects, as James remembered, was "the very brief stop and re-departure of the train at Epernay, with the ringing of bells, the bawling of guards, the cries of travelers, the slamming of doors and the tremendous pop as of a colossal champagne-cork, made all simultaneous and vivid by Mr. Smith's mere personal resources and graces." Of the many amusing characters along the way, one appreciative journalist fondly asked, "Who that heard them will ever forget undecided Mr. Parker, the man who could not ever make up his mind; or Mrs. Seymour in constant search for that black box from which she had been ruthlessly parted; or the two old ladies who, travelling in their own carriage, enjoyed Switzerland so much because they always pulled down the blinds when they came near any precipices? And, best of all, the thoroughly Dickensian character, Edwards the engineer in the service of the Austrian Lloyds, who was always impressing upon his hearer his grand discovery, 'What I says is, India isn't England, Mr. Smith!'"[13]

In the second act of *Mont Blanc*, Smith dramatized the daunting trek to the top of Europe's tallest mountain, followed by a triumphant, raucous descent. It was a tale of excitement, daring, and danger. The most fearsome obstacle to Smith and his Swiss guides was the formidable "Mur de la Cote," a nearly perpendicular wall of ice a hundred feet high near the pinnacle of the mountain. Smith told his breathless audience that every foothold had to be cut by an axe, that the slightest slip of a foot threatened to plunge them all into "an icy abyss so deep that the bottom is lost in obscurity."[14] By the time the climbers reached this critical point, however, they had also reached the limits of their physical strength, their "muscular powers already taxed far beyond their strength, and nerves shaken by constantly increasing excitement and want of rest."[15] A harsh, cold wind whipped around them. Thin air and lack of sleep robbed Smith of both his strength and his senses. He felt an overwhelming drowsiness, and, he assured his rapt listeners, if he had stopped even for a moment, he would have fallen asleep, dooming both himself and the three guides roped to him.

Pushed to the limit, Smith nevertheless managed to reach the top, where, by his own account, he immediately lost consciousness, spending his first seven minutes on the summit in a deep slumber. Carried away by the emotions of adventure, Smith's audience shared the storyteller's catharsis of bemusement and relief at this humorous and exhilarating climax. The descent was a festival of shouting, sliding, and tumbling along the snowfields leading straight to the show's grand finale, a fast-paced patter song called "Galignani's Messenger," in which Smith satirized current events by pretending to catch up on the news he had missed on his great adventure. In this way, Smith brought his audience full circle from humor to adventure and back to fun; and also from London to the mountaintop and back again.

Mont Blanc made Smith a superstar. As one magazine reported in 1860, with only slight exaggeration, "No one is more widely known in this country than Mr. Albert Smith, or enjoys a more extensive popularity. . . . Everybody has seen Albert Smith, and everybody else has seen his portrait."[16] Over seven years, between 1852 and 1858, Smith performed *Mont Blanc* more than two thouand times to a total audience of more than half a million people.[17] Prince Albert attended in 1853. Queen Victoria and the royal children attended three times, the final two at command performances, at Osborne in 1855 and Windsor Castle in 1856. More than any other man, Smith was responsible for the mountaineering craze that seized Britain in subsequent decades, and for the foundation of the Alpine Club in 1857.

Smith was successful because he was funny, dramatic, and entertaining but also because he appealed to the deepest aspirations of his era. To stand astride the frozen heights of Europe was the Victorian equivalent of slaying the dragon. Indeed, it was a feat beyond the capacity of a medieval knight. In this way, his story bespoke both heroism and progress. The eager crowds who flocked to Smith's shows discovered to their great delight that the age of machines, factories, and cities had not banished heroic manliness. On the contrary, there were new frontiers to cross and new quests to undertake. In Smith they saw the prototype of this modern manliness: independent, hearty, bold, and bearded.

9.3 Albert Smith, by Richard James Lane, Field Talfourd lithograph, 1854. Courtesy of National Portrait Gallery, NPG D22417.

The modern manliness that Smith embodied was in some respects old-fashioned. He faced the raw elements of nature, not the challenges of science or industry. On the other hand, his manliness was also modern and democratic. He demonstrated the power of personal character, and his triumph arose not from privilege and good fortune but from strength of body and will. It was precisely these qualities that men of the era honored most, and readily associated with the full, natural beard.

While London audiences thrilled to mountain climbing, American readers discovered a vigorous new voice for physical manliness on their own side of the Atlantic. Appearing in 1855, Walt Whitman's poetry collection *Leaves of Grass* urged Americans to find the spiritual in the material and the material in the spiritual, starting with their own bodies. "I am the poet of the body," Whitman wrote, "And I am the poet of the soul."[18] Two pages later he declares, "I am the poet of commonsense, and of the demonstrable, and of immortality, And am not the poet of goodness only . . . I do not decline to be the poet of wickedness also. Washes and razors for foofoos . . . for me freckles and a bristling beard." Whitman may have been interested in the good and bad, the body and soul, but he was not interested in shaving, which for him represented fear and escape from the rigors of life. His beard, and beards in general, bespoke a real and vital manliness that did not shrink from the terrors and joys of life, but grasped all it had to offer.

In Whitman's view, the meaning of life was rooted in the source of life itself, the body. He did not think the flesh was to be despised. On the contrary,

Divine am I inside and out, and I make holy whatever I touch or am
    touched from;
The scent of these arm-pits is aroma finer than prayer,
This head is more than churches or bibles or creeds.

He offered a poetic inventory of his own body, declaring each holy, including "mixed tussled hay of head and beard and brawn . . ."

Whitman thrilled his readers with a sense of freedom and discovery, as well as hope that there was more to life than routine and self-denial. The public response to these stanzas was ecstatic. One critic enthused that here was "an American bard at last! . . . One of the roughs, large, proud, affectionate, eating, drinking, and breeding, his costume manly and free, his face sunburnt and bearded, his postures strong and erect, his voice bringing hope and prophecy to the generous races of young and old."[19] A full-length photographic portrait of a rough, "sunburnt and bearded" Whitman graced every copy of *Leaves of Grass*, providing a crucial visual complement to his poetic self-portrait, helping make his face as recognizable in America as Smith's was in Britain. They were the bearded prophets of a modern manliness founded on physical vigor, fearless adventure, and personal resilience.

Whitman and his admirers believed he was describing an ideal American type, but as Louis Napoleon and Albert Smith proved, the admiration of bearded hardiness was by no means uniquely American. During the years between 1852, when Smith launched his show, and 1855, when Whitman published his song to himself, a wave of pro-beard manifestoes washed over Europe and the Americas. The British and American presses in particular grew hot churning out editorials and articles in favor of hair. The editors of the respectable *Tait's Edinburgh Magazine* led the charge in Britain, declaring themselves in 1852 "champions of the long beard."[20] In the following year, Henry Morley and William Henry Wills published a beard manifesto in Charles Dickens's widely read magazine *Household Words,* entitled "Why Shave?"[21] There were entire volumes as well, including *The Philosophy of Beards*, by the Englishman Thomas S. Gowing. Journals such as the prestigious *Westminster Review, Illustrated London News*, and *New York Times* commented extensively on these and other publications and pronounced the arrival of a "beard and moustache movement." The British humor magazine *Punch* happily joined the fray with a series of satirical cartoons.[22] One of these cartoons, drawn by John Leech, the magazine's chief cartoonist, poked fun at the shock produced by the sudden effusion of hair. A woman in a railway station believes herself beset by thieves when polite but hairy porters approach to assist her. Leech places in the background a visual clue to what he thinks is behind this surprising transformation: a placard with the words "Mont Blanc"—an advertisement for Albert Smith's show (figure 9.4).

American journals reproduced many of these British articles and added more of their own. A similar passion spread throughout Europe, though the French, as we have seen, had stolen a march on the rest. The 1850s emerged as a remarkable moment in masculine history. Never before had Western society become so invested in the question of beards, and never before had the faces of men changed so rapidly or so completely. As New York City's *Home Journal* observed with evident surprise in 1854, "Go where you will, the full, flourishing, ferocious beard presents itself!—in Broadway, or in the Bowery; in Fifth avenue, or along the quays; in the drawing room, or in the bar room; down in

THE BEARD AND MOUSTACHE MOVEMENT.

Railway Guard. "Now, Ma'am, is this your Luggage?"
Old Lady (who concludes she is attacked by Brigands). "Oh yes! Gentlemen, it's mine. Take it—take all I have; but spare, oh spare our lives!!"

9.4 Cartoon from *Punch* Magazine, 1854.

the oyster cellar, or up on the mast head. Nature has triumphed! and comfort and fashion at last coincide!"[23]

The flourishing commentary on hair in these years attempted to put into words the popular philosophy of beards and manliness. In this venture, apologists for hair were remarkably united and consistent, agreeing that God, providence, or nature had provided the beard to ensure manly dignity and authority in three primary ways: promoting physical health, representing manly virtues, and demonstrating the superiority of men over women.

The idea that beards are healthy fit easily with the general emphasis on physical manliness, and addressed concerns about industrialization, the growth of cities, and the many contemporary threats to public health. In reality, the health arguments of the 1850s were not much different from those proclaimed during the Renaissance beard movement three hundred years earlier. In 1851, for example, a French intellectual, Boucher de Perthes, voiced a common medical opinion that men without beards often had toothaches, whereas facial hair prevented "congestion and ailments of the throat."[24] The editors of the British medical journal *Lancet*, echoed by the American *Medical and Surgical Reporter*, pronounced in 1860, "We hope science and common sense will come to the rescue, and not only let soldiers and policemen continue to wear upon their faces the natural covering they have been given, but induce wheezing, sneezing, sore-throated, shivering mortals, who have trembled more at the keen edge of a January air or March wind than of a razor, to cease wasting their time."[25] A uniquely nineteenth-century idea was that beards and mustaches helped filter bad air. This idea was endorsed by many authorities, including the prestigious *Edinburgh Review*, which drew attention in an article on worker health to fumes and dust as a cause of disease, and recommended beards and mustaches as one defense.[26]

American writers produced the most eccentric theories, namely that hair helped the body maintain its electrical balance. New discoveries about the properties of electricity and the human nervous system sparked speculation about the electrical properties of hair. One notion, proposed by a contributor to the *American Phrenological Journal*, was that the high conductivity of hair allowed it to collect valuable electrical force for use by the brain and nervous system.[27] This explained why hairiness was commonly associated with "mental power and brilliancy." Another writer, noting, that hair is in fact an insulator, not a conductor of electricity, claimed that it helped keep the body's stores of electrical force from draining away into the air. Men who shaved lost electricity and thus vital energy.

Beard activists were always enthusiastic about the healthiness of hair, but they were even more excited about its moral force, in particular its power to express masculine character and authority. The beard, wrote French physician Auguste Debay, was a "natural ornament of the male visage" that "protects and enhances the luster of the skin with its silky shadows, and adds powerfully to the majesty of the human face."[28] An American journalist asserted in 1857 that even men who have not yet developed full and well-shaped beards "are ennobled by the look of strength and vigour which they newly wear."[29] A key feature of manly dignity in the democratic age was self-reliance and independence. In his 1853 book on hair, Englishman Alexander Rowland declared grandly that a bearded man was "a man of strongly-marked individuality . . . [who] will not fawn or cringe to any man."[30] This self-assertion of facial hair was the reason the legal and clerical professions often pushed back against the new trend. The battles of French lawyers for facial freedom inspired one among their number, Léon Henry, to produce a full-volume manifesto in 1879 entitled *La Barbe et la Liberté* (The Beard and Liberty), in which he defended every man's inalienable right to express his personality in hair.[31] All in all, there was widespread agreement among enthusiasts that men who grew their beards were tough, decisive, and independent, because, like Smith and Whitman, they were releasing and activating their natural strengths. As Thomas Gowing wrote in *The Philosophy of Beards*, the enterprising brow, sagatious eyes, firm lip, and bearded chin "proclaim a being who has an appointed path to tread, and hard rough work to do, in this world of difficulties and ceaseless transition."[32] A contributor to a usually sober-minded English journal, *The Westminster Review*, agreed: "The beard—identified as it is with sternness, dignity and strength—is only the becoming complement of true manliness."[33]

Like the fearless, mountain-climbing Albert Smith or the indomitable Walt Whitman, men could declare that their bodies were the solid foundation of both personal and political autonomy. By the same token, they could affirm their masculine prerogative over women. It was no mere coincidence that the era of beards corresponded closely with the emergence of the women's movement. The American women's rights movement was launched at Seneca Falls, New York, in 1848, followed two years later by the formation of the National Women's Rights Convention under the leadership of Lucy Stone. Also in 1848, German feminist Louise Otto-Peters founded *Frauen-Zeitung* (Women's News), and in 1849, the Englishwoman Elizabeth Blackwell became the first female physician practicing in her country. These were just early signs of greater things to come. Significant as these events were, the most profound change in the gender order involved not politics or the professions but the home. The so-called "cult of domesticity" relegated women to homemaking and child-rearing, while reserving public and commercial life for men. While this code limited women's sphere of action, it also imposed limits on men. As wives claimed sovereignty over home and children, the patriarch's domestic dominion was constrained.[34]

In these circumstances, it is no wonder that much of the discussion about beards centered on affirming a supposedly natural gender order that placed men in command. Facial hair provided a helpful argument in this cause. One American journal stated it succinctly: "The natural and appropriate spheres of man and woman, respectively, are plainly indicated by the hirsute, bristling image of the one and the less-protected face of the other."[35] The typical explanation of why women were less protected was, as Englishmen Henry Morley and William Henry Wills put it, that "man is born to work out of doors and in all weathers, for his bread; woman was created for duties of another kind, which do not involve constant exposure to sun, wind, and rain."[36] The English author of *An Apology for the Beard* (1862) offered beards, as guardians of the throat and voice, as proof of the masculine authority to speak, preach, and teach: "It is the man's duty to teach with his voice. It is the woman's to 'learn in silence.'"[37]

In their insistence that facial hair promoted health, demonstrated manly virtue, and validated the gender order, champions of the beard exposed deep-seated worries about the condition of men and manliness in the industrial age. As more and more people migrated to cities and towns in the early nineteenth century, men's work moved from fields and workshops to offices and factories. Work was less physical but often more competitive and stressful, and it usually took place away from home, wife, and children. In middle-class households especially, women assumed leadership of the home and of the children, and they were gradually gaining rights to their property, to divorce, and to custody of children. Women were also making their way slowly into the public sphere, as well as higher levels of educational and professional achievement. Women had by no means achieved equality with men, but traditional patriarchy was not on entirely sound footing either. Men had to work out anew what it meant to be a father and husband.

Feeling greater pressure to compete with each other and with women, men anxiously sought to establish more compelling notions of manhood. Increasingly, they chose to emphasize their "natural" physical, moral, and intellectual strengths. When men's work was less physical than ever, sports and beards helped them affirm the nobility of the male body. When business and politics were more open and competitive, a beard helped secure a sense of personal honor. When wives challenged male mastery over the home, a beard confirmed a husband's status as domestic patriarch. While men claimed that facial hair was a comfort to the throat and nerves, the real comfort was to their self-esteem. The nobility of facial hair was unique to men—with a few surprising exceptions.

Madame Clofullia Defies Belief

Between 1849 and 1854 Josephine Clofullia was an international sensation. A Swiss woman married to a Frenchman, she was a popular attraction in French shows, and Emperor Napoleon gave her gifts as tokens of his admiration. In 1851 she became a star attraction at the Great Exhibition in London, where she was seen by two hundred thousand astonished visitors over the course of two years. After her British triumph, she ventured to America, where she was greeted by equally great acclaim. "There has not been for years so great a curiosity to be seen in Boston," one American paper effused, "and we are told that it has been found difficult at times to accommodate the large concourse of persons who throng the hall to behold the bearded lady."[38] All the excitement was over a woman who, in the words of the normally restrained British journal the *Quarterly Review*, sported "a most glorious specimen" of a beard that "shamed any man's that we have ever seen."[39] P. T. Barnum, the great entertainment entrepreneur, knew a moneymaker when he saw it and immediately hired Clofullia to be exhibited at his American Museum in New York. She was his first bearded lady, a type of exhibit that would remain a fixture of his museum and circus shows until well after his death in 1891.

Today, the bearded lady is a faded cliché, and it is hard to imagine why dignitaries like Louis Napoleon, not to mention the public at large, were so fascinated by them. But in the mid-nineteenth century, as during the Renaissance, interest in beards ran high, and with it interest in bearded women. Once again, facial hair had attained great social importance, and bearded women became a fascinating intellectual and psychological challenge. Madame Clofullia and others like her were offered large sums to put themselves on display in fairs and stage shows throughout Europe and America, the demand so exceeding the supply of genuine bearded women that several men made careers of imper-

9.5 Josephine Clofullia. Photograph by Thomas M. Easterly, 1853. Courtesy of Missouri History Museum, St. Louis.

sonating them. As in the Renaissance, bearded women were generally accepted as genuine women. That was not really the issue.[40] The question was how a woman could possess a usually reliable symbol of manliness. For the latter half of the nineteenth century, bearded women were a puzzle that demanded explanation.

When Barnum hired Madame Clofullia, he understood very well how she could generate shock and excitement. To stir it up still more, he hired a man to stand up at one of her shows, proclaim that she was a man in disguise, denounce Barnum as a humbug, and demand his money back. Barnum then challenged the man to sue him, which, of course, he did. Excited crowds and newspapermen gathered at court to witness the testimony of the bearded woman's husband and father, as well as three physicians who were invited to examine her in private. The husband testified that he was Madame Clofullia's legal husband, and that she was the mother of his two children. The eminent doctors agreed that she was indeed a woman, and Barnum reveled in his staged legal vindication.[41] Many years later, when Barnum took his circus to London, he had a new bearded lady, Annie Jones, but the challenge for the audience remained the same: was she really a man? The London *Times* was almost incredulous, reporting that were it not for "Mr. Barnum's well-known professional rectitude," Jones "might be taken for a young man of somewhat effeminate cast."[42] Forced to accept that Clofullia and Jones were women, the nineteenth-century public cast them as freaks of nature to be ogled with the rest of their sideshow cohort, which in Barnum's show came to include a dwarf, a pair of giants, and skeletally thin man.

As aberrations of nature, bearded women provoked surprise and pity, but they also affirmed the natural order of things.[43] Just as midgets and giants reassured the majority of their normality, bearded women had the ironic effect of confirming the essential masculinity of beards. They were the exception that proved the rule. The shock of their oddity reminded everyone of how important norms were to happiness and good order. If anything, men would be even more inclined to prove they could produce facial hair, while women would be more determined to remove any vestige of their own, lest they themselves be considered freaks.[44] This feminine fear was no idle worry, for women with facial hair were widely regarded as deficient as women, even (or especially) by physicians who made a living helping them remove it. One American electrolysis specialist theorized in the 1890s that most of his hairy patients were unmarried women who suffered from "the inactivity of the uterus."[45] With the stigma of inadequate femininity looming over them, women in the late nineteenth and early twentieth centuries resorted to desperate measures. Despite being painful, expensive, and time-consuming, electrolysis emerged in the 1870s as the chief weapon against nature's imperfections.

Some women voiced objections to the craze for gender conformity. Annie Jones, the star bearded lady of the Barnum and Bailey Circus during the 1880s and 1890s, called a news conference in 1899 to protest the "freak" label ascribed to her and her fellow performers. She insisted that they should be referred to as "specialty artists" who "were created differently from the human family as the latter exist today, and that . . . in the opinion of many, some of us are really the development of a higher type, and are superior persons, inasmuch as some of us are gifted with extraordinary attributes not apparent in ordinary beings."[46] Whether this reflected a new self-respect on the part of the "specialty artists" or was merely a way for the circus to provoke interest in its performers—or both—is not really clear. What is certain is that interest in "freaks" had seriously declined by this time, along with the beard movement itself. The enduring legacy of freak shows is their reinforcement of the fiction of natural norms. The "bearded lady" may be gone, but not the notion that female facial hair is abnormal and rare; as one recent researcher has noted, the shame of female body hair persists as "the last taboo."[47]

Meanwhile, urbane men had worries of their own, particularly clergymen, professors, writers, artists, and physicians, whose success relied on seemingly feminine qualities of sensitivity, care, and feeling. Because neither their labors nor their products were physical, they had the hardest time affirming the "natural" masculinity of their work. What was more, women were clearly capable writers, artists and caregivers. It is no wonder, then, that professional men were the most loyal adherents of the beard movement from its beginning to its dying days, and sometimes even beyond that. No one better illustrates the meaning of facial hair for cerebral men than the British painter Luke Fildes.

Luke Fildes Paints the Ideal Man

Luke Fildes was a rare example of a financially successful visual artist. Rising from humble working-class origins, he was by the 1870s making a good living painting portraits of British elites, including several

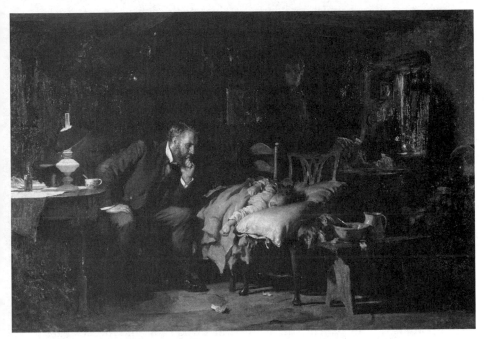

9.6 *The Doctor*, by Luke Fildes, 1891. Tate, London / Art Resource, NY.

members of the royal family. He was not entirely satisfied with his success, however. He yearned to make a statement. He got his opportunity when the wealthy art impresario Henry Tate commissioned from him a work of social significance to help launch his new gallery of English art. After years of thought, Fildes decided to "put on record the status of the doctor in our time."[48] In 1891, he completed *The Doctor*, one of the most widely admired and reproduced paintings of the past two centuries. In his subject matter, and the manner in which he addressed it, Fildes struck a chord. He had presented a deeply satisfying portrayal of the ideal professional man, and by the same token, a powerful version of the manly ideal (figure 9.6).

The subject of the painting was clear from the title and from the composition of the work. It was not about the sick child, the poverty of his surroundings, or his helpless parents in the background. It is about the doctor, who dominates the canvas, and the knowledgeable care he devotes to the innocent victims of disease. Fildes himself had lost a son to illness over a decade before, and the image reproduces this tragedy with all its anguish and pathos. Fildes projects his own emotions into the figure of the helpless but watchful father, and offers hope for a good outcome, indicated by the bright light illuminating the resting child, as well as the assuring competence of the doctor himself. With his knowledge of medicine, reflected in the bottles on the table, and his gentlemanly education and good reputation, suggested by his elegant clothes and top hat, the doctor leads one to feel the boy is in good hands. What is more, this gentlemanly physician has kindly sacrificed his own pleasures—perhaps a dinner party—to attend a needy family. The magic of this image is the seamless blending of caring and competence in the doctor's character.[49] Fildes was saying that neither training nor compassion is enough to make a good doctor; one must have both. The mother cares deeply but does not have the knowledge, and so she collapses in despair. The father has more fortitude but he too lacks expertise and looks anxiously to the doctor for help. Only the doctor can act effectively.

The action, such as it is, unfolds on the doctor's face as he leans toward his young patient. The slightly furrowed brow and focused gaze indicate concern. His pose is thoughtful, his peppery, full beard suggesting knowledge and experience. The anxious young father in the background, lacking this mark of manly wisdom, watches anxiously. The beard is the key to the doctor's character, granting him strength of mind and purpose he would lack without it. Fildes knew this intuitively. The primary model he used when painting the doctor was a clean-shaven actor, but the painter did not use his model's face. In fact, the doctor looks very much like Fildes himself.[50]

For this masterwork of a lifetime, Fildes thought long and hard about his subject and how to portray it. He chose to represent the skilled professional as the ideal of modern manliness. The doctor was neither an aristocrat, a soldier, nor a captain of industry, yet he deserved high honor. He cared like a mother, but he was not feminine. His beard made sure of that, and it underscored the painting's message that it takes a man to get things done when it counts the most, even in the care of children.

Luke Fildes was not alone in his imagination of hairy manliness. Physicians, artists, writers, and clergymen were particularly enthusiastic champions of the beard even after facial hair had fallen into general disfavor at the end of the century. What bearded writers and artists like Smith, Whitman, and Fildes hoped to prove was that work of the mind demanded the same masculine strength and vigor as any physical labor.

In several important respects, the nineteenth-century beard movement paralleled that of the sixteenth century. In both cases one finds renewed attention to the human body as the root of authentic manhood, and an inevitable fascination with its apparent contradiction in the existence of bearded women. Men of both eras esteemed facial hair as natural proof of male vitality, autonomy, and authority over women. In the nineteenth century, if not in the earlier period, this appeal to physical nature was animated by the increasing fluidity of social life, particularly in the urban middle ranks of society. Changing environments of work and family unsettled the patterns of home life, created new forms of female authority, and complicated the role of the man as master of his family. In this context, a beard was conservative and comforting, a signal that some things, at least, never change. Beards also bespoke masculine heroism: Louis Napoleon was not as accomplished as his uncle, but he *looked* impressive with his three-pointed imperial. Albert Smith and Walt Whitman cast themselves as brave adventurers. Luke Fildes painted a heroic healer in his own image. Even a small girl could see that Abraham Lincoln would seem a better leader with a more impressive face.

Late nineteenth-century champions of beardedness did not emphasize the aging effect of facial hair. Instead they spoke of energy and independence. Men were encouraged to become, like Whitman, the hero of their own story: "Washes and razors for foofoos . . . for me freckles and a bristling beard."

10

MUSCLES AND MUSTACHES

Beards helped men of the nineteenth century recover their primal manliness. Facial hair affirmed the "natural" fortitude that entitled a man to rule over his family and build empires. But hair alone was not enough to define the modern man. As the twentieth century approached, European and American men also embraced athletic competition and bodybuilding, activities that, like beards, were physical proofs of virility. It stood to reason that a bearded athlete would emerge at this time as an icon of the ideal man. It also stood to reason that this sportsman would be an Englishman, because the first industrial nation also took first place in its mania for games.

W. G. Grace Sports a Beard

The greatest cricket player of the Victorian age, William Gilbert Grace dominated Britain's most prestigious sport at a time when spectator sports were weaving themselves into the fabric of European life. For three decades, from the 1870s to the 1890s, cricket enthusiasts packed the stands for any game in which he played. He was famous as an all-around player, but especially for his achievements with the bat. The first generation of sports fans loved Grace's ability to fight off any sort and speed of bowls, and rack up astonishing run totals. He was revered also as a gentleman player, an amateur who played for glory rather than pay. For many of his active years he was a practicing physician, but the truth was he spent most of his time — and earned most of his money — playing cricket. He looked the part, too. Tall, thickly built, and heavily bearded, he was the quintessence of British sporting manhood.

One of the most fondly repeated stories about Grace involves a challenge to his legendary beard. It happened in a match between the English and Australian national teams, which was then, as now, the most emotionally charged rivalry in cricket. The tanned Australians were always eager to show the mother country what they were made of, and the pale Englishmen were equally keen to demonstrate that they retained the vigor of imperial greatness. When the Australians visited England for a series of test matches in 1896, Grace was forty-eight years old but still active and still captain of the English side. In one match, played in the hallowed turf of Lord's Cricket Grounds in London, the grandmaster of the cricket bat confronted a fresh-faced and dynamic Australian bowler named Ernest Jones. It would be hard to imagine two more appropriate representatives of the old country and the young colony. Excited to face the game's greatest player, Jones opened with a ballistic bowl that flew up from the turf and split the beard of the great man right below his chin. The crowd buzzed, and Grace barked back to the bowler, "Whatever are ye at?" "Sorry, Doctor, she slipped," the young colonial replied.[1] Accident or not, the English captain quickly regained his composure, redoubled his resolve, and sent crashing hits in all directions, propelling England to resounding victory. The colonials had mounted their challenge, but the English master was more than equal to the task. That, at least, was the story told by the home crowd.

Grace and his majestic beard were icons of England, and of the emerging passion for competitive sports that grew in tandem with industrialization and urbanization. London's Marylebone Cricket Club, which defined the modern game, held its first matches in 1787, just a few years after James Watt perfected the rotary steam engine and a few years before the outbreak of the French Revolution. The popularity of cricket and other sports mirrored the advance of urbanization thereafter. The first Oxford-Cambridge cricket match was held before a few hundred spectators in 1827, just as the industrial revolution was

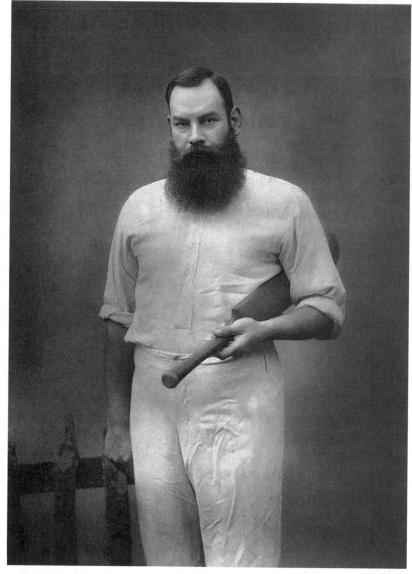

10.1 William Gilbert Grace in the late 1880s. Photograph by Herbert Rose Barraud.

hitting full stride. By contrast, a crowd of forty-six thousand gathered to watch the two universities square off in 1883.[2] Likewise, the annual match between the prestigious preparatory schools Eton and Harrow attracted only a few spectators in 1850, but drew a crowd of nearly ten thousand by 1864. There was a similar pattern in rowing, football, and rugby. One observer declared in 1870 that young men were "possessed by a perfect mania for every species of athletic contest."[3]

Athletic enthusiasm even took on theological dimensions. Influential English authors and clergymen embraced sporting competition as an expression of modern Christian manliness. Though critics mocked this attitude as "muscular Christianity," the label and its principles took a firm hold on the British mind. The single most influential expression of muscular Christianity was Thomas Hughes's blockbuster 1857 novel, *Tom Brown's Schooldays*. Set in Hughes's old school of Rugby in the 1830s, *Tom Brown* described games and sports as a key element of both school and moral life. A rugby match early in the novel is an opportunity for boys like Tom to demonstrate their pluck and courage. A final cricket match at the end of the novel, when Tom and his friends are eighteen and about to graduate, exhibits the maturity of Rugby's refined gentlemen. The young men play with skill and honor, and even the least athletic boys demonstrate an admirable nerve and perseverance that is a credit to their school and their sex. Playing, not winning, is the point, and this fictional cricket match concludes with an honorable defeat for Rugby as darkness descends.

W. G. Grace was nine years old when *Tom Brown* first appeared in print, and the novel's popularity helps to explain Grace's rise to fame. Hughes's story of sturdy manliness captured the English imagination and colored the popular view of sports and athletes. The story of the bowl that split Grace's beard echoes this theme precisely. Grace proved his fortitude and power in the face of challenge and danger, just as the fictional Tom Brown does by absorbing fierce rugby tackles or punishing fistfights. That Grace's beard was under assault was doubly appropriate, for it symbolically represented both moral character and physical strength. Grace's ability to defend the honor of his beard and his country was the triumph of natural manliness in the modern world.

In Grace's day, the British were proud of themselves for stealing a march on other nations in the field of physical culture. In 1859, Thomas C. Grattan, a British consul to the United States, dismissed Americans as less manly than the British because they did not play vigorous field sports, spending their leisure time instead chewing tobacco, smoking, and drinking. "They have no breadth either of shoulders, information or ambition," the consul declared. "Their physical powers are subdued and their mental capability cribbed into narrow limits."[4]

Forward-thinking Americans were duly alarmed about their own backwardness, and they urgently sounded the alarm. One of these was the Unitarian minister and reformer Thomas Wentworth Higginson, who in 1858 wrote an article decrying the common assumption that physical vigor was at odds with spiritual and moral virtues, and urging men of learning to take up the cause of physical culture. "Physical health," he argued, was "a necessary condition of permanent success" because bodily vigor was the foundation of moral courage. "Guarantee us against physical degeneration," he insisted, "and we can risk all other perils,—financial crises, Slavery, Romanism, Mormonism, Border Ruffians and New York assassins."[5]

In spite of these pleas, the British could still claim the lead in the 1860s, in part because of physical education advocates like William Penny Brookes, a physician who organized the first Olympic competitions in his hometown of Wenlock. In 1866, he organized a national Olympics in London that might have become an annual tradition had the powerful and jealous London athletic clubs allowed it. The winner of the hurdles race in this one-off national competition was a beardless eighteen-year-old named W. G. Grace. Brookes was passionate about his Olympics idea because he worried for modern manhood. In a speech at the close of the 1866 competition, he declared his fear that manliness in industrial nations was in decline and in desperate need of athletic invigoration. He thought the Americans and French were worse off than the British.[6] He noted that the French press had reported that military recruiters were forced to turn away a huge proportion of men as unfit for service, which at least one French newspaper attributed to overwork in factories and lack of physical education. It was a warning, Brookes concluded, that nations would survive only if their men remained active and fit.[7]

France's leading champion of physical education, Baron Pierre de Coubertin, was troubled by the same fears and inspired by the same ideals. Coubertin read *Tom Brown's Schooldays*, as well as Brookes's lectures and articles.[8] He traveled to Britain many times in the 1880s and 1890s, visiting Rugby and observing the Wenlock Olympic games for himself. The idea of a global Olympics competition to foster the peaceful regeneration of mankind percolated in his mind until the 1890s, when he secured enough support to put it into effect. Coubertin's vision was more about rebuilding manliness than it was about athletic competition as such, and that is why only amateurs were allowed to compete. Amateurs were the ideal sportsmen because, like W. G. Grace or Tom Brown, their athleticism manifested good character rather than mercenary training or calculation. Honor was more important than victory, and it was a matter of how one played the game rather than the results. Grace was a gentleman amateur, a physician, husband, and father first, and then a cricket player—or so the theory went. The problem with this notion of amateurism, and with the related notions of muscular Christianity, was that competition is ultimately defined by victory and defeat, and it is hard to reconcile sportsmanship with an indifference to winning. Already by 1896, when Grace's beard was clipped by Jones's high bowl, and when the first International Olympiad was held at Athens, professionalism was taking hold in cricket and other spectator sports in Europe and America. Grace successfully bridged the gentlemanly and professional eras by being both an amateur and a winner.

In retrospect, the reign of amateurism in spectator sports was relatively brief, as was the era of bearded athletes. W. G. Grace represented the happy conjunction of the beard movement and the gentlemanly athleticism in the Victorian era. As the century came to an end, a new formulation of manliness took precedence. Increasingly, the athlete became a man of muscle and speed rather than hair. To the extent that hair detracted from a youthful and muscular look, it had to be sacrificed. Even in the 1870s, when both Grace and the Victorian beard movement were in their prime, most young men of cricket, rowing, running, football, and gymnastics favored mustaches or even a clean shave in order to emphasize youth and vigor. The military mustache was a better fit than a beard for those who embraced teamwork, dash, and daring. The beard might denote maturity, wisdom, and stolidity, but those were not the ideals of fast-paced turn-of-the-century Europe.

The new passion for youth, speed, and strength was universal, whether in English football, French cycling, or German gymnastics. The French acquired an abiding zeal for bicycle racing at the end of the century, and this sport provides an excellent example of the conflict between hair and speed. The first French races were held in the 1860s, and velodromes sprang up around the country in the 1870s. Part of the fascination with bicycles was the opportunity they provided to combine muscular strength with modern technology. The writer and cycling promoter Baudry de Saunier joyously proclaimed in 1894 "the birth of a new human type, the cyclist . . . a man made half of flesh and half of steel that only our century of science and iron could have spawned."[9] Road races like the Tour de France, which was first run in 1903, had the additional benefit of inspiring a sense of national unity. This marvelous new masculine type, the bicyclist, had no use for billowing hair that might interfere with his machinelike muscles and wind-defying velocity.

We have seen how gymnastic exercises were cultivated in early nineteenth-century Germany by the bearded nationalist Friedrich Ludwig Jahn as a means to regenerate German manhood and reinvigorate a conquered land. After Napoleon's fall, the German states discouraged gymnastics because of its reformist overtones, but they reversed course in the 1840s. Danish and Swedish rulers blazed a new path, incorporating gymnastics into military training, with the Prussians and other German states following in their wake.[10] This training, built around drilling as well as floor and apparatus exercises, was intended to develop balance, discipline, and strength. Like English team games, it was thought to cultivate correct moral qualities through physical discipline. Though team sports eventually dominated the attention of continental Europe, gymnastics played a key part in the formation of twentieth-century manliness, particularly by contributing to the rise of bodybuilding. By placing increased emphasis on muscles, and on ancient Greek ideals of youthful beauty, bodybuilders contributed decisively to the demise of the beard as the visual standard of manliness. The greatest of all bodybuilders was the son of a Prussian grocer, Eugen Sandow.

Eugen Sandow Muscles His Way to the Top

In the summer of 1893, the World's Columbian Exhibition opened its doors. It was Chicago's great coming-out party along the shores of Lake Michigan, a fantastical "white city" of fanciful neoclassical exhibition halls, parks, fountains, and lagoons spread over six hundred acres. Millions of visitors flocked to see its marvels and to amuse themselves along the nearby Midway Plaisance, which featured countless concessions, amusements, rides, and the world's first Ferris wheel. For Chicago theater owners, it was a summer of golden opportunities. One variety-show producer, the youthful Florenz Ziegfeld Jr., became the envy of his peers when he staged the most popular act of that amazing summer, Eugen Sandow's performance as "the Perfect Man."

In the weeks before the show opened, Ziegfeld promised audiences something truly startling: the strongest man in the world. The public was to be treated to "a new Hercules," "a veritable Colossus of Rhodes."[11] Ziegfeld knew, however, that even this would not be enough of a draw. For Sandow to capture the public's imagination, he would need more than strength. A back story of gentlemanly character and romance would allow Ziegfeld to promote Sandow not simply as a spectacle, but as an ideal. Ziegfeld arranged for news accounts to describe the new Hercules as a gentleman of frock coats and tender feelings. The unscrupulous impresario even spread groundless rumors that Sandow was romantically involved with singing star Lillian Russell, America's greatest sex symbol at that time. To the bold go the spoils of victory. The strategy worked perfectly. People from all walks of life flocked to the Trocadero Theater to see this wonder for themselves.

"The Perfect Man" was the final act of Ziegfeld's variety show. It began with Sandow alone in the spotlight, striking poses that displayed his sharply defined, bulging muscles, which, according to Ziegfeld's program notes for the subsequent tour, were "without parallel, even in the ideal Greek statues."[12] After these poses he astonished his audience by making his muscles not only bulge but ripple and dance. Then it was time to demonstrate his strength. He pressed three hundred pounds over his head, performed somersaults with fifty-six-pound weights in each hand, and delighted the crowd with one of his signature acts, in which he lifted a gigantic barbell with a man in a basket at each end. Sandow held these two men over his head with just one arm, and then with two arms straight out from his chest. At times the audience was so entranced by these marvels they forgot to applaud.[13] The crowd laughed and cheered when he lifted his piano accompanist along with the piano itself. He closed his act with another elaborately devised stunt. Making an arch out of his body, chest upward, he balanced a platform on his chest upon which assistants loaded three horses, one by one. Observers admired the way in which every muscle in his body strained like a whipcord.[14]

10.2 Eugene Sandow, by George Steckel, ca. 1894. Library of Congress, LC-USZ62-101730.

Sandow's demonstration of form and power met and even exceeded the extravagant expectations Ziegfeld had drummed up on his behalf. Ziegfeld knew his audience well. He knew they would thrill to Sandow's indisputable skills as a weightlifter and showman. He also knew the public's hunger for symbols of masculine triumph. A few years before his Chicago success, Sandow had certified his claim to be the world's strongest man by winning the first official weightlifting competition in modern history. In this event, organized by the London Athletic Institute, he became the first man to lift a 250-pound barbell over his head. He was not merely strong, however. Before and after this victory Sandow had learned how to impress audiences with the look of his body alone and had extended his global fame by posing for dozens of enthralled artists and photographers.

To enhance his naturally smooth and marblelike skin, and to help define the impressive ripples and bulges of his musculature, Sandow carefully shaved all of his body hair other than his medium-length, blond mustache. Ziegfeld took advantage of this striking quality, and introduced a new element to Sandow's performances that would become a staple of his later career. Wealthy ladies and gentlemen who gave donations to charity were invited to touch the muscleman's body after the show. When Chicago theater critic Amy Leslie hesitated to touch his naked torso, Sandow gently took her hand and dared her to hit him. Leslie was clearly mesmerized. "He is a dangerously handsome man," she wrote later. Other men and women were not so shy and expressed amazement and delight at his washboard chest and velvety skin, which was "transparent white without blemish."[15] The bodybuilder encouraged them: "I want you to feel how hard these muscles are. As I stop before you, I want each of you to pass the palm of your hand across my chest."[16] "These muscles," he informed one lady, "are hard as iron itself, I want you to convince yourself of the fact." Taking her gloved hand in his own, he passing it slowly over his chest. "It's unbelievable!" she gasped, staggering backward, and an attendant rushed to her aid with smelling salts.[17]

The Perfect Man was decades in the making. A grocer's son, he was born in East Prussia with the mundane name Friedrich Wilhelm Müller. He left his homeland at the age of eighteen to avoid the draft and to join a traveling circus. By means of innovative physical training, a flair for showmanship, and the help of savvy impresarios, he honed his craft as a performing strong man. He changed his name to Sandow, which he derived by Germanizing his mother's Russian maiden name, Sandov. And he claimed rather more gentlemanly origins than he really had. With enhanced body and back story, Sandow gravitated first to London, Europe's greatest venue for mass entertainment, and then to New York and Chicago. In present-day terms, he was not a particularly remarkable specimen, standing five-feet-eight-inches tall and weighing in at 190 pounds. Though these measurements were more remarkable in his day than now, the important thing for his admirers was not his size but his well-developed physique, his shapely proportions, and his smooth white skin. He seemed to raise the body to an art form by becoming the living embodiment of classical ideals.[18]

As a fresh vision of primal manliness for modern city dwellers, Sandow offered living proof that men can improve themselves through physical culture. And he emphasized this point, urging other men to follow his example. By doing so, he almost single-handedly launched the bodybuilding movement. His example helped to fix a new ideal of manliness, emphasizing the beauty of muscular form and balance as well as strength. It was an ideal that explicitly excluded hair. Though Sandow kept his trimmed, blond mustache to match his supposedly genteel Prussian breeding, the remainder of his body was marble smooth. Later bodybuilders favored the metallic sheen of tanned skin and banished the mustache as well. Today, the Sandow Prize statuette, awarded each year to the world bodybuilding champions, presents a clean-shaven Sandow, deliberately correcting the Perfect Man's only imperfection.

In Sandow's time, however, a hairy lip remained the calling card of a vigorous officer or aristocrat who evinced a forceful discipline that commanded respect. Any young man at this time who hoped to make an impression, whether a grocer's son or an emperor, enhanced his lip with an honorable dash of hair.

Kaiser Wilhelm Asserts Himself

In March 1890, matters came to a head between the two men who would rule the German Empire. On one side stood the socially awkward thirty-one-year-old Wilhelm II, emperor for less than two years. On the other side stood the masterful Otto von Bismarck, the Iron Chancellor who had served Wilhelm's father, creating the German Empire through a policy of "blood and iron." The emperor deeply resented the old master's fame and presumption and believed that he, the Kaiser, could accomplish new and better things for Germany. In particular, Wilhelm wished to flex German military muscle in world affairs. He also believed it was time to extend political rights to the laboring classes in order to dampen class strife and secure the popularly of the throne. Bismarck disagreed, certain that the Kaiser failed to understand the risks of his ambitions. Germany, the old man insisted, would be better off under his steady hand.

At a political level, the confrontation was a battle over whose policies would prevail. At a personal level, it was what would later be termed a classic Oedipal struggle between a young monarch and the father of his nation. The final break came when Wilhelm discovered that Bismarck was negotiating important legislation without his knowledge, and indeed, the chancellor had instructed his cabinet not to speak with the emperor without his prior approval. Furious, Wilhelm ordered his coach early in the morning and sped to Bismarck's apartments, where he found the old man asleep. Not waiting even for the old man to dress, the young ruler threw down his hat and gloves on a table, demanding to know what his chancellor was up to. Bismarck stood his ground, and according to Wilhelm, slammed a notebook on the table, toppling an inkwell, insisting that, as chief minister of state, he was in charge of cabinet ministers.[19] Bismarck then played his trump card, threatening to resign. To his surprise, the emperor immediately accepted. He felt ready to rule on his own.

Bismarck had not expected to lose. He had underestimated his young sovereign. He knew that behind his impressively severe exterior, the Kaiser was nervous, sensitive, and frequently indecisive. What Bismarck did not fully understand was the emperor's white-knuckled determination to overcome these faults. To conquer Bismarck was his first great test, and there were many more in store as he willed himself to be more than he was. A key part of this effort was to make himself outwardly impressive. Wilhelm was passionate for parades, pageantry, and fiery speeches, but the signature feature of his newly invigorated image was his resplendent upturned mustache.[20]

Before settling on this fierce style, Wilhelm experimented with other looks. Twice he grew a full beard. The second occasion was a Scandinavian cruise in 1891, soon after firing Bismarck. Wilhelm was clearly pleased with the result, declaring to anyone who would listen that "with a beard like this you could thump on the table so hard that your ministers would fall down with fright and lie flat on their faces."[21]

10.3 Kaiser Wilhelm II, 1898.

It is interesting that he would put it that way, for this was the same forceful gesture he reported Bismarck using a year earlier in their fateful confrontation. Now Wilhelm would be the one to slam the table! He soon decided, however, that a beard would not do. Mustaches were the approved military and royal look of his day, and beards had come to seem old-fashioned. What to do? He needed a mustache like no other: something to make him stand above all others as a man among men. He turned to his court hairdresser, Francois Haby, for a solution, and the inventive coiffeur responded with his masterstroke, perfecting the technique needed to give the German ruler his uniquely erect and manly *schnurrbarte*. A delighted emperor kept Herr Haby close at hand anywhere he traveled.

The combination of the Kaiser's image obsession and Haby's styling skills produced the iconic look of the age. The story is told that when Haby first succeeded in creating the famous "erect" mustache, Wilhelm delightedly exclaimed, "Es ist erreicht!" (it is achieved!). This phrase entered the lexicon as the rather phallic name for the emperor's mustache, as well as the implements and ointments needed to accomplish it, which Haby was pleased to sell to thousands of eager customers clamoring to achieve their own spiky facial hair. Diederich Hessling, the title character in Heinrich Mann's 1919 novel *Der Untertan* (The Subject) exemplified this sort of hero worship. As Diederich watches the Kaiser parade on horseback through the Brandenburg Gate, "an intoxication, more intense and nobler than that stimulated by beer, raised his feet off the ground and carried him in the air . . . There on the horse rode Power, through the gateway of triumphal entries, with dazzling features, but graven as stone."[22] In a rush of ecstasy, he vows to devote his life to the nation and its ruler, and as a visible sign of his new commitment, he hastens to Haby's fashionable Berlin salon get an erect mustache for himself. "When this was done he could hardly recognize himself in the glass. When no longer concealed by hair, his mouth had something tigerish and threatening about it, especially when his lips were drawn, and the points of his moustache aimed straight at his eyes, which inspired fear in Diederich himself, as though they glared from the countenance of Power himself."[23]

The Kaiser's defeat in World War I put an end to spiky helmets and pointy mustaches, and this last stand of brave hair was swept away. The deposed emperor lived out the remainder of his life in quiet exile in the Netherlands, without uniforms, parades, or his court hairdresser. In retrospect, Germany would have been better off with Bismarck's unkempt walrus mustache and steady hand. Wilhelm's impatient aggressiveness had failed his country and himself. The demise of the Kaiser and his *es ist erreicht* magnificence was another turning point for Germany and for masculine hair. The "war to end all wars" did not, of course, end wars, but it did drop the curtain on facial hair. Germans abandoned this sign of the failed past as quickly as they had adopted it, and in doing so they joined the rest of Europe and America in renouncing—for the most part—the mustachioed image of military manliness.

The war was the final end, but not the cause of the beard movement's demise in the twentieth century. Decline had set in well before, driven by a collective reconsideration of the relation of manliness to the body. Hair seemed less relevant as men became increasingly literal in reading the male body as the source of masculine strength. More and more, it was muscles, performance, and a well-formed physique that mattered. W. G. Grace's facial magnificence was the exception rather than the rule on the cricket grounds, and was linked more to his identity as a gentleman than as an athlete. Eugen Sandow pointed the way to the new ideal, which seemed more impressively masculine because building muscles required real work and created actual, not just symbolic, strength. Even the Kaiser's mustache, though just hair, seemed to rise as if by its own power, and like a muscular frame, it too demanded significant effort to maintain. Mustaches held on as a limited form of hairy display, not entirely at odds with a youthful physique. Even this feature, however, was soon swept off men's faces by new pressures demanding conformist masculinity. The nineteenth-century bloom of patriarchal and militarist manliness wilted and dropped away, making way for a future built by men with firm muscles and clean-cut faces.

11

CORPORATE MEN OF THE TWENTIETH CENTURY

The twentieth century vied with the eighteenth as history's most clean-shaven. The reasons were not the same, however. In the eighteenth century, shaving was part of a code of gentlemanly good manners. In the twentieth century, it was important for men to exhibit youthful energy and disciplined reliability suited to corporate and professional employment. A smooth face made a man look younger and healthier. It also indicated honesty and sociability. The common English phrase "clean-shaven" neatly sums up these associations. A shorn man was neat, energetic, and dependable. Because society valued these virtues, men were eager to prove themselves with their razors.

Lawrence of Arabia Leads the Charge

Lieutenant T. E. Lawrence was a new hero for a new generation. He was a thoroughly modern, clean-cut, reliable soldier doing his small bit for the vast British military machine. But he became much more: a hardened desert chieftain who matched wits with wily bearded rivals, endured the raw elements, and fought the enemy hand to hand. For a European and American public scarred by the murderous quagmire of World War I, his story offered hope that brave and intelligent individuals still mattered in an age of mass armies and hellish mechanical firepower. It helped that Lawrence did not confront massed German forces on the dreary Western Front, but faced instead the more dispersed, less well-equipped troops of Ottoman Turkey in the desert expanse of Arabia. As an intelligence officer stationed in Egypt, Lawrence took the initiative in creating a new self, taking up Arab guise and guiding camel-riding commandoes on a string of unlikely desert victories. The curious anomaly of the beardless "blond Bedouin" was surprising enough, but when he proved also to be a conqueror, the legend was born of a modern man who had mastered a timeless and primitive land.

Lawrence's first great victory was the capture of Aqaba, a strategic Red Sea port (now part of Jordan). He and his Arab allies used speed, endurance, and toughness to surprise the city from the supposedly inaccessible northern wastes. First, however, they had to dispense with a Turkish battalion sent out to stop them at a remote settlement called Abu el Lissal. It was here that the Arab insurgents proved their true mettle.

On camel and horseback, the rebels reached Abu el Lissal on an unusually hot day in July 1917. Friend and foe were groggy from heat and thirst. Holed up in a narrow valley, the languid Turks failed to detect the approaching Arabs, who began firing down upon them hour after hour from the cliffs above. Long-range potshots would not do the trick, however, and Lawrence goaded his allies to charge. One chieftain initiated the engagement by galloping with fifty horsemen into the harried ranks of Turkish regulars, who fled straight into an even larger wave of camel cavalry led by Lawrence himself, white robes flying and guns blazing. "I had got among the first of them," Lawrence recalled later, "and was shooting, with a pistol of course, for only an expert could use a rifle from such plunging beasts; when suddenly my camel tripped and went down emptily upon her face, as though pole-axed. I was torn completely from the saddle, sailed grandly through the air for a great distance, and landed with a crash which seemed to drive all the power and feeling out of me."[1] Stunned, he recited to himself a favorite poem as he awaited death under crashing camel hooves. As he recovered his senses, however, he realized that the body of his fallen mount had saved him from the stampede, and that he had accidently shot his own poor beast with his gun. The Turks, meanwhile, had been swept away by the irresistible battering of four hundred camels galloping down the slope at thirty miles an hour.

The legend of "Lawrence of Arabia" was built upon this sort of daring, toughness, and luck. It rested also on Lawrence's uncanny ability to live in two worlds, British and Arab, and to navigate the contradictory complexities of modern guerrilla warfare involving daggers, camels, explosives, and airplanes. He was an Oxford-trained intelligence officer proud to serve his king and empire, yet he was also the blond Bedouin, an honorary Arab tribesman seeking to free a subject people from their foreign masters. Troubled by fear that he would be forced to betray his Arab friends in the end, he grasped onto the hope that it might be possible to be both sorts of man and to serve both sets of masters.

To perform his dual role, Lawrence had to be a great actor as well as a cunning strategist. Most men had to worry about how to define one manly identity; Lawrence had to contrive two at the same time. During the two years he was active in the desert, he always wore the white Arab robes and headdress presented to him by Prince Feisal of Mecca, the primary leader of the revolt. Even when he occasionally returned to Egypt to meet with his British superiors, Lawrence wore this costume. At the same time, he was meticulously British and un-Arab in his regular shaving, even when a lack of water forced him to scrape his face with a dry blade. This practice completed his heroic look, unique among British and Arabs alike. "It was notoriety to be the only clean-shaven one," Lawrence explained, "and I doubled it by wearing always the suspect pure silk, of the whitest (at least outside), with a gold and crimson Meccan head-rope, and gold dagger. By so dressing I staked a claim which Feisal's public consideration of me confirmed."[2] As he rode camelback in flowing white robes across a primitive, biblical landscape, his hairless face confirmed that he remained a thoroughly modern man.

Shaving was an ideal symbol of modernity precisely because it was the latest and most up-to-date mode for men. Less than a year before his raid on Aqaba, the British military had buckled to agitation within the ranks, issuing new rules permitting soldiers to be clean-shaven. For half a century, British soldiers, like most of their European counterparts, had been required to grow mustaches as a sign of military esprit de corps. In the years before World War I, however, British soldiers began pressing for the freedom not to grow them.[3] In 1915, in the midst of war, King George had been obliged to issue a stern warning that the hair regulations would be enforced. The following year, however, after the government implemented the draft, and worries about morale

11.1 Thomas Edward Lawrence in Arab garb. HIP/Art Resource, NY.

deepened, the general staff capitulated. They had no appetite to fight their own soldiers in addition to the enemy.[4]

Contrary to some later suppositions, the abandonment of mustaches had nothing to do with gas masks or trench hygiene. Nor was it a matter of improved shaving technology. The true cause of the downfall of beards and mustaches in the twentieth century was a social development even the military could not resist: the renovation of manliness to the specifications of urban and corporate society. Like the patriarchal beard, the chivalric mustache lost favor among men eager to display the virtues of a new century: youthfulness, energy, cleanliness, and reliability.

Before Lawrence, Tarzan was another heroic shaver. The creation of American author Edgar Rice Burroughs, the King of the Apes, who first appeared in print in 1912, was an orphaned English nobleman raised by hairy denizens of the jungle, unaware of his true identity. As he grew to manhood, his humanity and nobility asserted themselves, allowing him to command and subdue the beasts around him as well as his own primitive impulses. He taught himself both to read and to shave in order to claim his human birthright: "True he had seen pictures in his books of men with great masses of hair upon lip and cheek and chin, but, nevertheless, Tarzan was afraid. Almost daily he whetted his keen knife and scraped and whittled at his young beard to eradicate this degrading emblem of apehood. And so he learned to shave—rudely and painfully, it is true—but, nevertheless, effectively."[5] Here was a subtle but direct assertion of the ideals of a new era. Tarzan reasoned that, although civilized men had worn facial hair in the past, doing so risked introducing an element of wildness and disorder that he needed to resist.

Burroughs was not a great novelist, but he had a feel for the fears and fantasies of his times. Like Tarzan, men of the twentieth century were afraid of the ape within and worried about maintaining self-discipline. At the same time, modern city dwellers hoped that they, like Tarzan, might call upon a primitive potency within themselves when needed. As early twentieth-century icons of modernized manhood, Lawrence of Arabia and Tarzan were wildly popular because they suggested that men could have it both ways, as shaved men of the wild. Their stories also implied that steadfast loyalty to the male collective—the English nation for Lawrence, civilized Europe for Tarzan—were the foundation of true manliness.

The emergence of heroic shavers marked the end of the nineteenth-century beard and mustache movement. The year 1903 proved to be the tipping point. An enterprising reporter for the *Chicago Tribune* illustrated this fact by careful count. Standing on a busy street corner in downtown Chicago, he tallied in one hour 3,000 men, of whom 1,236 wore mustaches and 108 some kind of beard. The rest (1,656) were clean-shaven.[6] In other words, there was a rough balance, but the reporter also knew that the trend was moving strongly toward shaving. This was also the view of a contributor to the American journal *Harper's Weekly*, whose 1903 article "The Passing of Beards" was partly a eulogy for facial hair, partly a reluctant recognition of the virtues of a shaved face. The beard, he wrote, "really cannot be kept clean; but it was natural, and it was dignified." As for shaving, "there is gain for honesty if not beauty."[7]

It so happened that King C. Gillette secured a patent for his famous safety razor in 1904, which appears at first glance to fit the common narrative that improvements in shaving technology explain what was happening. Gillette's invention, however, was the beneficiary rather than the cause of the beard's demise. Facial hair was on the way out when Gillette entered the scene. Advertising by his and other shaving-products companies reflected the fact that they were serving rather than creating the desire for a smooth face. No effort was needed to persuade men to rid themselves of hair. There was instead a relentless focus on how their products made shaving easy and comfortable. The razor and shaving cream industry, with estimated annual sales of eighty million dollars by 1937 in the United States alone, provided the tools for middle-class mobility, enabling the common man to meet exacting grooming standards approved by corporate bosses.

Three powerful forces converged at this time to pressure men to shave: medical science, employers, and women. The understanding of disease was revolutionized in the late nineteenth century when it was discovered that contagious illnesses were caused by microorganisms. This prompted a dramatic about-face with respect to health and facial hair. In the nineteenth century, physicians routinely argued that beards and mustaches helped protect skin and nerves from the sun and weather, as well as filtering dust and bad air. Louis Pasteur's discoveries changed all that, and by the beginning of the twentieth century, doctors increasingly denounced facial hair as a haven for microbes. In the new century, newspapers, magazines, and medical journals were filled with increasingly alarming reports, such as that of a French scientist who described in 1907 an experiment showing that the lips of a woman kissed by a mustached man were polluted with tuberculosis and diphtheria bacteria, as well as food particles and a hair from a spider's leg.[8]

In 1909, a study in the British medical journal *Lancet* found clean-shaven men were less likely to suffer from colds. Their supposition was that removing facial hair removed a nursery of dangerous organisms, and allowed for the more effective use of soap.[9] The microbe fear was powerful, but not unchallenged. Many doctors continued to wear mustaches, and some persisted in arguing for their health benefits.[10] For most people, however, cleanliness was next to shavenness.

Employers were an even more effective force against facial hair. Fewer and fewer men in the industrialized world were independent or self-employed in the twentieth century. Increasingly, employees worked in professional, industrial, or corporate environments in which the prevailing virtues were teamwork, energy, cooperation, and good manners.[11] Men were eager to display these virtues, and to appear young, eager, and prepared. The man with a razor reaped the reward of being part of a team.

Businesses that introduced shaving codes justified their actions in terms of hygiene, professionalism, and the need to please customers. The Burlington Railroad, for example, banned facial hair on its conductors in 1907, at the same time introducing white linen collars, ties, and vests. The company's management announced that these changes would give its employees a uniform appearance and make them less likely to spread germs and contagion.[12] A few years earlier, the police department in Evanston, Illinois, had ordered its officers to shave their mustaches as part of a new insistence on drill and professionalism. The department issued a public statement, promising that "the inspector will see that each patrolman has clean shoes, clean gloves, a neat uniform, and that he is clean shaven. Slovenly or untidy dress at inspection will be considered a neglect of duty and will be entered against the officer."[13] In 1915, the Los Angeles Police Department stopped promoting any patrolman or detective who chose to wear a mustache, because, in the words of the superintendent, it gave "an untidy and irregular appearance to his men."[14] These were but samples of a sweeping international trend.

Women also made their desires known, sensing an opportunity to reinforce the message of regulated manliness. Alma Whitaker, in a column in the *Los Angeles Times* in 1920, complained about men who had returned from the war with "tricky little mustaches," an affectation she suspected "helps a fellow feel dashing and debonair, no matter how we happen to think he looks in it." In a half-serious tone, she urged her fellow women to put a stop to this trend, warning that "these ostensibly meager little hairy assertions on the male upper lip may become patriarchal whiskers before we know what has happened to us."[15] A few years later, a woman on a Chicago street echoed this antipatriarchal attitude when asked whether she liked mustaches. Absolutely not, she replied, "I want a modern husband, not one reared in Noah's ark."[16] As this comment suggests, changes at home as well as the workplace inclined men to adopt a more sociable shaved face. The Victorian domestic patriarch was no longer the ideal man.

The rise of this new ideal did not entirely eliminate facial hair, but it did establish a new configuration of meaning. Those choosing to grow a mustache were now, depending on their age, either quaintly old-fashioned or daringly unconventional. Mustaches remained a widely accepted style in continental Europe after the war, but the smooth look steadily gained ground because of what some Europeans described as the "Americanization" of men's faces.[17] The facial hair divide now distinguished two contrasting masculine types: sociable and autonomous. A man was neither wholly one nor the other, of course, but the presence and size of a mustache or beard—or their absence—served to move a man one way or another along the continuum. According to the twentieth-century gender code, a clean-shaved man's virtue indicated, as it had for Lawrence of Arabia, his commitment to his male peers and to local, national, or corporate institutions. The mustached or bearded man, by contrast, was much more his own man: a patriarch, authority figure, or free agent who was able to play by his own rules. These were stereotypes, of course, but like most stereotypes they carried real social power. This interpretive frame held firm for performer and audience alike, offering men with facial hair both risks and rewards, depending on who was watching.

For most urban men, a focus on sports and the muscled body diminished the importance of facial hair in the performance of manliness. This was particularly true for those influenced by Eugen Sandow and the "physical culture" movement, in that hair interfered with the display of both Grecian youthfulness and well-defined muscles. Americans were quicker than Europeans to adopt the new clean-shaven look, and many observers thought this reflected the Americans' particular enthusiasm

for both youthfulness and sports.[18] This idea was not without foundation. When a *Chicago Tribune* reporter asked about mustaches in 1925,
one man in the street opined that they were not good because "right
now everybody wants to look young and keep looking young, and we
all like to have everybody else looking young and feel young. And that's
a good sign."[19] Joseph Schusser, a New Yorker who managed America's
largest barbershop chain, believed the same thing and surmised that, in
America, youthfulness was associated with strength. "Every American
man," he argued, "wants to have 'a strong face;' square jaws, with a
clean-cut, firm mouth. This is our ideal, we try to present that kind of
face to the world."[20]

Americans may have been the quicker to abandon their facial hair,
but Europeans were not far behind. Beards survived only on the faces
of old or outmoded men who provided amusement in the 1920s for
children who spotted them in the street. Young Frenchmen played
games of "tennis-barbe," while British children delighted in games of
"Beaver," which was also scored like tennis, with greater point values
given for rarer beards, such as a red one, or the rarest sighting of all, a
royal beard—which scored as game, set, and match.[21] One legend has
it that the arrival of a bearded royal at an assembly at the University of
Cambridge prompted the undergraduates to rise to their feet and shout
in unison "Royal Beaver! Game, Set and Match!"[22]

Even those great champions of tradition, the British aristocracy, suc-
cumbed by the 1920s to the overwhelming compulsion of masculine
redefinition. The story is told of a sharp exchange between Lord Quickswood and his cousin Algernon Cecil. In spite of the fact that his father
was Lord Salisbury, Britain's last bearded prime minister, Lord Quickswood would not abide his cousin's anachronistic beard, inquiring,
"Algernon, why have you grown that beard?" Algernon replied, "Well,
why not? Our Lord is supposed to have been bearded." Quickswood
retorted, "That's no answer. Our Lord was not a gentleman."[23]

Clark Gable Doesn't Give a Damn

Clark Gable, or at least his film characters, were not perfect gentlemen
either, and that was his special charm. While European and American
manliness shifted toward well-regulated sociability after the Great War,

11.2 Clark Gable in the 1930s. HIP/Art Resource, NY.

masculine roguishness persisted in the cultural imagination, often in the form of mustachioed movie stars. In the land of wish-fulfillment called Hollywood, film studios produced visions of rugged and rakish individualism that was neither possible nor acceptable in everyday existence. For this reason it made perfect sense that many stars in the early decades of film history, including Adolphe Menjou, Ronald Colman, Errol Flynn, Douglas Fairbanks (Senior and Junior), and Clark Gable sported natty mustaches. In the 1930s, a dash of daring hair became the hallmark of swashbuckling romantic heroes. Its visual and metaphorical opposite was the dark smudge on the lip of Charlie Chaplin's tramp.

Clark Gable was the "King of Hollywood" in part because he was the most successful in deploying the romantic potential of mustached manliness. Unlike Chaplin, who was clean-shaven off camera, Gable cut the same dashing figure wherever he appeared, though he would make adjustments to his hair from time to time. For his best known role, as Rhett Butler in the blockbuster epic *Gone with the Wind,* he took pains to determine just the right sort of lip ornament, finally deciding on "a dashing thin line with spiked waxed ends."[24] This, Gable believed, was just the look for Butler, a resourceful, self-centered gambler and smuggler. Though a rogue and rule-breaker, Rhett was also honest and unpretentious. In short, he was fine example of Hollywood's rugged individualist. His forwardness in his first encounter with the vivacious and proud Scarlett O'Hara provokes her to declare, "Sir, you are no gentleman!" to which Rhett coolly responds, "And you, miss, are no lady. Don't think that I hold that against you. Ladies have never held any charm for me." This comment, of course, does not win Scarlett over. She is doggedly determined to prove herself a true lady by marrying the smooth-faced and gentlemanly Ashley Wilkes.

Audiences thrilled to see a rugged Rhett stand masterfully above the fray, immune to those who would question his character and judgment. In his second encounter with Scarlett, he brushes off her compliments about his service to the Southern cause:

> *Rhett:* I'm neither noble nor heroic.
> *Scarlett:* But you are a blockade runner?
> *Rhett:* For profit, and profit only.
> *Scarlett:* Are you trying to tell me that don't believe in the cause?
> *Rhett:* I believe in Rhett Butler; he's the only cause I know. The rest
>   doesn't mean much to me.

Here was the colorful nonconformist to match the strong-willed Scarlett O'Hara. After rescuing Scarlett from burning Atlanta, Rhett opens up: "I love you, Scarlett, in spite of you, me, and whole silly world going to pieces around us, I love you because we are both alike: bad lots, both of us, selfish and shrewd, but able to look things in their eyes and call them by their right names." Scarlett, unfortunately, cannot be so honest in her feelings. She is stuck on the unobtainable Ashley and her selfish dreams of being better than she is. Even after she marries Rhett, and he sweeps his pouty wife off her feet and has his way with her, Scarlett still cannot allow her obvious pleasure to interfere with her fantasy of being a true lady. In the end, Rhett leaves her, and Scarlett belatedly becomes aware that she has made a grave mistake. She beseeches her departing lover, "Where shall I go; what shall I do?" to which he famously replies, "Frankly my dear, I don't give a damn." This was a manly answer to the troubles of life, and to those who spurn you.

Long before these lines were written for him, Hollywood observers had noted that Gable's appeal as a leading man was built on his devil-may-care forcefulness. Hollywood reporter Ruth Biery declared in 1932 that he was "the epitome of the ruthless, handsome knock-'em-down, treat-'em-rough, virile, modern cave man," qualities that made him popular with men and alluring to women.[25] The year after this description appeared in print, Gable grew his trademark mustache, which he wore, with only a few exceptions, for the rest of his life. There was even a public kerfuffle in 1936 when Warner Brothers Studios, which had obtained Gable on loan from Metro Goldwyn Mayer, ordered him to shave for a movie. MGM formally complained to Warner Brothers that this would interfere with their star's image and lower the value of one of its prime assets.[26]

By the mid-1930s mustaches like Gable's were all the rage. According to the *Los Angeles Times*, half the leading men in Hollywood had joined the trend.[27] Even the mild-mannered Bing Crosby was urged by a flood of fan letters to enhance his upper lip, which he did in 1935 for his part in the musical *Mississippi*. The studios believed they were on to something, and they often ordered their leading men to meet the new standard. In 1939, a Hollywood reporter noted that "nearly every big-time, and small-time film star too, is wooing and winning the ladies with the aid of a bit of brush on his upper lip."[28] When, in 1940, a director insisted that the young star Robert Taylor grow a mustache for his film *Waterloo Bridge*, he did so "to make him appear more mature, rugged, and virile" instead of a "well-scrubbed choir boy."[29]

While Gable stuck with his mustache for the rest of his life, other movie actors began in the 1940s to abandon what detractors derided as "lip lettuce." Even in its heyday there were indications of resistance. In 1937 it was reported that Errol Flynn was receiving fan mail both for and against his mustache, and Flynn was unsure what he should do.[30] Some studios decided not to leave it to chance; in one case, a series of screen tests featuring Tyrone Power with different sorts of facial hair was shown to a sample audience of women.[31] This led to Power's clean-shaven appearance in his subsequent film, *Old Chicago*. A number of female stars were on record as disapproving of facial hair, including Marsha Hunt, Marlene Dietrich, Doris Nolan, Martha Raye, and Dorothy Lamour.[32] Actresses were no more unanimous than Errol Flynn's female fans, however. In 1940, for example, Rosalind Russell expressed approval for a hairy lip, while Barbara Stanwyck opined that "worn properly, the mustache can lend character and dignity to a man's face."[33]

If Clark Gable was the king of Hollywood, Charlie Chaplin was its court jester. Chaplin improvised this famous tramp character one day in 1914 during a break in filming. On a lark, to amuse his fellow actors, he put on parts of their costumes: the baggy trousers of a much bigger man, the tight-fitting coat of a thinner actor, and another's derby hat. According to one of those present, Chaplin dashed to the makeup room for a piece of crepe hair, cutting himself a mustache and trimming the sides to a rectangle small enough to wiggle when he made a face.[34] He was a huge hit with the actors and stagehands. The tramp was born.

The character was a fool, with a fool's motley costume. At a time when mustaches were falling from favor, and those that remained were pencil-thin, the tramp's square smudge, as ill-proportioned and ill-fitting as his jacket, served as their comedic opposite. This inappropriate and outdated style contributed to what Chaplin himself described as the tramp's "shabby gentility."[35] The tramp's mustache also hinted at the character's manic masculinity. In truth, Gable's "modern cave man" and Chaplin's tramp had more in common than one would first imagine. They were both rule-breakers and loners, and while the tramp was poor and weak, he was also, like Gable's characters, surprisingly and refreshingly resilient. Viewed in this light, Chaplin's lip smudge was not so absurd after all.

Hitler and Stalin Agree

In December 1939, as American audiences crowded into theaters to see Rhett and Scarlett face a disastrous war, an even greater cataclysm was commencing in Europe. Four months earlier, a triumphant Adolf Hitler hung up the phone at his Berghof retreat in Bavaria and exclaimed, "I have the world in my pocket!"[36] He had just received news that the Soviet leader Joseph Stalin had agreed to sign a nonaggression pact with Germany, giving the two tyrants a free hand to carve up Eastern Europe between them. Hitler confidante Albert Speer later intimated that "to see the names of Hitler and Stalin linked in friendship on a piece of paper was the most staggering, the most exciting turn of events I could possibly have imagined."[37] According to Winston Churchill, "the sinister news broke upon the world like an explosion."[38] For him it was the culminating failure of prewar British diplomacy. The nonaggression pact was the green light for Hitler to start World War II.

All the powers knew that the Nazis were planning to attack Poland in the summer of 1939, and Stalin was not certain what to do and whom to trust. In the end, he sensed that he could understand Hitler better than Britain and France, which were hesitating to strike an accord with the Soviet Union to counter Naziism. The western Europeans were counting too much on the historical and ideological animosity between fascist Germany and communist Russia. The British and French might have worked harder to forestall Hitler's diplomatic moves had they considered more thoroughly the ways in which Hitler and Stalin were alike, for it was these commonalities that allowed them to forge a deal. Neither Hitler nor Stalin recognized moral or political constraints on his pursuit of power. Each had a militaristic view of the world and favored military clothing and symbols, including mustaches, in presenting an impressive face to the world. Their mutual commitment to power and mustaches was not a simple coincidence, either. Both knew that an extraordinary and forceful face was essential for men who ruled through adulation and fear. Stalin and Hitler never met, but they believed they understood each other. When negotiations between them sputtered in 1939, Hitler circumvented diplomatic channels and wrote to the Soviet leader directly, and Stalin reciprocated. As only dictators could, they dispensed with formalities and got straight to business.

11.3 Joseph Stalin, ca. 1942. Library of Congress, LC-USW33-019081-C.

An analysis of mustaches might have alerted the western allies to the real possibility of German-Soviet agreement. Both dictators came by their look quite deliberately, and their choices offered important clues about their thinking. Each man made an effort with his hair to stand apart and above the men around him by refusing to conform either to past traditions or current trends.

As leader of the Soviet Union since 1922, Stalin's political fortunes were tied to the ideological and symbolic heritage of communism.

There was no specific leftist style as such, but beards of some kind were a common feature among the movement's leading men. Besides Marx and Engels, August Bebel, the longtime leader of the German Social Democrats, was also famous for his luxuriant beard. German labor leaders emulated Bebel's look in the decades before World War I, contrasting themselves to right-wing imitators of the Kaiser's mustachioed grandiloquence.[39] Another German socialist leader, Eduard Bernstein, though he renounced revolution in favor of constitutional reform, did not retreat on the hair front. In France, Jean Jaurés fit the mold as he railed against both the center and the right. In Russia, Vladimir Lenin and Leon Trotsky opted for smaller pointed beards, helpful in distinguishing themselves, on the one hand, from the hirsute tsars, priests, and peasants, and, on the other hand, from the clean-shaven Alexander Kerensky and his fellow professionals and industrialists who formed a centrist government after the tsar abdicated in 1917. Trotsky forged a particularly memorable style for himself, aptly described by a visiting English artist in the 1920s: "Full face he is a Mephisto. His eyebrows go up, at an angle, and the lower part of his face tapers into a pointed and defiant beard."[40]

Hair on the chin helped a balding Lenin appear wiser and more forceful. Ironically, he was beardless during the critical months of the Bolshevik revolution, having shaved to disguise himself from the police. As he pressed forward with revolution, Lenin adamantly refused to be photographed for many months afterward, until his mark of uniqueness and wisdom was fully restored.[41] He rightly understood the propaganda power of his bearded image. Trotsky confirmed this after Lenin's death, remarking in a review of children's writings about Lenin that for young people, "Lenin's beard becomes a very important element. It seems to symbolize maturity, manliness, and the fighting spirit."[42]

Stalin did not look like these paragons of the left. While Lenin and Trotsky favored civilian coats and ties, Stalin, from 1918 onward, opted for military-style tunics, trousers, and leather boots.[43] The mustache rather than the beard was the natural complement to this choice. His deportment declared that he was more militant and less cerebral than his communist predecessors.

Hitler's style was also explicitly militant. He served throughout World War I as a corporal stationed at field offices, where he cultivated a typical officer's adornment according to long military tradition. Germany's defeat, however, was also the downfall of the German mustache. Even the Kaiser reduced himself in 1918 to a small, pacific beard. Hitler rejected this humiliation and made it his life's mission to revive German military might and national fortunes. It made perfect sense for him to preserve the stiff upper lip, but he understood that Germany would not rise again by clinging to the past. He knew his country must modernize and that he must present himself as a modern leader. He needed new symbols and a new mustache.

The "toothbrush" mustache that he settled on was known before the war as a modern look, becoming popular at the beginning of the twentieth century as larger effusions of hair fell from favor. In Germany the new style was sometimes adopted as a more practical and hygienic version of the traditional style, but it was also derided on occasion as an undesirable American or English import.[44] The German military establishment was certainly opposed. In 1914, the commander of the German Guard Corps forbade this "modern fashion," declaring that "a trifling tuft of hair under the nose is unsuitable for Prussian soldiers and irreconcilable with the true German character."[45] After the war, however, such regulations and traditions were abandoned in the quest for a new German manliness. As he honed his skills and image on the rostrums of Nazi party rallies, Hitler experimented with different haircuts and mustache trims to get the right effect. The grandly upturned *kaiserbart*, the drooping walrus of Bismarck, and even the ordinary officer's trim all invoked the failed past. Clean shaving, on the other hand, though admirable for evoking youth and efficiency, also suggested the bland and unromantic modernity of Germany's western rivals. The famous square of dark hair under the nose became the ideal alternative. It delivered just enough of that forceful distinctiveness that Hitler needed to project an aura of command.[46]

No one was more alert to the power of symbols and propaganda than Hitler. As the embodiment of his movement, he needed always to appear imperturbably strong. Hair on his lip, even a small amount, helped him avoid betraying vulnerability. This was keenly perceived in 1931 by James Abbe, the first foreign photographer allowed access to Hitler. Abbe came away from his much-anticipated photo shoot frustrated by his failure to capture the inner dimensions of Hitler's personality. His camera, he said, simply could not penetrate the mustache mask. Abbe had previously photographed Charlie Chaplin and recalled that when the movie star removed his tramp costume and fake fuzz, Chaplin the man emerged before the camera. "But I couldn't ask Hitler to remove his mustache. Hitler, Hitlerism, and the entire Nazi movement, are identified with that mustache. Like the swastika, the brown shirt . . . it lures voters and adorers and baffles reporters and photographers."[47] Hitler could smile for others, Abbe discovered, but never for the camera. "Once or twice he started to smile in my direction, but each time he saw the camera the smile froze." Hitler remained barricaded behind his steely facade.

Besides this inscrutable defensive quality, Hitler's mustache had an unintentionally favorable effect for him. Hitler's resemblance to Chaplin's iconic tramp led western Europeans and Americans to underestimate the Fuhrer as something of a clown. Hitler scholar Hugh Trevor-Roper made this observation, and essayist Ron Rosenbaum has amplified it, accusing Chaplin himself of promoting this perception through his mockery of the Fuhrer in his film *The Great Dictator*.[48] There is ample evidence that Trevor-Roper and Rosenbaum are right. In 1931, for example, the editors of the *Boston Globe* found it incredible that "a man who would wear the little scrub of a mustache affected by Adolf Hitler could really be the rip-snorting, hard-boiled Fascist leader that he is, especially when one remembers some other famous German mustaches."[49] Even after the war had begun in 1939, there was a propensity to belittle rather than denounce the German dictator, prompting a correspondent to pen an eloquent letter to the *Times* of London complaining that official British programming on the BBC was aimed at mocking Hitler and his silly mustache, rather than exposing him as "a greater peril than ever Napoleon was."[50]

Stalin and Hitler presented a similar face to the world in part to show what they wanted to be, and also what they did *not* want to be. They refused to be men either of the bearded past or of the clean-shaven present. They intended to be modern warriors, blending cold ferocity with modern efficiency to carry out unprecedented destruction.

Thomas Dewey Fights for Votes

The famous mustaches of the 1940s did not generally inspire confidence. Hitler was evil, Chaplin's tramp was a fool, and Clark Gable

11.4 Campaign button for Thomas Dewey, 1948. Courtesy of Gene Dillman.

was a rogue. When Thomas Dewey, the mustachioed governor of New York, won the Republican presidential nomination in 1944 to challenge Franklin Roosevelt, and again in 1948, when his opponent was Harry Truman, many American voters could not help questioning his unusual style. Back in 1939, as Clark Gable was portraying devil-may-care Rhett Butler and Hitler was launching his war on Europe, Thomas E. Dewey was a young attorney general of New York and a rising political star. One admiring journalist effused that "in this clean-shaven age ... [Dewey's mustache] is little short of epic. It is fulsome, luxuriant, raven black, compelling, and curved in a way to gladden an artist's eye."[51] Dewey was, in that writer's opinion, "a Clark Gable of candidates" with more charm, personality, and political sex appeal than other Republicans. Neither this journalist, nor Dewey himself, understood the high cost any politician must pay for having the look of a charming rogue.

Murmurs began immediately when Dewey launched his campaign in 1944. Women writers were the most critical. The syndicated columnist Dorothy Kilgallen supported Dewey, though she admitted that mustaches did nothing for her.[52] Others were less tolerant. After attending the Republican National Convention in Chicago that July, Helen Essary, a syndicated political columnist, declared herself impressed by Dewey's intelligence and courage but hopeful that the candidate would get himself to a barber right away. "I have heard dozens of women make the same criticism of the gentleman from New York," Essary wrote. "It takes from the seriousness and strength of his face. Moreover it will not help with the women vote . . . You see only the mustache. You remember only the mustache. Without it, Governor Dewey would look a million per cent more real as the proper man for the White House job he is after."[53] Edith Efron, writing in the pages of the *New York Times Sunday Magazine* in August 1944, also concluded that Dewey "may be elected to office, but it will be in spite of his 'manly attributes'—not because of them."[54] To Efron, it seemed clear that whatever reasons a man had for wearing one, a mustache had a profound, often negative effect. "It plays many roles today," she wrote. "It is Chaplin-pathetic, Hitler-psychopathic, Gable-debonnair, Lou Lehr–wacky. It perplexes. It fascinates. It amuses. And it repels." The following month, the magazine published a letter from a well-known model named Cornelia Von Hessert who amplified Efron's thesis that mustaches connoted undesirable masculine traits. "The man who decides to sport lip adornment," Hessert wrote, "asserts his masculinity and desire to tyrannize over the home. No matter how prettily he waxes it, droops it, shingles it, at heart he's the Man's Man and ruler of his own roost."[55] Men in Britain and America were generally clean-shaven, she reasoned, because women rightly insisted on having their say.

Many male commentators agreed with these women that mustaches marked a strong, assertive type of man, but this was for them a positive quality. One syndicated columnist who contributed two articles on the subject declared that he felt "called upon to protect the fair name of gentlemen who wear mustaches, whether they're rather scraggly affairs like mine or strong, virile ones like Mr. Dewey's."[56] This squabble over hair had little effect. In the wartime election of 1944, the voters stuck with the shaven man they knew and trusted, awarding Franklin Roosevelt an unprecedented fourth term.

When he won the nomination a second time in 1948, Dewey stood a much better chance against the less popular Harry Truman. But again the Republican contender's small mustache loomed large in perceptions of him as a candidate. As before, articles appeared in the press musing on the fact that he would be the first president with facial hair since William Howard Taft left office in 1913. Other journalists speculated on whether he would start a new national trend in men's fashions. And again, Dewey's defenders took to the press, one assuring his readers that Dewey was not affecting "a trick trim . . . like some movie actors have. The Dewey mustache is merely a part of him."[57] When an Alabama businessman made a public appeal to Dewey to shave for the sake of southern votes,[58] another male columnist encouraged the candidate to stand firm, assuring him that he (the columnist) also had a mustache, yet had managed some years earlier to win the hand in marriage of a southern voter.[59]

The banter in the press hinted at innumerable private conversations and still more private feelings. Helen Essary had, four years earlier, mentioned hearing negative comments from dozens of women about Dewey's hairy lip. Who can say how many others shared this opinion? One we do know about is Emilie Spencer Deer, an Ohio wife and mother from a solidly Republican family. In 1948 she let her family know that she would vote for President Truman instead of Dewey because she could not vote for a man with a mustache.[60] An educated and conscientious woman, she was careful to read the masculine visual codes: a clean-shaven man was sociable and reliable, whereas a man with facial hair demonstrated willful independence that did not win her confidence.

When the votes were counted in 1948, Dewey had narrowly lost. The tallies were particularly close in California, Indiana, and Ohio, Emilie Deer's state. In those three states, Dewey lost by just 38,218 total votes out of the 8.6 million cast—just four-tenths of one percent. Had he won over half that tiny margin he would have become president.[61] Polling data is not available to prove that his mustache cost him the presidency, but anecdotal evidence suggests that it is certainly possible. Dewey himself could not ignore the possibility. When he ran successfully for reelection as governor of New York in 1950, Dewey was still explaining himself to female voters. Appearing in a televised forum, the very first question came from a woman who asked why he kept his mustache. The governor responded that as a young man he stopped shaving because it hurt his lip, and he kept it because Mrs. Dewey liked it.[62] Later that year, the wistful governor told a visiting group of boy scouts, "Remember fellows, any boy can become president—unless he's got a mustache."[63] It was a joke—sort of. Dewey had learned by bitter experience that being the "Clark Gable of candidates" had not worked out for him. No major candidate for the presidency has dared flaunt even a hint of facial hair since that time.

In the early twentieth century men were strongly encouraged to conform. It was important to be a reliable member of the masculine collective, whether it was the army, a company, or a sports team. A shaved face was part of the uniform, both clean and regular. Shaving was even heroic in some circumstances, as when Lawrence stood alone on behalf of his nation. There was, of course, a natural desire for men to test these limits, at least in their fantasies. Hollywood stars like Clark Gable gave expression to a daring and roguish spirit wishing to break free from social restraint. Hitler and Stalin were rogues on a profoundly sinister level, and though their mustaches were conservative in respect to military tradition, they underscored in the Western mind the danger of men who do not shave. Thomas Dewey was unable to overcome this headwind of mistrust. The only hope for a freer expression of manly hair was the emergence of a new spirit of political and social dissent.

12

HAIR ON THE LEFT

The strong association of cleanly shaved faces with conformity in the early twentieth century made it almost inevitable that critics of the status quo would again choose facial hair as a sign of protest. A spirit of restless independence, along with a few furry chins, emerged among beatniks soon after World War II. In the late 1960s, these iconoclasts were joined by thousands more, and the growth of hair paralleled the radicalization of the baby-boom generation. In the 1970s, a reaction against both radicalism and hair gained strength, leaving a mixed legacy for our times.

John Lennon Stays in Bed

The summer of 1969 was, if measured in terms of hair and beards, the longest summer of the twentieth century. Neil Armstrong and Buzz Aldrin arrived on the moon with crew cuts, but the Fab Four made an equally famous trek across Abbey Road in London with more hair on their heads and faces than ever before. All four Beatles had cultivated beards that summer, though Paul McCartney shaved his off before the photographer snapped the iconic *Abbey Road* cover in August. Just days later, across the Atlantic, the rock and drug utopia known as the Woodstock Festival opened on a farm in New York; there, long-haired, bearded, and mustachioed rockers such as Jerry Garcia, Jimi Hendrix, Country Joe McDonald, David Crosby, and Graham Nash performed for a massive assembly of American youth, many of whom paraded their own rebellious fuzz.

Not a few of these bearded, beaded, jeans-wearing youngsters looked up to the Jesus-in-wire-rims, John Lennon, as their model. That spring, before *Abbey Road* and Woodstock, Lennon had deployed his hair as a moral cause in a bizarre though strangely effective way, staging two "bed-ins" with his new wife, Yoko Ono. They conceived these demonstrations as performance-art honeymoons, one in Amsterdam in March, another in Montreal in May. The newlyweds hoped to exploit the frenzy over their love affair to publicize their call for world peace. On each occasion, a long-haired, fully bearded Lennon, dressed in pajamas, sat and lay in a hotel bed alongside frizzy and laconic Ono, holding court for a week before a rotating circus of journalists, well-wishers, and television crews. The cameras and interviews recorded long hours of the honeymooners philosophizing about the ills of the world and the need for peace and nonviolence.

On the window behind John and Yoko's heads were handwritten signs with the slogans "Bed Peace" and "Hair Peace." A short video they produced explained these themes. Appearing before the camera in pajamas, Lennon strums a few chords, trading chants with Yoko: "Stay in bed, grow your hair. Bed peace, hair Peace. Hair peace, bed peace." Then, speaking as he strummed, Lennon explains that "this is an alternative to violence: it's to stay in bed and grow your hair. If you are Mrs. Higgins living in Rotterdam, and you announced to your local paper, 'I'm staying in bed for peace, and growing my hair for peace,' they would be interested." The Montreal bed-in culminated in the recording of a new song with a catchy, mantra-like chorus: "All we are saying is give peace a chance." In contrast to Mohandas Gandhi, one of Lennon's heroes of nonviolence, he and Ono avoided the sufferings of prison and hunger strikes, opting instead for coffee and comfort. This pillowy protest bemused critics on both the left and right, but in significant ways it fit the times perfectly.

The year before had been especially violent. The Vietnam War had reached its zenith as the communist North launched the massive Tet Offensive. Meanwhile, Soviet tanks smashed popular uprisings in

12.1 John Lennon and Yoko Ono at their first "Bed-in," Amsterdam, March 1969. Keystone Pictures/ZUMA Press, Inc./Alamy.

Prague; students clashed with police in the streets of Paris, London, and Chicago; and assassins gunned down Martin Luther King Jr. and Robert Kennedy. The Beatles, following Lennon's lead, had responded to this horror with the song "Revolution," affirming that "we all want to change the world, but when you talk about destruction, don't you know that you can count me out." The Beatles opposed revolt and spoke for the majority of their young listeners in expressing a positive frame of mind: "Don't you know it's gonna be all right." Lennon's bed-in was a natural extension of this outlook. Lying in bed and growing long hair was protest to be sure, but it was passive and pleasant rather than dogmatic and angry.

The Lennons hoped to send other, less obvious messages as well. Their passivity mocked middle-class values of hard work and self-denial, while their "Bed Peace, Hair Peace" credo mimicked the catchy jingles of Madison Avenue advertisers. As both the beneficiary and prisoner of intense media fixation, Lennon, more than most leftists, was keenly alert to the psychological power of image and marketing. He and Ono were very clear that they believed people were moved by slogans and gestures rather than ideas and doctrines. At the bed-ins, Lennon openly rejected intellectualism and just as unapologetically embraced the superficiality of consumer advertising. We live in an era of "gimmicks and salesmanship," he asserted to reporters, and it was necessary to sell peace just like companies sold soap. Eventually everyone, including housewives and children, would think about peace just as much as they did about toys or televisions.

In spite of all the talk about salesmanship, however, Lennon saw himself as a spiritual messenger to the masses, readily comparing himself to Christ as prophetic and persecuted. In 1966, he had precipitated the Beatles' worst public-relations debacle when he proclaimed offhandedly to a reporter that "Christianity will go. It will vanish and shrink. . . . [The Beatles] are more popular than Jesus now. I don't know which will go first—rock 'n' roll or Christianity."[1] American conservatives took offense, and the Fab Four faced vehement protests during their subsequent North American tour. Now again in 1969, Lennon compared himself to the suffering Christ in the "The Ballad of John and Yoko," recorded between his two bed-ins. The playful lyrics describe his troubled quest to arrange a simple marriage to Yoko in France and then in Gibraltar, followed by their honeymoon-demonstration in Amsterdam. Now looking more like the conventional image Jesus than ever, Lennon sang this about himself:

> Christ you know it ain't easy
> You know how hard it can be
> The way things are going
> They're going to crucify me.

Things were really not all that bad, of course, though Lennon and Ono did attract as much criticism as praise for their oddball nonconformity. Even his fellow Beatles were beginning to wonder. With his wire-rim glasses, long hair, beard, and "Hair Peace" mantra, Lennon had established himself as a counterculture guru, the icon of youthful idealism and hippie rebellion.

While the John and Yoko show played to the TV cameras and radio microphones, New York and London audiences flocked to see Gerome

Ragni and James Rado's hit musical *Hair,* a lyrical celebration of love, liberation, and indulgence inspired by San Francisco's famous Summer of Love in 1967. Few of the thousands who had attended *Hair* and also witnessed the Lennons' demonstration could have missed the common themes of hair and beds. The final words of the Broadway show's signature song could double as a description of John Lennon:

> My hair like Jesus wore it
> Hallelujah I adore it
> Hallelujah Mary loved her son
> Why don't my mother love me?
>
> Hair, hair, hair, hair, hair, hair, hair
> Flow it, show it
> Long as God can grow it
> My hair

Before Lennon and Ono, the composers of *Hair* had struck upon the idea that a bed was the ideal place to mount a revolt against social and sexual repression. "You can lay in bed," the chorus sang. "You can die in bed; you can pray in bed; you can live in bed; you can laugh in bed, you can give your heart, or break your heart in half in bed . . . You can lose in bed; you can win in bed. But never, never, never, never, never, never, never, never can you sin in bed!" Parental repression be damned. The bed—laziness, sexual pleasure, and hairy independence—was true liberation.

The language of hair and rebellion that Lennon and the hippies exploited had emerged over time, beginning with the beatniks and restless university students of the late 1950s. In 1958, when the society editor of the *Chicago Tribune* decided to investigate a rise in beards, she found that "scholars, ecclesiastics, artists, bums, musicians, and frontiersman have been among the few who kept whiskers from dying out entirely," but that they had been "joined by increasing numbers of young men."[2] The best place to find youthful beards on either side of the Atlantic was on a university campus.[3] A reporter who interviewed bearded students at Columbia University in New York City found one student who admitted that he might have been expressing "antipathy to the Madison Avenue man." An undergraduate anthropology major summed up the cavalier self-satisfaction of the newly bearded with his response: "I look better with than without it—though, for all I know, it may be a sign of rebellion, but don't ask against what, at the moment I am feeling much too good just sitting here in this warm, spring sun."[4]

Bearded men may not have been protesting against anything in particular, but they still offended employers and other guardians of the social order. Eric W. Hughes, an employee of a large company in New York City, described what happened to him in 1958 when he showed up for work after vacation with a well-trimmed beard. His vice president was outraged, insisting that no man with a beard could appear presentable and that customers would stop using the company's services. After several confrontations along these lines, Hughes resigned, declaring that he would not conform to the executive's "rigid and narrow conception of an employee—a bland, beardless face, obedient as a machine, immaculate black or gray suit, and outrageous necktie."[5] It was the sort of confrontation that occurred with growing frequency. When a young insurance company trainee in Swansea, Wales, decided to adopt a more distinguished appearance in 1962, he was coolly informed by his manager that beards "were not the thing in the insurance business." He took his case to the top-level management and was rejected. Like the New York office worker, the woolly Welshman decided to resign before he was fired.[6]

Narrow-minded though they might have been, bosses on both sides of the Atlantic were surely right that customers disapproved of facial hair. A national poll in the United States, conducted by the syndicated magazine *This Week* in 1957, asked respondents whether they thought beards or mustaches were attractive. The results were definitive: 81 percent of men and 85 percent of women said no to beards, with 73 percent of men and 80 percent of women also opposed to mustaches.[7] A shaved face might be bland and featureless, but that is what the public wished to see. In the London *Times* in 1960, the Gillette Company produced a full-page advertisement featuring a small essay by Siriol Hugh-Jones, an editor for London's *Vogue* magazine, who sang the praises of shaven men. The author drolly warned against the untrustworthiness of beards, asserting that "bearded men are often dangerous, independent to a fault, and prone to stay out all night without revealing incriminating evidence around the jawline." On the other hand, "with a clean-shaven man you know—so far as such a thing is possible with men—smoothly where you are."[8] Hugh-Jones was impishly witty, but she artfully wove together the stereotypical fears of beards with a contrasting admiration for "honest" hairlessness.

As the 1960s got under way, it was still possible to be lighthearted about faddish facial hair. When, however, it spread beyond the bounds of bohemia and academia, the guardians of propriety reacted with alarm. By the middle of the decade, male hair had become a contentious and emotional issue. It was as if all the aspirations and anxieties of the era were manifest in mops, mustaches, bangs, and beards.

The crisis at John Muir High School in Pasadena, California, in 1963 is a striking illustration of this social fear. Paul Finot was a government teacher with a history of challenging his superiors. He had experimented with a beard in the 1950s at another high school, but when he was hired at John Muir, he promised to remain shaved. When he changed his mind and grew a Vandyke, the principal removed him from the classroom and assigned him to be a private tutor to homebound students. It did not matter that the school was named for a famous naturalist whose marble bust graced the entry of the school in full-bearded glory. The principal was worried that the predominantly black and Hispanic student population might be tempted to imitate their teacher's insubordination. Finot sued the school district, claiming an infringement of his constitutional rights of personal liberty and free speech.

In court, the principal testified that Finot's beard made discipline more difficult because it "might encourage Negro students to wear mustaches."[9] It was a rare moment of truth. The real issue was the danger that young black men might feel independent and resist authority. When some residents objected to the racist implications of this statement, the board of education issued a public statement of support for the principal.[10] The court subsequently ruled in favor of the school, affirming its right to require that teachers and students remain shaved.

What happened next was indicative of developments in subsequent years in Los Angeles, and in Western culture generally. Finot appealed his loss, and in April 1967 a higher California court reversed the earlier judgment, unanimously affirming the rights of facial hair. The three-judge panel acknowledged that the principal's regulations against beards were reasonable, but they held that the school district had not established that the social value of its restrictions outweighed the infringement of personal liberty, nor had the board proved that it lacked other means to enforce a ban on student beards. "A beard, for a man, is an expression of his personality," the judges wrote. "On the one hand it has been interpreted as a symbol of masculinity, of authority and of wisdom. On the other hand it has been interpreted as a symbol of nonconformity and rebellion. But symbols, under appropriate circumstances, merit constitutional protection."[11] The justices thus acknowledged that beards imply rebellion but ruled that such rebellion should be permitted as protected political expression. There were similar decisions in other courts around this time. A worker at Douglas Aircraft in California also won his right to wear a beard at work, and in 1969 a labor arbitrator allowed facial freedom for New York City bus drivers.[12] Still, the question remained: how much hairy rebellion could society accept?

The answer was that the public was nearing the limits of its tolerance. Finot won his appeal in the spring of 1967, but if the judges had known what was coming, perhaps they would have thought twice. Later that year, the dam burst. The "Summer of Love" in San Francisco exhibited a heady mix of drugs, music, hair, and rebellion. In England, the world's most famous rock band, the Beatles, appeared for the first time with long sideburns and mustaches on the cover of their experimental, drug-fueled musical voyage, *Sgt. Pepper's Lonely Hearts Club Band*. Later in the year, on the cover of the American release of the single "Hello, Goodbye," George Harrison had advanced to a full dark beard. The Beatles were not innovators in this respect, but they were powerful role models. When John, Paul, George, and Ringo grew mop tops in 1965, the youth of the world followed suit. The pattern was repeated in 1967, starting with mustaches, then with beards.

"Today, hair power is second only to black power as a driving force of American life," announced *Newsweek* magazine in 1968.[13] By this time long hair and beards, along with flared jeans and tie-died shirts, had become the emblems of a new liberal romanticism not unlike that which swept Europe in the 1830s and 1840s. Once again the rising generation declared its dissatisfaction with the social order by showing a contrary face to the world. For nineteenth-century romantics, hair expressed discontent with the lack of democratic progress in postrevolutionary Europe. In the 1960s, hair expressed a similar frustration with limits on personal freedom in the postwar West. In early 1968, for example, an underground newspaper editor in Detroit admitted that he viewed his bushy mustache as a "revolutionary, romanticist accouterment."[14] "Rebellion begins on your face," antiwar activist Jerry Rubin declared.[15] In jail in for his part in the Chicago riots outside the Democratic National Convention in 1968, Rubin suffered the humiliation of a forced haircut and shave. "Amerika asks us," Rubin declared afterward (using a Russianized spelling of his country), "'Why the beards, hairy legs, arms and long hair?' but we ask Amerika, 'Why do you do the unnatural act of cutting your hair and shaving the beautiful hair off your face and body?' Our hair prevents Amerika from seeing its reflection in our face—therefore we are a living rejection of its misdeeds and violence—our hair is our picket sign and our Molotov cocktail. Our hair hurts/offends them more than anything we can say or do."[16]

While Rubin fulminated in jail, rock singer David Crosby—he of flying hair and expansive mustache—wrote and performed this hit song:

> Almost cut my hair
> It happened just the other day
> It was getting kind of long
> I could have said it was in my way
>
> But I didn't and I wonder why
> I feel like letting my freak flag fly
> And I feel like I owe it to someone . . .

As long-haired, bearded bandmate Graham Nash later explained, men with long hair were proclaiming that "they were into good music, a reasonable life, and they probably hated the government."[17] Even those who were not particularly political could show sympathy with the spirit of the times by forgoing scissors and blades. In fact, growing one's hair was an excellent substitute for activism. It was relatively easy to do, and yet it rarely failed to deliver a strong message of defiance.

The battle of hair was fought in thousands of ways in thousands of places. A survey conducted in 1967 by the Student Union at the University of Hamburg in Germany found that residents strongly disapproved of long hair and beards and blamed students for undermining social values and wasting taxpayer's hard-earned money.[18] Employers also continued to resist. A survey of members of the New York City Administrative Management Society in 1968 found that 95 percent of the firms represented had rules against long hair, 74 percent disallowed beards, 54 percent banned long sideburns, and 27 percent disallowed mustaches.[19] Advertising campaigns were another tactic. Billboards appeared in New England declaring "Beautify America, Get a Haircut." Inspired, the *Christian Science Monitor* urged America's barbers to expand this effort and publicize "the handsomeness of cut, groomed, clean hair."[20] Even revolutionary Cuba and its bearded leader got in on the act. In 1968, Fidel Castro's government announced that Havana University would enforce military discipline, including a ban on beards, mustaches, and long hair.[21]

Often, the emotions generated by beards were immediate and personal. Travel writer Richard Atcheson cultivated a full beard before venturing across America in 1970 and soon found himself in a world of hostility. "I have been up the Zambesi without a paddle; I have flapped through the sky in a disabled helicopter over the Great Barrier Reef; I have been menaced by slitty-eyed pimps of Tijuana . . . but I have never been as scared in distant places as I was while traveling in my own country, in the summer of 1970, while wearing long hair and a beard."[22] In restaurants, bars, and motels in the South and West, many reacted with fear and aggression to a stranger they condemned only for his nonconformist appearance.

When John Lennon decided to cut his hair and shave his beard in 1970, it was major news. While on retreat in Denmark, he decided to adopt a less spectacular look for himself, trimming way back. He told a friend that he felt like a change and hoped it would "enable me to move about anonymously."[23] The following year the beard was gone for good. He was clearly burdened by the exposure, publicity, and symbolic weight of his hair. Lennon was stepping back, but many others stepped into the breach.

Paul Breitner Kicks Up a Fuss

The championship match of the 1974 World Cup soccer final, between the Netherlands and West Germany in the Olympic Stadium in Munich, was unusual in several ways. It opened with the quickest score in tour-

12.2 Paul Breitner playing for Bayern München, 1980. Werner Otto/Alamy.

nament history when the Dutch converted a penalty kick before their opponents had even touched the ball. It also featured the hairiest athletes in World Cup history. Today, football stars are more likely to appear with bald heads than long hair, but players in the early 1970s dared long sideburns, mustaches, and flowing manes. German star Paul Breitner stood out even among this furry crowd. His full beard and halo of curly hair were his calling cards, winning him epithets like "Krauskopf" (frizzy head) and "Mister Vollbart" (Mr. Full-beard). Fans seated in the highest seats could instantly recognize the iconoclastic kicker with flaring hair to match his outsized ego.

Though the huge worldwide audience was surprised at how quickly the Dutch had jumped ahead, they were not surprised that the team in orange was winning. The artful and powerful Dutch had marched to the final by overwhelming their opponents, while the more pedestrian West Germans had just scraped by. The early goal was not the beginning of a rout, however, and Germany soon evened the score. A German player was tackled in the penalty box, and Breitner stepped forward to take the penalty kick. Without doubt or hesitation, he smoothly chopped the ball into the left corner of the net. He later claimed that there was no advance agreement as to who should take the ball, and that he had stepped up simply because he happened to be closest.[24] When the Germans scored again and rode the turnaround to victory, his place in football history was assured.[25]

Before he helped his country win the World Cup, Breitner was a star defender for Bayern Munich, famous in equal measure for his stellar play, outspoken politics, and outlandish looks. Portraits of communist leaders Mao Tse Tung and Che Guevara graced the walls of his home, and visiting interviewers recorded streams of invective against capitalist exploitation of workers and athletes. Breitner portrayed himself as a working-class victim in spite of earning three hundred thousand deutsche marks ($92,000 in 2013 dollars) when he was only twenty years old, and more than half a million ($800,000) by age twenty-five.[26] He was a rebel at heart, railing against the modern "circus" of professional football, in which players were bought and sold, and toured from city to city to entertain heckling crowds. In the name of freedom, he fought team management, and within a year of his World Cup triumph he pressed successfully for a transfer from Munich to Real Madrid in Spain. Afterward, the young star petulantly proclaimed that he no longer felt like a German.[27] Further disputes led to his departure from the national team, which played the 1978 tournament without him. On and off the field, Breitner was sure to generate plenty of drama.

For admirers and detractors alike, Breitner's rebellious hair suited his iconoclastic personality. His defiance of convention and authority took visible form in his afro and beard, which in turn reinforced the cultural association between hair and nonconformity. In 1981, as a rehabilitated Breitner prepared to rejoin the German squad for the next year's World Cup, Joachim Wachtel rhapsodized in *Das Buch vom Bart* (The Book of the Beard) that "the full beard has for years been part of the image of this outspoken troublemaker and playmaker who makes wonderful passes. . . . Hasn't he now, when he sometimes resembles a highly trained, wrathful Viking, become his true self, Paul Breitner? What would Breitner be today without a beard? The full beard is part of this personality, it emphasizes the spirit of contradiction, the sense of everything unfitting."[28]

Breitner may have evoked the Viking spirit, but he more obviously channeled bearded revolutionaries from Marx to Che Guevara, whose fearsome figures adorned his walls. Guevara's reputation as a fighter and martyr has long stood as a challenge to the establishment; from 1967 (the year of his death) to the present day, the most famous photograph of the Cuban revolutionary has been a ubiquitous icon of the left, deployed in an astonishing number of forms and circumstances. In fact, the often highly stylized image—showing Che's piercing glare, flowing hair, dark, wispy beard, and starred beret—is said to be the most reproduced image in the history of photography.[29] By 1968 students in Paris, Berlin, Prague, Berkeley, and elsewhere had rallied around it, and Guevara-style beards sprouted on thousands of young chins, sometimes complemented by Guevara-style berets.[30] Che and his fellow Cuban communists originally grew their beards in their jungle bases, and became known during the guerrilla war as *los barbudas*, or the bearded ones. After their victory in 1959, Fidel, Che, and other leaders kept their hair as a symbol of the continuing worldwide struggle against bourgeois capitalism. Castro reminded his victorious followers that "your beard does not belong to you. It belongs to the Revolution."[31] This did not apply to the younger generation, however. When long hair, along with Che's image, became symbols of youthful challenge to authority in the West, the revolutionary old guard feared Cuban youth would imitate their antiestablishmentarianism. Castro's government decreed in 1968 that Cuban university students would be subject to military training and discipline, including a ban on beards and long hair.[32] Revolution had become the status quo, and the youth were now expected to obey.

Paul Breitner's emulation of Guevara represented all that twentieth-century society admired and feared in facial hair: the allure of freedom and the specter of anarchy. As the 1970s adavnced, utopian dreams of the Age of Aquarius faded. The decline of radicalism, however, did not mean a return to smooth faces and crew cuts. On the contrary, long hair advanced into the mainstream, along with sideburns and facial fuzz, as a kind of physical residue of a decade of upheaval. With respect

12.3 Poster of Che Guevara, Cuba, 2004. Robert Harding World Imagery/Alamy.

to the general population, the high point of facial hair in the twentieth century was not the 1960s but the 1970s, when it escaped the confines of rock music festivals and war protests. Breitner was part of this trend, as athletes, performers, teachers, scientists, civil servants, and even the occasional businessman tested the limits of social tolerance.

One measure of this trend was the transformation of Oakland Athletics baseball team. In 1971, the *New York Times* reported that a few basketball and football players had mustaches and small beards, but that hockey and baseball players were entirely clean-shaven. A spokesman for the baseball commissioner's office declared that this was unlikely to change until someone is "is good enough to make a real test of it."[33] Little did that official know, that man was already on deck. Reggie Jackson, like Paul Breitner, was a rising star with plenty of ego. When Jackson appeared in the Oakland A's training camp in the spring of 1972 with a mustache, the opinionated owner, Charlie Finley, instructed his young slugger to remove it. When Jackson resisted, Finley applied some reverse psychology, figuring it would deny Jackson his uniqueness if he could coax some of his other players to grow their own mustaches.[34] Though Finley was an effective club owner, he was not skilled in psychological trickery. Instead of a shaved Jackson, he ended up with a team that looked like a throwback to the 1890s.

At this point, however, Finley's salesman instincts took over, and he found a way to make the best of an awkward situation. He proclaimed that his club would celebrate "Mustache Day" in honor of Father's Day, and any man with a mustache would be admitted free to the game. He even offered cash bonuses to any player who grew a mustache. Some players complied only grudgingly, while others were more enthusiastic. Jackson advanced to a goatee, but relief pitcher Rollie Fingers grabbed the most attention with a natty handlebar mustache that was to make him the most recognizable face in baseball. What started as a psychological tactic became a marketing stunt, and then something much more. The freewheeling, gutsy A's had discovered a new identity and esprit de corps that set them apart from other teams.

This was the beginning of a dynasty. The A's won the World Series that year and in the following two seasons. Baseball writers could not resist interpreting their rise as a harbinger of the times, when a spirit of liberal individualism supplanted corporate conformity. This was especially true of the 1972 World Series, which pitted a team one reporter described as the "bad guys with mustaches and beards" against the straitlaced "good guys, the clean shaven Cincys,"[35] or in the phrase of another columnist, "the Bikers against the Boy Scouts." Cincinnati's crisp, by-the-book appearance matched its playing style, and the Reds were heavily favored to win the championship. Against all expectation the A's took the first two of the four games needed for victory in their opponent's home stadium. "The Hairs put the clippers to the squares," enthused one reporter, "and these throwbacks from the Gay Nineties have struck a damaging blow against the clean-cut American boy image."[36]

The eventual triumph of the A's that year, and in the succeeding two years, lent new prestige to facial hair by connecting it with athletic success. In this way, sports heroes played a big role in promoting bolder hair across Europe and the United States. Besides Paul Breitner and the Oakland A's, notable figures ranging from Gerd Müller, another German soccer star, to Olympic swimmer Mark Spitz, American football quarterback Joe Namath, and basketball great Wilt Chamberlain, graced the pages of newspapers and magazines with attention-grabbing mustaches or beards. It is fair to say that the celebrity of these figures resided to some degree in their reputation as nonconformist individualists as well as successful athletes, with all the positive and negative implications this identity carried.

It was not to last, however, and by the 1980s, long hair, sideburns, and beards were in full retreat, trimmed back by a powerful reassertion of the shaven ideal. Once again, Breitner exemplified the trend. In 1982, he contradicted his own spirit of contradiction by accepting 150,000 marks to cut off his famous beard, leaving only a modest mustache, to appear in an aftershave advertisement. Who knew that lurking behind the curly-headed communist was a smooth-faced capitalist? Pitralon, the company that talked him into it, understood that this turnabout would cause a sensation, that the taming of Germany's most famous beard would be a signal triumph for both shaving and their bottom line. "There were a few big titles in his life," the advertisement copy read, "but only one aftershave, Pitralon." The ad continued, "Since he doesn't wear a full beard any longer, he grooms himself with Pitralon with Cedar Oil. He learned about it from his father. 'He knew what felt good,' says Breitner, and strokes his well-groomed chin."[37]

To those who were disappointed at this apparent sellout, Breitner was unapologetic, insisting that his beard was just a beard, after all. Advertising was part of his job as an entertainer, even if he was also proud that his fame had boosted Pitralon's market share dramatically.[38] In retrospect, Breitner had never been an idealist so as much as a pragmatist, and surely that is what he meant when he said that his beard was just a beard. Freedom of action was for him more important than political purity. The defiant beard could be sacrificed if the money was right. The soccer star's reasons for abandoning his defiant hair were in line with the thinking of the 1980s. At one level the decline of facial hair was a matter of money, particularly the need to hold down jobs. Employers and other social authorities had adopted what one journalist called the doctrine of "shavism,"[39] deploying various means, including the law, to tamp down hairy nonconformity. The demand for reliability, regularity, and cooperation was reasserting itself.

Most of the time, the fight about hair was informal and unspoken, but on occasion it was quite public and explicit, particularly in that most litigious of societies, the United States. In its courtrooms, the impetus to individuality confronted an increasingly firm reaction bent on shoring up the shaven order of things. The fall of facial hair in the 1980s was not a simply a shift in fashion, but the result of a deliberate campaign of suppression.

The purest examples of corporate pressure to eradicate hair came from the quintessential American companies McDonald's and Walt Disney, which had built their businesses on wholesomeness and efficient service. In the wake of 1960s and 1970s rebelliousness, both companies remained entrenched in the 1950s. McDonald's insisted that its employees "must impress customers as being 'All-American' boys."[40] These teenagers, all male until 1964, were instructed to bathe and shave every day and were required to wear black pants, shiny shoes, a neat haircut, and a friendly smile. Workers (called "hosts") at Disney theme parks were given detailed instruction on achieving the "Disney Look," which for men required shaved faces and "neat natural haircuts" that did not cover the ears. In an odd phrasing, the guidelines stated that beards and mustaches were not permitted, "however, deodorant is required"—as though deodorant were a substitute for facial hair.[41] No instructions could more clearly express the corporate ideal of sanitized manliness in twentieth-century America. Hairiness was the unacceptable complement of untidiness, irregularity, and unreliability.

The stringent proscriptions at McDonald's and Disney were simply the most notable examples of an increasingly powerful backlash against the advance of hair in America. The legal right of private employers to regulate the grooming of their employees was rarely questioned, and when it was, employers' authority was generally vindicated. The sizable minority of American workers in private industry protected by union contracts had access to arbitration to challenge facial hair rules, but even in these cases, arbiters tended to favor company interests over those of individuals. A scholarly review of labor arbitration cases in the United States between 1967 and 1979 revealed that almost all involved rules designed to preserve a company's public image, and that arbitrators were divided on the issue of facial hair.[42] Workers had the best chance of overturning restrictions if they could demonstrate that their appearance would not harm an employer's business interests. Those employed in noncompetitive businesses like utilities or urban transport were more likely to win sympathy. A split decision involving utility workers in San Francisco in 1976 best illustrates the uncertain standing of beards in the workplace. In this case the arbitrator ruled that a company ban on sideburns, mustaches, and goatees was unreasonable because they could be kept neat and tidy, but its rule against full beards was reasonable because this type of beard "by its natural effulgence is much more difficult to keep neat and well trimmed than the more localized growths." As a result, the arbitration board concluded, bearded men were "most likely to provoke the angry public reaction which the Company fears."[43] One might say this was splitting hairs, but it was clear that the concerns for a company's image carried more weight than the need to preserve personal freedom.

Public workers in the United States repeatedly turned to the courts to win their rights, but the results were not encouraging. By the early 1980s, the right of both public and private employers to regulate facial hair had become enshrined in practice and in law. Men living the in the "land of the free" did not, and still do not, have the right to grow their own hair.

In the late 1960s and early 1970s, several groups of public employees initiated or threatened legal action to protect their right to wear beards or mustaches, including bus drivers and firemen in New York City, postal employees in Van Nuys, California, firemen and a school bus driver in Chicago, railway workers on Long Island, and policemen in Suffolk County, New York. In the early stages of some of these cases, the rulings favored workers' rights. The postal workers in California, for example got the facial-hair ban reversed before the suit was actually filed, and the New York bus drivers won their case in arbitration. As time went on, however, and as these cases rose higher in the courts, workers suffered stinging defeats. The key case involved the policemen of Suffolk County, outside New York City. The police commissioner there had imposed a strict code in 1972 banning hair below the collar and all facial hair beyond short sideburns and small mustaches. The police union, with help from the American Civil Liberties Union, filed suit, citing First Amendment guarantees of free speech, as well as Fourteenth Amendment protections of personal liberty against state regulation. Suffolk County responded with the argument that hair regulations made their officers recognizable to the public as policemen and contributed to the esprit de corps of the force.

The Federal District Court in New York ruled that the policemen's suit had no merit, but the Second Circuit Court reversed this decision, agreeing that the policemen should indeed have the freedom to choose their own appearance. The judges on the panel ruled that the county had failed to demonstrate a compelling public interest in infringing a policeman's personal liberties. Suffolk County then appealed to the United States Supreme Court, which decided the case, *Kelley v. Johnson*, in April 1976.

Writing for the six-member majority, Justice William Rehnquist rejected the police union's arguments. He denied that there was an absolute right to wear any hair style and insisted that it was the plaintiffs' responsibility to prove "that there is no rational connection between the regulation . . . and the promotion of safety of persons and property."[44] This was a far more difficult standard than that proposed by the appeals court, which had insisted that the county respect personal liberty unless it could demonstrate a "genuine public need."[45] With this more stringent test in mind, Rehnquist and the majority concluded that Suffolk County's desire to make its police officers "readily recognizable to members of the public," and its interest in promoting an esprit de corps, were both reasonable motives for establishing grooming regulations.[46] Two justices, Thurgood Marshall and William Brennan, dissented entirely. They held to the logic of the lower court, discounting the argument that long hair or beards would either damage morale or make a policeman less recognizable as an officer of the law.

As one would expect, policemen around the country objected to this ruling against them. The president of the New York City Patrolman's Benevolent Association complained that "this makes the police officer a second-class citizen because you are taking away his fundamental right of choice."[47] Many noted the irony that Justice Rehnquist himself, with his bushy sideburns and modish haircut, fell outside Suffolk County's grooming standards. When this was pointed out to him, the justice responded dismissively that, fortunately for him, he "never wanted to work for the Suffolk County Police Department anyway." Though this ruling technically applied to only to one police commissioner's rules, it was obvious that it would have much wider implications. A reporter for the *Los Angeles Times* immediately recognized that the Court's ruling was so broad that it would preserve virtually all grooming and dress codes regulating the nation's eleven million public employees.[48]

One unsurprising effect of the decision was to embolden police commissioners, fire chiefs, school principals, and other public officials to crack down on employees who were insufficiently exacting with their razors. In 1977, for example, the by-the-book police chief in Englewood, New Jersey, determined that the twenty-five bearded men on his eighty-one-man force needed to shave. "My face was mighty cold out there," one officer complained after a January patrol without his usual covering.[49] In the decades following the *Kelley* decision, federal courts affirmed and extended its application. A Texas case in 1978 and a Louisiana case in 1982 affirmed the power of school districts to enforce beard bans on employees as well as students. The Louisiana case, *Domico v. Rapides Parish School Board*, arose from a suit filed by bearded teachers and bus drivers who alleged that their civil rights were being violated. A federal circuit court applied the *Kelley* standard in ruling for the school board, concluding that "in the high school environment, a hairstyle regulation is a reasonable means of furthering the school board's undeniable interest in teaching hygiene, instilling discipline, asserting authority, and compelling uniformity."[50] Other rulings limited the rights of public employees in other categories, notably two cases from Arkansas involving a state park naturalist (1983) and emergency medical technicians (1992).[51]

The *Kelley* ruling passed another major test in 1992 when Massachusetts consolidated its state police forces into a single department. The new chief, in his first general order, banned all facial hair. Six of the more than 250 men who were forced to abandon their mustaches filed suit claiming, like the Suffolk County officers before them, that the state was violating their constitutional freedoms "by forcing them to sacrifice an integral aspect of their personal identities."[52] Unfortunately, the legal precedents were strongly against them. Noting the very low bar set by the Supreme Court for state agencies, a district judge ruled that the ban on facial hair easily met the reasonability test. The Supreme Court's judgment on facial hair held firm as decision after decision piled up against individual choice. The sole exception in all this litigation was a victory for public university instructors. It would seem that one reason it is common to see professors wearing beards is that they are among the few public employees who can do so by law.

The fading of hair toward the end of the twentieth century coincided with a renewed crisis of male confidence about masculinity. A notable expression of this trend in the United States was the so-called mythopoetic men's movement, inspired by poet Robert Bly and abetted by Jungian theorists and psychotherapists such as James Hillman, Robert L. Moore, and Michael Meade. Bly's 1990 book *Iron John* served as the manifesto of this movement and was for many years a best-seller. *Iron John* was an extended meditation on a Grimm Brothers folktale about the hairy Wild Man, which Bly took as a metaphor for the male psyche. Growing up, he wrote, men need to acquaint themselves with the wild man within themselves, in order to release positive "Zeus energy" — the strength, joy, and resilience of their masculine souls. The hairy man is frightening, "even more so now, when the corporations do so much work to produce the sanitized, hairless, shallow man."[53] This link between masculinity and hair permeates Bly's book. In one passage, he describes the Wild Man as the positive side of male sexuality: "The hair that covers his whole body is natural like a deer's or a mammoth's. He has not been clean shaven out of shame, and his instincts have not been so suppressed as to produce the rage that humiliates women."[54]

For the most part, this celebration of hair remained metaphorical. There were Wild Man weekend retreats, at which men were encouraged to bang drums, dance spontaneously, eat rabbit stew, tell stories, and cry, but growing actual hair was not much discussed or especially encouraged. Robert Moore had an impressive beard, but other movement leaders, including Reade, Hillman, and Bly himself, remained shaven. They were like the medieval monks who spoke of the "inner beard" as a spiritual rather than actual expression of manliness. As Bly said, the aim "was not to *be* the Wild Man, but to *be in touch with* the Wild Man."[55]

Though oriented to the left, Bly's movement was largely apolitical and not, in spite of its rhetoric, inclined to use hair as a form of personal expression. Even so, there was still life in leftist hair at the end of the century, particularly in Europe.

Frank Dobson Just Says No

When Frank Dobson, Labour Party candidate for mayor of London in 2000, was urged by party handlers to shave off his beard, he refused. He was losing badly, and a new look was suggested as a strategy for improving his personal appeal with voters. "I told them to get stuffed," Dobson told the press, "because, quite frankly, I am not in the image business. With me, what you see is what you get. If you don't like what you see, don't vote for me, but listen to what I've got to say."[56]

Dobson's defiant stand reflected several realities of political life at the end of the twentieth century: Europeans were less subject to "shavism" than their American counterparts, yet even in Europe the pressure to abandon beards was increasingly strong. Many prominent public figures, particularly on the left, persisted in wearing emblems of resistance to corporate conformity. This was true especially in France, where the victory in 1981 of Francois Mitterrand and the French Socialist Party opened the way for a small beard movement in the halls of power. Several leaders, including defense minister Charles Hernu, labor minister Jean Auroux, and more than thirty deputies in the new governing party—about 12 percent of the Socialist representation—wore beards.[57] At the time of the election, a writer for *Le Monde* noted the collar beards of several leaders, which had gained popularity during

12.4 Frank Dobson, M.P., Secretary for Health, 1998. Allstar Picture Library/Alamy.

the 1960s among Left Bank professors and intellectuals, and persisted
in spite of "advances in metal and electrical appliances."[58] The correspondent was bemused by the rise of a "Republic of professors."

As these jokes indicate, however, political beards hardly generated
wide admiration, even in France. The pressure against them was strong
and growing stronger in the final decades of the century. The election
of the British Conservative party in 1979 spelled the end of facial hair
in the British government for the next eighteen years, because the Conservative leader, Margaret Thatcher, was adamantly against it. The reign

of the Conservatives was finally ended in 1997 with the rise of the centrist "Lew Labor" party under the leadership of Tony Blair. New Labor promised to preserve some of the probusiness reforms of the Thatcher years while shifting gently to the left on social spending and other measures. One of the ways that politicians of the British left indicated to the public that they were ready for power in late 1990s was by abandoning their beards, so as to appear more like the blandly dependable politicians of the right. As the election of 1997 approached, the *Guardian* noted that "'New Labour, New Shave,' seems to be the fashion among rising stars."[59] Peter Mandelson, the formerly mustachioed Labour campaign manager and a future cabinet member, heeded surveys that revealed the unpopularity of facial hair with voters and convinced others to follow his smooth example, including Stephen Byers, soon to become secretary of trade for transport, and Geoffrey Hoon, who rose to defense secretary. Another Labour leader, Alistair Darling, though rightfully proud of his full, black beard, got rid of it after the election victory and his appointment as chief secretary of the treasury. A small band of three, David Blunkett, Robin Cook, and Frank Dobson, stuck with principle and kept their faces as they were.

Looking every bit like "Old Labour," Dobson was not Blair's first choice as Labour candidate for the newly created post of mayor of Greater London in 2000. Nor was he the first choice of the London electorate. Their favorite was Ken Livingstone, "Red Ken," a leftist with an outsize personality (and no facial hair). Londoners like outrageous personalities (they have since elected the even more eccentric Boris Johnson to replace Livingstone), and Dobson just didn't inspire any excitement. They also saw Dobson, in spite of his facial hair, as a functionary of puppet-master Tony Blair. In fact, the leak about Dobson's rebuttal of the suggestion to shave may have been a last-ditch ploy to prove to voters that he was *not* Blair's puppet.[60] If so, it did not work, and Dobson went down to crushing defeat.

The European battle over hair took on fresh urgency in 1991 as the opening of the Euro-Disney theme park, near Paris, approached. Euro-Disney was a wholesale transplantation of American popular culture into the heart of Europe, replete with everything that most annoyed the European intellectual elite, namely, the commercialization of culture, crass consumerism, and corporate standardization. Applicants for the twelve thousand jobs at the new park were surprised by regulations requiring "cast members," including ride operators and ticket takers, to smile constantly for the visitors. There was also general incredulity at Disney's strict no-alcohol policy. And then there was Disney's squeaky-clean dress code—spelled out in a detailed pamphlet titled "Le Euro Disneyland Look"—which, among many other regulations, specified short hair for men and a complete ban on facial hair.

To many of the French, already deeply suspicious of American corporate methods, the regulation of women's makeup and men's hair was an assault on individual liberty and the dignity of labor. How could the Americans be so inconsiderate of French cultural values? Disney officials assured the French public that they were well aware of the differences between France and the United States, but insisted that the Disney brand relied upon presenting an American-style experience for its customers. Without the clean-cut American dress code, the American director of hiring explained, "we wouldn't be presenting the Disney product that people would be expecting."[61] Unconvinced, labor unions filed an official complaint. In a local court, Disney went down to defeat, and in a final judgment in 1995, a Paris court slapped a small fine on the former executive directly responsible for the dress code. In the meantime, the code was withdrawn, though one union still complained that the American standards were being enforced indirectly.[62]

The Walt Disney Company came to realize that a more subtle approach would be less irritating, and generally just as effective. On the other hand, it learned that not all was lost if a few concessions were made. A greater variety of hair was a reasonable price to pay for labor peace, just as abandoning the prohibition of alcohol was a reasonable price to pay for larger crowds at the admission gates. Even so, it took another eighteen years for Disney to loosen the proverbial collar back home at its US parks, and to permit modest beards, so long as they maintained "an overall neat, polished and professional look."[63] While hardly a ringing endorsement for beards, this change signaled, more than any other, a true shift in attitudes as the century came to a close. If the most antihair company in the most antihair country could bend, even a little, one could say that "shavism" was finally waning, leaving both leftist hair and the reaction against it in a diminished condition as the new century began.

13

POSTMODERN MEN

In the twenty-first century, facial hair has attained greater social presence than in the previous century, but not to the extent that we can call it a new beard movement. The shaved face remains the established norm for sociable manliness. A bearded man must still face the slings and arrows of disapproval and distrust. Men still do not enjoy a fundamental right to wear facial hair, as civil and private institutions continue to enforce grooming codes. The primary statement a man makes with a beard, therefore, is that he autonomous, free to do as he pleases. Artists, musicians, and professors favor beards for this reason.

There are, of course, exceptions. For members of traditionalist religious groups, facial hair makes a statement about collective autonomy from mainstream society, not individual liberty within the group. And some men have more specific goals than the exercise of personal freedom. Culturally speaking, there are today four basic motives for growing beards besides personal autonomy: gender bending, social nonconformity, religious identification, and a special quest. These objectives often overlap in various ways. Men, for example, who are attempting to redefine gender, or to identify with a religious minority, are in many respects nonconformists.

The variety and uses of beards in the new millennium tells us a great deal about what men are thinking and how they are taking advantage of their hair to shape new understandings of manliness in a fluid and pluralist world. One recent formulation of masculine identity, for example, is the "metrosexual," a gender-bending type who finds self-expression in a carefully styled appearance.

Beckham Bends the Rules

On a sunny San Francisco day in June 2008, soccer star and celebrity icon David Beckham unveiled, on the front of Macy's department store, a massive, seventy-five-foot-tall photograph of himself posing in designer underwear. Thousands of fans and shoppers cheered and shrieked as his sultry, stubble-faced gaze was revealed, followed by a muscled and hairless body, bulging in tight Armani briefs. Even Beckham himself was impressed, confessing in his blog that he "was amazed by the huge billboard poster outside Macy's department store, but even more amazed by the amount of people who turned up to see it!"[1] The unveiling was yet another demonstration of Beckham's marketing star power, and another bold statement of his particular brand of masculine self-promotion.

Male athletes like Beckham have always put their bodies on display for the entertainment of others, but they have generally been admired for what they do on the field rather than how they look off it. Beckham was different. He wanted people to admire his body and his looks, and he positively invited discussion about the merits and demerits of a man's physical appearance in a way that was once reserved for women. The controversy in the tabloids about Beckham's suspiciously large bulge (was it real?) echoed past disputes about women's skin or breasts. Surely it was padded or Photoshopped? And what about those smooth, hairless legs? What sort of man would subject himself to the slow and painful waxing required to clean up the nether areas around those brief briefs? The answer is, a man who, according to Beckham himself, is willing to embrace an element of femininity in himself. At the launch of the Armani campaign he declared, "I always wear the Armani underwear. I've worn it in every game since joining the [Los Angeles] Galaxy . . . because it is comfortable. It's masculine but it has that feminine side."[2] Bulging but smooth: that is one model for masculine balance in the twenty-first century.

13.1 David Beckham posing in Armani underwear advertisement, San Francisco, 2008. Photo by Keith Parish.

Beckham's eagerness to bare himself as a sex symbol, and his unabashed passion for fashion, shopping, and grooming, cut against masculine stereotypes. For more than two hundred years, since the eclipse of wigs, silk stockings, and lace collars, the manly code rejected consumer indulgence as a form of feminine weakness and indiscipline. Luxuries made men soft and threatened to undermine the virtues of toughness, self-reliance, and hard work that helped a man fulfill his role as doer and provider.[3] Beckham didn't seem to care about all of this. If dressing well—and undressing well—meant that he was in some sense "feminine," he was willing to accept that. He was, in other words, happy to bend more than his trademark free kicks to attain a goal. He also directed the conversation about masculinity and the male body in new, and often controversial, directions.

Trend spotters and social commentators fumbled around for new words to describe men like Beckham. Peter Hartlaub, the pop culture critic for the *San Francisco Chronicle* who interviewed Beckham during his visit, described him as "man-tastic," particularly in respect to his crisp clothes and stylish facial hair. Years before, the British cultural critic Mark Simpson had coined a different term that was to prove more enduring. In a widely read 2002 article in the online magazine *Salon*, Simpson "outed" Beckham as neither straight nor gay but "metrosexual."[4] Simpson was responding to Beckham's recent publicity hat trick, when, while captain of the English national football team, he appeared simultaneously on the covers of three prominent nonsports British publications, the women's monthly *Marie Claire*, the British version of *GQ*, and the gay magazine *Alliance*.[5] The distinguishing feature of a metrosexual, according to Simpson, was his love of being looked at. This reversed the usual gender dynamic, in which men look at, and objectify, women. For Simpson, this reversal was not a good thing; it constituted a retreat to vanity, consumerism, and objectivization, in effect introducing into normative masculinity the worst aspects of traditional femininity and homosexuality.

Simpson and other observers agreed that metrosexual eagerness to impress was driven in part by the increasing power of women. Men who wish to attract independent women must, as one group of sociologists put it, "learn some new tricks," in terms of grooming, appearance, and attention to their feelings.[6] Both the cause and the effect of these shifts in gender behavior have discomfited many men and women. Simpson viewed metrosexuality as a form of masculine surrender, and others have voiced their consternation as well.[7] Morgan Spurlock's 2012 documentary *Mansome*, for example, presents a critical and sardonic assessment of male vanity. One anonymous woman opines on-screen that "I think if you try really hard, it looks really bad." At another point a man declares, "Looking good for yourself . . . I find really fucked up."

More sympathetic observers, agreeing that codes of manliness are moving in a more feminist or queer direction, have seen the shift, and Beckham's role in it, in a positive light. Rather than casting Beckham as a poster child for narcissist self-indulgence, these critics have focused on other aspects of his personality that depart from the hypermasculine culture of elite sports. Rather than boozing it up with the "lads," for example, Beckham has preferred shopping and vacations with wife and children. By all appearances, he has abandoned the impulsive misogyny and homophobia of the locker room and pub, expressing instead a perfect ease with his role as a sex symbol for both women and gays. His "feminine side," the smooth nudity, the smoldering gaze, and even an occasional willingness to wear makeup and nail polish, are deliberate affronts to normative masculinity. Beckham biographer Ellis Cashmore enthuses that the soccer star has modeled a life in which "traditional insecurities over sexuality melt away" and "the traditionally rigid male/ female divide disappears."[8] The academic David Coad goes still further, arguing that at the core of metrosexuality is the idea that power can be shared between the sexes, rather than being seen exclusively as a sign of virility or as naturally pertaining to the male sex."[9] In this sense, the new urban man is a progressive response to modern feminism. Still other academics have looked ahead, fantasizing about a new and improved version of metrosexuality to come. Sociologists Marian Salzman, Ira Matathia, and Ann O'Reilly have trumpeted the coming of the "übersexual," a straight man like George Clooney who has all the sensitivity of the metrosexual without the self-doubt and narcissism.[10]

Is metrosexuality regression or progress? As with other examples of masculine reconfiguration, it is helpful to consider what hair can tell us about meanings and motives. Simpson himself made disparaging reference to the shaving of face and body as signs of male renunciation and passivity. If, however, Beckham is to be taken as the quintessence of metrosexuality, beards play an important part in the image of the new man. At the time the steamy Beckham banner was unveiled in San Francisco, journalist Peter Hartlaub reported that Beckham's hair was "cut short and simple, ceding attention to his long stubble, which covers his face except for two Band-Aid-size vertical stripes shaved clean on either side of his goatee."[11] As a male sex symbol, Beckham has devoted a great deal of thought to every aspect of his presentation, and almost always sported some form of facial hair. A survey of his style over the years confirms that though the length and shape of his beard have constantly changed, it is as important to him to have hair on his face as it is to remove it everywhere else.

The metrosexual is not averse to the beard. Far from it. Michael Flocker and other metrosexual style gurus have encouraged its growth even as they urge careful and extensive removal of body hair. "Beards, goatees, soul patches and moustaches provide endless options," Flocker has instructed, "but should always be kept reasonably trimmed and cleanly edged. Even when going for a casually stubbled look, shaving beneath your jaw line is a subtle way to keep it looking clean and strong."[12] As Beckham and other borderline metrosexual celebrities such as Brad Pitt and George Clooney demonstrate, beards have enjoyed a small renaissance on the faces of fashionable men in the early years of this millennium.

There are several reasons beards have made a comeback on the toney streets of major European and American cities. To an extent, heterosexuals like Beckham have taken their cue from urban gays, many of whom turned to beards in recent decades to help counteract cultural affiliations between homosexuality and effeminacy.[13] Men in touch with their "feminine side" can affirm their masculine side with their hair. Another reason for metrosexual men to grow moderate facial hair has been the sense that it might make them more sexually alluring. Studies of women's attitudes, discussed in chapter 1, bear this out. Many young women have expressed a preference for men with short or stubbly beards. Not too much, mind you, but also not too little. This has been Beckham's approach precisely. Whether fashion celebrities like Beckham have influenced female respondents in psychological studies, or the other way around, there does seem to be something of a consensus of the sexes on this score.

This is not the whole of it, however. The metrosexual beard is extensively groomed and is treated much like clothing. As with clothing, the wearer can shape and experiment, trying out different effects from month to month or year to year. For this reason there has been no single metrosexual style for facial hair. Change and variation are the guiding principles. In the late nineteenth century, by contrast, men favored beards as a sign of unchanging masculine qualities, and a beard's natural fullness was its most helpful and popular quality. The fashionable men of our day have a different agenda. They wish to please as well as impress, and to draw attention rather than deflect it. A modern man uses his hair to project individual distinctiveness more than masculine privilege. In this respect, the metrosexual beard is a paradox: while a well-groomed beard is undoubtedly manly, it also epitomizes a concern with looking good for oneself and for others that Beckham and others view as expressive of a man's "feminine side." To some extent this paradox arises from the contradictions of uncritically labeling behaviors as "feminine" or "masculine." It is not necessary, after all, for sexual display to be feminine, and that is really the point Beckham and his kind have been trying to make. The carefully maintained beard bridges the theoretic gender divide.

While urban men have experimented with facial hair, they have relentlessly fought body hair. It is tempting to think, as Mark Simpson has, that this antipathy represents a feminine quality, but readers of this book will know better. Body shaving, since Eugen Sandow, is all about muscle. In his *Metrosexual Guide to Style*, Michael Flocker enunciates this principle, urging his readers to trim their chest, stomach, and underarm hair "to enhance a well-defined body." Advertisements for home exercise equipment, he notes, consistently show the "before" look as chubby and hairy, the "after" as muscular and "miraculously hairless."[14] In Spurlock's film *Mansome*, Shawn Daivari, an American professional wrestler of Middle Eastern descent, is shown laboriously shaving his extensive body hair to meet the expectations of his television audience. Admiring his newly shaved torso, Daivari explains that "it gives somewhat of the illusion of being in better shape than I actually am."[15] Shaving is about the shape of the body and also, in a classical Greek sense, the vitality of youthfulness. The metrosexual's interest in body shaving is not essentially feminine, or really new, but rather, an infusion of old ideals into the bloodstream of popular culture.

Cultivating facial hair while eradicating body hair, then, is a coherent approach to enhancing masculine physical presentation. The beard can help, but muscles are important too. To these the metrosexual adds still another form of masculine display, as evidenced by Beckham's famous bulge. As this aspect of male anatomy has drawn more attention, it too has become subject to hair removal. So-called Boyzillians, or depilation of "crack, back, and sack," have become increasingly popular in the new millennium. In 2012, the *New York Times* reported the increasing popularity of men's Brazilians in New York: "It's the gay community, it's the straight community, it's very conservative guys, it's very liberal guys," said the president of a prominent depilation provider. "All different age groups are coming in. It's much, much bigger than we ever thought."[16] Sales of specially designed body grooming electric razors have also surged. Surveys in Germany have found that about a fifth of young men regularly remove their pubic hair, declaring it dirty and unhygienic.[17] An editor at British *GQ* theorizes that "there's a cleaner look that is really present in fashion today, and people pick that up in their subconscious."[18] Another salon director states the point more graphically: hair removal around the genitals "accentuates it, because there's nothing to obscure the, you know, implement down there."[19] The competition between hair and genitals has joined that between hair and muscle. To remove hair is to remove that which might obscure the form underneath, even if, in the case of Beckham's giant poster, that "form" is covered by designer underwear.

This tripartite focus of physical presentation—face, muscle, and genitalia—reflects the urgent need many men feel to shore up self-confidence and win approval. The "great renunciation" of the early nineteenth century may finally have run its course. Two hundred years ago, European and American men abandoned colorful clothing and reduced physical display to a minimum—except for beards—in order to reduce competition between themselves and solidify the distinction between the sexes. Drably outfitted men stood as observers and judges of elaborately adorned women who competed with one another for male attention. To some extent, this distinction has lessened, and women have come to embrace their new role as observers. It is telling, for example, that the most famous moment of the popular 1995 BBC production of Jane Austen's *Pride and Prejudice* was a thoroughly modern display of the male body. Modern women thrilled to see Darcy's plunge into a pond and his subsequent wet-shirted encounter with Elizabeth. Even this demure display would have been unthinkable in Austen's time, but it helped make the actor Colin Firth an international sex symbol.

Contemporary urban men, labeled metrosexual or not, have come to embrace a sexually liberated and consumer-oriented modernity. In discovering that modest beards can be just as attractive as well-defined muscles, they have given facial hair fresh validity. By the same token, they have redefined the beard as the sign of a sensitive sophisticate rather than a stolid patriarch, bending normative masculinity into territory previously delimited as feminine.

This move has not been easy or universally accepted. On the contrary, there seems in recent years to have been a retreat from this sort of urbane refinement. So-called hipsters and lumbersexuals have offered a different approach to bearded manliness. "Lumbersexual" is a term introduced in 2014 to describe urban men who favor plaid shirts, heavy boots, and full beards.[20] The term is a play on "metrosexual" and suggests something similar in respect to the urban straight man's self-conscious effort to find a convincing display of manliness. The metrosexual is sporty and trim, while the lumbersexual is outdoorsy and burly. Both are very deliberate about their looks, but the lumbersexual and the similarly bearded hipster aspire to appear unselfconscious, as though free of consumerist narcissism. The booted and full-bearded man adopts the nineteenth-century logic of historic and natural manliness, showing greater concern to dispense with femininity than to please women. At least one avowed lumbersexual has acknowledged in print that the lumbersexual look, along with the hipster and gay "bear" styles upon which it is based, is a carefully calculated effort to sharpen the line between the masculine and feminine in a shifting gender landscape.[21]

Many gay men have felt a similar urgency to reinforce their masculine bona fides by combatting cultural associations between homosexuality and femininity.[22] For two groups in particular, "bears" and "leathermen," beards have become an essential accessory, along with clothes, pastimes, and sexual practices, in cultivating a sort of gay hypermasculinity. Both of these communities emerged in the aftermath of the Stonewall riots in New York City in 1969, when homosexuals marched out of the political shadows and staked their claim to recognition and acceptance. Bears are men who associate themselves with unambiguously manly, working-class traits, including flannel shirts, guns, and pickup trucks. Their periodicals and retreats appeal particularly to heavy, hairy men, and they glory in these qualities that are often denigrated by the larger society. By the same token they fuse same-sex attraction with these normative qualities, effectively challenging both stereotypes.

One of the most important gatherings of leathermen is the International Mr. Leather convention, held in Chicago since 1979. In recent years it has attracted some twenty thousand attendees. As one journalist describes them, these are generally gay men who are "white-collar but prefer their sex with a leather collar."[23] They also overwhelmingly prefer beards, and their annual procession in the city's Grant Park has long been a notable display of masculine hair. With both hair and leather, this gay subculture evokes the ethos of biker gangs, including the association with violence (rough sex) and risk-taking. Like metrosexuals, bears and leathermen make an ostentatious display of the sexualized male body, positioning men as objects of sexual desire rather than simply the ones who desire. In each case, the fortress of masculine decorum and restraint is breached, though the extent to which it constitutes liberation for men or women is still a matter of debate.

A still more radical use of facial hair to upend gender boundaries is the arresting style of Austrian cross-dresser Thomas Neuwirth, who triumphed in the 2014 Eurovision Song Contest in his drag persona, Conchita Wurst. Conchita's most remarkable feature, besides her sequined dress, earrings, long hair, and eyelash extensions, was her thick, dark beard. The confusion of masculine and feminine provided a striking visual counterpoint to the theme of personal transformation in her song "Rise Like a Phoenix." Conchita swept to victory, winning votes even from conservative eastern European countries. In this venue, at least, Europe seemed ready to embrace her statement of personal liberation, particularly liberation from gender norms. "It was not just a victory for me," she said on her return to Austria, "but a victory for those people who believe in a future that can function without discrimination and is based on tolerance and respect."[24]

The challenges to the social and sexual order presented by metrosexuals, gays, and transvestites are just the sort of thing that frightens social conservatives. Ironically, conservative men's anger has put them in a contrarian mood to the extent that they too are experimenting with nonconformist beards. Even in the most hostile ground for facial hair, evangelical America, a new face of masculinity has emerged to challenge the right of urban metrosexuals and gays to define what it means to be a man. Pastor Rick Warren and TV star Phil Roberston, both Southern Baptists, are prominent representatives of two overlapping, if partially contradictory, sorts of bearded nonconformity within the heart of Christian conservatism.

Rick Warren Hosts a Contest

In the spring of 2013, Rick Warren, the goateed Baptist preacher, invited the men of his twenty-three-thousand-member Saddleback Church in California to grow facial hair and submit photographs of themselves to win a spot in the finals of a beard contest. In July, Warren himself, identified by many as America's most influential pastor, would hand out hundred-dollar gift certificates to those with "the most magnificent" and "the most pathetic" beards.[25] The occasion for this "Beardup Saddleback" hoopla was a visit by "Duck Commander" Phil Robertson, the heavily bearded patriarch of the hit reality television series *Duck Dynasty* and a noted proponent of conservative evangelical piety. After that day's services, church members were treated to a party featuring Cajun food, zydeco music, a crawfish cooking demonstration, and *Duck Dynasty* prize giveaways, as well as the beard awards.

The Southern Baptist tradition, of which both Warren and Robertson are a part, has a long history of resistance to male hair. Now, paradoxically, conservatives were eagerly experimenting with this countercultural style. The simplest explanation for this about-face would be that long hair and beards are no longer considered liberal or rebellious, and that the Saddleback beard contest, like the fulsome beards of the *Duck Dynasty* men, were more stunt than statement. But that answer would only be partly true. Beards, especially large ones, retain their daring and nonconformist quality, and this is an important part of their appeal to conservative as well as liberal men. A generation ago, conservative evangelicals began appropriating rock music into their worship. Now,

13.2 Rick Warren, 2005. Aurora Photos/Alamy.

finally, it is time for hair. Is it possible to be a conservative rebel? Why not? That is precisely what many young American men aspire to be today.

Warren and Robertson have, to a great extent, attained the influence they have by embracing a dynamic and contrarian spirit (along with beards). In the early 1970s, the teenage Rick Warren was the good son of a Baptist preacher who aspired to be a preacher himself, but on his own, decidedly contemporary terms. When he started a Christian club at his high school in 1970, he was guided by the example of the "Jesus Movement," which adapted the style and expression of the 1960s rock and roll culture to conservative religious sensibilities.[26] Warren looked every bit the Christian John Lennon, long-haired, with wire-rim glasses, soulfully strumming his guitar to contemporary folk rock tunes. His semi-hippie style did not sit well with everyone, however. Still in high school, he appeared before a review committee of his home church to obtain his lay preaching license, the first step toward a career as a Southern Baptist minister. His answers to questions about his salvation experience and doctrinal beliefs were satisfactory, but the senior pastor objected to his appearance. It seemed to him that the gangly young man looked more like a war protester than a Baptist minister.

Warren defended himself; his hair was not a political statement, he said, but a youthful style that would help him connect with people his age.[27] The committee saw his point and granted him a license to preach. In later years, Warren remained committed to presenting a modish California appearance. In the 1980s and 1990s, while building his new church in suburban Los Angeles into one of America's most successful megachurches, he reduced the length of his hair but added a mustache, and later a goatee. In the 2000s, a closet full of Hawaiian shirts further enhanced his presentation as the laid-back man of God.

All this was a subtle way of breaking conventional boundaries and suggesting that he and his church would not be bound to outmoded customs. Warren's approach was well suited to the denizens of southern California's disconnected maze of colorless subdivisions, cut off from their historical and communal roots. Warren offered a conservative faith that seemed attuned to modern conditions. His choice was not simply a matter of style, nor was it limited to him. Sociologist John D. Boy has incisively observed that a new crop of bearded evangelicals emerged around the turn of the century, eager to exchange the rigid doctrines and codes of the past for uplift and "conversation."[28] "The goateed proselytizer," Boy opines, "appears more of an authentic man of God than his well-groomed, overly politicized, GOP-loving fore-bears." True to form, Warren has demonstrated less patience with the right-wing fixation on family and sexual morality, and directed more attention to wider social problems such as poverty and global warming. It was this unconventionality that inspired newly elected president Barack Obama to invite Warren to deliver the opening prayer at his 2008 inauguration.

Warren and Duck Commander Phil Robertson are not exactly birds of a feather, but they are alike in more than just their affinity for facial hair. In their different ways, both offer resistance to modern, secular culture. Robertson, the camouflaged guru of cornpone wisdom, abandoned the path of conventional respectability as a young man, though his departure from the straight and narrow was, like his beard, more dramatic than Warren's. Robertson was the star quarterback on the Louisiana Tech football team for two years in the late 1960s, skillful enough to keep future hall-of-famer Terry Bradshaw on the bench. With his square jaw and crew cut, Robertson was the picture of the middle-American ideal, but he quit football because it interfered with what he cared about most: duck hunting. Rejecting the socially approved and richly rewarded model of sporting manliness, he opted instead for the leave-me-alone masculinity of the outdoors. The problem for Robertson was that he let himself get lost in the wilderness, so to speak. Married, with young children, he fell into a self-defeating pattern of carousing and alcoholism, to the point that he abandoned his family for a time.[29] Having hit bottom, he found Jesus and a way back to sobriety and his family. Even then, Robertson refused to be entirely domesticated, holding tenaciously to his hunting lifestyle and his outdoorsman beard. It was a badge of manly independence and defiance that he later turned into marketing magic.

The basis of Robertson's business success was his collection of uniquely successful duck calls, but his real genius was in selling the hunting lifestyle, packaged in clothing, gear, videos, and his own bearded hunter image. When Roberston's sons, now grown, began running the business, they did not at first emulate their father's example, believing it was important for businessmen to maintain a clean-cut look.[30] Around 2005, however, they realized that beards made them distinctive and got their company attention. According to son Willie, a long beard was "the best marketing gimmick anybody's ever thought of and it didn't cost."[31] Even so, they tended to grow beards only for sales shows and duck hunting season.[32] Once they hit the big time, however, the sons had an image to protect, and they committed themselves full-time to their patriarchal manes, to the regret of several of their wives.[33] The women endured the change because, in the *Duck Dynasty* show, the men are the stars, while the women are the support crew.

Duck Dynasty's nostalgic call to the rugged life echoes key themes in the great beard movement of the 1850s, when mountain climbing and big-game hunting also attracted urbanized men worried about the authenticity of their manhood. Phil Robertson and his sons recognized a similar impulse in contemporary society and have, directly and indirectly, addressed the perceived need to strengthen male self-confidence while reinforcing traditional gender roles.[34] Willie Robertson recently contributed a forward to Darrin Patrick's conservative (though not conservatively titled) *The Dude's Guide to Manhood* (2014), in which he declared that he came "from a family who not only have mature facial hair but more importantly are mature men who know how to live life and love their wives and kids. . . . We don't need more boys, we need real men. Strong, godly, mature men."[35] Precisely what he meant by this distinction between boys and men is not entirely clear, particularly when he followed his disapproval of "boys" with this appeal: "Oh yeah, and by the way, get to growing those beards out, Boys!!!" The terminology may not have been consistent, but the clear message of the duck hunters to suburban men was to hold fast to their embattled manliness and wear it with defiant pride.

The newly sprouted beards of American evangelicals are a social rather than a religious statement. Neither Warren nor the Robertsons have promoted facial hair for specifically biblical or theological reasons. They could hardly do so when, for the vast majority of conservative Christians, short hair and a shaven face remain the conventional signs of moral and religious rectitude. The most dramatic promoter of this attitude is the Mormon church, which generally interprets facial hair as a form of disobedience. Brigham Young University, Mormonism's flagship university, positively forbids beards for students. A recent study has revealed that, in spite of intense pressure, a small minority of faithful Mormon men maintain mustaches and beards. These men are not reformers or rebels, but their decisions, for whatever personal or psychological reasons, to wear facial hair, forces them into the role of nonconformist.[36] The case of Mormon beards thus demonstrates that beard-wearing can become a defiant act even when that is not the original motivation.

Most conservative Christians still view facial hair as discordant with tradition, but for other conservative religious groups in Europe and America, it has precisely the opposite significance, namely, as a sign of religious obedience and group identity. Amish, Orthodox Jewish, and fundamentalist Muslim men rely on beards to affirm and advertise their religious piety and ethnic identity. In these settings, piety and masculine honor are inseparably bound, which makes a beard an especially powerful symbol, as well as a target for those who might wish to do harm.

Mullet's Men Take Their Revenge

Asleep in their rural farmhouse, forty-five-year-old Myron Miller and his wife Arlene were roused by pounding at their door. Six men were waiting outside. When Myron opened the door just a crack to see who it was, a man grabbed his beard and pulled him through the door. Myron grabbed the other man's beard as well, tearing some of it out as still more men jumped from the shadows to wrestle him to the ground. Arlene screamed for the their children to call for help as one of the attackers, brandishing scissors, chopped away Miller's chest-length beard until less than two inches were left. As quick as that, the attackers retreated into the dark, leaving their victim stunned and humiliated.[37]

This strange crime would seem to be ripped from the pages of ancient history, but in fact it was perpetrated in Ohio on October 4, 2011. Miller was an Amish bishop embroiled in a dispute with a break-away group of fellow Amish living a settlement called Bergholz and led by their own angry and eccentric bishop, Sam Mullet. The attack on Miller's beard was Mullet's version of revenge, an idea that is generally rejected in the Amish community. It was neither the first nor the last time Mullet's men attacked. Over a period of about two months, the "Bergholz barbers," though not Mullet himself, committed five attacks, cutting the beards of eight men and the hair of one woman, all of whom were perceived to have insulted and betrayed them and, by extension, the Christian faith. The early victims of these attacks refused to press charges, but Miller and a later victim decided to press charges when it appeared that nothing less would stop Mullet's men. Un-Amish behavior demanded an un-Amish response.

What followed was a sensational and groundbreaking trial that drew international attention and led to the first-ever conviction under the 2009 Shepard-Byrd Act, which made it a federal offense to cause bodily injury to any person on the basis of his or her actual or perceived race, color, religion, sexual orientation, or national origin. For the wider world, the trial presented the curious spectacle of violence within a bucolic community, as well as a striking illustration of the religious resonance of beards for traditionalist faith communities. The hate-crime case that federal prosecutors brought against the attackers was built on the understanding that a beard was not just a beard. Cutting an Amish man's beard was a form of religious hatred, they argued, and was thus far more serious than temporary disfigurement.

In many regards, Sam Mullet's group was a cult, and he was a cult leader. A taciturn sexagenarian who held his followers in thrall through a regime of fear, Mullet told his followers that he was a prophet who

13.3 Followers of Sam Mullet leave federal court in Cleveland, August 2012. epa european pressphoto agency b.v./Alamy.

spoke with God and that any who opposed him were sinners. He ordered his followers to abandon traditional Sunday worship as unnecessary, presenting his own pronouncements as sufficient revelation. He also promoted the notion of individual and communal penance, denouncing his followers for individual and collective spiritual failings, and ordering unusual forms of penance, including beating with paddles and long stays in goat pens or chicken coops. Often the wife of a man thus interned was ordered to move into Mullet's home, and into his bed for "sexual counseling," during which Mullet would demonstrate to the wife how better to please her husband.

Beard- and hair-cutting was introduced as another form of humiliation and penance for sins at Bergholz. From their origins in seventeenth-century Europe, the Amish have set themselves apart from the corrupted world about them and made it an article of faith to renounce artificial, indulgent, carefully groomed modernity in favor of simple beards and bonnets. The significance of removing a faithfully grown beard or feminine long hair is understood in terms of Old Testament references to the ancient practice of tearing or shaving hair as a sign of mourning or disrespect. Sinners in Bergholz were encouraged to have themselves trimmed voluntarily as a sign of their eagerness to purge themselves of evil thoughts and renew their spirits. Then Mullet and his followers conceived the idea that such humiliating penance might be visited upon "hypocrites" who had left the community or spoken ill of them.[38]

At trial, Mullet's lawyers argued that shearing away hair did not amount to bodily harm, as required by the federal statute. The court therefore needed to determine the nature of the harm caused. Testimony made it clear that the attacks had achieved their desired effect, deeply distressing the victims. One man confessed to being heartbroken. "I was depressed. It was not the Amish way of living to go around without hair and beard."[39] He reported taking an assortment of vitamins in the hope his hair would grow back faster. Another victim told the court, "I'd rather have them beat me black and blue than take my hair."[40] The harm was real, even if it was more spiritual and psychological than physical in nature. After deliberating for four days, a federal jury in Cleveland found Mullet and fifteen of his followers guilty as charged. A few months later, Mullet was sentenced to fifteen years in prison, and others to sentences ranging from one to seven years.[41] In the fall of 2014, however, the defendants had their hate-crime convictions overturned when an appeals court decided that the assaults resulted from personal disputes rather than religious hatred.[42] The case may be retried and the religious meaning of beards reconsidered.

The case of the Bergholz barbers illuminates the prominent role beards can play in establishing religious and ethnic identities. The Amish isolate themselves, hold fast to old customs, and demonstrate their religious commitment with their hair. Fundamentalist Jews and Muslims follow a similar script, also preferring plain, old-fashioned clothing and untrimmed beards. While the Amish have retreated to unelectrified homesteads, conservative Jews and Muslims have established urban enclaves, such as the Hasidic Jews who, in novelist Chaim Potok's vivid words, "walked the Brooklyn streets like specters, with their black hats, long black coats, black beards, and earlocks."[43] Religious separatists of all stripes reach deep into the past to shape their antimodern religious identity, and in the matter of facial hair, Jews can stake a claim to the oldest of all written directives.

As mentioned in chapter 2, the ancient Hebrews left us with history's first beard-preservation law. Ironically, this ancient teaching has proved more significant in recent centuries than at any other time since it was written down. For most ancient and medieval Jewish communities, the commandment in Leviticus not to "shave off the edge of their beards" was unremarkable and uncontroversial because facial hair was commonplace and few were tempted to contravene it. The Talmud, a collection of postbiblical rabbinical writings generally took the view that, as a God-given adornment, the beard was meant to distinguish men from women and should not be removed.[44] On the other hand, it was not a matter that rose to the level of great legal or religious significance, and rabbinic writings also softened the impact of the biblical ban by interpreting it to refer only to the use of razors, and not scissors, clippers, or other cutting implements.

An important exception to this easygoing attitude, however, was the mystical Kabbalist school of Jewish thought, which had its roots in a thirteenth-century Spanish book called the *Zohar*. In its complex scheme of relationships between divine, human, and earthly substances, the *Zohar* assigned the beard an exalted status as a physical manifestation of the highest dimension of God's creative power and mercy. Even now, rabbis influenced by Kabbalistic thought instruct their male followers to preserve all of the hair of their beards, lest they cut off one of the conduits of God's grace.[45]

Though their tradition is definitely favorable to facial hair, most Jews living in Western Europe and the Americas over the past three centuries have accommodated themselves to the modes and tastes of a shaven society. Even highly observant and Orthodox Jews of the eighteenth and early nineteenth centuries often chose to make themselves as smooth-faced as their Christian neighbors.[46] Samson Raphael Hirsch, an influential early nineteenth-century German rabbi and one of the founders of modern Orthodoxy, shaved himself until the middle of the century, when that era's beard movement inspired Jews and non-Jews alike to acquire a more patriarchal aspect.[47]

For both observant and secular Jews, the late nineteenth century was an important turning point. Just as the bearded style was once again in retreat in the non-Jewish world, both Ultra-Orthodox and secular Zionist Jews pushed strongly in the opposite direction, opening an increasingly visible divide between assimilators and separatists. An influential early Jewish fundamentalist, the Hungarian rabbi Moses

Sofer, and his even more strident Ultra-Orthodox successors erected a bulwark against the erosion of tradition by stressing the equal importance of every religious stricture found in Jewish law and writings.[48] Two important consequences of this stance were a refusal to relativize or minimize biblical directives on hair, and an inclination to interpret obedience to these and other regulations as a sign of commitment to the Jewish way of life.[49]

Secular Jews were also increasingly disillusioned with late nineteenth-century European society. Educated and professional Jews in nineteenth-century European cities typically sought to integrate themselves into the larger culture, but found as the century progressed that the social barriers against them were stiffening. This was the experience of Theodor Herzl, a Viennese banker's son and journalist. As a young man, Herzl was sophisticated and stylish, showing an affinity for German literature and music, as well as a distain for the old and seemingly uncouth Jewish folkways, including drab, untrimmed beards. As a young man, he adopted the grand sideburns and shaved chin modeled by the Austrian emperor.[50] With the rise of explicitly anti-Semitic politics in Europe in during the 1890s, however, Herzl changed his mind about the prospect of Jews' integration, concluding instead that the Jews needed their own nationalist movement and their own state. In 1896, he spelled out his ideas in a book, *The Jewish State*, that launched the modern Zionist movement and helped lead eventually to the creation of modern Israel.

Any nationalist movement, Jewish or otherwise, needs symbols, icons, and images to rally around. Herzl understood that he must himself be a symbol as well as a leader for his movement, and he carefully reconsidered his appearance. He abandoned his stylish sideburns in favor of a luxuriant, square-cut beard of the sort found in the ancient Assyrian and Babylonian monuments installed in European museums. In the hands of Zionist artists and publicists, Herzl's grandiloquent figure was deployed to popularize Zionist ideas.[51] By reclaiming their identity as heirs of an ancient civilization, secular Jews sought to reinforce a non-European identity, as well as their claim to a homeland in the Middle East.

In these ways, both secular and observant Jews in the twentieth and twenty-first centuries have found reasons to adopt beards as a sign of Jewish identity. This practice, in turn, has led to disputes between Orthodox communities and secular, non-Jewish states. In 2012, for example, a Hasidic student in the New York City police academy was dismissed when he refused for religious reasons to trim his beard to the required one-millimeter length. "I don't understand what the problem would be," the recruit said.[52] The issue, of course, was not his hair, but whether the regulations of state or religion should prevail.

Symbols of segregation, like long beards, affirm distinct values that stand in contrast to the more liberal values of Western society. It may be, as the admittedly unbearded New York City rabbi Meir Soloveichik has argued, that Jewish beards stand as an honest rebuke to the modern tendency to deny aging and mortality. On the other hand, long Orthodox beards say even more loudly that religious identity is paramount, and that traditionalists refuse to be defined by the values—progressive or otherwise—of a liberal and secular society.[53]

A similar pattern has emerged on a rather larger scale in the Muslim world. Here again, the majority of Muslims worldwide take a pragmatic approach to hair, while an increasingly adamant conservative element insists that traditional directives be strictly followed.[54] For these fundamentalists, beards are one of several bulwarks against Western power and culture, including its unwelcome tendency to weaken male authority. As in the cases of the Amish and Orthodox Jews, conservative Muslims rely on both ancient and modern religious sanctions that make facial hair a signifier of identity, commitment, and the proper ordering of society.

"Every day when I shaved, I used to ask God for forgiveness." Those were the words in 2012 of Ahmed Hamdy, an Egyptian police officer torn between the regulations of his employment and what he believed to be his religious obligations as an observant Muslim.[55] Hair had become the front line in the cultural battle between modernists and traditionalists in the Muslim world. After Egyptian leader Hosni Mubarak was forced from power in the Arab Spring uprisings in 2011, Hamdy dared to show up to work unshaved, joining thousands of others clamoring to embrace their faith in this very public way. He was immediately placed on leave at reduced pay. In the summer of 2012, Mohamed Morsi, leader of the Muslim Brotherhood, became both the first democratically elected and the first bearded president of modern Egypt. The triumph of the traditionalists, however, was too much for the secular elites to accept. Morsi and his bearded supporters were violently forced from power in 2013, and men like Hamdy were required to return to their razors and prayers for forgiveness.

This back-and-forth pattern has been repeated throughout the Middle East, China, and central Asia in recent years, as secular governments attempt to establish discipline and loyalty to the state with shaving decrees, while radical groups press men of all ages to eschew impious razors.[56] In recent years, the Iraqi government has required all men in its military and police forces to shave, contributing to resentment among enlistees.[57] At the other extreme, the militant Islamic State in Iraq and Syria has instructed its followers to maintain a beard at least two fists in length — longer even than other Islamist groups — to prove their commitment to the cause.[58]

Civilians are often caught up in this ideological struggle. When the Taliban held Afghanistan under its puritanical rule, cigarettes, television, drinking, and music were all banned. Women were required to cover themselves from head to toe in public, and men were required to keep their hair short but maintain beards of at least four inches. Religious police monitored barbershops to see that this decree was enforced, and residents were warned not to let their hair look like that of an American. After the Taliban defeat in 2001, barbers ran a brisk business, as men lined up to cut off this talisman of oppression. "I've got nothing against beards," one customer explained. "The problem is when someone tells you that you have to have one. That's why I hated it."[59]

The requirement to wear beards has become increasingly important to both Sunni and Shia conservatives for the same reasons it had among Orthodox Jews since the late nineteenth century, as a matter of preserving folkways and identity in the modern world. In Iran, a return to beards was a visible feature of the overthrow of the shah's secular regime in 1978 and a return to Islamic law. The clamor for religious beards began before that, however. Moroccan scholar Muhammad al-Zamzami, for example, published in 1967 a pamphlet entitled *Clear evidence that he who shaves his beard is cursed, and that his prayers are of no value.*[60] Indian scholar Muhammad Zakariya Kandhlawi, similarly angry about seeing young Muslim men shaving in 1970s India, produced a tract entitled *The Beard of a Muslim and Its Importance*, which was later translated into English and French for the benefit of the faithful living in the West. According to the South African institute that produced the English translation, Kandhlawi's tract would help "many who desire to uphold Islamic symbols in an anti-Islamic environment."[61] In more recent years, conservative authors from different schools of thought have published similar discourses, which are readily available in translation on the Internet.[62]

Kandhlawi, al-Zamzami, and other Muslim fundamentalists build their cases around a rich trove of beard references in the Hadith, traditional collections of the sayings and actions of Muhammad.[63] Some Hadith simply report that Muhammad commanded men to trim their mustaches while letting their beards grow. Others describe the Prophet's beard and his practice of cutting it at a fist's length. Some attest that Muhammad commanded faithful men to trim their mustaches and grow beards so that men might be distinguished from women and the faithful from pagans, Jews, or Christians. Still others describe the Prophet as warning those who failed to follow these rules that they were sinning against God and the faith. Kandhlawi, for one, insists that even barbers who shave others' beards are sinning.

Some conservative authors provide more practical arguments to bolster ancient authorities. To Kandhlawi in particular, it is clear that Muhammad wished to establish with his grooming regulations a sort of uniform that would help preserve Muslim fidelity. Every religion and nation creates uniforms, flags, and other symbols, he reasons, and any group that loses them will be quickly absorbed into other nations. The preservation of Islam therefore depends on maintaining distinctive traditions, including facial hair.[64]

As in the case of Orthodox Judaism, the preservation of the symbols of commitment and segregation can lead to conflict with secular states. A notable instance is the laws enacted in France in 2004 forbidding religious displays, potentially including beards, in public schools. On the other hand, the United States Supreme Court ruled unanimously in January 2015 that a Muslim prisoner in Arkansas had the right to a half-inch beard as a matter of religious expression.[65] In the United States, arguments of religious liberty clearly have a better chance of undoing antibeard legal precedents than claims of individual or labor rights. The US military has already made accommodations for some Sikh soldiers,

allowing them their beards and turbans, even as it refuses similar concessions to other groups.[66] There will be many such challenges in the
years ahead.

Boston Believes Again

A recurring use for facial hair in modern society is to establish a temporary brotherhood, lasting only as long as it takes to complete a goal or
mission. This is the quest beard, dramatically exemplified by 2013 Major
League Baseball champions the Boston Red Sox.

No one is quite sure why they did it, but baseball fans in Boston are
glad they did. At the start of the season, most of the players decided to
grow out their beards, not just tidy trimmed ones but untamed manes in
whatever form nature permitted. Not coincidentally, in many people's
view, the team's playing was transformed, allowing it to rise from one
of the worst season records in 2012 to become a powerhouse, sweeping
aside opponents relatively easily on its march to the championship. On
the way, supporters jumped on the bandwagon, wearing T-shirts with
beard themes and all manner of real and fake whiskers. One journalist
recounted a brief episode of this madness, when he stopped in his car at
a traffic light next to another car containing a man, woman, and child,
"all of them wearing baseball caps and outfitted with something strange
and gray and hideous on their faces."[67]

By all accounts, the brotherhood of the beard began at training
camp in March, when a few players on a lark decided to stop shaving.
Others joined in, sensing that it was a way to bond as teammates.[68] A
few weeks into the new season, Boston's famous marathon was struck
by homemade terrorist bombs, which killed three and wounded hundreds. The city, including its baseball players, rallied to the slogan "Boston Strong," and though it was not the inspiration for their beards, the
tragedy added a layer of emotional intensity that persisted through the
entire season, symbolized by a special "B strong" patch on the team's
uniforms. The success of the Red Sox seemed more important than
ever.

The remarkable look and success of Boston's baseball club inevitably raised questions about these "rally beards." What were they for, and

how did they work? The most common answer was that they helped the players form a tight bond by sharing a distinctive look. Teammates also created a new form of celebration in which they pulled each other's beards after a great play. Another explanation of the power of the "basebeards" was that it represented sacrifice and toughness, what star player David Ortiz called a "go-for-broke approach" and "rebellious streak."[69] One psychologist suggested that it triggered a "Samson" factor, projecting hairy warrior strength. Underlying both of these dynamics was a seriousness of purpose, described by a commentator as "a kind of solemnity."[70] It was a combination of social bonding, strength, and purpose that gave the Boston quest beards their power. As one local columnist concluded, "The beard represents all that was good with this team—unity and ruggedness."[71] There was still one more dimension. The team's supporters had a new means to identify with their team and their city, deploying any sort of wool, string, or marker ink to play along.

Pulling together in common sacrifice and special effort is the hallmark of the quest beard. Players' wives had to make sacrifices too, patiently waiting for the season to end in order to get their neatly groomed husbands back. The season following their championship, the Red Sox players returned to their previous selves, by and large, having trimmed most if not all of their distinctive hair.[72]

The seriousness underlying the success of the quest beard is readily visible in another prominent example—"Movember," an international cause that encourages men to grow a mustache during the month of November to raise awareness of men's health issues. Technically, this is a quest mustache; beards are not allowed according to the Movember Foundation's rules. It is the same idea, however. The rules state that one must start the month clean-shaven. In other words, it is explicitly a temporary gesture that, like the playoff beard, symbolically unites a group in a common mission. According to the organization's official history, a few Australian men came up with the mustache-growing idea in 2003, and only later did they link it to a particular quest—fighting prostate cancer.[73] It has worked brilliantly. Movember can boast that in its first decade it has registered over four million people from twenty-two countries who made $559 million in contributions.

Karl-Heinz Hille Sets a Record

By definition, the quest beard is provisional and short-term. There are many bearded and mustachioed men, however, who are in it for the long haul, and not for religious or gender-bending reasons. As contrarians to the norm, they simply see their hair as liberating. Their primary impetus is the expression of autonomy. Nevertheless, as a visible minority, men of the beard often band together for mutual support and admiration in beard clubs and beard contests. Given Germany's long history as a bastion of facial hair (recall Pastor Schönland, Georg Kirchmaier, Prince Albert, Friedrich Ludwig Jahn, Kaiser Wilhelm, and Paul Breitner), it is unsurprising that the modern World Beard and Mustache Championships has its origins in a German club formed in 1986. Nor is it unexpected that the most the most decorated competitor over the past three decades is a German, Berliner Karl-Heinz Hille (figure 13.4). After winning both the "imperial partial beard" category and his second overall title at the Carson City Championship in 2003, Hille, dapper in a shimmering grey tuxedo and top hat, declared rather incongruously that he was "as happy as a pig in mud."[74] Another victory in his category at the 2013 championships in Leinfelden-Echterdingen, Germany, gave him a streak of six straight triumphs and a place in the *Guinness Book of World Records*.[75]

Beard clubs and competitions are a relatively recent phenomenon, often nostalgic in style but fundamentally quite modern. At one level, they are a response to the decline of fraternal organizations and other traditionally male-dominated bastions, such as labor unions. At another level, they celebrate male dignity in an age of increasing gender equity. Somewhat like the quest beard of the Red Sox, the clubber's hair is a source of personal and collective pride. The qualities of which these bearded men are most proud are individuality and independence. Gary James Chilton, for example, a contestant at the 2003 World Beard and Mustache Championships, described a bearded man as "open-minded, non-judgmental and a free spirit," whereas a clean-shaven man is "someone who has been told what to do."[76] There is often talk of expressing one's authentic self. "I think," one contestant wrote, "that your face is not your real face if you shave every day."[77] Sociologist

13.4 Karl-Heinz Hille competing at the World Beard and Mustache Championships, Carson City, Nevada, 2003. Brian Cahn/ZUMA Press, Inc./Alamy.

Paul Roof, longtime president of the Holy City Beard and Mustache Society in Charleston, South Carolina, echoed this theme of liberated authenticity in declaring that he finds that men with "beards and the mustaches are the most interesting people at any party."[78]

For middle-class professionals in particular—and this is the primary constituency of beard and mustache clubs—social groups are not a given but must be built around common proclivities and interests. Clubs and contests are an opportunity for men to socialize and engage in community work, along with their spouses and partners. In a sense, beard clubs hope to accomplish over a longer term what the quest beard accomplishes in the short run. Hair becomes a common symbol and the premise for a set of activities that bring people together for common ends. Not that it always works smoothly. From the inception of international competition, there have been intense disputes, splits, and jealousies concerning venues, categories, and judging. A serious rift opened in 2014, when Phil Olsen, the prime mover of Beard Team USA, organized his own world championship in Portland, Oregon, without the approval of the World Beard and Mustache Association.

Beard clubs are the most explicit example of the social uses of facial hair in the postmodern world, though other men's associations, not built specifically around facial hair, have also made it a key feature of masculine autonomy and socializing. These include the gay subcultures already mentioned, like bears and leathermen, and also motorcycle clubs, which the leathermen emulate. In these contexts, hair works in tandem with other symbols and practices. Motorcycle clubs have established a powerful alliance between facial hair and leather, both evincing toughness and assertiveness to the point of menace. Often times, the medal-studded and hairy men attending gatherings like the annual Sturgis Motorcycle Rally in South Dakota are professional men living out a masculine fantasy of liberation, if only for week.

A lot of men want this fantasy. The Sturgis rally, which has its origins in a motorcycle race in 1938, became a cultural phenomenon after Hollywood galvanized the image of the liberated and rebellious biker in *The Wild One* (1954), starring Marlon Brando, and later *Easy Rider* (1969), starring Peter Fonda. From the 1970s onward, the Sturgis rally and other biker gatherings have grown dramatically in Europe as well as North America. The Sturgis event has boasted almost half a million attendees in recent years, many from Europe and other regions, offering powerful testimony of men's desire to defy the constraints of ordinary life in riding out, bold and bearded, on the open road.

In our times, the cracks in the smooth façade of the shaven norm run in many different directions. Whether gay, straight, liberal, conservative, religious, secular, urban, or rural, men have found reasons to encourage beards and mustaches to grow. In one sense or another, men have found in facial hair a form of masculine liberation. In a shaven world, it is statement of personal autonomy, but not only that. For consumer-oriented urban men like David Beckham, carefully sculpted beards help bridge the divide between supposedly masculine and feminine qualities, while for other gay and straight men, a furry face clarifies that distinction. Conservative men worried about the dissolution of traditional gender and family norms are experimenting with hairy rebelliousness. For deeply conservative religious communities, including the Amish, Orthodox Jews, and fundamentalist Muslims, ancient laws prescribing long beards are enforced to symbolize a social collective in opposition to secular modernity, including its threat to masculine privilege. For nonreligious groups too, facial hair is a means to bond men with each other in teams, clubs, or causes for the short or long term. The quest beard has proven very popular in recent years because it offers men the option of having it both ways. It marks a special time during which men can escape social rules, join a tight-knit brotherhood, and do something daring and special. Later they can return to the smoother course of their regular lives.

CONCLUSIONS

One intent of this work has been simply to marvel at the extraordinary lives of men and women in history. The personalities considered here are a diverse bunch, to be sure. Another aspiration has been to shed light on dark corners of our understanding, dispelling common misperceptions about facial hair and its history. The most significant myth to be set aside is the notion that changes in facial hair are the meaningless product of fashion cycles. Beard lore is full of bogus explanations for changes in style that have distracted us from a far more interesting reality. Alexander did not order his men to shave simply to prevent beard pulling; he inviting them to see themselves as extraordinary and heroic. Hadrian did not grow a beard to cover a skin problem; instead, he was attempting to redefine masculine and imperial authority in terms of philosophic reasoning. King Francis I of France did not grow hair on his cheeks because his face was injured by a snowball; he was, rather, expressing Renaissance pride in humanity. Beards did not become popular in the nineteenth century because of the Crimean War or the American Civil War, nor did they disappear in the twentieth century because of Gillette's safety razor. These great shifts marked, rather, varying strategies to assert appropriate and compelling forms of manhood in the altered political, economic, and family patterns of industrial society. To explain the prevalence of the shaven idea in the

West, one must look first to Alexander the Great, then to the medieval church, and finally to the seventeenth-century royal courts, all of which promoted beardlessness as the mark of a superior sort of man.

The variability of the male face in history testifies to the mutability and variety of ideas of manhood within a given period, and across time. This observation confirms a central tenet of gender theory that masculine and feminine identities are created, not natural, and are subject to continuous historical transformation. The difficult part is tracking and explaining these changing formulations. Considering facial hair is one way to do this.

In the broadest terms, beard history offers a chronology of masculine history marked by major shifts in attitudes to facial hair. In the history of the West since classical times, shaving has been the default position, punctuated by four great beard movements. The term "movement" is appropriate because a historic shift toward beards required in every case a certain amount of deliberation and conscious effort, while subsequent reversions to shaving have proceeded with little comment. In some periods, particularly in the Middle Ages, opposing styles of hair representing differing ideals of manhood have coexisted in a single society. These situations, however, are exceptional.

One fundamental idea proved remarkably resilient over the course of Western history, and that is the association of hair with nature and, conversely, the removal of hair with the control or transcendence of nature. Champions of the beard movements in the second, sixteenth, and nineteenth centuries (and of smaller efflorescences along the way) have all made explicit reference to a masculine persona grounded in the physical body. It is the male body, they argued, and the mental and moral strengths latent within it, that ultimately justifies masculine claims to authority, pride, and dominion.

By contrast, shaving the beard has been consistently associated with some kind of transcendence of the body. This alternative idea posits that true manhood is grounded in powers and ideals beyond the self, whether God, community, nation, or corporation. The quintessential shavers from the beginnings of civilization were the priests. The logic of priestly shaving—cutting away the sin and corruption of our physical natures to approach a higher plane of being—was manifest in the earliest practices of Western civilization, and was reinvented by the Christian church in the Middle Ages, as well as many non-Western religious traditions. This idea of masculine transcendence was not, however, limited to the priestly context. By shaving himself Alexander the Great was declaring that he was not subject to the limits of his human body, or even to his humanity, but that his powers emanated from the realm of the divine. For less heroic men, shaving has been an acknowledgment of one's reliance on membership in a masculine collective. An eighteenth-century gentleman, for example, carefully conformed to elegant taste to prove his social worthiness, while a twentieth-century man employed a razor to win trust and secure employment.

The prevalence of the shaving standard since Alexander is strong evidence of the cultural preference for manliness grounded in social approval rather than the physical body. This does not mean that bearded men are not socialized or that shaved men fail to be individuals. It means simply that, over time, shaving has proved to be a useful cultural practice in shaping a masculine identity properly oriented to its social foundations. T. E. Lawrence was a striking example of this effect. Immersed in Arabian life, he symbolically retained his connection to the source of his identity and strength—Britishness—by scraping his face with a dry razor.

The case of the military mustache is an interesting variation on these basic themes. Its staying power between the eighteenth and twentieth centuries indicates that its symbolism was truly powerful. It staked out an ideal middle ground on the spectrum of shaving that elegantly expressed the position of the soldier—subject to the discipline of his superiors (shaved chin and cheeks), yet also reliant on his own physical and moral fortitude (hairy upper lip). In modern civilian life, this same compromise has made mustaches more socially acceptable than beards.

The shape of beard history helps us gain perspective on our own times, first by alerting us to the social power of facial hair. As in the past, the condition of our own times is visible on men's faces. What is immediately apparent is an increased variety and experimentation indicative of an ongoing renegotiation of what is expected of men, and of what men wish for themselves. Much of this communication is nonverbal or even subconscious, but there are a wide variety of issues at play, including personal autonomy, social regulation, religious identity, gender roles, and sexual attraction. We live in interesting times.

This book cannot hope to offer a complete evaluation of the subtle, complex language of hair. There is much more to be said and done, particularly in the consideration of hair on the head and body. More discoveries are yet to be made as the historical hair code is deciphered.

ACKNOWLEDGMENTS

I am grateful to the many people who supported me and this project over many years. This book exists because of the enthusiasm and professional guidance of my agent Malaga Baldi and acquisitions editor Doug Mitchell. Special thanks also to editor Joel Score, as well as Ashley Pierce, Kyle Wagner, Isaac Tobin, Joan Davies, and the rest of the talented staff of the University of Chicago Press. I can say with all truthfulness that this book would not have been possible without the invaluable wisdom and encouragement of my scholarly buddies in the "Vickies": Carol Herringer, Rick Incorvati, Barry Milligan, Tammy Proctor, and Laura Vorachek. I am deeply grateful to others who have read and critiqued all or parts of this manuscript: Alun Withey, Christopher Forth, Michael Leaman, Amy Livingstone, Claudia E. Suter, Sean Trainor, and my wife, Jennifer Oldstone-Moore. I owe unending thanks to several talented linguists for translations from many languages: J. Holland, Allison Kirk, Katie Derrig, Daniel Koehler, Maria Hickey, Shaydon Ramey, David T. Barry, Anjelika Gasilina, and Daniele Macuglia. A big thank-you also to my student research assistants, Evan Weiler and Maria Hickey. I am grateful for the help and encouragement in this venture of my colleagues in the history department at Wright State, especially Paul Lockhart, who taught me the ropes of the publishing world. Many thanks also to those who provided me with photographs for this book: Claudia E. Suter, Noël Tassain, Gene Dillman, and

Keith Parish. Leanne Wierenga helped me navigate key foreign negotiations. Friends and family members have offered insights and beard lore wherever they found it. Thanks to Lynn Rigsbee, Donald Deer, Jim Secord, Reynold Nesiba, Glenn Short, and many others. Love and unending appreciation to my parents Stanley and Elizabeth Moore and my in-laws Michael and Elizabeth Oldstone for their intellectual, moral, and financial support for this venture. Finally, loving thanks to my brilliant wife Jennifer and long-suffering daughters Caroline, Aileen, and Marilee. I know a lot of words, but not enough to express my love for you all.

NOTES

Introduction

1   Sean Trainor, "The Racially Fraught History of the American Beard," *Atlantic*, 20 January 2014, http://www.theatlantic.com/national/archive/2014/01/the -racially-fraught-history-of-the-american-beard/283180/.

2   Judith Butler, *Gender Trouble* (New York: Routledge, 1990), 16–25.

Chapter 1

1   "Effects of Sexual Activity on Beard Growth in Man," *Nature* 226 (30 May 1970): 869–70.

2   Sterling Chaykin, "Beard Growth: A Window for Observing Circadian and Infradian Rhythms of Men," *Chronobiologia* 13 (1986): 163–65.

3   Charles Darwin, *Descent of Man*, 2nd ed. (London: John Murray, 1890), 597–604, babel.hathitrust.org.

4   Ibid., 603. Darwin emphasizes this point more strongly in the second edition than in the first.

5   Nancy Ectoff, *Survival of the Prettiest: The Science of Beauty* (New York: Doubleday, 1999), 24.

6   Amotz Zahavi, "Mate Selection: A Selection for a Handicap," *Journal of Theoretical Biology* 53 (1975): 205–14. See also Amotz Zahavi and Avishag Zahavi, *The Handicap Principle: A Missing Piece of Darwin's Puzzle* (Oxford: Oxford University Press, 1997), 25–40.

7   Ivar Folstad and Andrew John Karter, "Parasites, Bright Males, and the

Immunocompetence Handicap," *American Naturalist* 139 (1992): 616. See also Randy Thornhill and Steven W. Gangestad, "Human Facial Beauty: Averageness, Symmetry, and Parasite Resistance," *Human Nature* 4 (1993): 249–50.

8   Daniel G. Freedman, "The Survival Value of the Beard," *Psychology Today*, October 1969, 36–38.

9   Samuel Roll and J. S. Verinis, "Stereotypes of Scalp and Facial Hair as Measured by the Semantic Differential," *Psychological Reports* 28 (1971): 975–80.

10   Charles T. Kenny and Dixie Fletcher, "Effects of Beardedness on Person Perception," *Perceptual and Motor Skills* 37 (1973): 413–14. See also Robert J. Pellegrini, "Impressions of the Male Personality as a Function of Beardedness," *Psychology* 10 (1973): 29–33.

11   Saul Feinman and George W. Gill, "Females' Response to Males' Beardedness," *Perceptual and Motor Skills* 44 (1977): 533–34.

12   S. Mark Pancer and James R. Meindl, "Length of Hair and Beardedness as Determinants of Personality Impressions," *Perceptual and Motor Skills* 46 (1978): 1328–30.

13   Elaine Hatfield and Susan Sprecher, *Mirror, Mirror: The Importance of Looks in Everyday Life* (Albany: State University of New York Press, 1986), 227–28.

14   J. Ann Reed and Elizabeth M. Blunk, "The Influence of Facial Hair on Impression Formation," *Social Behavior and Personality* 18 (1990): 169–76.

15   Micheal L. Shannon and C. Patrick Stark, "The Influence of Physical Appearance on Personnel Selection," *Social Behavior and Personality* 31 (2003): 613–24.

16   Frank Muscarella and Michael R. Cunningham, "The Evolutionary Significance and Social Perception of Male Pattern Baldness and Facial Hair," *Ethology and Sociobiology* 17 (1996): 109–13.

17   R. Dale Guthrie, *Body Hot Spots: The Anatomy of Human Social Organs and Behavior* (New York: Van Nostrand Reinhold, 1976), 5.

18   Freedman, "Survival Value."

19   See especially Pellegrini, "Impressions of the Male Personality," and Douglas R. Wood, "Self-Perceived Masculinity between Bearded and Nonbearded Males," *Perceptual and Motor Skills* 62 (1986): 769–70. German researcher Christina Wietig was surprised that even well-educated men in her survey believed that fuller beards indicated greater virility. Wietig, "Der Bart: Zur Kulturgeschichte des Bartes von der Antike bis zur Gegenwart" (dissertation, Universität Hamburg, 2005), 112–13, http://www.chemie.uni-hamburg.de/bibliothek/2005/DissertationWietig.pdf.

20   Muscarella and Cunningham, "Evolutionary Significance," 109–13.

21   Barnaby J. Dixson and Paul L. Vasey, "Beards Augment Perceptions of Men's Age, Social Status, and Aggressiveness, but Not Attractiveness," *Behavioral Ecology* 23 (May 2012): 481–90.

22   Michael R. Cunningham, Anita P. Barbee, and Carolyn L. Pike, "What Do

Women Want? Facialmetric Assessment of Multiple Motives in the Perception of Male Facial Physical Attractiveness," *Journal of Personality and Social Psychology* 59 (1990): 61–72.

23   Ectoff, *Survival of the Prettiest,* 158–60.

24   Christina Wietig, *Der Bart,* 112–13. The English research is reported in Nick Neave and Kerry Shields, "The Effects of Facial Hair Manipulation on Female Perceptions of Attractiveness, Masculinity, and Dominance in Male Faces," *Personality and Individual Differences* 45 (2008): 373–77.

25   Barnaby J. Dixson and Paul C. Brooks, "The Role of Facial Hair in Women's Perceptions of Men's Attractiveness, Health, Masculinity and Parenting Abilities," *Evolution and Human Behavior* 34 (May 2013): 236–241.

26   Christian Bromberger, "Hair: From the West to the Middle East through the Mediterranean," *Journal of American Folklore* 121 (2008): 380.

Chapter 2

1   The significance of beards is not simple or certain. See Claudia E. Suter, "The Royal Body and Masculinity in Early Mesopotamia," in *Menschenbiler und Körperkonzepte im Alten Israel, in Ägypten und im Alten Orient,* ed. Angelika Berlejung, Ian Dietrich, and Joachim Friedrich Quack (Tubingen: Mohr Siebeck, 2012), 442–45.

2   Many scholars now identify this carving as Shulgi. See Claudia E. Suter, "Ur III Kings in Images: A Reappraisal," in *Your Praise Is Sweet: A Memorial Volume for Jeremy Black by Students, Colleagues and Friends,* ed. Heather D. Baker et al. (London: British Institute for the Study of Iraq, 2010), 335–36.

3   Samuel Noah Kramer, *History Begins at Sumer,* 3rd ed. (Philadelphia: University of Pennsylvania Press, 1981), 277–88. See also Marc Van De Mieroop, *A History of the Ancient Near East,* 2nd ed. (Malden, MA: Blackwell, 2007), 76. See also H. W. F. Saggs, *Babylonians* (Norman: University of Oklahoma Press/British Museum Press, 1995), 85–89.

4   Kramer, *History Begins,* 287. For another translation, see Mario Liverani, *The Ancient Near East: History, Society and Economy,* trans. Soraia Tabatabai (London: Routledge, 2014), 167–68. The story is set in Shulgi's seventh year on the throne, according to the official name given for that year in another text "in which the king travelled from the city of Ur to the city of Nippur (and back)." See Nicole Brisch, "Changing Images of Kingship in Sumerian Literature," in *The Oxford Handbook of Cuneiform Culture,* ed. Karen Radnor and Eleanor Robson (Oxford: Oxford University Press, 2011), 709.

5   For a description of purification priests in Babylon, see Gwendolyn Leick, *The Babylonians: An Introduction* (London: Routledge, 2003), 137. Physicians were known to shave. See Jean Bottéro, *Everyday Life in Ancient Mesopotamia,* trans. Antonia Nevill (Baltimore: Johns Hopkins University Press, 2001

[1992]), 163. See also Dominique Collon, *Ancient Near Eastern Art* (Berkeley: University of California Press, 1995), 508.

6   Georges Contenau, *Everyday Life in Babylon and Assyria* (New York: Norton, 1966 [1877]), 281.

7   Collon, *Ancient Near Eastern Art*, 514.

8   Numbers 8:5–7. See also Saul M. Olyan, "What Do Shaving Rites Accomplish and What Do They Signal in Biblical Ritual Contexts?" *Journal of Biblical Literature* 117 (1998): 614. Olyan emphasizes the importance of marking a transformation from one state or role to another.

9   Ann Macy Roth, "The Social Aspects of Death," in Sue D'Auria, Peter Lacovara, and Catharine H. Roehrig, *Mummies and Magi: The Funerary Arts of Ancient Egypt* (Boston: Museum of Fine Arts, 1988), 56.

10   Edna R. Russmann, "Fragment of Funerary Relief," in D'Auria, Lacovara, and Roehrig, *Mummies and Magi*, 192.

11   Jeremiah 41:5.

12   Liverani, *Ancient Near East,* 79–80. See also De Mieroop, *History of the Ancient Near East*, 43–45.

13   Wolfram von Soden, *The Ancient Orient,* trans. Donald G. Schley (Grand Rapids, MI: William B. Eerdmans, 1994), 63–64.

14   Liverani, *Ancient Near East,* 137. See also Thorkild Jacobsen, *Toward the Image of Tammuz* (Cambridge, MA: Harvard University Press, 1970), 155. See also Saggs, *Babylonians*, 70.

15   Henri Frankfort, *The Art and Architecture of the Ancient Orient,* 4th ed. (New Haven, CT: Yale University Press, 1970), 84.

16   Liverani, *Ancient Near East,* 137.

17   Caroline Waerzeggers, "The Pious King: Royal Patronage of the Temples," in Radnor and Robson, *Oxford Handbook of Cuneiform Culture*, 739.

18   Samuel Noah Kramer, "Kingship in Sumer and Akkad: The Ideal King," in *Le palais et la royauté (Archéologie et Civilisation),* ed. Paul Garelli (Paris: Librairie Orientaliste Paul Geuthner, 1974), 171.

19   O. R. Gurney, *The Hittites* (London: Penguin 1952), 152.

20   Quoted in Joyce Tyldesley, *Hatchepsut* (London: Viking, 1996), 143.

21   James Henry Breasted, *Ancient Records of Egypt,* vol. 2, *The Eighteenth Dynasty* (Champaign: University of Illinois Press, 2001 [1906]), 112.

22   W. C. Hayes, quoted in Tyldesley, *Hatchepsut,* 3. See also Peter F. Dorman, "Hatshepsut: Wicked Stepmother or Joan of Arc?" *Oriental Institute News and Notes,* no. 168 (Winter 2001), 1.

23   Quoted in Tyldesley, *Hatchepsut,* 157.

24   Saphinaz-Amal Naguib, "Hair in Ancient Egypt," *Acta Orientalia* 51 (1990): 11.

25   Bob Brier and Hoyt Hobbs, *Daily Life of the Ancient Egyptians* (Westport, CT: Greenwood Press, 1999), 135.

26   The transformation of Hatshepsut is examined in Dorman, "Hatshepsut," 5–6.

27   I Chronicles 19. See also II Samuel 10.

28   Isaiah 50:5–6 (NRSV).

29   Contenau, *Everyday Life*, 65. See also A. T. Olmstead, *History of Assyria* (Chicago: University of Chicago Press, 1960 [1923]), 120.

30   Marie-Thérése Barrelet, following Ruth Opificius, refers to this style as "roi héroïsé" in her article "La 'figure du roi' dans l'iconographie et dans les textes depuis Ur-Nanse jusqu'à la fin de la primiere dynastie de Babylone," in Garelli, *Le palais et la royauté*, 104.

31   Theodor H. Gaster, *Myth, Legend, and Custom in the Old Testament* (New York: Harper, 1969), 437.

32   Robert D. Biggs, "The Babylonian Sexual Potency Texts," in *Sex and Gender in the Ancient Near East*, ed. S. Parpola and R. M. Whiting (Helsinki: Neo-Assyrian Text Corpus Project, 2002), 71–78. See also Bottéro, *Everday Life in Ancient Mesopotamia*, 99.

33   Judges 13:3–5.

34   Judges 16:16–18.

35   Judges 16:28–30.

36   J. E. Curtis and J. E. Reade, eds., *Art in Empire: Treasures from Assyria in the British Museum* (New York: Metropolitan Museum of Art, 1995), 43.

37   Ibid., 44. See also Irene J. Winter, "Art in Empire: The Royal Image and the Visual Dimensions of Assyrian Ideology," *Assyria 1995*, 371.

38   Winter, "Art in Empire," 372–73.

39   Steven W. Cole and Peter Machinist, eds. *Letters from Priests to the Kings Esarhaddon and Assurbanipal* (Helsinki: Helsinki University Press, 1998), 36.

40   Susan Niditch, *My Brother Esau Is a Hairy Man: Hair and Identity in Ancient Israel* (Oxford: Oxford University Press, 2008), 49–50, 59.

41   For a thorough discussion of these hair codes, see Niditch, *My Brother Esau*, 106–11.

42   Leviticus 21:5–6 (NRSV).

43   Leviticus 19:27.

44   Deuteronomy 14:1–2 (NRSV).

45   Numbers 8:7.

Chapter 3

1   John Maxwell O'Brien, *Alexander the Great: The Invisible Enemy* (London: Routledge, 1992), 94.

2   Arrian, *Anabasis Alexandri*, trans. E. Iliff Robson (Cambridge, MA: Harvard University Press, 1967), 1:251.

3   Plutarch, *Moralia*, trans. Frank Cole Babbitt (Cambridge, MA: Harvard University Press, 1931), 3:57.

4   Plutarch, *Plutarch's Lives*, vol. 7, trans. Bernadotte Perrin (Cambridge, MA: Harvard University Press, 1967), 231.

5   Aristophanes, *Women at the Thesmophoria*, trans. Eugene O'Neill Jr., in *The Complete Greek Drama*, vol. 2 (New York: Random House, 1938), lines 231–32.

6   Theopompus, fragment 225a, in *Homosexuality in Greece and Rome: A Sourcebook of Basic Documents*, ed. Thomas K Hubbard (Berkeley: University of California Press, 2003), 74.

7   Homer, *Iliad*, I.500.

8   Helen King, *Hippocrates' Woman: Reading the Female Body in Ancient Greece* (London: Routledge, 1998), 9–10.

9   Hippocrates, *Nature of the Child*, trans. I. M Lonie, in *Hippocratic Writings*, ed. G. E. R. Lloyd (London: Penguin 1983 [1950]), 332.

10 Aristotle, *Generation of Animals* (V.iii), trans. A. L. Peck (Cambridge, MA: Harvard University Press, 1963), 523–25.

11 Andrew F. Stewart, *Faces of Power: Alexander's Image and Hellenistic Politics* (Berkeley: University of California Press, 1993), 75. Paul Cartledge discusses the many uses of Lyssipus's work in *Alexander the Great: The Hunt for a New Past* (London: Macmillan, 2004), 235.

12 Katherine Callen King, *Achilles: Paradigms of the War Hero from Homer to the Middle Ages* (Berkeley: University of California Press, 1987), 3.

13 Homer, *Iliad*, 24:337–39, trans. Stephen Mitchell (New York: Free Press, 2011), 402.

14 K. J. Dover, *Greek Homosexuality* (London: Duckworth, 1978), 86–87.

15 Plato, *Charmides*, in *Plato in Twelve Volumes,* vol. 8, trans. W. R. M. Lamb (Cambridge, MA: Harvard University Press, 1955), 154b.

16 Many scholars have noted that in later classical literature interest in Heracles as an indefatigable slayer of monsters and beasts declines, while interest in him as a man of virtue worthy of emulation and eternal life with the gods increases. This trend toward a more "spiritualized" Heracles is mirrored in art. See Rainer Vollkommer, *Herakles in the Art of Classical Greece* (Oxford: Oxford University Committee for Archeology, 1988), 79–81. See also T. B. L Webster, *Potter and Patron in Classical Athens* (London: Methuen & Co., 1972), 261–63.

17 Every *kouros* statue followed the same stylized design, meant to allow the commemorated deceased man, in Robin Osborne's words, "to place himself as a model of humanity before the gods." See Osborne, "Men without Clothes: Heroic Nakedness and Greek Art," in *Gender and the Body in the Ancient Mediterranean*, ed. Maria Wyke (Oxford: Blackwell, 1998), 86. Some have argued that nudity in art was meant to imitate the nudity of athletes, but the reverse is more likely the case. See Andrew Stewart, *Greek Sculpture: An Exploration* (New Haven, CT: Yale University Press, 1990), 106. Another context for nudity was initiation rituals. Many Cretan and Greek rites of passage involved young men shedding their clothes of childhood and revealing their true nature as men strong enough to fight and act as full citizens. See Gloria Ferrari, *Figures of Speech: Men and Maidens in Ancient Greece* (Chicago: University of Chicago Press, 2002), 117–25.

18   Quoted in Stewart, *Faces of Power*, 341.

19   Varro, *De Re Rustica,* trans. W. D. Hooper (Cambridge, MA: Harvard University Press, 1937), 419.

20   Pliny the Elder, *Naturalis Historia* 59:1–4. Roman historian Aulus Gellius confirms that shaving became common in Scipio's day. See Aulus Gellius, *Attic Nights* (Cambridge, MA: Loeb Classical Library, 1946), 1:253.

21   A. E. Astin, *Scipio Aemilianus* (Oxford: Clarendon Press, 1967), 15.

22   Quoted in Astin, *Scipio Aemilianus,* 30.

23   Suetonius, *The Lives of the Caesars,* trans. Alexander Thomson (London: George Bell and Sons, 1890), 30–31.

24   See Thorsten Opper, *Hadrian: Empire and Conflict* (London: British Museum Press, 2008), 69.

25   Anthony Birley concludes that Hadrian grew his beard after staying with Epictetus. Birley, *Hadrian: The Restless Emperor* (London: Routledge, 1997), 61.

26   Paul Zanker, *The Mask of Socrates: The Image of the Intellectual in Antiquity,* trans. Alan Shapiro (Berkeley: University of California Press, 1995), 108–13. See also Harry Sidebottom, "Philostratus and the Symbolic Roles of the Sophist and Philosopher," in *Philostratus,* ed. Ewen Bowie and Jas Elsner (Cambridge: Cambridge University Press, 2009), 81–83, 95.

27   Quotes are taken from *Musonius Rufus,* trans. Cynthia King (CreateSpace .com, 2011), 79–81.

28   Dio Chrysostom, *Dio Chrysostom,* trans. H. Lamar Crosby (Cambridge, MA: Harvard University Press, 1951), 3:331.

29   Epictetus, *Discourses as Reported by Arrian,* vol. 2, trans. W. A. Oldfather (Cambridge, MA: Harvard University Press, 1959), 15.

30   Galen, *On the Usefulness of the Parts of the Body,* trans. Margaret Tallmadge May (Ithaca, NY: Cornell University Press, 1968), 530–31.

31   Aurelius is quoted in G. W. Bowersock, *Julian the Apostate* (London: Duckworth, 1978), 102. Bowersock declares that Julian was "a man of ostentatious simplicity" (14).

32   Quotes from Julian are taken from *The Works of the Emperor Julian,* vol. 2, trans. Wilmer Cave Wright (London: William Heinemann, 1913), 423–25.

Chapter 4

1   Robin Margaret Jensen, *Face to Face: Portraits of the Divine in Early Christianity* (Minneapolis: Fortress Press, 2005), 23–26. See also John Lowden, *Early Christian and Byzantine Art* (London: Phaidon, 1997): 57.

2   Jaroslav Pelikan, *Jesus through the Centuries* (New Haven, CT: Yale University Press, 1985), 86.

3   Robin Margaret Jensen, *Understanding Early Christian Art* (London: Routledge, 2000), 38–40.

4   Thomas F. Mathews, *The Clash of Gods: A Reinterpretation of Early Christian Art*, rev. ed. (Princeton, NJ: Princeton University Press, 1993), 126–28.

5   Ibid., 127.

6   Jensen, *Face to Face*, 161.

7   Deborah Mauskopf Deliyannis, *Ravenna in Late Antiquity* (Cambridge: Cambridge University Press, 2010), 156–58. See also Robin Margaret Jensen, "The Two Faces of Jesus," *Bible Review* 18 (October 2002): 50, 59. See also Jensen, *Face to Face*, 159–63.

8   Kurt Weitzmann, ed., *Age of Spirituality: Late Antique and Early Christian Art, Third to Seventh Century* (New York: Metropolitan Museum of Art, 1979), 606–8.

9   Ibid., 515.

10   Jensen, *Understanding Early Christian Art*, 106–7.

11   Clement of Alexandria, *Christ the Educator* (*Paedagogos*), trans. Simon P. Wood (New York: Fathers of the Church, 1954), 214–15.

12   Tertullian, *The Apparel of Women*, trans. Edwin A. Quain, in *Tertullian: Disciplinary, Moral and Ascetical Works*, ed. Rudolph Arbesmann, Emily Joseph Daly, and Edwin A. Quain (New York: Fathers of the Church, 1959), 139.

13   Peter Brown, *The Body and Society: Men, Women, and Sexual Renunciation in Early Christianity* (New York: Columbia University Press, 1988), 169, 174.

14   Ibid., 382.

15   Augustine, *City of God against the Pagans* (Cambridge, MA: Harvard University Press, 1972), 7:289–301. Augustine discusses the body and bodily resurrection in book 22, chaps. 19–20.

16   Augustine, *St. Augustine on the Psalms*, trans. Scholastica Hebgin and Felicitas Corrigan (London: Longmans, Green and Co. 1961), 2:156, 161.

17   Augustine, *Expositions on the Book of Psalms*, in *Nicene and Post-Nicene Fathers of the Christian Church*, ed. Philip Schaff (Grand Rapids, MI: Eerdmans, 1974), 8:623. See also Cassiodorus, *Cassiodorus: Explanation of the Psalms*, trans. and ed. P. G. Walsh (New York: Paulist Press, 1990–1991), 3:334. Concerning Psalm 133 (132 in the old Latin enumeration), Cassiodorus (ca. 485–580) follows Augustine closely: "We do well to interpret *beard* as the apostles, for a beard is the mark of the most forceful manliness, remaining immovable below its head. In overcoming many sufferings by divine kindness, the apostles proved themselves to be most steadfast men through Gods' grace."

18   Augustine, *City of God*, 7:335 (book 22, chap. 24).

Chapter 5

1   D. D. R. Owens, "Beards in the *Chanson de Roland*," *Forum for Modern Language Studies* 24 (1988): 175–79. See also Susan L. Rosenstreich, "Reappearing Objects in *La Chanson de Roland*," *French Review* 79 (2005): 358–69.

2   *Song of Roland* [61], trans. C. H. Sisson (Manchester: Carcanet Press, 1983), 37.

3   Ibid., 135.

4   This is what Paul Edward Dutton has determined in his study of hair in the Carolingian era. See Dutton, *Charlemagne's Mustache and Other Cultural Clusters of a Dark Age* (London: Palgrave, 2004), 21–26.

5   Herbert Kessler, *Old St. Peter's and Church Decoration in Medieval Italy* (Spoleto: Centro italiano di studi sull'alto Medioevo, 2002), 7.

6   Matthias Becher, *Charlemagne*, trans. David S. Bachrach (New Haven, CT: Yale University Press, 2003), 7.

7   I Corinthians 11:14 (NRSV): "Does not nature itself teach you that if a man wears long hair, it is degrading to him."

8   Louis Trichet, *La tonsure: Vie et mort d'une pratique ecclésiastique* (Paris: Les Éditions du Cerf, 1990), 45.

9   Gregory the Great, *Morals on the Book of Job* (Oxford: John Henry Parker, 1844), 1:123–24. A generation earlier, another Christian writer, Cassiodorus, had expressed a similar idea in reference to the razor of wicked men in Psalm 51, concluding that a razor "can shave off any external attributes like hair, but in so doing it makes the inner part of the soul more beautiful, since it strives to deprive it of worldly things." Cassiodorus, *Cassiodorus: Explanation of the Psalms*, trans. and ed. P. G. Walsh (New York: Paulist Press, 1990), 2:3.

10   Quoted in Bernard Lewis, *The Muslim Discovery of Europe* (New York: W. W. Norton, 1982), 280.

11   See Tia M. Kolbaba, *The Byzantine Lists: Errors of the Latins* (Urbana: University of Illinois Press, 2000), 56–57, 195.

12   Ratramnus Corbeiensis, *Contra Graecorum Opposita Romanum Ecclesiam Infamantium Libri Quatuor*, book 4, Apud Acherium, in *Library of Latin Texts Online* (Turnhout: Brepols, 2005) (trans. Katie Derrig, 2008).

13   Gregory VII, *The Correspondence of Pope Gregory VII*, trans. Ephriam Emerton (New York: Columbia University Press, 1932), 164–65.

14   Quoted in Giles Constable, "Introduction to *Apologia de Barbis*," in *Apologiae Duae: Gozechini Epistola ad Walcherum; Burchardi, Ut Videtur, Abbatis Bellevallis: Apologia de Barbis*, vol. 57 in *Corpus Christianorum: Continuatio Mediaevalis* (Turnhout: Brepols, 1985), 103–4.

15   *Collectio Canonum in V Libris*, in *Corpus Christinorum, Coninuatio Mediaevalis*, vol. 6, ed. M. Fornasari (Turnholt: Brepols, 1970), 412. See discussion in Trichet, *La tonsure*, 100. See also Constable, "Introduction," 106–7.

16   A study of Spanish manuscripts reveals the continuing popularity of beards for laymen in the eleventh and twelfth centuries, particularly among the royalty and nobility. See Philippe Wolff, "Carolus Glaber," *Annales du Midi: Revue archéologique, historique et philologique de the France mérodionale* 102 (1990): 375–82. The Roman theologian (later canonized) Peter Damien (d. 1072) worried that the absence of facial hair was too often the *only* thing that distinguished a priest from a laymen, because so many priests had become

immersed in worldly affairs. See Peter Damien, *Peter Damien: Letters 91–120*, trans. Owen J. Blum (Washington, DC: Catholic University Press, 1989), 55.

17   H. Platelle, "Le problème du scandale: Les nouvelles modes masculines aux XIe et XIIe siècles," *Revue Belge de Philologie et d'Histoire* 53 (1975): 1073–76.

18   Othlonus S. Emmerammi Ratisponensis, *Narratio Olthoni de Miraculo, quod Nuper Accidit Cuidam Laico* in *Library of Latin Texts Online* (Turnhout: Brepols, 2005) (trans. Katie Derrig, 2008).

19   Alan of Lille, *The Plaint of Nature*, trans. James J. Sheridan (Toronto: Pontifical Institute of Medieval Studies, 1980), 187.

20   Giles Constable provides a thorough analysis of the background and themes of Burchard's *Apologia*. See Constable, "Introduction," 47–150.

21   Burchardi, *Apologia de Barbis*, in *Apologiae Duae*, 179 (trans. Katie Derrig, 2008).

22   Hildegard of Bingen, *On Natural Philosophy and Medicine: Selections from "Cause et cure,"* trans. Margaret Berger (Cambridge: D. S. Brewer, 1999), 69.

23   Ibid., 51.

24   Burchardi, *Apologia de Barbis*, 187.

25   Bruno Astensis, *Expositio in Pentateuchum: Incipit Expoistio in Leviticum*, chap. 19 in *Library of Latin Texts Online* (Turnhout: Brepols, 2005) (trans. Katie Derrig, 2008). See also Constable, "Introduction," 70.

26   Burchardi, *Apologia de Barbis*, 162.

27   Ibid., 166.

28   Orderic Vitalis, *Ecclesiastical History of England and Normandy*, vol. 3, trans. Thomas Forester (London: Henry G. Bohn, 1854), 72.

29   Quoted in Lewis, *Muslim Discovery*, 280–81.

30   Serlo's sermon is described by the medieval monk and historian Oderic Vitalis. See Orderic Vitalis, *The Ecclesiastical History of Orderic Vitalis*, vol. 6, ed. and trans. Marjorie Chibnall (Oxford: Clarendon Press, 1978), 63–67.

31   Pauline Stafford, "The Meanings of Hair in the Anglo-Norman World," in *Saints, Scholars and Politicians: Gender as a Tool in Medieval Studies*, ed. Mathilde van Dijk and Renée Nip (Turnhout: Brepols, 2005), 153–71. Stafford emphasizes the clerical defense of masculine standards of the previous generation and analyzes the role of facial hair in distinguishing Normans from Saxons. See also Platelle, "Le problème du scandale," 1071–96.

32   William of Malmesbury, *Gesta Regum Anglorum*, ed. and trans. R. A. B. Mynors, R. M. Thomson, and M. Winterbottom (Oxford: Clarendon Press, 1998) 1:451.

33   William of Malmesbury, *Gesta*, 1:451, 455–59. Pauline Stafford is certainly right to note William's attempt to link Norman virility with priestly virtue. Though she believes this was an attempt to valorize the shaved priesthood, the reverse is equally possible; that is, that he ascribed moral virtue to the shaved Normans army. See Stafford, "Meanings of Hair," 167.

34   Alison Weir, *Eleanor of Aquitaine* (London: Jonathan Cape, 1999), 43. See

also Augustin Fangé, *Mémoires pour servir a l'histoire de la barbe de l'homme* (Liege: Jean-Francois Broncart, 1774), 98–99. The clean-shaved style of kings after Louis VII is evident in manuscript images. See Colette Beaune, *Les manuscrits des rois de France au moyen age* (Bibliotheque de l'Image, 1989).

35 Fred S. Kleiner, *Gardner's Art through the Ages: The Western Perspective* (Boston: Cengage Learning, 2010), 1:341.

36 For a description of Louis's crisis of conscience, and Bernard's influence, see Yves Sassier, *Louis VII* (Paris: Fayard, 1991), 109–31. See also Francois Gervaise, *Histoire de Suger, Abbé de S. Denis* (Paris: Francois Berois, 1721), 95.

37 Illustrations in medieval manuscripts typically showed Westerners without beards, in contrast to Byzantines and Muslims of the Middle East. See Jaroslav Folda, *Crusader Manuscript Illumination at Saint-Jean d'Acre, 1275–1291* (Princeton, NJ: Princeton University Press, 1976).

38 Robert Bartlett, "Symbolic Meanings of Hair in the Middle Ages," *Transactions of the Royal Historical Society*, 6th series, vol. 4 (1994): 46–47.

39 Giles Constable, *Crusaders and Crusading the Twelfth Century* (Farnham: Ashgate, 2008), 333.

40 Thomas Asbridge, *The Crusades* (New York: Echo Press, 2010), 414.

41 Malcolm Barber and Keith Bate, eds., *The Templars: Selected Sources* (Manchester: Manchester University Press, 2002), 42. See also J. M. Upton-Ward, ed., *The Rule of the Templars: The French Text of the Rule of the Order of the Knights Templar* (Woodbridge: Boydell Press, 1992), 25.

42 Helen Nicholson, *The Knights Templar: A New History* (Stroud: Sutton, 2001), 124–27.

43 Caire Richter Sherman, *Imaging Aristotle: Verbal and Visual Representation in Fourteenth-Century France* (Berkeley: University of California Press, 1995), 184–98.

44 *Pero Tafur: Travels and Adventures (1435–1439)*, trans. and ed. Malcolm Letts (New York: Harper & Brothers, 1926), 175.

Chapter 6

1 R. J. Knecht, *Renaissance Warrior and Patron: The Reign of Francis I* (Cambridge: Cambridge University Press, 1994).

2 Elliot Horowitz, "The New World and the Changing Face of Europe," *Sixteenth Century Journal* 28 (Winter 1997): 1196.

3 Francis Hackett, *Henry the Eighth* (New York: Liveright Publishing, 1945), 112; Horowitz, "New World," 1197.

4 Knecht, *Renaissance Warrior*, 105.

5 Horowitz, "New World," 1198.

6 Knecht, *Renaissance Warrior*, 105.

7   Glenn Richardson, *Renaissance Monarchy: The Reigns of Henry VIII, Francis I and Charles V* (London: Arnold, 2002), 173. See also Knecht, *Renaissance Warrior*, 125.

8   Jean-Marie Le Gall locates the origin of the beard renaissance at the papal court in Rome in the 1510s, as evidenced by Raphael's artwork in particular, in *Un idéal masculin: Barbes et moustaches, XVᵉ–XVIIIᵉ siècles* (Paris: Payot, 2011), 33–34.

9   Mark J. Zucker, "Raphael and the Beard of Pope Julius," *Art Bulletin* 59 (1977): 526.

10   Ibid., 530.

11   John Julius Norwich, *The Popes: A History* (London: Chatto & Windus, 2011), 294.

12   Pierio Valeriano, *The Ill Fortune of Learned Men*, trans. Julia Haig Gaisser, in *Pierio Valeriano on the Ill Fortune of Learned Men: A Renaissance Humanist and His World*, ed. Julia Haig Gaisser (Ann Arbor: University of Michigan Press, 1999), 93–95.

13   Gaisser, *Pierio Valeriano on the Ill Fortune of Learned Men*, 38. See also Zucker, "Raphael," 532.

14   Zucker, "Raphael," 532.

15   Pierio Valeriano, *A Treatise Written by Iohan Valerian a Great Clerke of Italie, Which Is Intitled in Latin "Pro Sacerdotum barbis"* (London: Tho. Bertheleti, 1533), 8–9.

16   Pierio Valeriano (Pierii Valerianii), *Pro Sacerdotum Barbis* (Rome: Calvi, 1531), 18–19 (trans. J. Holland, 2012).

17   Ibid., 19.

18   Mark Albert Johnston, *Beard Fetish in Early Modern England: Sex Gender, and Registers of Value* (Farnham: Ashgate, 2011), 34.

19   Le Gall, *Idéal masculine*, 57.

20   *Mémoire pour Mer André Imberdis et Charles Pacros* (Paris: Pillet, 1844), 18–19. See also Léon Henry, *La barbe et la liberté* (Niort: Ve H. Echillet, 1879), 74–76.

21   Gentian Hervet, *Orationes* (Veneunt Aureliae apud Franciscum Gueiardum Bibliopolam, 1536), 55 (trans. J. Holland, 2012).

22   Ibid., 61.

23   Le Gall, *Idéal masculine*, 132–40.

24   Ibid., 47–48.

25   Diarmaid MacCulloch, *The Reformation* (New York: Viking, 2003), 627–28.

26   Quoted in Steven E. Ozment, *Reformation in the Cities: The Appeal of Protestantism to Sixteenth-Century Germany and Switzerland* (New Haven, CT: Yale University Press, 1975).

27   Quoted in Horowitz, "New World," 1186.

28   Sergio Rivera-Ayala, "Barbas, fierros y masculinidad dentro de la mirada columbiana," *Bulletin of Hispanic Studies* 87 (2010): 609.

29   Horowitz, "New World," 1186.

30   Merry Wiesner-Hanks, *The Marvelous Hairy Girls* (New Haven, CT: Yale University Press, 2009), 35.

31   Frederick William Fairholt, ed., *Satirical Songs and Poems on Costume: From the Thirteenth to the Nineteenth Century* (London: Percy Society, 1849), 121–24. Also quoted in Johnston, *Beard Fetish*, 257–58. Scholars have dated this poem to 1597; see Johnston, *Beard Fetish*, 167.

32   William Shakespeare, *As You Like It* II.7.149–56.

33   Robert Greene, *A Quip for an Upstart Courtier: Or a Quaint Dispute between Velvet-Breeches and Cloth-Breeches*, ed. Charles Hindley (London: Reeves and Turner, 1871 [1592]), 38. See also Le Gall, *Idéal masculine*, 45–46.

34   Johannes Barbatium, *Barbae Maiestas hoc est De Barbis* (Frankfurt: Michaelis Fabri, 1614), 7. Ovid, book 13 of the Metamorphoses, trans. Frank Justus Miller (London: William Heinemann, 1958), 2:289.

35   William Shakespeare, *Much Ado about Nothing* I.1.245–46. Shakespeare quotes are from *The Riverside Shakespeare*, ed. G. Blakemore Evans (Boston: Houghton Mifflin, 1974).

36   Ibid., II.1.29–39.

37   Ibid., III.2.48–49.

38   Ibid., V.1.192.

39   William Shakespeare, *King Lear* II.4.193, p. 1272.

40   Ibid., III.7.34–41, p. 1280.

41   Ibid., IV.6.96–99, p. 1286.

42   Shakespeare, *As You Like It* II.7.139–40, p. 381.

43   Ibid., II.7.149–56, p. 382.

44   Will Fisher suggests that the theatrical use of false beards in this era reflected a general recognition that even real beards were prosthetic: a costume of masculine performance. Fisher, Materializing Gender in Early Modern English Literature and Culture (Cambridge: Cambridge University Press, 2006), 85–93.

45   William Shakespeare, *A Midsummer Night's Dream* I.2.90–96, p. 226.

46   Paul F. Grendler, *The Universities of the Italian Renaissance* (Baltimore: Johns Hopkins University Press, 2002), 154–56.

47   Marcus Antonius Ulmus, *Physiologia Barbae Humanae: De Fine Barbae Humanae* (Bononiae: Apud Ioannem Baptistam Bellagambam, 1603), 82 (trans. J. Holland, 2012).

48   Ibid., 257.

49   Ibid., 199.

50   Ibid., 256.

51   Ibid., 197.

52   Ibid., 198.

53   John Baptista Van Helmont, *Oriatrike, or Physick Refined*, trans. J. C. (London: Lodowick Loyd, 1662), 666.

54   Ibid., 667. See also J. Crofts, "Beards and Angels," *London Mercury* 14 (1926): 134–36.

55   Faegheh Shirazi, "Men's Facial Hair in Islam: A Matter of Interpretation," in *Hair: Styling, Culture and Fashion*, ed. Geraldine Biddle-Perry and Sarah Cheang (Oxford: Berg, 2008), 116.

56   Adam is beardless in Michelangelo's Sistine Chapel ceiling (1512) and in Raphael's *Adam and Eve* ceiling fresco of the *Stanza della Segnatura* (1519). The same is true of Lucas Van Leyden's *Expulsion from Paradise* (1510), Tintoretto's *Temptation of Adam* (ca. 1550), Veronese's *Expulsion from Paradise* (ca. 1580), and several other paintings and engravings from the fifteenth and sixteenth centuries.

57   Quoted in Fisher, *Materializing Gender*, 115. See also Will Fisher, "The Renaissance Beard: Masculinity in Early Modern England," *Renaissance Quarterly* 54 (2001): 171.

58   Mark Albert Johnston also discusses this painting but argues that it clearly demonstrates Magdalena's subordination to her husband, because his beard "looms" over hers. See Johnston, *Beard Fetish*, 201–4.

59   The case of the Gonzales sisters is thoughtfully explored in Wiesner-Hanks, *Marvelous Hairy Girls*. For a discussion of Vanbeck (Userlein), see Johnston, *Beard Fetish*, 204–12. See also Chistopher Hals Gylseth and Lars O. Toverud, *Julia Pastrana: The Tragic Story of the Victorian Ape Woman*, trans. Donald Tumasonis (Stroud: History Press, 2005), 51–53.

60   The story of St. Galla is related in St. Gregory the Great, *Dialogues*, trans. Odo John Zimmerman (New York: Fathers of the Church, 1959), 205–7. For discussion of other legends, see Jane Tibbetts Schulenburg, *Forgetful of Their Sex: Female Sanctity and Society, ca. 500–1100* (Chicago: University of Chicago Press, 1998), 152–53. See also Vern L. Bullough, "Transvestism in the Middle Ages," in *Sexual Practices and the Medieval Church*, ed. Vern L. Bullough and James Brundage (Buffalo: Prometheus Books, 1982), 50; also Wiesner-Hanks, *Marvelous Hairy Girls*, 38–41.

61   Wiesner-Hanks, *Marvelous Hairy Girls*, 3–11.

62   Valeriano, *Treatise*, 10.

63   John Bulwer, *Anthropometamorphosis: Man Transform'd: Or the Artificiall Changling Historically Presented* (London: W. Hunt, 1653), 215.

64   Barbatium, *Barbae Maiestas*, 6.

Chapter 7

1   I am siding with the fourth of Alun Withey's suggested explanations for the triumph of shaving, namely that beards were rejected because they "came to symbolise an opposing model of roughness and rugged masculinity." See Withey, "Shaving and Masculinity in Eighteenth-Century Britain," *Journal for Eighteenth-Century Studies* 36 (2013): 231.

2   Louis de Rouvroy, duc de Saint-Simon, *Memoirs of the Duke of Saint-Simon*, vol. 3, trans. Bayle St. John (London: Swan Sonnenschein & Co., 1891), 21.

3   John Woodforde, *The Strange History of False Hair* (London: Routledge & Kegan Paul, 1971), 15.

4   Samuel Pepys, *The Diary of Samuel Pepys*, ed. Henry B. Wheatley, vol. 3, part 2, (New York: Croscup and Sterling, 1893), 302 (entry for 30 October 1663), Hatitrust Digital Library.

5   Ibid., 306 (entry for 4 November 1663).

6   Ibid., vol. 6 (1895), part 2, 233 (entry for 31 March 1667).

7   For a discussion of the social significance of wigs, see Michael Kwass, "Big Hair: A Wig History of Consumption in Eighteenth-Century France," *American Historical Review* 111 (June 2006): 643.

8   Quoted in Maria Jedding-Gesterling, "Baroque (ca. 1620–1715)," in *Hairstyles: A Cultural History of Fashions in Hair from Antiquity to the Present Day*, ed. Maria Jedding-Gesterling, trans. Peter Alexander and Sarah Williams (Hamburg: Hans Schwarzkopf, 1988), 105.

9   Bulwer devotes a chapter to beards in his book surveying human customs around the world. See John Bulwer, *Anthropometamorphosis: Man Transform'd: Or the Artificiall Changling Historically Presented* (London: W. Hunt, 1653), 193–216.

10   Poet John Hall, who supported Parliament, referred to royalist clerics as "distinguished by their Beards and Cassocks." Quoted in Nicholas McDowell, *Poetry and Allegiance in the English Civil Wars: Marvell and the Cause of Wit* (Oxford: Oxford University Press, 2008), 162.

11   Georg Caspar Kirchmaier, *De Majestate Juribusque Barbae* (Wittenberg: Christiani Schrödteri, 1698), 2.

12   Boni Sperati [Samuel Theodor Schönland], *Barba Defensa, sive Dissertatiuncula de Barba* (Leipzig and Dresden: Christophor Hekelium, 1690), 30 (trans. J. Holland).

13   Ibid., 31.

14   Ibid., 47.

15   Johann Freidrich Wilhelm Pagenstecher, *De Barba Prognosticum Historico-politico-juridicum* (Burgo-Steinfurt: Arnoldinis, 1708), 6–7.

16   Quoted in Donald B. Kraybill, Karen M. Johnson-Weiner, and Steven M. Nolt, *The Amish* (Baltimore: Johns Hopkins University Press, 2013), 34.

17   Richard S. Wortman, *Scenarios of Power: Myth and Ceremony in Russian Monarchy* (Princeton, NJ: Princeton University Press, 1995), 1:44.

18   Lindsey Hughes, "'A Beard Is an Unnecessary Burden': Peter I's Laws on Shaving and Their Roots in Early Russia," in *Russian Society and Culture and the Long Eighteenth Century*, ed. Roger Bartlett and Lindsey Hughes (Münster: Lit Verlag, 2004), 22. See also Paul Bushkovitch, *Peter the Great: The Struggle for Power, 1671–1725* (Cambridge: Cambridge University Press, 2001), 204.

19   Quoted in Hughes, "Beard," 22.

20 Bushkovitch, *Peter the Great*, 207.

21 Hughes, "Beard," 24.

22 John Perry, *The State of Russia under the Present Czar* (London: Benjamin Tooke, 1716), 196.

23 R. Atorin, *Problema bradobritiia v pravoslavnoi traditsii* (The Problem of Beard-Shaving in the Orthodox Tradition) (Moscow: Arkheodoksiia, 2009), chap. 4 (trans. Anjelika Gasilina, 2012).

24 Hughes, "Beard," 28.

25 Ibid., 26.

26 Atorin, *Problema*, chap. 4.

27 Jean-Jacques Rousseau, *The Confessions of Jean-Jacques Rousseau*, ed. A. S. B. Glover (New York: Heritage Press, 1955). Rousseau's original phrase is "J'étois ce jour-là dans le meme equipage négligé qui m'étoit ordinaire; grande barbe et perruque assez mal peignée." See *Les Confessions*, vol. 2 in *Oeuvres de J. J. Rousseau* (Paris: E. A. Lequien, 1872), 155–56. Another English translation renders "grande barbe" as "a beard of a few days' growth," which is a reasonable interpolation. See Rousseau, *Confessions*, vol. 2, ed. P. N. Furbank (New York: Alfred A. Knopf, 1992), 28–29.

28 Withey, "Shaving and Masculinity," 225–43.

29 In addition to those discussed, a notable contribution to beard literature is the posthumous publication of German physician Christian Franz Paullini's *Tractatus de Barba*, within Wilhelm Friedrich von Pistorius, *Amœnitates historico-ivridicæ* (Frankfurt and Leipzig: A. J. Felssecker, 1731). Another notable work is Francis Oudin, "Recherches Sur La Barbe" *Mercure De France*, March–April 1765.

30 Giuseppe Valeriano Vannetti, *Barbalogia: Ovvero ragionamento intorno alla Barba* (Roveredo: Francescantonio Marchesani, 1759), 6–7 (trans. Daniele Macuglia, 2010).

31 Ibid., 111–12.

32 Augustin Fangé, *Mémoires pour servir a l'histoire de la barbe de l'homme* (Liege: Jean-François Broncart, 1774), 52.

33 Ibid., 52–62.

34 Jacques A. Dulaure, *Pogonogogia, or a Philosophical and Historical Essay* (Exeter: R. Thorn, 1786), iv.

35 Marcellin Boudet, *Les Conventionnels d'Auvergne: Dulaure* (Paris: Auguste Aubry, 1874), 40–41.

36 Dulaure, *Pogonogogia*, 9.

37 Ibid., v–vi.

38 Ibid., 11.

39 Ibid., 141.

40 Jean-Joseph Pithou, *The Triumph of the Parisians* (n.p., 1789), quoted in Antoine de Baecque, *The Body Politic: Corporeal Metaphor in Revolutionary France, 1770–1800*, trans. Charlotte Mandell (Stanford, CA: Stanford University Press, 1997), 139.

Chapter 8

1   Daniel A. McMillan, "Energy, Willpower, and Harmony: On the Problematic Relationship between State and Civil Society in Nineteenth-Century Germany," in *Paradoxes of Civil Society: New Perspectives on Modern German and British History*, ed. Frank Trentman (New York: Berghahn Books, 2003) 181. See also Heikki Lempa, *Beyond the Gymnasium: Educating the Middle-Class Bodies in Classical Germany* (Lanham: Lexington Books, 2007), 78–85.

2   Hans Ballin, "Biographical Sketch of Friedrich Ludwig Jahn," *Mind and Body* 1 (October 1894): 3. See also Lempa, *Beyond the Gymnasium*, 87.

3   Frederick Hertz, *The German Public Mind in the Nineteenth Century*, trans. Eric Northcott (Totowa, NJ: Rowman and Littlefield, 1975), 37; Asa Briggs, *The Nineteenth Century* (New York: Bonanza Books, 1985), 157.

4   Friedrich Ludwig Jahn, *Deutsches Volksthum*, in *Friedrich Ludwig Jahn Werke*, vol. 1, ed. Carl Euler (Hof: G. A. Grau, 1884), 293 (trans. David T. Barry, 2014).

5   Horst Ueberhorst, *Friedrich Ludwig Jahn and His Time*, trans. Timothy Nevill (Munich: Moos, 1982 [1978]), 51–58.

6   Ibid., 63.

7   J. C. Flügel, *The Psychology of Clothes* (London: Hogarth Press, 1930), 74–76. See also Philippe Perrot, *Fashioning the Bourgeoisie: A History of Clothing in the Nineteenth Century*, trans. Richard Beinvenu (Princeton, NJ: Princeton University Press, 1994), 30–32. See also Christopher E. Forth, *Masculinity in the Modern West: Gender, Civilization and the Body* (Houndmills: Palgrave Macmillan, 2008), 48–55.

8   Victor Hugo, *Les misérables*, trans. Julie Rose (New York: Modern Library, 2009), 574.

9   Victor Hugo to Theophile Gautier, 1845, in *The Letters of Victor Hugo*, vol. 3, ed. Paul Meurice (Boston: Houghton, Mifflin, 1898), 36. Hugo does not say that he wrote the article praising beards, but his phrasing strongly implies it.

10   Ibid., 37.

11   Theophile Gautier, *Histoire du romanticisme*, 2nd ed. (Paris: Carpentier, 1874), 101.

12   Hugo, *Les misérables*, 905.

13   A. J. S., *Histoire des moustaches et de la barbe* (Paris: Hernan, 1836), 12. See also Maxime du Camp, *Recollections of a Literary Life* (London: Remington and Co., 1893), 1:35–36.

14   Clara Endicott Sears, *Bronson Alcott's Fruitlands* (Boston: Houghton Mifflin, 1915), 54. See also Stewart Holbrook, "The Beard of Joseph Palmer," *American Scholar* 13 (Autumn 1944): 453–54.

15   Sears, *Bronson Alcott's Fruitlands*, 67.

16   [William Lloyd Garrison], "Reform Extraordinary," *Genius of Universal Emancipation* 4 (2 October 1829): 30.

17   "Beard, Whiskers and Moustaches, Etc.," *Southern Literary Journal and Magazine of Arts* 4 (December 1838): 411.

18   Quoted in Joachim Wachtel, *Das Buch vom Bart* (Munich: Wilhelm Heyne Verlag, 1981), 63 (trans. Daniel Koehler, 2006).

19   Mark Girouard, *The Return to Camelot: Chivalry and the English Gentleman* (New Haven, CT: Yale University Press, 1981), 90–93.

20   Ibid., 112.

21   Quoted in Stanley Weintraub, *Uncrowned King: The Life of Prince Albert* (New York: Free Press, 1997), 78.

22   Quoted in Weintraub, *Uncrowned King*, 88.

23   Robert Spencer Liddell, *The Memoirs of the Tenth Royal Hussars* (London: Longmans and Green, 1891), 75.

24   Aubril, *Essai sur la barbe et sur l'art de se raser* (Paris: E. Dentu, 1860), 44–45.

25   Liddell, *Memoirs*, 75.

26   Nevil Macready, *Annals of an Active Life* (London: Hutchinson & Co., 1924), 1:258.

27   Jean-Baptiste-Antoine-Marcelin Marbot, *The Memoirs of General Baron de Marbot*, trans. Arthur John Butler (London: Longmans, Green & Co., 1892), 1:42–43.

28   "Military Moustaches" (letter to the editor), *Times*, 23 May 1828, 3. See also Henry Sutherland Edwards, *Personal Recollections* (London: Cassell and Co., 1900), 3.

29   Girouard, *Return to Camelot*, 112.

30   Quoted in Girouard, *Return to Camelot*, 115.

31   A. J. S., *Histoire*, 9. See also "Histoire de la Barbe en France," *Magasin Pittoresque* 1 (1833): 158.

32   Quoted in Scott Hughes Myerly, *British Military Spectacle from the Napoleonic Wars through the Crimea* (Cambridge, MA: Harvard University Press, 1996), 149.

33   Fernando Diaz-Plaja, *La vida española en el siglo XIX* (Madrid: Prensa Española, 1969), 155.

34   Charles Mackay, *Memoirs of Extraordinary Popular Delusions* (London: Richard Bentley, 1841), 353.

35   Terrell Carver, *Friedrich Engels: His Life and Thought* (New York: St. Martin's Press, 1990), 14–15.

36   Quoted in Iorwerth Prothero, *Radical Artisans in England and France, 1830–1870* (Cambridge: Cambridge University Press, 1997), 197.

37   "Ireland," *Times*, 5 October 1843, 5.

38   Paul A. Pickering, "Class without Words: Symbolic Communication in the Chartists Movement," *Past and Present* 112 (1986): 160.

39   Richard Mullen and James Munson, *The Penguin Companion to Trollope* (London: Penguin, 1996), 36.

40   Elizabeth Davis Bancroft, *Letters from England, 1846–49* (New York: Scribners, 1904), 177.

41   Richard S. Wortman, *Scenarios of Power: Myth and Ceremony in Russian Monarchy* (Princeton, NJ: Princeton University Press, 1995), 1:401–2.

Chapter 9

1   Arthur Schopenhauer, *Essays and Aphorisms*, trans. R. J. Hollingdale (London: Penguin, 2004), 223.

2   Paul F. Boller Jr., *Presidential Anecdotes* (New York: Oxford University Press, 1981), 125.

3   Quoted in Doris Kearns Goodwin, *Team of Rivals* (New York: Simon & Schuster, 2005), 258.

4   Quoted in Abraham Lincoln, *Collected Works of Abraham Lincoln*, ed. Roy P. Basler (New Brunswick, NJ: Rutgers University Press, 1953), 4:130.

5   Ibid., 4:129.

6   "Editorial Correspondence," *Zion's Herald and Wesleyan Journal*, 1 June 1864, 86.

7   Donald B. Kraybill, *The Riddle of Amish Culture* (Baltimore: Johns Hopkins University Press, 2001), 63–65.

8   William H. Herndon and Jesse W. Weik, *Abraham Lincoln, the True Story of a Great Life* (New York: D. Appleton and Co., 1909), 2:197–98. See also "Abraham Lincoln's Beard," *New York Times*, 5 November 1876, 8.

9   Napoleon described these events in a letter quoted in Henry Walter De Puy, *History of Napoleon Bonaparte* (New York: Hurst & Co., 1882), 242–44. See also Pierre Hachet-Souplet, *Louis-Napoleon, prisonnier au Fort de Ham* (Paris: E. Dentu, 1893).

10 Hachet-Souplet, *Louis-Napoleon*, 215.

11 Guy de Maupassant, *Les dimanches d'un bourgeois*, in *The Life Work of Henri René Guy de Maupassant* (London: M. Walter Dunne, 1903), 15:2.

12 Henry James, *A Small Boy and Others* (New York: Charles Scribner's Sons, 1913), 317.

13 Edmund Yates, "Bygone Shows," *Fortnightly Review*, n.s. 39 (1886): 641.

14 Albert Smith, *The Story of Mont Blanc* (New York: G. P. Putnam & Co., 1853), 189.

15 Ibid., 190.

16 *The Musical World* 38 (14 January 1860): 28.

17 Walter Goodman, *The Keeleys on the Stage and at Home* (London: Richard Bentley & Son, 1895), 229; Peter H. Hansen, "Albert Smith, the Alpine Club, and the Invention of Mountaineering in Mid-Victorian Britain." *Journal of British Studies* 34 (July 1995): 300–301.

18 Walt Whitman, *Leaves of Grass* (Brooklyn, 1855), 26. All Whitman quotes are taken from pages 26–30.

19 "Walt Whitman and His Poems," *United States Review*, September 1855, 205.

20 "A Few Words upon Beards," *Tait's Edinburgh Magazine* 19 (October 1852): 611–14.

21 [Henry Morley and William Henry Wills], "Why Shave?" *Household Words* 13 (August 1853): 560–63.

22 "The Beard and Moustache Movement," *Illustrated London News* 24 (4 Feb-

ruary 1854): 95. See also "Beard and Moustache Movement," cartoon in *Punch* 25 (1853): 188.

23   FUM, "Letter to the Editor," *Home Journal*, 14 January 1854, 414.

24   Boucher de Perthes, *Hommes et choses: Alphabet des passions et des sensations* (Paris: Treuttel et Wurtz, 1851), 3:335. A contributor to a Cincinnati newspaper offered a typical formulation: a man's throat, neck, lips, cheeks, and nostrils "are all filled with many smaller or larger glands of secretion, in which some of the most important processes of the system are carried on," and to guard against a cold or inflammation in these glands, it was necessary to shield them from extremes of hot and cold, wet and dry. See "Wearing Nature's Neckcloth," *Christian Inquirer* [from the Cincinnati *Columbian*] 8 (31 December 1853): 1. Physicians reported clinical evidence of this theory. See Mercer Adam, "Is Shaving Injurious to the Health? A Plea for the Beard," *Edinburgh Medical Journal* 7 (1861): 568.

25   "The Uses of Hair," *Lancet* 76 (3 November 1860): 440. See also "Plea for Beard," *Medical and Surgical Reporter* 5 (1 December 1860): 234.

26   "The Effects of Arts, Trades and Professions, and Civic States and Habits of Living on Health and Longevity," *Edinburgh Review* 111 (January 1860): 5.

27   "Wearing the Beard," *American Phrenological Journal* 20 (August 1854): 37.

28   Auguste Debay, *Hygiène Médicale des Cheveaux et de la Barbe*, 3rd ed. (Paris: Chez l'Auteur, 1854), 200.

29   "Topics Astir," *Home Journal* 11(11 March 1854): 422.

30   Alexander Rowland, *The Human Hair, Popularly and Physiologically Considered* (London: Piper, Brothers & Co., 1853), 106.

31   Léon Henry, *La barbe et la liberté* (Niort: H. Echillet, 1879), 9.

32   Thomas S. Gowing, *The Philosophy of Beards* (Ipswich: J. Haddock, 1854), 17.

33   "The Beard," *Westminster Review*, n.s. 6 (1854): 67.

34   John Tosh analyzes the problem of domesticity for men in *A Man's Place: Masculinity and the Middle-Class Home in Victorian England* (New Haven, CT: Yale University Press, 1999), 145–69. See also Tosh, *Manliness and Masculinities in Nineteenth-Century Britain* (Harlow: Pearson, 2005), 61–82.

35   "Concerning Beards," *Every Saturday*, 15 July 1871, 66

36   Morley and Wills, "Why Shave?" 562. Other examples include "Wearing Nature's Neckcloth," *Christian Inquirer* [from the Cincinnati *Columbian*] 8 (31 December 1853), 1.

37   Artium Magister, *An Apology for the Beard, Addressed to Men in General, to the Clergy in Particular* (London: Rivingtons, 1862), 70.

38   *Gleason's Pictorial Drawing-Room Companion*, 23 April 1853, 268.

39   "Human Hair," *Quarterly Review* (April 1853).

40   Sean Trainor, "Fair Bosom/Black Beard: Facial Hair, Gender Discrimination, and the Strange Career of Madame Clofullia, 'Bearded Lady,'" *Early American Studies* 12 (Fall 2014): 550.

41   Morris Robert Werner, *Barnum* (New York: Harcourt, Brace and Co., 1923),

205–7. See also Neil Harris, *Humbug: the Art of P. T. Barnum* (Chicago: University of Chicago Press, 1973), 67.

42 *Times*, 12 November 1889, 7.

43 Leslie Fiedler also makes this point in *Freaks: Myths and Images of the Secret Self* (New York: Simon & Schuster, 1978), 31.

44 Theorist Judith Halberstam argues that the uncertain boundaries of male and female help propel the cultural effort to confirm and harden gender binaries. See Halberstam, *Female Masculinity* (Durham, NC: Duke University Press, 1998), 27.

45 Plym S. Hayes, *Electricity and the Methods of Its Employment in Removing Superfluous Hair and Other Facial Blemishes* (Chicago: McIntosh Battery and Optical Co., 1894), 33–34.

46 *Times* (London), 7 January 1899, 6. See also Fiedler, *Freaks*, 15.

47 Karin Lesnik-Oberstein, ed., *The Last Taboo: Women and Body Hair* (Manchester: Manchester University Press, 2006), 1–17. Modern bearded lady Jennifer Miller has fought this taboo in feminist themed sideshows and circus acts, asserting with her words and body that facial hair is normal for women and does not represent any sort of masculine distinction or privilege. See Rachel Adams, *Sideshow U.S.A.* (Chicago: University of Chicago Press, 2001), 219–28.

48 Quoted in Y. Michael Barilan, "The Doctor by Luke Fildes: An Icon in Context." *Journal of Medical Humanities* 28 (2007): 63.

49 Barry Milligan, "Luke Fildes's *The Doctor*, Narrative Painting, and the Selfless Professional Ideal," *Victorian Literature and Culture* 44 (2016).

50 L. V. Fildes, *Luke Fildes, R.A.: A Victorian Painter* (London: Michael Joseph, 1968), 121. See also David Croal Thomson, *The Life and Work of Luke Fildes, R.A.* (London: J. S. Virtue, 1895), 30.

Chapter 10

1 Quoted in Robert Low, *W. G. Grace: An Intimate Biography* (London: Metro, 2004), 254–55.

2 Bruce Haley, *The Healthy Body and Victorian Culture* (Cambridge, MA: Harvard University Press, 1978), 126.

3 F. Napier Broome, quoted in Haley, *Healthy Body*, 136.

4 Quoted in Elliott J. Gorn and Warren Goldstein, *A Brief History of American Sports* (Urbana: University of Illinois Press, 1993), 81.

5 Thomas Wentworth Higginson, "Saints, and Their Bodies," *Atlantic Monthly* 1 (March 1858): 585–86.

6 William Penny Brookes, quoted in David C. Young, *The Modern Olympics: A Struggle for Revival* (Baltimore: Johns Hopkins University Press, 1996), 71.

7 Ibid.

8   Ibid., 31.

9   Christopher S. Thompson, *The Tour de France: A Cultural History* (Berkeley: University of California Press, 2006), 27.

10   Roland Naul, "History of Sport and Physical Education in Germany, 1800–1945," in *Sport and Physical Education in Germany*, ed. Roland Naul and Ken Hardman (London: Routledge, 2002), 17–20.

11   David L. Chapman, *Sandow the Magnificent* (Urbana: University of Illinois Press, 2006), 60.

12   Ibid., 73.

13   John F. Kasson, *Houdini, Tarzan and the Perfect Man* (New York: Hill and Wang, 2001), 53.

14   Ibid., 28.

15   Chapman, *Sandow*, 64.

16   Kasson, *Houdini*, 57.

17   Chapman, *Sandow*, 75.

18   George L. Mosse, in *The Image of Man* (New York: Oxford University Press, 1996), explored the role that revived interest in classical Greek aesthetics played in shaping modern European ideals of physical and moral manliness.

19   Lamar Cecil, *Wilhelm II: Prince and Emperor, 1859–1900* (Chapel Hill: University of North Carolina Press, 1989), 163–64. See also Giles MacDonogh, *The Last Kaiser: The Life of Wilhelm II* (New York: St. Martin's Press, 2000), 162.

20   Isabel V. Hull, *The Entourage of Kaiser Wilhelm II, 1888–1918* (Cambridge: Cambridge University Press, 1982), 17–21; see also Thomas A. Kohut, *Wilhelm II and the Germans: A Study in Leadership* (New York: Oxford University Press, 1991), 162–67.

21   Quoted in John C. G. Röhl, *Wilhelm II: The Kaiser's Personal Monarchy, 1888–1900* (Cambridge: Cambridge University Press, 2004), 386.

22   Heinrich Mann, *The Loyal Subject* (Der Unterdan), ed. Helmut Peitsch (New York: Continuum International Publishing, 1998 [1919]), 42.

23   Ibid., 70.

Chapter 11

1   T. E. Lawrence, *Seven Pillars of Wisdom* (Garden City, NY: Doubleday, Doran & Co., 1935), 304.

2   Ibid., 547. Graham Dawson observed that Lawrence's shaving was a carefully contrived sign of Englishness that counteracted his Arab dress and helped him "establish the combination of 'mystery,' purity and authority that distinguished him from the Arabs." See Dawson, "The Blond Beduin," in *Manful Assertions: Masculinities in Britain since 1800*, ed. Michael Roper and John Tosh (London: Routledge, 1991), 135. Lawrence himself wrote, "We English, who lived years abroad among strangers, went always dressed in the pride of our remembered country." See Lawrence, *Seven Pillars*, 544.

3   *New York Times*, 20 July 1913, 4. "An Old Shaver: Thoughts on Razors and Beards," *Times* (London), 18 April 1959, 8. The Kaiser was fighting a similar battle among his own officers. See "Kaiser Decrees Mustaches: Displeased with Army Officers Who 'Americanize' Themselves," *New York Times*, 3 December 1913, 1. See also "Small Mustache Barred," *New York Times*, 13 February 1914, 4. The Canadian military likewise enforced the wearing of mustaches before the war. See "Must Wear Mustaches," *New York Times*, 21 November 1905, 1.

4   Nevil Macready, *Annals of an Active Life* (London: Hutchinson & Co., 1924), 1:257–59.

5   Edgar Rice Burroughs, *Tarzan of the Apes* (New York, Modern Library, 2003 [1912]), 104–5.

6   "Types of Chicago Beards," *Chicago Tribune*, 3 April 1904, 42.

7   "The Passing of Beards," *Harper's Weekly* 47 (1903): 102.

8   George Harvey, "Reflections Concerning Women," *Harper's Bazaar* 41 (December 1907): 1252–53.

9   "Shaving Guards Heath," *New York Times*, 5 December 1909, C3.

10   "Most British Physicians Stick to the Mustache," *New York Times*, 2 August 1926, 19. For a defense of beards, see "Shall We Stop Shaving?" *Literary Digest* 66 (11 September 1920): 125–28.

11   For discussions of how the corporate economy affected masculinity, see Peter Stearns, *Be a Man! Males in Modern Society* (New York: Holmes & Meier, 1979), 112–15. See also Michael Kimmel, *Manhood in America: A Cultural History*, 3rd ed. (New York: Oxford University Press, 2012), 61–86; also Christopher Forth, *Masculinity in the Modern West: Gender, Civilization and the Body* (Houndmills: Palgrave Macmillan, 2008), 154–55.

12   *New York Times*, 26 April 1907, 1.

13   "Orders Police to Shave," *Chicago Daily Tribune*, 10 July 1905, 5.

14   "Mustaches Irregular," *Los Angeles Times*, 12 December 1915, II, 1.

15   Alma Whitaker, "Hairy Wiles," *Los Angeles Times*, 10 April 1920, II, 4.

16   "Inquiring Reporter," *Chicago Tribune*, 9 May 1925, 25.

17   Already by the first decade of the twentieth century, European traditionalists had gained the habit of identifying undesirable cultural trends such as shaving as "Americanization." See "Parisians Fear Their City Is Americanized," *New York Times*, 12 February 1911, SM14. See also "'Toothbrush' Mustache: German Women Resent Its Usurpation of the 'Kaiserbart,'" *New York Times*, 20 October 1907, C7. See also "Kaiser Decrees Mustaches."

18   Associated Press, "Sport Face of American the Rage in Berlin," *Davenport Democrat and Leader*, 8 March 1923, 15.

19   "Inquiring Reporter," *Chicago Tribune*, 9 May 1925, 25.

20   Allan Harding, "Do You Know a Man under Forty Who Wears Whiskers?" *American Magazine* 96 (September 1923): 60.

21   Andre Fermigier, "Les mystères de la barbe," *Le Monde*, 13 July 1978. See also "Beaver," *Living Age* 314 (9 September 1922): 674–75. See also Harding, "Do You Know?" 178.

22   *New Statesman* 19 (12 August 1922): 509–11.

23   Lord Altrincham [John Grigg], "Beards," *Guardian*, 2 August 1962, 16.

24   "Gable Grows Spiked Mustache as Rhett," *Oakland Tribune*, 29 January 1939, 4B.

25   Biery is quoted in Timothy Connelly, "'He is as he is—and always will be': Clark Gable and the Reassertion of Hegemonic Masculinity," in *The Trouble with Men: Masculinities in European and Hollywood Cinema*, ed. Phil Powrie, Ann Davies, and Bruce Babington (London: Wallflower Press, 2004), 39. Gable's masculine allure is analyzed in Joe Fisher, "Clark Gable's Balls: Real Men Never Lose Their Teeth," in *You Tarzan: Masculinity, Movies and Men*, ed. Pat Kirkham and Janet Thumim (New York: St. Martin's Press, 1993), 36–37.

26   "Items of Hollywood Moment," *New York Times*, 17 May 1936, X3.

27   "Mustache Can Either Make or Break the He-Man's Face," *Los Angeles Times*, 2 September 1934, A3.

28   "Romantic! Mustache Said to Add to Male 'Oomph,'" *Pittsburgh Post-Gazette*, 3 December 1939, 9.

29   Paul Harrison, "Bob Loses That Choir-Boy Look with Whiskers," Newspaper Enterprise Association, *Ogden Standard-Examiner*, 3 March 1940, 8B.

30   "Mustache . . . or Clean Shave for Errol?" *Ames Daily Tribune*, 31 July 1937, 8.

31   Henry Sutherland, "Film Romeo May Put On a Mustache," *Pittsburgh Press*, 2 July 1937, 20.

32   Associated Press, "Top Lip Fringe in Style, but Girl Stars Don't Approve," *Spokane Daily Chronicle*, 31 March 1937, 1.

33   Alexander Kahn, "Hollywood Film Shop," United Press, *Dunkirk* (NY) *Evening Observer*, 4 March 1940, 14.

34   Joyce Milton, *The Tramp: The Life of Charles Chaplin* (New York, 1996), 60.

35   Ibid., 61.

36   Anthony Read and David Fisher, *The Deadly Embrace: Hitler, Stalin, and the Nazi-Soviet Pact, 1939–1941* (New York: W. W. Norton, 1988), 225.

37   Quoted in Read and Fisher, *Deadly Embrace*, 228.

38   Winston Churchill, *The Gathering Storm* (Boston: Houghton Mifflin, 1948), 394.

39   Hendrick de Man, *The Psychology of Marxian Socialism*, trans. Eden and Cedar Paul (New Brunswick, NJ: Transaction, 1985 [1928]), 152.

40   Clare Sheridan, quoted in Robert Service, *Trotsky: A Biography* (London: Macmillan, 2009), 265.

41   Robert Service, *Lenin: A Biography* (London: Macmillan, 2000), 313, 393. Lenin's early balding and adoption of a beard helped him to look wiser and older than his years, contributing to his enduring nickname, "Old Man." Service, *Lenin*, 105. See also Christopher Read, *Lenin: A Revolutionary Life* (Milton Park: Routledge, 2005), 27.

42   Leon Trotsky, *On Lenin: Notes towards a Biography*, trans. Tamara Deutscher (London: George G. Harrap & Co., 1971), 187.

43   Robert Service, *Stalin: A Biography* (London: Macmillan, 2004), 167. The contrast between Lenin's civilian look and Stalin's military posturing is dramatically apparent in propaganda posters. See Victoria E. Bonnell, *Iconography of Power: Soviet Political Posters under Lenin and Stalin* (Berkeley: University of California Press, 1997).

44   "'Toothbrush' Mustache: German Women Resent Its Usurpation of the 'Kaiserbart,'" *New York Times*, 20 October 1907, C7. The newspaper was reporting on letters written by women to the *Berliner Tageblatt*.

45   "Small Mustache Barred," *New York Times*, 13 February 1914, 4.

46   Rich Cohen has raised the intriguing possibility that Hitler was inspired by German infantry lieutenant Hans Koeppen's heroic performance in the first round-the-world automobile race from New York to Paris. Yet Koeppen's adornment is rather wider and more traditional than the look Hitler finally adopted. See Cohen, "Becoming Adolf," *Best American Essays 2008*, ed. Adam Gopnik (Boston: Houghton Mifflin, 2008), 16. Another explanation, proposed by Robert Waite and adopted by George Victor, was that Hitler was imitating the look of the warrior god Wotan in Franz von Stuck's painting *The Wild Chase*. See Waite, *The Psychopathic God* (New York: Basic Books, 1977), 77–78; Victor, *Hitler: The Pathology of Evil* (Washington, DC: Brassey's, 1998), 88–89.

47   James Abbe, "Trying to Make Hitler Smile," *Daily Boston Globe*, 31 July 1932, B3/6.

48   Ron Rosenbaum, *The Secret Parts of Fortune* (New York: Random House, 2000), 494–98.

49   "Editorial Points," *Daily Boston Globe*, 16 July 1931, 18

50   R. S. Forman, "The Dangers of Humour," *Times*, 25 October 1939, 6.

51   J. P. H., "This and That," *Hutchinson News*, 27 April 1939, 4.

52   Dorothy Kilgallen, "Dorothy Kilgallen," *Lowell Sun*, 25 October 1944, 17.

53   Helen Essary, "Inside Washington," *Vedette-Messenger* (Valparaiso, IN), 17 July 1944, 4.

54   Edith Efron, "Saga of the Mustache," *New York Times Sunday Magazine*, 20 August 1944, 21–22.

55   "Cornelia B. Von Hessert, "Shorn Samsons," *New York Times Sunday Magazine*, 24 September 1944, 23.

56   ELM, "After All," *Hutchinson News-Herald*, 7 October 1944, 4.

57   ELM, "After All," *Hutchinson News-Herald*, 29 July 1948, 4.

58   Associated Press, "Dewey Weighs Mustache against Southern Votes" *New York Times*, 29 July 1948, 13.

59   Frederick C. Othman, "Some Advice to a Candidate on Retaining His Mustache," *Chester Times*, 2 August 1948.

60   Donald Deer, letter to Christopher Oldstone-Moore, 22 April 2010.

61   Calculated from figures published in Dave Leip's *Atlas of U.S. Presidential Elections*, uselectionatlas.org/RESULTS/state.php?year=1948&fips=6&f=0&off=0&elect=0.

62   "Dewey on Television," *New York Times*, 1 October 1950, 1.

63   Richard Norton Smith, *Thomas E. Dewey and His Times* (New York: Simon & Schuster, 1982), 559.

Chapter 12

1   Quoted in Philip Norman, *John Lennon: The Life* (New York: HarperCollins, 2008), 446.

2   Eleanor Page, "Does a Beard Add to Manly Charm?" *Chicago Daily Tribune*, 20 July 1958, E1.

3   At the universities of West Germany in the early 1960s, youthful independence took a similar form, including pipe smoking, beards, and long scarves, see Eckard Holler, "The Burg Waldeck Festivals, 1964–1969," in *Protest Song in East and West Germany since the 1960s*, ed. David Robb (Rochester, NY: Camden House, 2007), 97.

4   Joseph Deitch, "Chins Sprout on Campus," *Christian Science Monitor*, 10 May 1958, 3.

5   Eric W. Hughes Jr., "Bearding the Corporation" (letter to the editor), *Nation* 186 (3 May 1958): 380, 393.

6   "Chose to Keep His Beard and Lose His Job," *Guardian*, 28 August 1962, 3.

7   "Beards—What Do *You* Think," *Los Angeles Times*, 28 July 1957, L1, 20.

8   Siriol Hugh-Jones, "Shining Morning Faces," *Times*, 28 September 1960, iv.

9   "Beard Handsomer Now, Fellow Teachers Say," *Los Angeles Times*, 20 December 1963, 32.

10   "School Board Backs Educators," *Los Angeles Times*, 30 January 1964, H1.

11   *Finot v. Pasadena City Bd. of Education* (California Court of Appeals, Second Dist., Div. Three, 250 Cal.App.2d 189 [1967]).

12   "Modern Beards Gain Esteem," *Los Angeles Times*, 30 April 1967, L5. See also Damon Stetson, "Bearded Bus Drivers Travel in Good Company," *New York Times*, 17 November 1969, 49.

13   William Zinsser, "Some Bristly Thoughts on Victory through Hair Power," *Life*, 19 January 1968, 10.

14   "The Mustache Is Back," *Newsweek*, 22 January 1968, 81.

15   Jerry Rubin, *We Are Everywhere* (New York: Harper and Row, 1971), 42.

16   Ibid., 41.

17   Quoted in Terry H. Anderson, *The Movement and the Sixties* (New York: Oxford University Press, 1995), 261.

18   Nick Thomas, *Protest Movements in 1960s West Germany* (Oxford: Berg, 2003), 116.

19   "Management Views Office Fashion," *New York Times*, 14 July 1968, F17.

20   "The Hirsute Pursuit," *Christian Science Monitor*, 3 May 1968, 20.

21   "Castro Regime Insists Students Shave Beards," *New York Times*, 4 April 1968, 17.

22   Richard Atcheson, *The Bearded Lady: Going on the Commune Trip and Beyond* (New York: John Day Company, 1971), 12–13.

23   Associated Press, "Lennon's Haircut," *Washington Post*, 22 January 1970, C16.

24   "Paul Brietner on Golden Goal," https://www.youtube.com/watch?v= mlw7jMbdWes.

25   Scott Murray, "On Second Thoughts: The 1974 World Cup Final," *Guardian*, 19 September 2008, www.theguardian.com/sport/blog/2008/sep/19/ger manyfootballteam.holland.

26   "Es Ist Idiotisch," *Der Spiegel*, no. 43 (18 October 1976), 208, http://www .spiegel.de/spiegel/print/d-41125199.html. For a report of his affinity for leftist thought, see Henry Kamm, "Soccer Star a Hero to the German New Left," *New York Times*, 20 July 1972, 15.

27   Peter Brügge, "Ich waere auch nach Griechenland gegangen" *Der Spiegel*, no. 35 (26 August 1974), 92–93, http://www.spiegel.de/spiegel/print/d-41651442 .html.

28   Joachim Wachtel, *Das Buch vom Bart* (Munich: Wilhelm Heyne Verlag, 1981), 208 (trans. Shaydon Ramey, 2013.)

29   Hannah Charlton, "Introduction," in *Che Guevara: Revolutionary and Icon*, ed. Trisha Ziff (New York: Abrams Image, 2006), 7; Michael Casey, *Che's Afterlife* (New York: Vintage, 2009), 28–29.

30   Casey, *Che's Afterlife*, 125–33.

31   Fidel Castro quoted in David Kunzle, *Che Guevera: Icon, Myth and Message* (UCLA Fowler Museum of Cultural History, 1997), 49.

32   *New York Times*, 4 April 1968, 17. See also Kunzle, *Che Guevera*, 49–50.

33   Richard W. Wertheim, "More Hair Now More Acceptable, but There Is a Cutoff Point," *New York Times*, 23 February 1971, 32.

34   Bruce Markusen, *Baseball's Last Dynasty* (Indianapolis: Masters Press, 1998), 84–85.

35   Ibid., 171.

36   Arthur Daley, "Long and Short It" *New York Times*, 17 October 1972, 49.

37   Andreas Ballenberger, *Alles, was man nicht wissen muss: Das Lexikon der erstaunlichen Tatsachen* (Norderstedt: Books on Demand, 2009), 139 (trans. Maria Hickey, 2013). See image of the advertisement at www.flickr.com/photos /retroads/2242113892/lightbox/.

38   "Den Bart hochzujubeln passt nich zu mir," *Berliner Morgenpost*, 9 February 2011, http://www.morgenpost.de/newsticker/dpa_nt/infoline_nt/sport _nt/fussball_nt/article1751699/Den-Bart-hochzujubeln-passt-nicht-zu-mir .html.

39   Mickey Kaus, "Washington Diarist: Facially Correct," *New Republic*, 4 March 1991, 42.

40   J. Anthony Lukas, "As American as a McDonald's Hamburger on the Fourth of July," *New York Times Magazine*, 4 July 1971, 25.

41   Quoted in Janet Wasko, *Understanding Disney: The Manufacture of Fantasy* (Cambridge: Polity Press, 2001), 94.

42   Michael Marmo, "Employee's Pursuit of the Hirsute: The Arbitration of Hair and Beard Cases," *Labor Law Journal*, July 1979, 416–26.

43   Pacific Gas and Electric/International Brotherhood of Electrical Workers Review Committee Arbitration Case #34, September 17, 1976, http://www .ibew1245.com/PGE-docs/RC-01405.pdf [9-3-13].

44   James M. Maloney, "Suits for the Hirsute: Defending against America's Undeclared War on Beards in the Workplace," *Fordham Law Review* 63 (May 1995): 1209.

45   Linda Matthews, "Justices Uphold Police Ban on Long Hair, Beards," *Los Angeles Times* 6 April 1976, B13.

46   Pranay Gupte, "Hair Codes for Police Upheld by Supreme Court," *New York Times*, 6 April 1976, 1, 25.

47   Ibid.

48   Matthews, "Justices Uphold Police Ban," B1.

49   Robert Hanley, "Freshly Shorn Officers Fight Crew-Cut Chief's Beard Ban," *New York Times*, 11 January 1977, 31.

50   Quoted in Maloney, "Suits for the Hirsute," 1214.

51   *Lowman v. Davies* (US Court of Appeals, Eigth Circuit, 704 F.2d 1044 [1983]); *Hottinger v. Pope County, Ark.* (US Court of Appeals, Eigth Circuit, 971 F.2d 127 [1992]).

52   *Weaver v. Henderson* (US Court of Appeals, First Circuit, 984 F. 2d 11 [1993]).

53   Robert Bly, *Iron John* (Reading, MA: Addison Wesley, 1990), 6.

54   Ibid., 223–24.

55   Ibid., 227.

56   Barry McIntyre, "Dobson Beards Image Makers," *Guardian*, 13 March 2000, 8.

57   Jeanneney Jean Noel, "Barbes de 1853 et barbes de 1981," *Le Monde*, 17 July 1987.

58   Yves Agnès, "La Barbe!" *Le Monde*, 31 August 1981.

59   David Hencke, "Hair Today—and Gone Tomorrow?" *Guardian,* 5 February 1997, 5. See also Ed Lowther, "A History of Beards in the Workplace," *BBC News Magazine* 14 August 2013, www.bbc.co.uk/news/magazine-23693316.

60   Andrew Rawnsley, *Servants of the People: The Inside Story of New Labour* (London: Hamish Hamilton, 2000), 366.

61   "A Disney Dress Code Chafes in the Land of Haute Couture," *New York Times,* 25 December 1991, 1.

62   *Irish Times,* 20 January 1995, supplement 1.

63   Jason Garcia, "After Nearly 60 years, Disney to Let Theme-Park Workers Grow Beards,"*Orlando Sentinel,* 23 January 2012, http://articles.orlandosentinel .com/2012-01-23/travel/os-disney-beards-20120123_1_theme-park-disney -spokeswoman-andrea-finger-walt-disney-world.

Chapter 13

1   "'Amazed': David Beckham Emporio Armani Underwear Billboard," *Pop-crunch*, 26 June 2008, http://www.popcrunch.com/amazed-david-beckham -emporio-armani-underwear-billboard/.

2   "David Beckham Brings His Hotness to Town," *Popsugar*, 19 June 2008, http://www.popsugar.com/David-Beckham-Unveils-His-New-Armani-Ad -Macy-San-Francisco-1722146.

3   Christopher Forth skillfully discusses this key historical development in modern society in *Masculinity in the Modern West: Gender, Civilization and the Body* (Houndmills: Palgrave Macmillan, 2008), 1–18, 201–2.

4   Mark Simpson, "Meet the Metrosexual," *Salon*, 22 July 2002. http://www .salon.com/2002/07/22/metrosexual/.

5   David Coad, *The Metrosexual: Gender, Sexuality, and Sport* (Albany: SUNY Press, 2008), 184.

6   Marian Salzman, Ira Matathia, and Ann O'Reilly, *The Future of* Men (New York: Palgrave Macmillan, 2005), 60, 79.

7   Michael S. Rose complains that the metrosexual is "nothing more than a feminized man—effete, insecure, and socially emasculated—seeking to re-empower himself in a world in which the sexes are artificially converging." Quoted in Coad, *Metrosexual*, 32.

8   Ellis Cashmore, *Beckham*, 2nd ed. (Cambridge: Polity Press, 2004), 155.

9   Coad, *Metrosexual*, 197.

10 Salzman, Matathia, and O'Reilly, *Future of* Men, 76–77.

11 Peter Hartlaub, "A Brief Encounter with David Beckham," *SFGate*, 22 June 2008. http://www.sfgate.com/living/article/A-brief-encounter-with-David -Beckham-3279965.php.

12 Michael Flocker, *The Metrosexual Guide to Style* (Boston: Da Capo, 2003), 108.

13 Peter Hennen, *Faeries, Bears, and Leathermen: Men in Community Queering the Masculine* (Chicago: University of Chicago Press, 2008), 9–13. See also Allan Peterkin, *One Thousand Beards: A Cultural History of Facial Hair* (Vancouver: Arsenal Pulp, 2001), 128–39.

14 Flocker, *Metrosexual Guide to Style*, 111–12.

15 Morgan Spurlock, *Mansome* (quote at 44:45).

16 Rachel Felder, "A He-Wax for Him," *New York Times*, 10 April 2012, http:// www.nytimes.com/2012/04/12/fashion/men-turn-to-bikini-waxing.html?_r =4&ref=style&.

17 Manfred Dworschak, "'Back, Crack and Sack': Pubic Shaving Trend Baffles Experts," *Spiegel Online International,* 13 July 2009, http://www.spiegel.de /international/zeitgeist/back-crack-and-sack-pubic-shaving-trend-baffles -experts-a-636711.html.

18 Quoted in Helen Pidd, "Men Seeking Beckham Effect Go Wild for Boyzil-

ians," *Guardian*, 25 January 2008, http://www.theguardian.com/uk/2008 /jan/26/fashion.lifeandhealth.

19   Ibid.

20   Tom Puzak, "The Rise of the Lumbersexual," *GearJunkie*, 30 October 2014, http://gearjunkie.com/the-rise-of-the-lumbersexual. See also Puzak's "Lumbersexuality: An Explanation," *GearJunkie*, 28 November 2014, http:// gearjunkie.com/lumbersexuality-article.

21   Denver Nicks, a self-described lumbersexual, declared, "If my beard is a trend-inspired attempt to reclaim a semblance of masculinity in a world gone mad, then so be it. It beats scrotum jokes." See Nicks, "Confessions of a Lumbersexual," *Time*, 25 November 2014, http://time.com/3603216/confessions -of-a-lumbersexual. Logan Rhoades insists that "Lumbersexual men have a CALCULATED look with the desire to be (and be seen) as rugged and the heteronormative version of 'manly.'" See Rhoades, "Introducing the Hot New Trend among Men: 'Lumbersexual,'" *BuzzFeed*, 13 November 2014, http:// www.buzzfeed.com/mrloganrhoades/introducing-the-hot-new-trend-among -men-lumbersexual#.vlVG8Rw3z. Luke O'Neill argues that this "performative sort of manliness" is actually the continuation of the well-established hipster style. See O'Neill, "Lumbersexual Is Not a Thing," *Bullett*, 14 November 2014, http://bullettmedia.com/article/lumbersexual-thing.

22   Hennen, *Faeries*, 9–13. Hennen's work explores the modes and motives of the bears' and leathermen's hypermasculinity and finds evidence for and against the notion that these groups are challenging normative masculinity. Sean Cole also discusses the value of beards and body hair in the masculinizing strategies of gay men since the 1970s. See Cole, "Hair and Male (Homo) Sexuality," in *Hair: Styling, Culture and Fashion*, ed. Geraldine Biddle-Perry and Sarah Cheang (Oxford: Berg, 2008), 81–95.

23   Tyler Gillespie, "My Weekend at Mr. Leather," *Chicago Reader*, 28 May 2013, http://www.chicagoreader.com/Bleader/archives/2013/05/28/my-weekend -at-international-mr-leather.

24   Quoted in Caroline Davies, "Conchita Wurst Pledges to Promote Tolerance after Jubilant Welcome Home," *Guardian*, 11 May 2014, http://www.theguard ian.com/tv-and-radio/2014/may/11/conchita-wurst-pledges-to-promote -tolerance.

25   Rick Warren blog, 2013. http://saddleback.com/visit/about/pastors/blog /rick-warren/2013/05/25/news-views-5-25-13. See also Lauren Leigh Noske, "Duck Dynasty' Stars to Speak at Saddleback Church," *Gospel Herald*, 16 July 2013, http://www.gospelherald.com/article/church/48423/duck-dynasty -stars-to-speak-at-saddleback-church-rick-warren-to-return-next-week.htm.

26   Paul Boyer, "The Evangelical Resurgence in 1970s American Protestantism," in *Rightward Bound: Making America Conservative in the 1970s*, ed. Bruce J. Schulman and Julian E. Zelizer (Cambridge, MA: Harvard University Press, 2008), 41–43. See also Jeffery L. Sheler, *Prophet of Purpose: The Life of Rick Warren* (New York: Doubleday, 2009), 57–59.

27   Sheler, *Prophet of Purpose*, 64.

28   John D. Boy, "Icons of the New Evangelism: Why All the Little Beards?" *Killing the Buddha*, 6 September 2009. http://killingthebuddha.com/mag /dogma/icons-of-the-new-evangelicalism/.

29   Drew Magary, "What the Duck," *GQ*, January 2014, http://www.gq.com /entertainment/television/201401/duck-dynasty-phil-robertson?current Page=1.

30   Vi-an Nguyen, "Duck Dynasty's Willie Robertson on Beard Maintenance, Life on Reality TV, and Fame" *Parade*, 20 March 2013, http://parade.conde nast.com/31704/viannguyen/20-duck-dynasty-willie-robertson-beard -maintenance-reality-tv-dealing-with-fame/.

31   "The Secret behind the Beards," *Outdoor Life Online*, 24 October 2007, http:// www.outdoorlife.com/blogs/strut-zone/2007/10/secret-behind-beards.

32   Ibid.

33   "Why Do the Duck Dynasty Guys Have Beards?" *Fear the Beards* (2013), http://www.fear-the-beards.com/why-do-duck-dynasty-guys-have-beards/. See also "Secret behind the Beards."

34   Phil Robertson has provoked controversy on several occasions for his out-spokenly antigay sentiments and for his suggestion during a Georgia Chris-tian retreat that men would be wise, when picking a wife, to chose a younger woman who carries a Bible, cooks meals, and is willing to pick your ducks. For this latter comment, see https://www.youtube.com/watch?v= FDhCxER2fqM.

35   Willie Robertson, foreword to *The Dude's Guide to Manhood* (Nashville: Nel-son Books, 2014), xi–xii.

36   Michael E. Nielsen and Daryl White, "Men's Grooming in the Latter-day Saints Church: A Qualitative Study of Norm Violation," *Mental Health, Reli-gion and Culture* 11 (December 2008): 821–24.

37   Donald B. Kraybill, *Renegade Amish: Beard Cutting, Hate Crimes, and the Trial of the Bergholz Barbers* (Baltimore: Johns Hopkins University Press, 2014), 11–12. See also Thomas J. Sheeran, "Ohio Beard Victim Testifies against Fellow Amish," Associated Press, *Seattle Times*, 6 September 2012, http:// seattletimes.com/html/nationworld/2019082140_apusamishattacks.html (accessed 28 January 2014). See also Erik Eckholm and Daniel Lovering, "Amish Renegades Are Accused of Bizarre Attacks on Their Peers," *New York Times*, 17 October 2011, http://www.nytimes.com/2011/10/18/us/hair-cutting -attacks-stir-fear-in-amish-ohio.html?_r=0.

38   Kraybill, *Renegade Amish*, 67–78.

39   Quoted in James F. McCarthy, "Rival Amish Bishop Testifies He Feared 'Cultlike' Activities of Sam Mullet's Clan," *Cleveland Plain Dealer*, 6 Septem-ber 2012, http://www.cleveland.com/metro/index.ssf/2012/09/rival_amish _bishop_testifies_h_1.html (accessed 28 January 2014).

40   Kraybill, *Renegade Amish*, 84.

41   Erik Eckholm, "Amish Sect Leader and Followers Guilty of Hate Crimes,"

New York Times, 21 September 2012, A14, 17. See also Trip Gabriel, "Amish Sect Leader Sentenced to 15 Years in Hair-Cutting Attacks," *New York Times*, 9 February 2013, A11.

42   John Caniglia, "Federal Court Overturns Amish Beard-Cutting Convictions, Citing Erroneous Jury Instructions," *Cleveland Plain Dealer*, 27 August 2014, http://www.cleveland.com/court-justice/index.ssf/2014/08/federal _appeals_court_overturn.html.

43   Chaim Potok, *The Chosen* (New York: Ballantine, 1967), 3.

44   "Beard and Shaving," q.v. *Encyclopedia Judaica*, 2nd ed., vol. 3, ed. Fred Skolnik (Detroit: Thompson Gale, 2007).

45   Elliott Horowitz "The Early Eighteenth Century Confronts the Beard: Kabbalah and Jewish Self-Fashioning," *Jewish History* 8 (1994): 97. For a contemporary expression of this idea, see "Mystical Significance of Hair," *Kabbalah Online*, http://www.kabbalaonline.org/kabbalah/article_cdo/aid /750313/jewish/Mystical-Significance-of-Hair-Part-1.htm.

46   Horowitz "Early Eighteenth Century," 95–115.

47   Shnayer Z. Leiman, "Rabbinic Openness to General Culture in the Early Modern Period in Western and Central Europe," in *Judaism's Encounter with Other Cultures: Rejection or Integration?* ed. Jacob J. Schacter (Lanham: Rowman and Littlefield, 1997), 197. See also "Hirsch, Samson Raphael," in *Encyclopedia of Judaism*, ed. Sara E. Karesh and Mitchell M. Hurvitz (New York: Facts on File, 2006), 213–14.

48   Michael K. Silber, "The Emergence of Ultra-Orthodoxy: The Invention of Tradition," in *The Uses of Tradition: Jewish Continuity in the Modern Era*, ed. Jack Wertheimer (New York: Jewish Theological Seminary of America, 1992), 48–49.

49   Ibid., 52–61.

50   Artur Kamczycki, "Orientalism: Herzl and His Beard," *Journal of Modern Jewish Studies* 12 (March 2013): 90–92.

51   Ibid., 98.

52   Associated Press, "Hasidic Jew Fired from NYPD over Beard Length," 10 June 2012 (Points of View Reference Center).

53   Meir Soloveichik, "Why Beards?" *Commentary*, February 2008, 43–44.

54   Sjoerd van Konigsveld, "Between Communalism and Secularism," in *Pluralism and Identity: Studies in Ritual Behavior*, ed. Jan Platvoet and Karel van der Toorn (Leiden: E. J. Brill, 1995), 327–45. See also "Sha'r," *Encyclopedia of Islam*, 2nd ed., ed. P. Bearman, T. Bianquis, C. E. Bosworth, E. van Donzel, and W. P. Heinrichs (Brill Online, 2014).

55   Steve Hendrix, "In the New Egypt, Beards Appear Where They Were Once Banned," *Washington Post*, 17 July 2012, http://www.washingtonpost.com /world/middle_east/in-the-new-egypt-beards-appear-where-they-were -once-banned/2012/07/17/gJQAWaEurW_story.html.

56   Faegheh Shirazi, "Men's Facial Hair in Islam: A Matter of Interpretation,"

in *Hair: Styling, Culture and Fashion*, ed. Geraldine Biddle-Perry and Sarah Cheang (Oxford: Berg, 2008), 118–20.

57 Raheem Salman, "Beard Ban Fuels Iraq Religious Debate," *Ottawa Citizen* (Reuters), 24 June 2012, 48.

58 Dominique Soguel, "To Trim or Not to Trim? For Syrian Men, Beards Matter under Militant Rule," *Christian Science Monitor*, 17 July 2014 (Academic Search Complete).

59 Dexter Filkins, "In a Fallen City, a Busy, Busy Barber" *New York Times*, 13 November 2001, B3.

60 See Konigsveld, "Between Communalism and Secularism," 340.

61 Muhammad Zakariya Kandhlawi, *The Beard of a Muslim and Its Importance* (Waterval Islamic Institute, n.d. [1976]), http://www.sajedeen.org/resources /youth-section/173-the-beard-of-a-muslim-and-its-importance. For a French translation, see Mohammad Zakariyyah, *L'importance de la barbe* (Saint-Pierre: Centre Islamique de la Réunion, 1984).

62 Notable examples are Syed Badi-ud-Din al-Rashidi, *The Status of Beard in Islam*, trans. and ed. M. Saleem Ahsan (Lahore: Dar-ul-Andlus, 2007); also Allamah Murtada al-Baghdadi, *The Islamic Perspective of the Beard*, translation of *Tahrim Halq Al-Lihyah* (Unlawfulness of the Shaving of the Beard) by Shaykh Mubashir Ali (Birmingham: Al-Mahdi Institute of Islamic Studies, 1999); reproduced at http://www.al-islam.org/articles/islamic-perspective -of-the-beard. Tallal Alie Turfe, an American Muslim businessman, offers his theological support for beards in *Children of Abraham: United We Prevail, Divided We Fall* (Indianapolis: iUniverse, 2013), 125–29.

63 Faegheh Shirazi reproduces a list of relevant Hadith in "Men's Facial Hair in Islam," 117.

64 Kandhlawi, *Beard of a Muslim,* chap. 2.

65 *Holt v. Hobbs* (574 US [2015]). See Adam Liptak, "Ban on Prison Beards Violates Muslim Rights, Supreme Court Says," *New York Times*, 20 January 2015, http://www.nytimes.com/2015/01/21/us/prison-beard-ban-gregory-holt -ruling.html?_r=0.

66 James Dao, "Taking On Rules So Other Sikhs Join the Army," *New York Times*, 8 July 2013, A9.

67 Wesley Morris, "Sportstorialist: Basebeards: Understanding Baseball's Facial Hair Explosion," *Grantland*, 8 October 2013, http://grantland.com/features /the-red-sox-baseball-beards.

68 Scott Cacciola, "Chin Music," *New York Times*, 9 September 2013, D1, D3. See also Peter Abraham, "Red Sox 'Beard Bonding' Symbolic of Attitude Adjustment," *Boston Globe*, 2 October 2013, http://www.bostonglobe.com /sports/2013/10/02/beards/BAQGj2IcEckzCq5Z0Piy3N/story.html.

69 Cacciola, "Chin Music," D3.

70 Morris, "Sportstorialist: Basebeards."

71 Bill Burt, "For Tightknit Team, It's All about 'The Beard,'" *North of Boston*

Media Group: One for the Beards [supplement], 5 November 2013, S2. The "Samson factor" is discussed by Stuart Vyse, "Five Reasons Why the Red Sox Grew Their Beards," *Psychology Today*, 26 October 2013, http://www.psychology today.com/blog/believing-in-magic/201310/five-reasons-why-the-red-sox -grew-their-beards.

72 Peter Kerasotis, "After World Series Win, Red Sox' Beards and Memories Are Short," *New York Times*, 20 March 2014, http://www.nytimes.com/2014/03 /21/sports/baseball/fresh-start-and-faces-for-red-sox-after-a-championship -season.html.

73 http://us.movember.com/about/history.

74 "German Crowned World Beard Champion," BBC News online, 2 November 2003, http://news.bbc.co.uk/2/hi/americas/3233833.stm.

75 "Happy Movember! Moustache Champion Karl-Heinz Hille Makes It into Guinness World Records 2014 Book," *Guinness World Records*, 8 November 2013, http://www.guinnessworldrecords.com/news/2013/11/happy-movem ber!-moustache-champion-karl-heinz-hille-makes-it-into-guinness-world -records"-2014-book-52755/.

76 Quoted in Vincent M. Mallozzi, "Sideburns to Fu Manchu, the Best and Brightest," *New York Times*, 28 December 2003, Sports, 9.

77 Bryan Nelson, "My Real Face," in *Beard*, ed. Matthew Rainwaters (San Francisco: Chronicle Books, 2011), 45.

78 Paul Roof, Beardcon (Ohio) panel: "The Social Significance of Facial Hair," 6 October 2012 (quote at 10:25), https://www.youtube.com/watch?v=dxh LpODj6jo.

INDEX

Aaron, 22, 77
Abbe, James, 229–30
Achilles, 3, 43–48, 52, 61, 300
Adam, 124, 146, 308n56
Agamemnon, 42
Akkad, 23–24, 298
Aksakov, Constantine, 173
Aksakov, Ivan, 173
Alain of Lille, 89
Albert (prince consort, Great Britain),
     164–70, 285
Alcott, Amos Bronson, 161
Alexander the Great, 3, 38–45, 48, 50, 52,
     58, 61, 148, 289–90
Alpine Club, 183
Al-Zamzami, Muhammad, 281–82
American Civil Liberties Union, 253
Amish, 1, 137, 176, 274–77, 280, 288
Ammann, Jacob, 137
An, 20–21
androgens, 5–6, 11
angels, 72–73, 124
Antioch, 60–61
Antioch Chalice, 71–72
Apelles, 44
Apollo, 45, 66
Aristophanes, 42–43
Aristotle, 44, 54, 101–4, 121

art: Alexander imitates, 3, 45; ancient
     Roman, 52–53, 55, 57–60, 62, 65–72,
     82–83; archaic Greek, 45, 47–48;
     baroque, 133; Christ in, 63–74, 77;
     classical Greek, 3, 40–41, 44–52, 62,
     77, 204–5, 266, 300nn16–17, 316n18;
     inspires Renaissance beards, 108–9,
     306n8; medieval, 102–4; Renaissance,
     108, 124; 125–27, 306n8, 308n56;
     romantic, 158–59; Victorian, 194–97;
     Zionist, 279
Asclepius, 68
Assurnasirpal II, 34–35
Assyria, 26–27, 32–36, 279
Atcheson, Richard, 244
Atorin, R., 140–42
Augustine, Saint, 77, 92
Augustus (Roman emperor), 52–53, 59,
     66, 83
Aurelius, Marcus, 57–59
Auroux, Jean, 256
Austria, 138, 152, 172–73, 269, 279

Babylonians, 24, 26, 32–33, 36, 279
baldness, 5–6; in ancient Mesopotamia,
     23; Aristotle's theory, 44; athletes', 245;
     Caesar's, 52; Lenin's, 228, 318n41; Louis
     XIII's, 134; of tonsure, 84, 104

Ballad of the Beard, 115–16

Bancroft, Elizabeth, 171

Barbatium, Johannes, 116–17, 128

barbers: common in Hellenistic Greece, 48; introduced to ancient Rome, 50–51; of Louis XIII, 134; in Renaissance, 116; in Russia, 140–41; in Taliban Afghanistan, 281; urged to promote shaving in United States, 244

Barnum, P. T., 191, 193–94

Bassus, Junius, 68

Bayern Munich, 245–46

Bayeux Tapestry, 96

beard: artificial, 29, 34, 120, 283, 307n44; assertiveness of, 13–15, 17, 32, 148–49, 162, 174, 188–89, 240, 287; attractiveness of, 7, 9–17, 81, 240, 268, 292; and autonomy, 161, 183, 189, 197, 233, 235, 239–41, 260, 273, 285, 287–88, 292; bestows honor, 31–34, 37, 42–43, 57, 104–5, 112, 114, 117–20, 128, 136, 139, 148, 153, 164, 173, 187, 189–90, 274, 285; in Christian theology, 62, 75–77, 92–94, 122–24, 302n17, 303n9; clubs, 3, 115, 285–88; evolution of, 7–17; favored by religious conservatives, 260, 270–83; Freudian interpretations, 18, 33–34; and gender bending, 260–69, 285; goatee, 156, 249, 252, 265, 270, 272; and health, 11–12, 111–13, 136, 148, 150, 187–88, 190, 218–19, 314n24; and heroism, 42, 111, 154–55, 164, 173, 183, 197, 211; imperial 160, 166, 180, 197, 285; and individuality, 174, 188, 222–23, 249, 251, 259, 266, 285; as intimidating, 13–15, 17, 24, 106; laws about, 4, 48, 84, 88–89, 109, 170, 189, 251–55, 279, 281–82, 288; legal proceedings, 1, 189, 241–42, 251–55, 275–77, 282; *mouche*, 160, 170; and nonconformity, 144, 160, 283, 240, 244, 246, 250–51, 260, 270–74; promoted as God-given, 75, 92, 114, 117, 120, 122, 128, 135–36, 141–42, 146, 157, 187, 239, 278, 282; promoted as natural, 56–58, 105, 110–11, 135, 145, 156, 187–90, 201, 218, 243, 255, 268; quest, 283–88; scientific views, 5–17, 43–44, 57–58, 92, 121–24, 135, 188,

218–19; as social protest, 156–61, 172–73, 235–49, 271, 320n3; spade, 115–16; square-cut, 32, 279; as sign of strength, 16, 20, 32, 37, 40, 43–44, 75, 77, 92, 111, 129, 153, 184, 188–90, 196–97, 201, 284, 290; stiletto, 115–16; stubble, 15–17, 58, 95, 116, 261, 265; tax, 140; and virility, 43–44, 122–24, 149, 198, 224, 232, 296n19, 304n304; women's, 5, 28–31, 43–44, 123, 125–29, 146, 148–49, 191–94, 197, 315n47. *See also* beardlessness; beard movement; mustache; sideburns (*favoris*)

beardlessness: of Adam, 124, 146, 308n56; of Alexander, 3, 45, 61; blandness of, 240; of Christ, 65–66, 72–73; and goodness, 101, 109, 113; and holiness, 84–85, 87–89, 93–94, 97, 99, 101; and honesty, 213, 218, 241; of Lawrence of Arabia, 214–15; of Lenin, 228; as mark of superiority, 29, 48, 89, 93–94, 97, 290; and immortality, 45, 47–48, 52, 66; and youthfulness, 3, 42, 45–6, 47, 52, 66, 117–18, 203–4, 213, 217, 219–21, 229 266, 280. *See also* shaving

beard movement, 2–4, 260, 290; first, 52, 54, 55, 62, 75; medieval, 81, 88, 97; Renaissance, 109–10, 115, 128, 130, 137, 187; nineteenth-century, 163, 174, 180, 186–87, 194, 203, 212, 217, 273, 278

Beard Team USA, 287

bears (gay culture), 268, 324n22

Beatles, 23, 237–38, 242

Beaver (game), 221

Bebel, August, 228

Beckham, David, 261–67, 288

Bedell, Grace, 175–76

Beethoven, Ludwig van, 151

Berlin, 152, 155, 172–73, 211, 247, 285

Bernard of Clairvaux, Saint, 98–99

Bernstein, Eduard, 228

Bible, 22, 31–34, 36–37, 64, 68, 74, 92, 115, 118, 121, 137, 146, 185, 278–79; Genesis, 92; Leviticus, 36–37, 142, 278; Numbers, 22, 36; Deuteronomy, 36; Judges, 33; II Samuel, 32; I Chronicles, 31; Psalms, 77; Jeremiah, 23; Isaiah, 31, 90;

Matthew, 66; Luke, 64–65, 68; John, 66; I Corinthians, 83
Bismarck, Otto von, 208–9, 211–12, 229
Blair, Tony, 258
Blunkett, David, 258
Bly, Robert, 255–56
bodybuilding, 204–8. *See also* sports
bonobos, 5–6
Borromeo, Cardinal, 113
Boston Red Sox, 1, 283–85
Boy, John D., 272
Breitner, Paul, 244–51, 285
Bromberger, Christian, 18
Brookes, William Penny, 202
Bruno, Bishop of Segni, 93, 104
Bulwer, John, 128, 135–36, 146
Burchard, Abbot, 89–94, 97, 104
Burnside, Ambrose, 176
Burroughs, Edgar Rice, 217
Butler, Judith, 2

Caesar, Julius, 51–52
Callisthenes, 44
Calmet, Antoine Augustin, 146
Cashmore, Ellis, 264
Cassiodorus, 302n17, 303n9
Castiglione, Baldassare, 108
Castro, Fidel, 244, 247
Catherine of Aragon, 107
Cecil, Algernon, 221
Cecil, Hugh (Lord Quickswood), 221
Chamberlain, Wilt, 250
Chaplin, Charles, 223, 225, 229–30, 232
Charlemagne, 79–85, 94, 97
Charles I (king of England), 135
Charles II (king of England), 134
Charles V (Holy Roman emperor), 105–6, 109
Charles V (king of France), 102
Charles X (king of France), 157–58
Chartists, 171–72
Chicago, 12, 14, 204, 206–7, 217, 220–21, 225, 232, 237, 239, 243, 253, 269
Chilton, Gary James, 285
chivalry, 148, 153, 163–64, 170
Chrysippus, 48
Cistercians, 89–94, 98

Civil Liberties Union, 253
Civil War (Britain), 130
Civil War (US), 176
civil wars (France), 114, 130, 133
Clement of Alexandria, 75
Clement VII, Pope, 109–10
Clofullia, Josephine, 191–93
Clooney, George, 264–65
clothing: of 1960s youth, 242; Amish 137, 276–77; of bears, 269; of Beckham, 261–63; of Charlemagne, 82; in Disney dress code, 259; eighteenth-century, 149, 130–33, 145; of fundamentalist Muslims, 277; of Hatshepsut, 29–30; of Hitler, 226, 228; of Lawrence of Arabia, 214–15, 316n2; of Louis XIV, 130–33; of lumbersexuals, 268; of Magdalena Ventura, 125; masculinity of dark, 155–56, 267; in McDonald's dress code, 251; medieval, 89–90, 97, 103–4; of metrosexuals, 266; of Orthodox Jews, 277; of Rick Warren, 272; of romantics, 153, 157; Russians adopt Western style, 139, 142; and spirit of the age, 174; of Stalin, 226, 228; tearing in grief, 22–23. *See also* wigs
Coad, David, 264
Colman, Ronald, 222
Columbus, Christopher, 114
Conservative Party (Britain), 257–58
Constantia, 65
Constantine (Roman emperor), 59–60, 65, 82–83
Constantinople, 72–73, 104
Cook, Robin, 258
Copernicus Nicholas, 121–22
Coubertin, Baron Pierre de, 202
court cases, 241–42, 251–55, 259, 275–77, 282; *Kelley v. Johnson*, 1, 253–55; *Domico v. Rapides Parish School Board*, 254
cricket, 198–99, 201, 203, 212
Crimean War, 289
Crosby, Bing, 224
Crosby, David, 236. 243
Crusades, 95, 99–101, 104
Cunningham, Michael, 15
Cynics, 55

Daivari, Shawn, 266
Darius, 39
Darling, Alistair, 258
Darwin, Charles, 7–10
David (king of Israel), 31–34, 77
Debay, Auguste, 188
Declaration of Independence (US), 155
Declaration of the Rights of Man and
    Citizen (France), 155
Deer, Emilie Spencer, 233
Deir el-Bahri, 28–30
Delacroix, Eugène, 158–59
Delilah, 33
Dewey, Thomas, 230–34
Dickens, Charles, 182, 186
Diderot, Denis, 145
Dio Chrysostom, 56
Diocletian (Roman emperor), 58–59
Dionysus, 66
Disney. See Walt Disney Company
Dobson, Frank, 256–57
Doctor, The, 195–96
Doryphoros, 48–49, 52
Duck Dynasty, 1, 270–74
Dulaure, Jacques, 147–49

Ectoff, Nancy, 10, 16
Edward III (king of England), 170
Efron, Edith, 232
Eglinton, Lord. See Montgomerie,
    Archibald (Earl of Eglinton)
Egypt, ancient 3, 19, 22, 24, 27–31, 34, 37,
    39–40, 74; modern, 214–15, 280
Eleanor of Aquitaine, 97–98
electrolysis, 193–94
Emerson, Ralph Waldo, 161
Enfantin, Barthélémi-Prosper, 159
Engels, Friedrich, 170–71, 228
Enlightenment, 130, 145–49
Enlil, 20–21, 24
Epictetus, 54–57
Epicurians, 55
erastes, 46
eromenos, 46
Essarhaddon, 34
Essary, Helen, 232–33
eunuchs, 35–36, 123

Euripides, 42
Euro-Disney, 258–59. See also Walt Disney
    Company
Eusebius, Bishop, 65, 68
Evangelicals, 270–74

Fairbanks, Douglas, Jr., 222
Fairbanks, Douglas, Sr., 222
Fangé, Augustin, 146, 148
fashion cycle, 1–2, 38, 289
femininity: creation of, 2, 290; and long
    hair, 96, 137, 276; and metrosexuality,
    261–66, 268–69; of shaving, 42, 56–57,
    61, 71, 89, 96, 111–12, 114, 264–66, 276.
    See also women
Field of Cloth of Gold, 106–8
Fildes, Luke, 194–97
Fingers, Rollie, 249
Finley, Charlie, 249
Finot, Paul, 241–42
Firth, Colin, 268
Flandrin, Hippolyte, 179
Flocker, Michael, 265–66
Flynn, Errol, 222, 225
Francis I (king of France), 105–9, 148, 289
Frankfurt Parliament, 172
Franks, 79, 81–82, 94–95, 149
French Revolution, 147 149–52, 155, 199
French Revolution of 1830, 157–60
Freud, Sigmund, 18, 33–34
Furetière, Antoine, 146

Gable, Clark, 221–25, 230–32, 234
Galen, 57–58, 121–22
Galla, Saint, 127
Gandhi, Mohandas, 236
Garrison, William Lloyd, 162
Gaugamela, 39–40
gays, 263–65, 267–70, 287–88
George V (king of Great Britain), 215
Gericault, Theodore, 168–69
Gillette, King C., 218, 289
Gillette Company, 240
Gone With the Wind, 223–24
Gonzales sisters, 127–28
Gospels, 64–66, 68, 77. See also Bible
Gowing, Thomas S., 186, 189

Grace, William Gilbert, 198–203, 212
Grant, Ulysses, 176
Grattan, Thomas C., 201
Greece, ancient, 3, 38–57, 61–62, 111, 148, 157
Greene, Robert, 116
Gregory I (the Great), Pope, 84–85, 93
Gregory II, Pope, 83
Gregory VII, Pope, 85–89, 104, 148
Guevara, Che, 246–48
Günzburg, Johan Eberlin von 114
Guthrie, R. Dale, 13–14
gymnastics, 152–55, 203–4. *See also* sports

Haby, Francois, 211
Hadrian (Roman emperor), 3, 52—57, 62, 148, 289
hair: of Amish, 137, 275–77; ancient Greek theories about, 43–44; athletes remove, 203–4, 207–8, 220; of Beckham, 265–66; of the body, 36, 75, 117, 125, 127, 146, 194, 207–8, 243, 255, 261, 264–67, 315n47; Caesar removes, 51–52; of Christ, 63, 66, 68–69, 71–72, 74; churches favor short, 82–83, 88, 274; of conservative Muslims, 280–81; electrical properties, 188; of Francis I, 107; of Franks, 82, 94, 150; of Henry VIII, 108; of Hussars, 168; as impurity, 19, 22–24; and libido, 34; linked to sin, 84, 93, 113; magic qualities, 32–33; and manly honor, 37, 57, 128, 153–54; medieval theories about, 92–93; in mourning rituals, 22–23; and myth of the wild man; 115, 255–56; Olmo's theory about, 122; opposition to long hair, 88, 96, 243–44, 247, 250–53, 259, 271; in Ovid, 116–17; philosophers and, 55–57; preserved in afterlife, 77, 94; of priests, 22, 36, 83–84; protest and long hair, 150, 158–60, 235–40, 242–47, 251, 270; pubic, 267; Renaissance pride in, 115; as representing worldly thoughts, 84–85, 93, 303n9; in the resurrection, 77, 94; return to natural hair, 155; in Russia, 142; sanctified, 36; Schopenhauer's theory of, 174; in Shakespeare's

plays, 120; sociological study of, 18; and strength, 33–34, 40, 42–43, 45, 255, 284; styles reflect gender ideals, 2; of Templars, 100–101; as threat device, 14; transition to false, 134–35; of women, 43–44; 92, 96, 125–29, 137, 146, 194; 275–77, 315n47. *See also* baldness; beard; hypertrichosis universalis; mustache; wigs
Hair (musical), 239
Hamburg, 243
Hamdy, Ahmed, 280
handicap principle, 11
Hartlaub, Peter, 263, 265
Hārūn ibn Yahā, 84
Hatshepsut, Queen of Egypt, 28–31
Hauff, Hermann, 162
Hebrews, ancient, 22, 31–34, 36–37, 106, 148, 277
Henry, Léon, 189
Henry II (king of England), 94–96
Henry IV (king of the Germans), 86–87
Henry VIII (king of England), 105–9
Heracles, 3, 45–47, 52, 61, 300n16
Hermes, 46, 65–66
Hernani, Battle of the, 158
Hernu, Charles, 256
Hervet, Gentien, 112–14
Herzl, Theodor, 279
Higginson, Thomas Wentworth, 202
Hildegard of Bingen, 92
Hillman, James, 255–56
Hippocrates, 43, 57, 128
hipsters, 268
Hitler, Adolf, 226–32, 234
Hittites, 27–28
Hollywood, 2, 221–25, 234, 287
Holy City Beard and Mustache Society, 286
Holy Roman Empire, 85–89, 105, 109
Homer, 42–43, 45, 106, 157. See also *Iliad*
Hospitallers, 99
Hughes, Eric W., 240
Hughes, Thomas, 201
Hugh-Jones, Siriol, 240
Hugo, Victor, 156–59
Hussars, 168
hypertrichosis universalis, 127

Ibbi-Sin, 26–27, 37
icons, 72–75
Iliad, 40, 42–43, 45–46
immunocompetence theory, 11–12
Iran, 281
Iraq, 281. *See also* Mesopotamia
Islam: beards required by, 280–82; and
  mustaches, 282. *See also* Muhammad;
  Muslims
Islamic State, 281
Israel: ancient, 22, 31–33, 64; modern
  287. *See also* Hebrews, ancient; Jews;
  Zionism
Ivan V (tsar of Russia), 137–39

Jackson, Reggie, 249
Jahn, Friedrich Ludwig, 152–56, 161, 172,
  204, 285
James, Henry, 182
Jaurés, Jean, 228
Jefferson, Thomas, 155
Jerome, Saint, 76–77
Jesus Christ, 63–78, 84, 111, 113, 127, 161, 236,
  238–39, 271, 273
Jews, 36, 64, 157, 274, 277–82, 288. *See also*
  Hebrews, ancient
John VIII (Byzantine emperor), 104
Jones, Annie, 193–94
Jones, Ernest, 199, 203
Julian (Roman emperor), 59–62
Julius II, Pope, 108

Kandhlawi, Muhammad Zakariya, 281–82
Kelley v. Johnson (1976), 1, 253–55
Kerensky, Alexander, 228
Khomiakov, Alexei, 173
Kilgallen, Dorothy, 232
Kirchmaier, Georg Caspar, 136, 285
Korniliy, Metropolitan, 143
kouros, 47–48

Labour Party (Britain), 256–58
Lamarck, Jean Baptiste, 7
Las Casas, Bartolomé de, 114
Lawrence, Thomas Edward (of Arabia),
  213–17, 316n2
leathermen (gay culture), 268–69

Leech, John, 186
Leinfelden-Echterdingen, 285
Lenin, Vladimir, 228
Lennon, John, 235–39, 244, 271
Leo III, Pope, 82
Leonardo da Vinci, 106, 108
Lincoln, Abraham, 174–78, 197
Livingstone, Ken, 258
London, 134, 168, 170–71, 181–83, 185, 191,
  193, 199, 202, 207, 235, 237–38, 256, 258
Los Angeles, 219, 224, 241, 254, 272. *See also*
  Hollywood
Louis I (the Pious), 84
Louis VII (king of France), 97–99, 104
Louis IX (king of France), 99–101, 104
Louis XIII (king of France), 134
Louis XIV (king of France), 130–34, 137,
  148–49
Louis XV (king of France), 144
Louis Philippe (king of France), 159
lumbersexuals, 268, 324n21
Luther, Martin, 113–14
Lysippus, 40, 45

Majlisi, Mohammad Baqir, 123
Mandelson, Peter, 258
Mann, Heinrich, 211
Mao Tse Tung, 246
Marbot, Jean-Baptiste, 168
Marcello, Cristoforo, 110
Marcus Aurelius. *See* Aurelius, Marcus
Marx, Karl, 170–71, 228, 247
Mary, mother of Jesus, 72, 239
masculinity: in afterlife, 76–77, 93–94; of
  Christ, 75, 77–78; in Christian thought,
  75–78, 92–97, 104, 201; creation of,
  2–4, 38, 264, 290; conservative views
  on, 270, 273–74; in Enlightenment,
  130–31, 133, 148–49; established by
  nature, 56–58, 110–11, 113–14, 117–20,
  123, 127, 135–37, 146, 148, 187, 193, 197,
  290; gay 263–70, 287–88; hypermasculinity, 264, 268, 324n22; lumbersexual,
  268, 324n21; manifest in facial hair,
  12, 14, 75, 77, 92, 117, 123, 136–37, 140,
  186–91, 196–97, 220, 232, 242, 255–56,
  268; metrosexual, 263–64, 268; and

priesthood, 110–14; in Renaissance, 105, 109–10; and romanticism, 153, 155, 163, 173; sociable, 212, 217, 219 221, 228, 251–52, 260, 291; and sports, 190, 201–4, 220, 234, 264, 273; of Stoicism, 54, 56–57, 62; threatened, 61, 76, 111–12, 136, 148, 190, 194, 202, 263, 273, 280, 288; of women, 29, 43, 123, 125–28, 191–94, 197
Matathia, Ira, 264
Maupassant, Guy de, 179–80
McCartney, Paul, 235
McClellan, George, 176
McDonald's Company, 251–52
Meade, Michael, 255–56
Menjou, Adolphe, 222
Mennonites, 137, 176
Mesopotamia, 3, 19–27
metrosexuals, 3, 261–70, 323n7
Michelangelo, 108–109, 308n56
Miller, Myron, 274
monks, 84–85, 87–95, 99, 101, 256
Montgomerie, Archibald (Earl of Eglinton), 163–64
Moore, Robert L., 255–56
Morley, Henry, 186, 190
Mormons, 274
Morsi, Mohamed, 280–81
Moscherosch, Johann Michael, 135
Moscow, 139, 142, 173
Movember, 1, 284
Mr. Leather convention, 269
Muhammad, 282
Müller, Gerd, 250
Mullet, Sam, 274
muscular Christianity, 201
Muslims: conservatives insist on beards, 36, 274, 277–82, 288; contrast with Christians 18, 96, 99; and Crusades, 99, 101; reaction to Western shaving, 84, 94–95; views on Adam, 124; win right to have beard in prison, 282. See also Islam
Musonius Rufus, 55–56
mustache: assertiveness of, 158–60, 176, 209–11, 168–69, 171, 220–33, 241–43, 249–50, 291; aristocratic, 164, 168, 170, 208; artificial, 168–69, 225, 230; and athletes, 203, 208, 249–50; attractive-

ness of, 12, 166, 168, 220, 223–25, 231; Charlemagne's, 80, 82–83; Dewey's, 231–34; fall from favor, 130, 216–21; handlebar, 249; and health, 188, 218; Hitler's, 228–30, 319n46; in Islam, 282; Kaiser Wilhelm's, 211–12; military, 156, 164, 168–72, 176, 203, 211–12, 215–17, 226, 228–29, 291, 317n17; November, 1, 284; opposition to, 12, 93, 122, 162, 219–21, 225, 232–34, 240–42, 244, 251–55, 274; Prince Albert's, 166–70; Stalin's, 228, 319n43; toothbrush, 229–31; walrus, 212, 229; women's opinion of, 12, 14, 16, 219–20, 224–25, 232–33, 240–41, 319n44
mythopoetic men's movement, 255–56

Nabu-suma-iskun, 24
Namath, Joe, 250
Napoleon, Louis (Napoleon III), 178–81, 186, 191, 197
Napoleon Bonaparte, 150–52, 160, 168, 178, 204, 230
Naram-Sin, 23–26
Nash, Graham, 236
Native Americans, 114–15
Nebuchadnezzar, 36
Neuwirth, Thomas (Conchita Wurst), 269
Newton, Isaac, 130
New York City, 186, 191, 202, 207, 221, 232, 238, 239, 240, 242, 244, 253–54, 267–68, 280
Nicholas I (tsar of Russia, 172–73
Nippur, 20–21, 24, 26
Normans, 94–96
Notre Dame Cathedral, 97
nudity, 45, 47–48, 52

Oakland Athletics, 249–50
O'Connell, Daniel, 171
O'Connor, Feargus, 171
Old Believers, 140, 142–44
Olmo, Marco, 121–24, 128, 135, 146
Olsen, Phil, 287
Olympics, 202, 250
Ono, Yoko, 236
O'Reilly, Ann, 264

Origen, 76
Orthodox Christianity, 73, 84–85, 139–143, 172, 228, 274
Orthodox Judaism, 277–80, 282. *See also* Jews
Ortiz, David, 284
Othlonus, 88
Ovid, 117

Pagenstecher, Johann F. W., 137
Palmer, Joseph, 160–62
Paris, 97, 106, 112, 134, 147, 149, 156–60, 170–72, 178, 237, 247, 258–59
Patrick, Darrin, 273
Patroclus, 46
Paul, Saint, 65, 72, 76, 83
Paula of Avila, Saint, 127
Pepys, Samuel, 134
Peripatetics, 55–56
Perry, John, 140
Persia, 3, 23, 36, 38–40, 60, 124, 148
Perthes, Boucher de, 187
Peter the Great (tsar of Russia), 137–44, 148–49
pharaohs, 24, 28–31, 34, 37, 40
Philip IV (king of France), 101
Philip of Macedon, 42
Philippa (queen of England), 170
philosophers, 38, 43–44, 48, 50, 52–59, 61–62, 65, 111, 113, 122, 136, 174
Phoenicians, 33
Pitt, Brad, 265
Plato, 113
Plutarch, 39–40
policemen, 188, 219, 253–55, 280–81
Pompey, 51
popes, 82–87, 89, 93, 98, 101, 104, 108–11, 148
Portugal, 83
Poseidon, 45
Potok, Chaim, 277
Power, Tyrone, 225
Praxiteles, 48–49
priesthood, 290–91; Hebrew, 22, 32, 36–37; Mesopotamian, 19–29, 32, 37; Orthodox Christian, 85, 139–43, 172, 228, 274; Roman Catholic, 83–89, 109–114,

304n33; and shaving, 19–29; 32, 36, 84–85, 87–88, 96, 109–14, 290. *See also* monks
Procter & Gamble Company, 1
professors, 112, 121, 194, 255, 257, 260
Protestants, 112–14, 133, 136–37. *See also* Amish; Evangelicals; Mennonites
Prussia, 152, 155, 170, 204, 207–8, 229
Punch, 186–87

Rado, James, 239
Ragni, Gerome, 238–39
Raphael, 108, 306n8, 308n56
Ratramnus, 85
Renaissance, 4, 105–30, 137, 157–58, 171, 187, 191–92, 289
revolutions of 1848, 173, 181
Ribera, Fernando Afán de, 125
Ribera, Jusepe de, 125–26
Rigaud, Hyacinthe, 131–33
Robert, Duke of Normandy, 95
Robertson, Phil, 270, 325n34
Robertson, Willie, 273–74
romanticism: of the 1960s, 242–43; of the aristocracy, 163–70; of Beethoven, 151; and chivalry, 160, 163–64, 170; confronting conservatives in France, 156–60; of Friedrich Jahn, 152–56, 161, 172, 204, 285; look to history, 152–55, 160, 163–64, 173; in military, 166–69; and Napoleon, 151; of Saint-Simonians, 160; of Victor Hugo, 157–59; of Young France, 158, 172
Rome, ancient, 3, 48–62, 64–65, 68, 72, 75–77, 83, 113, 116; medieval, 82–84, 86, 88; modern, 173; renaissance, 108–10, 113
Rosenbaum, Ron, 230
Rousseau, Jean Jacques, 144–45
Rubin, Jerry, 243
Russia, 137–45, 149, 166, 172–73, 226
Russian Orthodox Church, 139–44

Saint Apollinaire Nuovo (Ravenna), 70–71
Saint-Simonians, 159
Salzman, Marian, 264
Samson, 33–34, 284
Sandow, Eugen, 204–8

San Francisco, 239, 242, 252, 261–63

Santa Costanza, Church of (Rome), 72

Sarcophagus of Junius Bassus, 68–69

Sargon of Akkad, 23–27

Saunier, Baudry de, 204

Saxony, 136–37

Scaliger, Julius Caesar, 122

Schönland, Samuel Theodor, 136–37

Schopenhauer, Arthur, 174

Schusser, Joseph, 221

Scipio Aemilianus, 49–52

Scipio Africanus, 50

Scott, Walter, 157, 163

Serlo, Bishop of Séez, 95–97

Seymour, Jane Georgiana, Duchess, 163–64

Shakespeare, William, 116–20, 123–24

shaving: as default mode in history, 3, 290; healthfulness of, 213, 218–19; heroic, 3, 45, 47–48, 51–52, 215, 217, 234, 289, 316n2; manliness of, 2–4, 20, 40, 44–45, 48, 50, 52, 61–62, 79, 87, 93–94, 104, 109, 131, 140, 145, 203, 208, 217, 219–20, 233, 260, 289–91; and piety, 83–85, 88–89, 93, 96–97, 99, 110, 274; pubic hair, 267; purity, 19, 23, 29, 32, 36–37, 84, 316; and sacrifice, 22–23, 96; shamefulness of, 32, 41–42, 44, 56, 88–89, 112, 255; technology, 2, 216, 218; unmanliness of, 3, 42–43, 56–57, 61–62, 89, 96, 111–12, 135, 148, 264; virtuousness of, 12, 17, 61, 79, 83, 96, 101, 104, 109, 113, 145, 157, 213, 217–20, 232, 240–41; and youthfulness, 3, 42, 45, 48, 52, 59, 89, 118, 203, 213, 217, 219–20, 229, 266, 280. See also beardlessness; electrolysis; priesthood; tonsure

shavism, 251, 256, 259

Shulgi, 19–28, 32, 37, 297

sideburns (favoris), 156, 160, 176, 181, 242, 244–45, 247, 250, 252–54, 279;

Sikhs, 1, 282

Simpson, Mark, 263–64

Sistine Chapel, 109

slavophiles, 172

Smith, Albert, 181–84, 186

Socialist Party (France), 256–57

socialists, 159, 161, 171, 226–28, 256–57

Sol Invictus, 66

Soloveichick, Meir, 280

Song of Roland, 79

Sophia, Regent of Russia, 138–39

Sophists, 54

Soviet Union, 226–27

Spain, 80–81, 99, 106, 145, 152, 158, 170, 246, 303n16

Speer, Albert, 226

Spitz, Mark, 250

sports, 60, 190, 198–208, 220–21, 234, 250, 264, 266, 273, 283–84 300n17; American football, 249, 272; baseball, 249–50, 283–84; bodybuilding, 204, 204–8; cricket, 198–99, 201, 203, 212; cycling, 203–4; gymnastics, 152–55, 172, 204; Olympics, 202–3, 250; soccer, 200, 203, 244–46, 251, 263–64

Spurlock, Morgan, 264, 266

Stalin, Joseph, 226–28, 230, 234, 319n43

Standard of Ur, 23

Statuta ecclesia antiqua, 88

St. Catherine Monastery, 73–74

St. Denis, Abbey of, 97–98

Stoicism, 48, 54–57

St. Peter's Basilica (Old), 82–83

Sturgis Motorcycle Rally, 287

Suger, Abbot, 97

Sulla, 51

Sumerians, 19–27, 22–27, 32, 37

Summer of Love, 242

Supreme Court of the United States, 253–55

Syria, 39, 281

Tafur, Pero, 104

Taliban, 281

Tarsus, 56

Tarzan, 217

Tate, Henry, 195–97

Taylor, Robert, 224

Templars, 99–101

Tertullian, 75

Thatcher, Margaret, 257

Thélin, Charles, 178

Theodoric, 82

Theopompus, 42

Thetis, 43

Thomasius, Jakob, 136
Thorburn, Robert, 170
Thoreau, Henry David, 161
Tom Brown's Schooldays, 201
tonsure, 83–84
Tour de France, 204
Trevor-Roper, Hugh, 230
Trotsky, Leon, 228
Tuthmose III, 31

Ur, 20, 26, 32
Ur-Nammu, 26

Valeriano, Pierio, 109–14
Van Helmont, Jan Baptiste, 124
Vannetti, Giuseppe, 146
Varro, 48
vaudeville, 170
Ventura, Magdalena, 125–27
Versailles, 133
Vesalius, Andreas, 121–22
Victoria, Queen of Great Britain, 164–66, 170, 183
Vitalis, Orderic, 94
Von Hessert, Cornelia, 232

Wachtel, Joachim, 246
Walt Disney Company, 251–52, 258–59
Warren, Rick, 270–72, 274
whiskers. *See* sideburns (*favoris*)
Whitman, Walt, 185–86, 189, 197
wigs, 29, 131, 133–37, 144–45, 148–49, 263
Wilgefortis, Saint, 127
Wilhelm II, Kaiser, 208–11, 285
William V of Bavaria, 127

William of Malmesbury, 96–97
William of Volpiano, 88
William the Conqueror, 95–96
Wills, William Henry, 186, 190
women: bearded, 5, 28–31, 43–44, 123–29, 146, 148–49, 191–94, 197, 315n4; beardlessness thought to indicate inferiority of, 43–44, 77–78, 92, 187, 189–90, 197; disapprove of facial hair, 9, 12–17, 219–20, 225, 232–34, 240–41, 273, 284; explanations for beardlessness of, 43–44, 58, 92, 146, 190; favor facial hair, 7, 9, 11–17, 174, 224–25, 265, 267; fear their own facial hair, 193–94; men shave to please, 56, 96, 232, 263; increasing power of, 189, 263, 267. *See also* femininity
women's movement, 189–90
Woodstock Festival, 235–36
World Beard and Mustache Competition, 285–87
World's Columbian Exhibition, 204
World War I, 211–21, 228
World War II, 226–27, 230, 232, 235
Wurst, Conchita. *See* Neuwirth, Thomas (Conchita Wurst)

Young France, 157–59

Zahavi, Amotz, 11
Zeigfeld, Florenz, Jr., 205–7
Zeno, 56
Zeus, 43, 45, 68, 73, 255
Zionism, 278–79
Zohar, 278